# The pheno

**For my father and mother**

**I am bipolar; you do not understand, may be you do not know how, all that I ask for is empathy.**

**By Avshalom Rapp**

1

# Table of Contents

2

# The time 09:00 Psychosis

From the Greek ψυχή "psyche" for mind or soul and -ωσις "-osis" for abnormal condition.

Literally, psychosis is an abnormal state of the soul, and in psychiatric terms, it denotes a conscious state that is bound by "losing touch with reality". It means, there is an extreme state of partial or full loss of contact with reality and therefore, the loss of "control of reality".

By a wide definition, a mental patient is in a psychotic state when due to lack of control of reality he has difficulties functioning in daily life, and hallucinations and delusions appear for a period of at least one month as well as a serious thought disorder and disorders of perception and behaviors needed to maintain a normal way of life.

People who are undergoing a psychosis are experiencing hallucinations and delusions and may undergo a confused thinking and a change in behavior i.e. strange behavior as well as difficulties in interaction with other people and malfunctioning in the performance of the daily assignments.

A psychotic disorder actually always indicates the existence of a malfunction in the brain in one or more of the following areas: sensing, perception, communication, thinking, feeling or all of the above. Sometimes the reasons for it are known and sometimes are not.

Psychosis is identified and appears mainly in schizophrenia, manic depressive and major depressive disorder. Psychotic events might be affected by mood; e.g. people who experience a psychotic event in a context of mania may create delusions of grandeur, namely megalomania followed by paranoia.

Pressure and mental stress are known to be the causes and accelerators of a psychosis. A history of a traumatic psychological event or an experience that was happening lately of mental stress and pressure could cause a development of a psychosis.

A short lived psychosis that is accelerated by pressure and stress is known as a short reaction of psychosis that could drag for two weeks after which patients can recuperate and return to normal functioning. In very rare cases a person could remain in a psychotic state for several years.

Sometimes it is hard to draw the line between psychosis and a personality disorder known as psycho neurosis (neurosis) since neurosis might be so severe, paralyzing and confusing in its influence, so it becomes very similar to psychosis. Nevertheless, generally, patients that are diagnosed and suffer from psychosis display a malfunction or a disorder in contact with reality and lack of organization in their personality that distincts them from neurosis.

Patients of psychosis really believe that they do not have any problem in spite the evidence that shows otherwise.

In common terminology, "psychosis" is wrongly confused with "psychopath" which is a general term for personality disorders that are characterized by indifference, social manipulativeness and violent behavior. In spite of the phonetic resemblance between psychotic and a psychopath, there is a big difference between the two; psychotics are usually not violent and they undergo hallucinations and delusions. Actually, psychopathy indicates a person with a tendency to violent and anti social behavior that does not involve hallucinations and delusions.

## 09:15 Hallucinations

Hallucinations are defined as sensual perceptions lacking an external stimulation. Hallucinations are conscious perceptions lacking external stimulation and have the qualities of real perceptions in the sense that they are sharp and alive like an external perception.

They differ from illusions or wrong perception in the sense that they are erroneous or constitute a wrong interpretation of a perception with external stimulations.

A Mirage is an illusion, not a hallucination; the person sees heat waves or hot air interpreting it as a pool of water or he may hear the blowing wind interpreting it as a crying child.

Hallucinations may take place through any one of the five senses (visual, vocal, olfactory, tactile, and gustatory and even the proprioceptive system, meaning the receiving of information by the sensual systems relating to the position of the body, its movement etc.). They may take almost any form starting from simple perceptions of light, color, tastes and smells ending with very complex experiences like actual seeing and coming into touch and interact with nonexistent people, hearing meaningful voices and come into touch with complex physical objects that, again, are nonexistent; In brief, a psychotic person may see, hear, touch, taste and smell objects that are nonexistent outside his consciousness.

Vocal hallucination is characterized by psychosis e.g. schizophrenia in which the patient is hearing voices speaking or ordering him. Vocal hallucinations, particularly the experience of hearing voices, are very common and well known in psychosis. Hallucinatory voices can talk about..., or materialized as human being or in the extant like God.

Vocal hallucinations are especially disturbing when humiliating or obsessive or ordering. However, the experience of hearing voices does not have to be always negative. Many people not defined as psychotics or mentally ill are hearing voices but are not in need of a psychiatric treatment.

Research shows that the experience of hallucinations exists worldwide. A survey and research conducted on more than 13,000 people between 1996 and 1999 shows that 39% of the people reported that they have experienced hallucinations, 27% of which were during the day and particularly not attributed to a mental illness or use of drugs.

Olfactory hallucination is an experience in which a person smells nonexistent smells existing only in his consciousness. The research shows that olfactory and gustatory hallucinations are the most common among the general public.

As aforesaid, hallucinations can materialize in different forms; different forms of hallucinations influence the various senses, sometimes they even materialize in parallel into a complex hallucination or synthesis of some "senses" into one synthetic hallucination, e.g. a person "sees" someone; he can "smell" him, "hear" and "touch" him, meaning the person or the patient is realizing a hallucination that is a person even if no person exists outside his consciousness.

## 09:25 Delusions

Psychosis includes false thoughts or misbeliefs; e.g. paranoia, the thought or the belief that someone is chasing you and is conspiring against you to inflict harm upon you, like this person over there at the corner that is stalking you in the attempt to kill you.

Delusions are defined as false misbeliefs fixated or obsessive. In layman terms they describe false beliefs, imaginary or derived from error.
In psychiatry, the definition is more precise: the belief is pathological, a result of an illness. As pathology, the beliefs differ from beliefs that are based on a lie or on partial information or certain outcomes of perceptions that are better described as illusions. Delusions take place in a context of a mental illness.

A special trait of patients suffering from delusions is their willingness to accept even flimsy evidence to support their beliefs and the inability to seriously accept evidence to the contrary.
They are characterized especially in psychosis and particularly in schizophrenia and manic depressive disorder in the manic stage.

Notwithstanding the fact that for thousands of years there were no clear concepts of insanity, the psychiatrist and philosopher Karl Jaspers was the first to define three criteria for a delusion to be considered as such.

In his book General Psychopathology he defines the three criteria:
- Certainty, meaning a belief that is held by convincing and complete recognition;

15

- Non variation, meaning the belief of the psychotic is not changed even if arguments and evidence to the contrary are being produced;
- Impossible belief or a belief with false content, meaning not reasonable and strange.

Jaspers' criteria are still valid today; in the Diagnostics and Statistical Manual of Mental Disorders, the definition is 'false belief that is based on a wrong conclusion derived from the external reality and that is held firmly although, almost everybody else believes in the contrary and in spite of what constitutes evidence or irrefutable evidence to the contrary. The belief as such is not accepted by other members of the community or of the culture to which the psychotic belongs'.

It is duly noted that there is a controversy about the definition especially about 'although, almost everybody else believes' which indicates that a person, who believes in something that almost everybody else do not believe in, is not a candidate to become delusional.

Moreover, there is a certain irony, in spite of the fact that the three criteria are ascribed to Jaspers, he himself says and describes them as fuzzy and external (General Psychopathology, Volume 1, p. 95).

He has, also, written that since the real criteria or the 'intrinsic' criteria for delusions exist in a fundamental experience of delusions and in the change of personality (and not in the three fuzzy criteria), it may be considered that delusions may be right in their content without ceasing to be delusions, e.g. a world war is happening (General Psychopathology, Volume 1, p. 106).

The modern definitions and the original criteria of Jaspers are standing for criticism. Clinical research conducted on patients show that delusions may be seen as gradually changing over time in level and in convincing which indicates that certainty and non variation are not essential ingredients in delusions.

Delusions are not necessarily false or a wrong conclusion of an external reality. Some religious or mental beliefs in their nature do not have to be refutable, and therefore we cannot describe them as false or wrong.

In other cases the thoughts can come out as true and real, e.g. delusional thoughts of jealousy, when a person believes that a person is not loyal to him (and can even stalk him) and as a result the loyal partner is forced into betrayal by the unreasonable pressure that is exerted upon him by his delusional partner.

In this case the thought does not cease to be a delusion just because the content has become real and true.

As aforesaid a delusion is a type of a thought disorder that expresses itself in the existence of erroneous thoughts that are not accepted culturally. The patient that suffers under the delusion cannot be persuaded of their wrongfulness. Delusions are a trait of a psychotic state.

There are several types of delusions:

- **Delusions of persecution or paranoia**: a syndrome that can be a trait of schizophrenia (Paranoid Schizophrenia) and manic depressive disorder or it can exist separately without them.

Paranoia is a psychotic state in which a person feels persecuted, although it is not based in reality. Paranoia is a trait common with schizophrenia (Paranoid Schizophrenia).

In such state the paranoid is convinced that someone wants ill or is trying to cause him harm. For example: "Every evening, Daddy is putting poison in the food being served to me".

The sense of persecution expresses itself in the paranoid being over suspicious. In extreme situations the paranoid might imprison himself in one room for long hours out of fear that he is being stalked through cameras and even go so far and having thoughts of spying from out of space, a fear from aliens or secret agents that might kidnap him.

In cases of paranoid schizophrenia, the paranoid tends to fear that hostile elements are trying to take control of his mind by transmitting different messages to him by means of implanting various electronic chips under his skin or in other organs and as a result he might even refuse to any urgent and needed chirurgical procedures.

Paranoia originates from the Greek word παράνοια meaning insanity and that from "para" which is a state of "*beside*" and "noos" which is mind or soul.

In our culture and language it is often confused between paranoia and phobia; e.g. a person will have fear from flying because of a fear from aerial accident. This is not enough to be defined as paranoia, but if someone is afraid of flying because the stewardess will make an attempt on his life, then he is a paranoid.

The focal point is a feeling of guilt! In various phobias there exists no feeling of guilt as opposed to paranoia where it does exist.

The stewardess wants to make an attempt on my life or terrorists will hijack the plane in which I fly and hit the twin towers although I do not have any evidence to support it.

The clinical definition describes a delusion as a state when a person believes that he is being persecuted and the following two elements exist:

1. Such person thinks that harm is coming or is about to come upon him.

2. That person believes that the persecutor intends to cause harm.

- **Delusions of relation**: the special significance of neutral stimulation. For example: "the television presenter is talking to me", or: "a car driving the street was signaling - this is a sign from God that I am telling the truth!"

- **Somatic delusions**: a person is sure that he has some kind of a physical problem, and he cannot be persuaded that he is wrong.
This is different from a hypochondriac that is fearful of having a physical problem but he is not sure of it.

- **Erotomanic delusions**: the person is sure that someone, usually a celebrity, is in love with him.

- **Delusions of greatness**: 'Megalomania' comes from the Greek word μεγαλομανία; the term Megalomania comprises of the word "mania" meaning insanity and of the word "megalo" meaning obsession of greatness.
Since the megalomaniac is someone important and big, he is making enemies and that is why, in many cases, he turns out to be paranoid.
This is a state characterized by fantastical delusions of happiness, power, genius quality, omnipotence; such person is convinced that he has special abilities although he was not trained for them (e.g.: he can lecture mathematics in the university although he did not graduate in mathematics), or he is convinced that he has a special role (e.g. "I am a special emissary for the prime minister to the negotiations with Syria").

The megalomaniac may think that he is the Messiah and that he plays a political or a social role (I am the Messiah Ben David and I have come to redeem the people of Israel).

- **Bizarre delusions**: the person is convinced of facts that cannot exist in reality, not for him and not for anybody else. E.g. - "I am a son of an alien", "I am King David", "I have a pair of eyes at my back which enable me to see what goes on behind my back without turning my head or turn around".

## 09:40 Types of psychosis

There are three groups of psychotic disorders that are more common with which are incorporated few similar psychotic disorders and this under the assumption that they are linked to schizophrenia, among them are acute and transient psychotic disorders, delusional disorders and schizoaffective disorders.

## 10:00 Acute and transient psychotic disorders

These are difficult to define and in order to avoid ambiguity and confusion, three criteria were chosen through which a diagnostic sequence and a list of priorities for diagnostics will be constructed and added to them are additional traits.

The basic criteria for diagnosis:

1.  An acute psychotic outbreak within a time frame of two weeks - meaning a fast and clear transition from clinical state that does not have any psychotic symptoms, to a clear and active psychotic state within a time frame of two weeks or less. At this time the psychotic symptoms become clear with a potent force that disables the daily functioning and work abilities in one aspect or more.

2.  Typical syndrome indicators - according to the American classification manual for diagnostics 4-DSM - only one short lived psychosis disorder was defined.
    The presence of one of the positive indicators of schizophrenia is needed such as hallucinations, delusions, disorganized speech and disorganized behavior.
    On the other hand the international classification manual for diagnostics ICD-10 is expanding the internal division that is based on various clinical indicators: most of the polymorphic

indicators are changing quickly with or without accompanied symptoms of schizophrenia such as delusions, hallucination, and acute disorders of disorganized behavior and of lack of judgment.

In spite of the short term of the psychosis, the impact on the functional level during the event is evident, that is why the patient is in need of supervision of hygiene, eating, and preventing dangerous behavior and lack of judgment, by which the patient might cause harm to himself or to his fellow men, commit suicide or react impulsively to delusions and hallucinations.

3.  The presence of an acute stress state or the absence thereof - an acute social state like an unexpected loss of a spouse, war trauma, terror and torture acts, career or marriage crisis. Prolonged stress states are not to be included.

    In most cases there is a connection and relation between the causes of the stress and the psychotic outbreak. There is a need for comprehensive analysis and for additional information from family and friends on the level of functioning before the outbreak of the event and on similar reactions in the past. Upon an identification of a cause for stress, it should be described.

Complete recovery - within a time frame of two to three months, sometimes within couple of weeks even days. The recovery is usually good and swift. Only few patients develop a permanent state of disability.

In the American classification, acute and transient psychotic disorders are not detailed; all are classified under one disorder. In the international classification, the reason for the detailing is the frequency of these various psychotic disorders in developing countries.

## 10:30 An acute polymorphic psychotic disorder

This disorder shows suddenly and it is furious, fast changing from time to time and short lived.

Basic criteria for diagnosis:

1.  Clear diagnosis: the psychosis is developing quickly and dramatically and without warning, it reaches its peak within forty eight hours or within few days up to two weeks. It has short duration and lasts up to one month after which a full recovery occurs.

2.  The clinical syndrome: this disorder expresses itself in delusions and hallucination of various types. The mental state is changing from time to time, its strength is not constant and it expresses itself in an emotional storm of joy and elation or anxiety and bad temper. These symptoms vary in character and in strength from day to day or during the same day.

3.  A preliminary stress factor: a stress factor exists only in part of the cases. The disorder is usually typical to young people without evidence of prior mental disorders.

## 10:45 An acute psychotic disorder schizophrenia -like

This disorder is developing within a time frame of up to two weeks from a non psychotic state to a clear and acute psychotic state. Here, the symptoms are more stable and fixed and conform to the criteria of schizophrenia, while, still exists a certain level of instability and sensual diversity.

The main difference from schizophrenia is the duration of the disorder. According to the international classification a course of up to one month is needed for complete recovery, otherwise the diagnosis has to be changed to schizophrenia.

A patient will be diagnosed as suffering from schizophrenia already after one month into the course of the illness. According to the American classification, which prefers to keep the old term schizophreniform disorder, the disorder will be diagnosed based on a duration that is over one month and less than six months.

A patient who suffers from schizophrenia will be diagnosed only after six months from the start of the mental disorder, a period that includes duration of the prodromal indicators and the residual phase.

## 11:00 An acute delusional psychotic disorder

A stormy disorder that starts, suddenly, following a significant psychosocial stress event which severely impacts a person, his self image and esteem. This event can be a loss of a loved one, a war trauma etc. An outbreak is also possible without a stress state. The illness usually breaks out in a young age. The seizure breaks out in an acute or sub acute form within few days up to two weeks from a stress event.

The acute seizure includes an extreme emotional turmoil that expresses itself in powerful ups and downs and sharp passages between emotions such as depression, elation, anxiety, embarrassments and confusion.

The accompanying psychotic symptoms are a severe thought disorder, with associative laxity and damage to the coherency. The delusions and hallucinations are relatively stable and must be present most of the time since the state has been unequivocally defined as psychotic. The duration of the acute seizure is relatively short - few hours up to few weeks and rarely over one month.

The swift recovery happens usually after three months. The prognosis is good and the level of general functionality returns to its formal state. However the patient might still suffer from mild depression and reduced self esteem. The diagnosis has to be changed if the delusions persist more than three months.

## 11:20 An induced delusional disorder

This is a psychotic disorder of two people or more who share the same system of delusions, supporting each other and strengthening each other in such thoughts.

These people live very close emotionally for a long period of time but live in isolation and detachment from their social and cultural environment. Actually only one person from the two is suffering from a real psychotic disorder and his delusions are induced in his fellowman.

A proof must be present that the original illness has began before the development of the secondary joint disease induced in his mate who did not show any prior symptoms. The inducing patient is the dominant and always suffers from prolonged schizophrenia accompanied by delusions.

The receiving mate is passive, dependant and influenced by the patient as a result of the close relationship between them. Mostly, the induced mate is a woman. The psychotic disorder in the induced mate may not be explained by schizophrenia or any other psychotic disorder. The disorder can be developed in any age and is chronic in its course. The severity of impairment in the induced mate is less than that of the original patient.

When the mates separate the induced mate leaves the pathological state and gives up the delusions. After the separation the recovery may be sometimes quick and sometimes slow. The treatment focuses on both mates while temporarily separating them until an improvement occurs in the situation of the primary patient.

## 11:40 A schizoaffective disorder

Traits of the diagnosis of this disorder are predominant and unequivocal schizophrenic symptoms together with predominant and unequivocal affective symptoms appearing simultaneously or within days of each other during the same episode of the illness.

However, the patient does not conform to all the criteria of schizophrenia and of the affective disorder.

When it comes to an episode, it means the period of time in which active symptoms of the disorder including negative indicators exist until the time of a swift recovery.

The illness starts in the adolescence age and the young adolescence age. The course of the illness is characterized by **returning waves**, partly schizo- depressive or schizo- manic and partly mixed affective and schizophrenic.

The professional functioning is reduced, the social connection is limited, the level of personal observation is low and the risk of committing suicide is high. There is a risk of developing a severe depression syndrome and dependency on drugs and alcohol. The disorder is more common among women, the bi polar type is common among the young and the depressive type is common among the elderly.

1.  **Schizo- manic wave**: manic and schizophrenic symptoms exist in that acute wave of the illness.

    The manic state is characterized by the following symptoms: elated mood, excessive and energetic activity, sometimes aggressiveness and bad temper, exaggerated self esteem, ideas of reference and delusions of grandeur, difficulties of concentration and reduction in social inhibitions.

    Patients can describe their thoughts being transmitted or disrupted from outside, or that foreign powers want to take control over them. They can report that they hear voices of different types that express recognized thoughts and not only thoughts of grandeur and persecution.

The schizophrenic symptoms require at least two main groups of symptoms such as delusions of persecution, control or the transmission of thoughts and vocal hallucinations. During the course of the illness there could be one or more waves. The recovery is swift and the prognosis is good.

2. **Schizo- depressive wave**: the depressive state is characterized by major symptoms such as: depression, feelings of guilt, lack of concentration, helplessness, lack of hope, languidness, lack of appetite, insomnia and suicidal thoughts.

   The schizophrenic symptoms require at least two main groups of symptoms such as delusions of transmission of thoughts and control by foreign powers, delusions of persecution and vocal hallucinations that are degrading and giving orders, commands and even threats to commit murder. The seizure tends to be more prolonged and the prognosis is less than good.

## 12:15 Schizophrenia

Schizophrenia from the Greek word schizein (σχίζειν) for split and phren (φρήν, φρεν) for mind, soul and spirit.

Schizophrenia is a common chronic mental illness that belongs to the group of psychotic illnesses. It harms most of the mental and social functions; mood, sensations and effect, perception, thinking (content and manner), as well as cognitive functions.

Schizophrenia is an illness with a chronic course with outbreaks. The term "Schizophrenia" was coined by Swiss psychiatrist Eugen Bleuler (until than it was called Dementia praecox). This is psychiatric diagnosis that describes a mental illness which is characterized by irregularities in perception or in expressing reality.

The illness expresses itself, mainly, in hallucinations, paranoia, delusions, disorganized speech and thought, social and occupational disfunctioning.
The diagnosis is based on the patient's own reporting of his experiences and behavior; it is the result of reporting of first-person (the patient) about his inner experiences, meaning the diagnosis is **phenomenological**.

Due to more than one combination of symptoms there is a scientific controversy as to whether the diagnosis represents one disorder or a number of separate syndromes that appear together. This is why Eugen Bleuler who coined the term in 1908, used it in the plural form.
It is important to understand that schizophrenia is a wide and heterogenic illness which includes a "basket" of diagnoses and that no one indicator or symptom is exclusive, meaning, it can be found in other psychiatric and neurological disorders. It is also important to understand that the symptoms shown by the patient may change with time. For example, hallucination may appear and disappear.
The illness causes harm and affects, mainly, the consciousness, but not exclusively, it has a chronic effect on behavior and emotions. People with schizophrenia are in risk of developing deep depression and anxieties. Social problems like employment

and poverty are common as well. There is a certain tendency to commit suicide.

As I have mentioned before, people who are diagnosed as suffering from schizophrenia show hallucinations, delusions, disorganized or weird speech and thought, this phenomenon of disruption of thought and senseless sentences that create lack of coherency by the listener, is called, in acute cases, 'word salad'. Moreover, there is isolation and social seclusion for several reasons:
Deficiency of the social consciousness, as well as other symptoms of paranoia, delusions, hallucinations and negative symptoms of indifference and lack of motivation which are attributed to the illness.

There is no one indicator that forms a diagnosis for schizophrenia, but there are several, all of which may appear in other mental states. Often, indicators and symptoms appear in the prodromal stage of the illness. Schizophrenia patients are often described as children who were quiet, passive and introvert; as children they did not have many friends; as youth they avoided social activity and prefer, for example, to watch television or listen to music (not determining that all, or even most of the children and adolescents that fit this description will ever be diagnosed as suffering from schizophrenia).

The indications and symptoms that appear prior to the first hospitalization may appear months even years before it and include: various physical complains, problems with social and occupational functioning, renewed interest in abstract ideas, in philosophy, mystic and religion, weird behavior, abnormal effect, change in speech, bizarre ideas and weird perceptual experiences. This period prior to the outbreak of the illness is called the prodromal period. The present classification of psychosis defines that symptoms must be present at least during one month in a period of at least six months of disfunctioning.

The illness breaks out during the late adolescence period or at the beginning of adulthood; it is an important period in the life of adolescent youth or young adults in which their social and professional life is developing. A great deal of work has been done in order reduce the influence of the illness before its outbreak and to identify and treat the illness in the prodromal period which can start up to 30 months before its outbreak.

These people, who suffer under the outbreak of the illness, undergo an unspecific experience of social seclusion, anxiety and bad temper, depression and restlessness in the prodromal period; also, weak symptoms of the psychosis appear prior to it reaching its peak. It is important for me to emphasize that notwithstanding the etymology, schizophrenia is not identical to Dissociative Identity Disorder also known as multiple personality disorder or multiple personalities.

Schizophrenia is mistakenly confused with split personality; this is not the case.

## 12:20 Thought disorder

These are the core symptoms of schizophrenia grouped as the disorder of content of thought comprise of delusions of different types: persecution, grandeur, relation, religion, jealousy, love or somatic delusions.

**Delusion of persecution** might, for example, be the belief that the Israeli Shabak is looking after the patient. At this state he might walk the street and be certain that every person walking behind him is an agent.

**Delusions of grandeur** may express themselves in the patient considering himself to be the Messiah, and that he might, for example, take a donkey and ride it toward Jerusalem.

**Relation thoughts** might express themselves in the patient believing that the anchor man on television is talking to him.

**Delusions of jealousy** might make the patient extremely jealous on his spouse, to suspect that his spouse is cheating on him, or is planning to leave; he, then, might forbid her to socialize and all of that based on meaningless details.

**Delusion of love** leads the patient to believe that a person loves him; often the imaginary person in love is a celebrity or an authoritative person (e.g. the treating physician).

**Somatic delusions** might be bizarre physical beliefs e.g., the patient might believe that aliens reside in his testicles destroying his fertility or that they control his behavior and mind. Patients might believe that other people control their minds and "transmit" thoughts to them, or, alternately, that they themselves control, supernaturally, external events like causing the sun to rise and set or causing an earthquake.

An interesting point is the deviation in lingual communication - the spoken and written language of the schizophrenia patient constitutes, sometimes, one of the relevant indicators to it. Sometimes the patient develops his own language in which the words have a totally different meaning from the usual.

## 12:20 Negative and positive symptoms

In 1980 T. J. Krew has offered a classification of schizophrenic patients into types I and II based on the existence or the lack of positive and negative symptoms. Although the classification was not accepted by the DSM, this is an important classification that has heavily influenced psychiatrics.

Consequently, schizophrenia is characterized and described in terms of positive and negative (deficit) symptoms.

The term **'positive symptoms'** includes delusions and hallucinations.
Delusions, for example, can manifest in a person believing that he is the Messiah, or that the Shabak is chasing him (paranoid delusion).

Hallucinations can be visual; the patient sees things that do not exist in reality, or a more common type, vocal hallucinations, the patient hears voices talking to him. There are also olfactory and tactile hallucinations.

**'Negative symptoms'** reflects the loss or the non presence of traits and abilities that normally are present, they include traits like impassiveness, poverty of speech (alogia), meaning a partial or a complete inability for one to express himself properly, the inability to experience pleasure (anhedonia), and the lack of motivation (avolition), personal neglect and social withdrawal (asociality).

An additional negative symptom is the lack of organization syndrome; it is described as including chaotic speech, thoughts and behavior.

**Type I** patient: this patient will, mainly, show positive symptoms, normal brain structures will shows on image scans and relatively good reaction to treatment.

**Type II** patient: this patient will, mainly, show negative symptoms, brain abnormality will show on image scans and limited reaction to treatment.

**12:40 Standard criteria**

The accepted standards for the diagnosis of schizophrenia are defined by the Diagnostic and Statistical Manual of Mental Disorder published by The American Psychiatric Association, version DSM- IV- TR and by the World Health Organization's International Statistical Classification of Diseases and Related Health Problems, the ICD-10. The last classification (ICD-10) is being used by the European countries while the DSM is being used in the USA and the rest of the world.

Standards for diagnosis of schizophrenia:

1. Typical symptoms are two or more of the following, when each one is present most of the time during a period of one month or less if the patient is being treated:

   a) Delusions.

   b) Hallucinations.

   c) Disorganized speech which is a reflex of disorganized thought (switching subjects back and forth and 'word salad').

   d) Disorganized behavior.

   e) Negative symptoms: decline or deficit in emotional reactions, decline or deficit in speech, decline or deficit in motivation.

2. Social or occupational disfunctioning manifesting at work, in an interpersonal relationship or self care.

3. Duration: the presence of indicators of the disorder for at least six months out of which, the presence of symptoms of type I for at least one month.

**12:45 Sub types**

The DSM- IV- TR manual contains five sub classifications of schizophrenia.

1. The **paranoic type**: there are hallucinations, delusions and misbeliefs without the disorganized speech and behavior and a lack of an emotional response.

This type is characterized by intensive occupation in one or more delusions (mainly persecution or grandeur) or vocal hallucinations.

It should be said that paranoiacs are very rational and have emotional reactions and normal cognitive abilities (memory, judgment and drawing conclusions); the delusions are organized into one coherent framework.

Paranoiacs are functioning on a higher level than the other sub types. The patients are mostly suspicious, defensive and sometimes hostile and aggressive. Mostly, these patients behave properly in social circumstances. An illness of this type will outbreak mostly in a later stage of life.

2.  The **disorganized type**: is classified in the ICD as hebephrenic schizophrenia where thought disorder and the lack of emotional response are present.

3.  The **Catatonic type**: the patient is statue -like. This type is characterized in, at least, two of the following traits:

    - Immobility - the patients may remain in an uncomfortable position and not change it. They will remain in any position even In the case of another person changing it.

    - Hyper mobility - the movement will be purposely and unaffected by external stimuli.

    - Stereotype movements, conspicuous behavior, permanent giggle and weird posture.

    - Echolalia, the repetition of words; Echopraxia, the repetition of movements.

4.  The **undifferentiated type**: psychotic symptoms are present but the criteria for paranoid, disorganized, or catatonic types have not been met.

5.  The **residual type**: shows usually in chronic patients. The type is characterized, mainly, by negative syndromes, by the absence of positive syndromes or by the presence of relatively low intensity positive syndromes.

The classification of sub types of schizophrenia does not exclude the combination of sub types. Patients may show a mixture of symptoms that defy the subdivision. There can be schizophrenic symptoms mixed with symptoms of other psychosis e.g. manic depressive disorder.

## 12:55 Epidemiology and factors

Schizophrenia is present equally among man and women notwithstanding an early onset by man;

The peak ages of onset are 15–28 years for males standing higher risk of developing 'negative' syndromes and 25–35 years for females standing higher risk of developing 'positive' syndromes. Onset in childhood is much rarer, as is onset in middle age.

Schizophrenia is an illness of the young. The proportion of the population expected to experience the disease is given at 1%. The variation in appearance between different areas in the world is relative small.

Schizophrenia has some genetic components. An identical twin to a patient, as opposed to the general population, is at 47 times higher risk to experience the illness. A child of two parental patients is at 40 times higher risk compared to brothers of a patient who are at 8 times higher risk.

Evidence show that genetics and environment, both acting together, are factors of schizophrenia. Research show that the genetic component is important and hereditary but the outbreak is influenced and dependant on environmental factors like stress and mental pressure.

The Diathesis Hypothesis- Stress holds that people, who tend to it, will start a response to the stress state. The primary tendency may be biological, genetic or acquired (substance abuse like drugs). The stress may be biological, like illness or injury, or psychological (e.g., psycho- social state, a death of a significant person or a trauma). The social elementa are interesting; living in the city, social distress state, poverty, immigration, racial discrimination, broken family and unemployment are risk factors of schizophrenia.


## 12:59 Prognosis and treatment


The course of the illness is changing: there are patients who undergo one acute episode and then recuperate; they function quite well and can live independently; others suffer from repeating episodes with remissions between them and negative symptoms and having more difficulties to properly function in daily life; and still there are patients that become chronic psychotics and must be permanently hospitalized.

The prognosis of the schizophrenia patients was improved by the use of medication and the support by the community. The symptoms of schizophrenia may be treated by anti psychotic drugs like Risperdal that causes the positive symptoms to disappear (misbeliefs, hallucinations, thought disorder, bad temper and violence, if at all exists); psychotherapy can help in alleviating stress and pressure and help the patient to cope with the illness, for example in cases of loneliness and helplessness or in strengthening health tendencies. The aim of psychotherapy is to return the patient to a normal course of life.

**The time 13:01 Semantics and logic**

Husserl considered phenomenology as a basis for logic; what is called by Husserl pure logic is being called, by present philosophers, semantics which is a system that coordinates between language, sense and the world. Semantics is a system that coordinates between forms of expression in language through sense (intentional content) and external objects. The semantic or the logical system is linked to the structure of intentionality of consciousness by the sense of our experience that represents the things around us. Therefore, expressions, sense and truth of a certain situation are linked to each other exactly the same way as logic is relating to sense that is given to an expression in a language which receives sense from conscious acts. This way logic is linked to the world, to conscious acts and their objects.

David Woodruff Smith[1] defines phenomenology as follows: phenomenology is a semantic theory of ideal sense, or in other words, a semantic theory of an intentional content. Husserl's phenomenological theory is dealing in ideal contents (meaning or sense) that are logically linked to consciousness, or to the content of the consciousness. For Husserl, phenomenology is the science that describes and analyzes different forms of consciousness where such analysis will be performed on the objective contents of conscious states or different experiences. Sense or contents may include sensual perceptions, concepts, metaphors, thoughts or assertions, desirability and passions. A conscious act is intentional through its content thus by sense toward the specified object. Intentionality is the consciousness 'about something' or 'of something'; it is the ideal sense that represents external objects.

Knowledge takes place in intened expressive act. Intentionality is an experience, that is, a conscious act that is being intended toward an external object through the sense that represents such object.

Every sign (Zeichen) signify something. Through the sense, a connection is created with the object. To use an expression significantly is the same as to indicate the object by using an expression (logical investigations, investigation I page 289[2]). Logic

[1] David woodruff smith, Husserl, Rutledge

is interested in expression, in the expressed meaning and their formal interconnections, relations of inference, their essential kinds and differences (logical investigations I p.29). Expressions express meanings; they carry an ideal expressive meaning or sense. Through the sense or meaning there is a relation to an object in the world. Each expression which has sense indicates or stands for an object, but **"it does not matter whether the object exists"** (logical investigations, investigation I page 293). Therefore, the object may not exist and it may be, actually, a hallucination of the psychotic, meaning there exists an object in the consciousness that does not relate to anything external, it does not stand for anything transcendental. Husserl distinguishes between the sense-given and sense-fulfilling acts. He also distinguishes between meaning or sense and its objective correlate, the "objectivity" to which it refers. An expression "means something, and in so far as it means something, it relates to what is objective" (logical investigations I p.280). The relation between an expression and its meaning is an ideal relations, meaning are ideal, self-identical unities which are not temporal, that is they do not come or pass away and which may be shared between different speakers. Therefore intentional contents (meaning) of such or other experiences, that is, contents that may be expressed in a language are ideal senses. Ideal objects are not temporal; they may not cease to exist or created as well as they may not change.

Meanings are different from the mental images that accompany to the act of thinking. Meaning express an object-something; they refer to an object in the world. Therefore expressions, then, not

---

2 Edmund Husserl, Logical Investigations, Routledge & Kegan Paul 1970

only have "meaning", they also have reference (Beziehung). Sense is an ideal being or beings in the sense that different experiences of different consciousness can be of the same content. Two expressions can refer to the same object by two efferent meanings; 'the vanquished at Waterloo' and the 'victor at Jena' refer and stand for the same object, Napoleon. In the same way two expressions with the same meanings can refer to two different objects. I can use the expression "cat" to refer to two different cats. Expressions not only refer to names or objects but may also refer to more complex situations like state of affairs, for example "the cat on the mat". This account of logic is more or less similar to Frege, with which Husserl was familiar since the early 1890s. For both the reference is made through the meaning. For Husserl the reference of propositions will be the state of affairs that they affirm as holding through intuitions fulfillment. Expressions, in so far as they have sense, also have intended references which are specified by context, and for some expressions, for example "round square" the reference is incapable of being fulfilled. Expression like "round square" does not luch meaning, but it lacks referential fulfillment. "The present king of france" is a meaningful expression which at the past had true object to which it referred, but today it cannot be intuitively fulfilled. States of affairs are ontological counterparts of propositional contents, which may contain as their parts individual things. They may hold or not hold, when they hold they are true, when they are not hold they are not true. If, for example, I say: "Napoleon was defeated in Waterloo" and in reality, it was the case, Napoleon was in fact defeated in Woterloo, then the expression holds, that is, it is a true statement. An expression like "Napoleon was defeated in Waterloo" is objectively representing a situation in the world.

In summary, Language is being supported by intentionality because language expresses thoughts which are directed through sense on something, i.e, (intentional objects). The ideal sense of the expressed sentence is the content of a thought; the sentence expresses the content or the sense of my thinking act (intentional act)! The ideal intentional content of my experience is sense. "Sense" is that conscious content by which I intend and experience something external. The role of sense is to represent or to logically point to a suitable external object. In Ideas I[3] (1913), Husserl presents the Greek term "Noema" for the ideal intentional content of a conscious act; he names it "noematic sense".

We need to investigate the consciousness and its acts, exactly as they are being experienced by us, from a personal "first person" viewpoint using the theory of Phenomenology! I will investigate the psychotic consciousness by Phenomenology!

## 13:25 Phenomenology

Husserl's phenomenology is a new method in philosophy in particular and in science in general: the science of consciousness.

---

[3] Edmund Husserl, ideas pertaining to a pure phenomenology and to a phenomenological philosophy, Translated by f.kersten, 1998 Kluwer Academic Publishers

He developed the concept of phenomenology as a new philosophical method to analyze and research consciousness, intentionality and sense.

What is phenomenology? Phenomenology is a theory about consciousness from a personal "first person" viewpoint, e.g. I experience phenomena in my consciousness and anybody else are experiencing in their consciousness from their own personal point of view. You could say phenomenology investigates how it feels to have a particular experience; how it feels to experience a taste of a fruit, it can be for example sweet or sourish, in short, how it feels to experience something.

Phenomenology is investigating the *Phenomenon,* i.e. the world around us that is being experienced by us, that is, when I undergo sensual experiences of it. I, for example, *see* the fruit on that tree in front of me; I see the fruit, i.e. experience it, I also experience its round shape and his greenish color, when I tap on the fruit I *hear* a certain sound, I *smell* its smell, I *touch* the fruit before I bite it and then I *taste* it.

A fruit is a structure of color, shape, smell, touch, taste and sound; this is my experience of the fruit! We experience the fruit as we experience anything else starting with simple objects like stones ending with lightning, thunders and galaxies. I experience the lightning through my eyes, hearing the thunder in my ears, all of which is part of the way by which we are experiencing the world; the world in this context is a phenomenon in my consciousness, it appears in my consciousness as the fruit appears in my consciousness in its specific form.

Phenomenology investigates the sense of the phenomena, the way by which objects appear before us in an experience, as well as the way by which we experience it in the world around us. We are realizing phenomenology each time we are asking ourselves "what do I see?", "what do I feel?", "what am I thinking about?", "what do I want?", "what do I intend to do?", all this is right *for us* as long as we answer the questions in a "first person" point of view when we define our experience by visual, auditory, tactical, olfactory and gustatory senses.

The psychotic patient, who is the subject of this paper, is also experiencing phenomenology wise, objects of various types; for example, a fruit on a tree: in his hallucinating consciousness he sees it, smells it, touches and tastes it. All of these acts are united by a synthesis to one conscious act which is a complex hallucination.

As an answer to the above mentioned questions, we, also, refer to our emotions, our thoughts, our feelings and our desirability. We give a phenomenological recounting of experiences when we report "I see the fruit on the tree", "I feel satiated after I have been tasting the fruit", "I am angry on what she has been telling me", "I think that Moses was a political leader", "I want to start a diet tomorrow", "I desire her", "I imagine the mountain", "I intent to start engaging in sports next week" and so forth.

Phenomenology, therefore, is describing the consciousness from a "first person" viewpoint, meaning, when we report on something subjectively. On the other hand, Neurology, a science that deals with the nerve system and the brain, investigates how the consciousness is created in the brain of someone, thus describing a neurological-mental state from a "third person" viewpoint-objectively. Neurological researchers investigate what neurotransmitters (like Dopamine in the case of delusions of psychotic patients) are being discharged in the brain when one thinks, or feels hunger etc., i.e. what parts of the brain are active when one is at such conscious state or another. As aforesaid, compared with the neurological viewpoint, phenomenology describes the objects of one's experience; "I see the fruit on the tree", "I feel tooth ache".

Today, philosophers dealing with consciousness who conduct their research together with cognitive researchers acknowledge the phenomenological analysis of the consciousness and acknowledge the fact that consciousness originates in brain states. The physician diagnoses the psychotic patient using phenomenology, i.e. the patient reports to the treating physician, from "first person" viewpoint, about his delusions, his hallucinations, his emotions, his emotional state and his desirability.

Philosophers of the consciousness or cognitive psychologists think that phenomenology deals mostly in the subjective quality of the sensual experience, as for example to see red. Husserl, however, did not refer to the sensual experience and its qualities as the exclusive object of the phenomenological analysis; Husserl referred to our perceptional experience as having a significant conceptual content which represents things around us in a richer form than just sensations. For him, phenomenology deals with a structure having sense of experience which is above and beyond sensations; phenomenology deals not only with sensations but also with imagination, passion or will and thought; all that while we are coming in contact with the world.

Sense is in the center of the phenomenological discourse. Sense is the content of a *conscious* experience. Sense distinguishes between all of our experiences; it also makes the link as a relation of the experience to something. Only through sense, consciousness is presenting us with a world made of an organized structure. Husserl characterizes phenomenology as transcendental. The central role played by the sense in our experience brings phenomenology to be positioned beyond the natural sciences including psychology.

As opposed to "natural" sciences, also called the precise sciences (physics, chemistry, biology) that deal in research by empirical observations and generalizations, the sense and logic in phenomenology is being researched in a different manner.

Husserl wanted to develop his method as pure science with a defined field of research and its own methodology. Sciences like physics, chemistry and biology are being developed by a systematical methodology in which we collect observations (which can be repeated continuously) and includes generalizations while performing a scientific analysis that includes also hypotheses and testing them in reality, meaning we validate the hypothesis using the facts in reality. By this methodology, the body of science is growing.

Phenomenology differs from the methodology of the precise sciences by the fact that the field of research, "the conscious experiencing" includes the experiences of the subject of the research, i.e. subjective; he is experiencing from a "first person" point of view. Therefore, phenomenology is a research from a "first person" point of view.

In phenomenology, we, therefore, are interested not in a specific experience, but in the *shape and form or in the structure of conscious experiencing* in general, objective forms of *experiences that are being realized in subjective experiencing, mine or yours.*

The objective phenomenological structure of experiencing includes, as said, the *sense that represents the object in the consciousness as was experienced by the subject.* The semantics and logic of conscious experiencing make the phenomenological investigation objective i.e. converting subjective experiencing to objective experiencing.

In Ideas I, Husserl specifically says (§ 34) that phenomenology is a science about the essence of consciousness. The essence of consciousness has two characteristics; the first is that each experience or a conscious act is happening in awareness; the experiencing subject is aware of performing the act i.e. I, for example, am aware of my thinking, I am aware of my fantasy, I am aware of my passions etc.

The first characteristic is, therefore, the awareness of each act in the consciousness. (Still, there are, apparently, acts of consciousness that are not aware, for example Freud divides the soul to three parts: conscious, sub conscious and non conscious, where there are non conscious impulses that affect our behavior and thoughts; phenomenology does not deal in these).

The second characteristic is that each conscious act is being conscious of something; in my sensual perception, I see or hear something; when I am imagining, I am imagining something; when I want, I want something, when I judge, I judge something being in a certain situation and so forth. This trait of the consciousness is relating always on something which is called by Husserl Intentionality; therefore, consciousness intends on something.

The experience is being intended toward something or onto something, an object of some kind. A conscious state or act stands for or represents some object (e.g. a thing- a fruit, an event- the war of independence, or a state of things- the fruit on the tree and so forth) through sense; therefore, intentionality is characterized by representativeness.

Intentionality, in everyday language, means that we intend our will or passion toward something, I, for example, intend to take ten kilograms off my weight. Most of our experiencing, as aforesaid, takes the form of *consciousness on or of something.* Husserl is using an *"act"* or *conscious act to indicate states or processes which are intentioned, a consciousness of or on something.*

In summary, Phenomenology, the research of the essence of consciousness as we are experiencing it, researches mainly the structure of intentionality i.e. sensual perception, imagination, judgment, emotions, desirability and passions, the consciousness of time-space, experiencing others i.e. in other "selves" and so forth. Phenomenology is dealing mainly in the way of which sensual perception, thought, feelings and act are being intended on something external.

## 13:30 Intentionality

In the fifth and sixth investigations of the logical investigations, Husserl deals with awareness or what is *consciousness* or *cognizance* in itself.

Husserl is not interested in neurology or physiology but in epistemology, he is interested in the cognitive element; that is, the term *"cognizance"* describes the phenomenon of the human knowledgeability (knowledge or information in the possession of a person) and its acquiring process, its processing and application. The phenomena which are included in the term *cognizance* are, among others, thinking, perception, understanding, learning, attentiveness, memory, creativity, representation, knowledge, drawing conclusions, making decisions and problem solving. The term cognizance describes, also, thoughts, ideas, opinions, beliefs, intentions, desirability, wishes, emotions and behaviorism.

Husserl is trying to describe cognizance as our awareness, that is, our experience as defined to us from a "first person" viewpoint (not in what is happening in the brain at the same time! He is not interested in the physiological and causal elements in the consciousness or cognizance).

Phenomenology is committed to depiction of what is given in the consciousness whether it is a subjective act or an external object. While analyzing the structure of our experience, he discovers that in most cases it is possible to characterize the experiencing as being *aware* of something, that is, the intentionality toward a thing or an object. Each conscious act is an intentional experience; however not every experiencing is a conscious act. "That not all experiences are intentional is proven by (the existence of) emotions and complex emotions" (logical investigations, V page 556). When we are itching, for example, we have an experience that is not an intentional act; there is no intentionality toward an object of some kind i.e. emotions of pleasure and the lack of pleasure, feelings of pain etc., must remain subjective and can never produces the representation of an object.

Intentionality is the trait of the consciousness in which it is being intended toward or onto an object or an external occurrence. Somebody is not just in love or is afraid or sees and judges, but

50

somebody is in love in somebody else, is afraid of something, desires something, imagines something, sees an object and judges a state of things. Whether we are dealing in perception, thought, judgment, fantasy, doubt, memory or hope, all these forms of consciousness (awareness) are characterized by the intentionality toward objects and are impossible to be analyzed without "it" that is perceived, "it" that is thought of, "it" that is doubted and "it" that is fantasized by us.

Most of the interpreters consider Husserl of 'Logical Investigations' as a realist i.e. if I observe that fruit in my hand therefore it is the real fruit which I am being intended onto and not only a mental picture, a copy or a representation of the fruit; I perceive the fruit itself; its existence is independent of my perception of it.

Husserl contends that in case of perception we have an immediate acquaintanceship with the object. By this assertion, in 'Logical Investigations', Husserl is protecting the perceptual realism. Realism in philosophy means that there is external object outside of our consciousness that does not dependent on it to exist.

In Husserl's opinion, so contends Zahavi, *there is no need of an intermediary image because we perceive the fruit of the tree itself, we intend directly onto real external objects. This intentionality is direct and not intermediary by any conscious representation.* Therefore, instead of contending that we are experiencing representation, we may say that our experience intend directly on the external world.

As opposed to the realist picture of phenomenology there is a question concerning objects that do not exist here and now in reality. When I think of absent objects, impossible objects, nonexistent objects, and objects existing in the future, it is clear that I do not intend toward them since they have influenced my consciousness in a causal way; that is, if I am thinking now about a fruit even though it does not exist now and here, then it is not possible that this fruit caused, through a causal chain, the creation of the thought or the image of the fruit in my consciousness.

Husserl's assertion, according to Dan Zahavi[4], is that the conscious acts are intentional whether or not the objects exist. The physical objects that exist in the physical reality around us comprise only of a small part of what I can be conscious of. Now, when I am sitting and working at my computer, I can imagine the moon or imagine myself eating ice cream, or calculate the root number of 9, or even imagine centaurs.

When I think of a centaur (In the Greek mythology, a race of creatures with a human torso and the lower body part of a horse), I do not think of anything but on something. In the phenomenological analysis we discover that fantasies or hallucinations are also intentional.

It is possible to intent to a nonexistent object, there is no need that the centaur will come out from mythology and will materialized in order to influence my consciousness in a causal way and will cause me to intend onto it. My intentionality does not end if it turns out that its object is nonexistent.

Intentionality is a relation between the consciousness and its object (that may not exist as in the case of a hallucination). Since the object does not always exist in reality, intentionality has to relate, primarily, to an intrinsic object i.e. an object that exists in

---

[4] Husserl's Phenomenology, Dan Zahavi, Stanford University Press (2003)

my consciousness; this is a subjective interpretation of intentionality.

The subjective interpretation of phenomenology is the intrinsic logic of hallucinations. In the case of hallucination, we see, touch, hear, smell and taste nonexistent external objects. Hallucinations are intentional; they intend something although it does not exist in reality here and now. Hallucination is a picture in my head without external input. However, and this is the important point, through the memory we touch the real thing; I, for example hallucinate the painting by Van Gogh 'starry night', my hallucination, then, is a recycled memory of the real painting I have seen yesterday in flesh. Husserl's assertion, according to Dan Zahavi, is that the conscious acts are intentional whether or not the objects exist. In psychosis, the logic of the hallucination is indeed the representation of the fruit, an intrinsic picture without an external stimulus; it is, in fact, a memory of a real fruit from the past, an object that was in existence in time-space in the *past* except *now* it is reconstructed to an intrinsic image; the intrinsic image of the fruit in its consciousness has touched the real fruit itself in the past but now it does not. The psychotic conscious act, according to its intrinsic logic, is being intended onto a memory of a fruit and through the conscious act of memory it is touching the fruit itself which simply exists in nature in flesh. Hallucinations are, therefore, an active imagination i.e. an image or an imitation; an image of a real fruit that we are remembering from the past.


How should we understand the position of Husserl when he says that intentionality is not only a characterization of actual objects, but also something that is the trait of our fantasies, our memories and so forth? Through direct perception and according to realistic interpretation, there exits an external object i.e. real transcendental object which we are touching instantly as opposed to the case of a psychotic where the logic is indeed the logic of the 'representing perceptual theory'; in hallucination or in fantasy, there exists an intrinsic image which is a memory or 'a thought on something from the past' which is, actually, an intentional content that mediates to an external transcendental object.

In a case of hallucinations in psychosis there are, as said, intrinsic representations; an images. In this sense the psychotic is an idealist which means that the existence of the object depends on the consciousness of the psychotic. What the psychotic has in his mind are only "pictures" or images; representations of an object and not the object in itself. The representation is what is present in the phenomenological consciousness of the psychotic; however it is an *image from the real past.* In the psychotic past he held the real fruit in his hands (realism) which is absent from his present. In hallucinations of the psychotic, *there is* an intrinsic image, the linguistic expression "the man over there at the corner" is a noetic content (sense) which is a representation (idealism) of a man at the corner that was there in the past; the image mediates between the perceiving subject and the perceived external object. The representation mediates between the past and the present. Therefore the psychotic was realist in the past; he perceived the real object, which means realism; but now at the time of hallucination he is an idealist since he "sees only images".

The content of hallucination is a memory and as such originates in the past; the image of the man that is being seen now does not exist in the present but originated in the man who we have seen yesterday and which arose and appears in the present of the

54

psychotic; or for example, the voice of the man is an echo from the past.

The hallucination is similar to the phenomenon of watching a movie; we are sitting in the movie theatre and watching a figure in the movie, this figure is an authentic and original photograph of a real man external to the movie—the actor (that was given to us as himself), but at the moment in which the movie is played we do not see the actual man but only the figure which represents the real man.

The figure that appears before us was united with or is identical to the real man in the past during the filming; now there is a gap of temporality between it and the real man. During the watching, the figure is present in the movie theatre but the man (the actor) is not, he is absent. I hear the man's voice through the figure, the voice is the same by the man (the actor) and by the figure since they are identical but now at the time of listening, I hear a voice that was recorded a day earlier. At that time, the real actor is not present, but the figure is.

The figure in the movie is not being united with the man because time has passed from the time of filming to the time of projecting the movie. That is, using the movie metaphor, the figure is a hallucination that was, in the past, a real actor.

What is left to us is to give a phenomenological linguistic description of the movie! A semantic noetic description!

The figure is an intrinsic image of the actor in the movie i.e. the actor exists externally to the movie, in reality, and he creates the image of the figure, but they do not coincide in time. The image which exists on the screen in the metaphor is the consciousness of the psychotic, the ego describes the movie by way of phenomenological analysis; the psychotic is, therefore, a temporal idealist;

I coin this stance idealism of temporality. In a hallucination the intentionality toward an object is characterized by the intentionality onto a transcendental object exactly the same as a perception is being intended toward or is denoting a transcendental object. However, as opposed to regular perception the object does not exist in the present. Zahavi contends that in a regular perception the consciousness is being intended toward an existing transcendental object, whereas in a fantasy or a hallucination, the consciousness is being intended toward a nonexistent transcendental object; but at the end the hallucinating consciousness is being intended onto an external object as well that was in existence in the past but is absent now in the present; it is being intended onto an intrinsic object (an intrinsic image) which is a recycled memory of an external real object from the past.

One more important comment is that the object of intentionality is never given to us in full but always through a certain perspective. When i *think* of an object, i will always think of it under certain descriptions and through certain terms, Husserl calls those perspectives phenomenological descriptions.
We cannot perceive an object totally through one appearance only; the object is never given to us in one perception, it is not being epitomized in one appearance, it remains always in a partial form. While it is possible to experience the object from different perspective then from the one that is being used now, the situation is different when we try to perceive the consciousness

itself. Trying to perceive the consciousness by a reflexive observation, I shall have a total perception without different perspectives. We discover that consciousness is intentional!

Husserl contends that the sense of the verb "intended" is that the consciousness is being intended onto something. The subject ("I") is being intended onto some object in an experience of any kind. For example, I am being intended onto the lion; in my conscious act I am being intended on an object of some kind. While we intend on the object under several perspective, I perceive the "I", the ego, immediately and in fullness.

When I think of the "The victor of Jena" and later I think of "The one who was defeated in Waterloo", I think of the same object who is Napoleon but I think of him in two different ways. That is, to imagine, to think, or to point out someone as the victor of Jena is to act differently than to think or to imagine or to point out someone as the one who was defeated in Waterloo. The sense that is expressed is different although the object that was being intended onto is the same (Logical Investigations, I page 287). The sense of the first thought is the assertion "The victor of Jena" whereas the sense of the second thought is the assertion "The one who was defeated in Waterloo". These two assertions or terms are different ways to signify the same object, in that case a person named Napoleon. Those are the two ways of the phenomenological description, that is, two different contents of my consciousness, the one "The victor of Jena" and the second "The one that was defeated in Waterloo". The content or the sense is semantically linked to contents and additional senses that are linked to napoleon, for example, the fact that he was a Corsican. These senses or contents define the outline of the object that is represented in my thought of Napoleon.

While conscious acts as seeing a tree or a roaring lion carry a sense or content that describes the perceptual object, the conscious acts themselves occur in a flow of sensual experiencing. We live "through" a flow of sensual experiencing that includes a synthesis or a link of all senses to one experience; the sense of vision, the auditory sense, the tactition sense, the olfaction sense and the gustatory sense create with us an intentional experiencing that is perceived as one flow of consciousness while the flow is an event occurring in time. In the sensual consciousness we are experiencing a structure of *temporality*. The temporal flow of the sensual consciousness plays a decisive role in our experiencing of the world surrounding us.

In the flow of *temporality* we are aware of events that flow in time surrounding us (roaring lion, rolling thunder, a blooming flower). In the same flow of our experiences we, also, are aware of events- our own conscious experience that flows in time.

Our daily experiencing of physical things links between space and temporality; when I see the fruit on the tree and I am experiencing it as a temporal spatial object in nature. We are experiencing physical things positioned in relation to our body through which we make contact with objects. When I reach my hand to pluck the fruit, I perceive it in relation to my body; I see it, I reach my hand to it, I have the feeling of movement.

I am always experiencing things as positioned in relation to me; I am the point of reference. When I see the fruit on the tree I perceive the tree moving in the wind and the fruit on it in front of my eyes. My field of vision defines my sense of movement; when I see the fruit I turn or raise my head and watch it through my eyes. Therefore, the world around me is temporal as well as spatial. We are the point of reference! When I am experiencing the tree I am

58

not only experiencing it as a visual object, I am also smelling it, tasting it and even hearing myself biting it. Nowadays cognitive psychologists are speaking about the union of the whole of the sensual perceptions by the brain that creates a body of information which comprises of visual, auditory and tactile information (Husserl puts the brain in "brackets" and turns his attention to our experiences or experiencing the fruit).

We perceive all objects around us as temporal and also as positioned in space in relation to us. The object of my consciousness *is being formed* "as the same object" as I have been intended onto by various acts of perception.

We intend and are experiencing the "same object" from different perspectives, from different intentional acts. Moreover, the object is being formed as the same object, also, as far as one is concerned, by additional perceptions. That is, I perceive the fruit, now, on the tree one meter away from me; I can move further away and then the fruit is being formed two meters away from the position it was formed before.

"The same object" (the fruit) is being formed in different ways of intentional experiencing, one way is from a close distance, another way is from afar, however, this is still the same fruit on the tree! Moreover, my intentional experiencing of the fruit is also a perception of the fruit with other possibilities. I can experience the falling of the fruit thus experiencing the fruit on the ground and then again it is the same fruit! The fruit is the *same* fruit that is being formed into something else in my experiencing of it.

This formation of the same fruit in different perceptions is possible or actually is linked to our experiencing of time-space. Time and space are linked to each other in our experiencing of the physical things.

On one hand, time compels the formation of objects in space; on the other hand, space compels the formation of objects in time. For example, in sensual experiencing, "the same object" is being formed when I am moving around it in space and at the same moment I am also "surrounding" it in time; that is, time passes while I am experiencing it in space, when I am moving around it, a certain period of time is passing.

I perceive the "same object", the fruit as a spatial object of which falling has taken time. The fruit is falling down from the tree, "the fruit is in front of my eyes now", and it is always in time-space especially when I am moving.

Physical or spatial objects are being formed "as the same object" also when I perceive them in the future, I am experiencing them now and in the future while they are being formed and changed or I am changing the angle by which I am observing them. In Ideas I, Husserl emphasizes the importance of the term the *formation* of physical objects; he analyzes the consciousness of "the same object" in different experiences. I can experience different perceptions of the object from different perspectives and angles.


### 13:35 Act, sense and object


According to Husserl, intentional experiencing may be analyzed in the following manner: the mental process itself is an intentional act; the intrinsic intentional content of the act; and the sense of the experience focusing on what was intended on, i.e. on the intended object as it was and which we are aware of.

The intentional content is what gives the consciousness its intentional trait, that is, to intend on something. There are different types of consciousness, for example belief, desirability, doubt etc. Taking an example used by Zahavi: I believe that the dead see is healthy, I may want to swim in it and I may be afraid to swim in it. All these types of experiences (belief, desirability, and fear) are different contents of the conscious act.

Every intentional experiencing is of a certain type, experiencing hope, experiencing fear, experiencing passion, experiencing remembrance, doubtfulness, judgment etc. Husserl names this aspect of experiencing as 'intentional quality'.

In addition to the first qualitative "moment" there is the second material "moment". Every intentional experiencing is intended on something, it is about something, a green fruit, the number 5 or about a triangle.

Husserl names the component, which describes the subject of the experiencing 'the intentional material' of the experience. That 'intentional quality' can be integrated with a different 'intentional material' and that 'intentional material' can be integrated with different 'intentional qualities'.

I can have fear from lions, or have fear from a horror movie or have fear of dying. On the other hand, I can judge that the 'green fruit'…, desire the 'green fruit' or negate that the 'green fruit'…; the 'intentional quality' and the 'intentional material' are abstract components which cannot exist separately.

According to Husserl the 'intentional material' is what gives the conscious act its trait 'being intended on an object' while the 'intentional quality' only empowers the intentionality but is not founding it. The 'intentional material' is what gives the conscious act its sense; we intend an object by making a meaningful saying about it. The link to an object is created by giving it a sense, that is, to use an expression or, identically, to denote it in a meaningful way. The sense is what gives the consciousness its intentionality on an object. An expression is with sense if it denotes an object, if it exists. The 'intentional material' does not merely determines toward which object it intended but also how the object is perceived, that is, how do we perceive the fruit in our consciousness. We are not just aware of the object but we are aware of the object in a certain manner, for example to be aware of the fruit in a certain manner from a certain angle in space.

We intend (perceive, imagine and judge) the object as something, i.e. by terms, descriptions or by certain perspectives. For example, the man over there at the corner is an assassin or a secret agent; we describe the object in a certain manner. To think about "the morning star" or "the evening star" is to think about Venus, about the same object by different descriptions.

To think about the sum of 2+2 or to think about the sum of 3+1 is to think about the number 4 by different ways.

We think about the same object by terms, descriptions and different perspectives, that is, by a different 'intentional material'. One 'intentional material' cannot be intended in different objects, on the contrary, different "intentional materials" can denote the same object. Zahavi says that although we always intend an object by way of sense, we have to distinct between the conscious act, the sense and the object. The object, either a physical object as a fruit or an ideal object as the number 5 is different from the conscious act i.e. from the process of intentionality.

## 13:40 Phenomenological description

We are applying phenomenology each time we describe from a "first person" point of view a conscious experiencing. For example, "I see the cat over there", here I am experiencing an intentional vision of the cat in my consciousness; the cat is what the consciousness intends to. "I hear that thunder from afar", here the thunder is the object of the intentionality of my consciousness by way of hearing, I am experiencing the thunder as a noise in my ears; "Now I think of venus", here, again, Venus is the object to which my consciousness intends by way of thought; "I admire venus", now I intend on my admiration for Venus; "I feel fear when I hear the thunder", here I fear the thunder; "I remember my first love and the face of my beloved", here, my phenomenological experience is a memory that also intends to an object that is my beloved; "I imagine myself as someone like Abraham who is very important", in this case my experience is an imagination; "shortly, I want to light a cigarette", that is, I intend the cigarette which is the object of my desire; "I intend to start a diet next week", in this case the object of my intentionality is the intention to loose weight, etc.

These descriptions of conscious experiencing are called, as aforesaid, "phenomenological descriptions"! Each description that was given by me describes an act or a conscious act from a "first person" point of view. The subject or the "I" which Husserl calls ego, is being intended with his consciousness onto something; the description captures the sense of the consciousness' experience. These descriptions are called by Husserl "transcendental" phenomenology. The phenomenological method of Husserl is, as aforesaid, a reflexive method, being aware i.e. describing conscious experience.

I have to "put in brackets" the question of whether the world outside my consciousness exists, that is, I am supposed to put a question mark as to the existence of the object that I see (or desire or think about) "before my eyes". I am supposed to focus on my consciousness and on the object as it appears in it, on my experiencing it and to describe a phenomenological description of my consciousness on that object.

The method of Husserl "to put in brackets" (which will be developed in more detailes later) is meant to divert my attention from the objects to my consciousness of the objects and the way by which I am experiencing them. I am focusing on how my experiencing is being intended on the world and on the objects as I am experiencing them.

Please think about the experiment of "the brain in the vat" by Hillary Putnam that may be possible in the future. We have a brain in the vat suspended in a fluid material called CSF (the material in which the brain is suspended inside the skull).

Let us assume that the scientists have succeeded by applying electrical signals into the brain's nerve cells to cause the brain to create images of a fruit and of, for example, the skies and oceans; of course, no fruit is in existence outside the brain! There are only electrical signals that create in the brain images of a fruit or a sound of thunder etc. It may be that nothing exists "in the outside" and that the sights and sounds that I "see" or "hear" are only like hallucinations because hallucinations do not have any external input;

I am not contending that there are no fruits in the world "outside" the brain, but we want to focus on what is the consciousness of the fruit, that is, what taste it has, smell, color, texture or how am I experiencing the sky, how is it to swim in the ocean and so forth. In this state I am aware of things, I "see", "feel", "want", "desire" etc. Let us assume that the brain will be connected to a super computer; the brain with the help of a language by the computer can describe its experience to us. The computer will describe a phenomenological description about what it "sees", "feels", "wants", "desires" etc.

The description will be linguistic! In "Logical Investigations" (1900-1) Husserl shows how our experience of the consciousness is logically linked to a language. He shows the link between consciousness, assertions and the world. By using a language we can describe and analyze a phenomenological analysis.

In logical investigations, Husserl makes a distinction between the content and the object of intentional experiencing. When I think of "the man that took the sons of Israel out of Egypt", I think of Moses, which is the object of my consciousness, I can also think "the prince of Egypt that was pulled out from the river Nile" but then the *object* of my thought or my consciousness (Moses) has to be noticeable from the *content* of my thought because different assertions or terms can describe or represent the same object.

The two contents of my consciousness, "the prince of Egypt that was pulled out from the river Nile" and "the man that took the sons of Israel out of Egypt", are different, that is, different thoughts or phenomenological description, but the object is one, Moses.

In addition to the phenomenological analysis of ideal contents of different experiences, phenomenology will also research the ways by which different experiences are united into one conscious flow in one's ego. I see the pictures in the movie, listen to the sound track, sit on a chair, intend to eat salted pop corn and feel pleasure. All these contents are united into one conscious act *(watching a movie)* in the ego of a person.

The ego also perceives spatial objects and it is the point of reference. We are aware by a sensual perception of things in time and space around us. We see things, hear things and come in contact with things around us. These things have traits, for example, color, form and texture. They are positioned in a spatial link (in time and space) to other things and in relation to us. Moreover, we are aware in a sensual perception to processes or events that occur in time, as well to objects persisting in time. A rock, for example, exists thousands of years in spite of the fact that it can undergo erosion but still we think of it as the same rock. Likewise, we see other people and talk to them. We feel love, fear, awe and hatred. Likewise the acts or our conscious acts occur in time, we are also aware of the passing time. I have a memory of experiences from the past and expectations of future experiencing and at the same time I have awareness to my conscious experiencing in the present. My consciousness of time is dependent on these links between memory, expectations for the future and awareness to my past experiences.
At this state I am aware at the same time to the temporality of things in the world around me and also to the flow of my intrinsic time, that is, to the temporality of our experiencing, we ourselves and others, all exist in time-space.

The sum of all my experiences exists in the flow of consciousness. The experiencing inside the flow of consciousness is coherent, thus I have different experiences of the same object: when I walk around the table, I see it, touch it, I walk away from it, all that time I am aware of the same table. All of these experiences from the different perspectives are of the same table. Without forms or that structure of the intentionality projected from that subject ("I") toward the same object (the table), my consciousness did not have the coherence needed to create one coherent experience. The *uniformity of the consciousness* is a precondition to anything else that I am doing, I see, hear and touch and as a result I can walk and talk, feel, think of various things, join with others etc.

The concept of intentionality is an Archimedean point in the account given by Husserl on phenomenology as a science of the sense of consciousness. The concepts of act, content and object of consciousness are being developed in investigation V of Logical Investigations.

Let us assume that I am walking in the field on a sunny day enjoying the walk. Suddenly I hear a roar and to my amazement I see a lion with his mouth open moving through the bushes.

My sensual experiencing is a visual consciousness (that acts on the senses) of a lion; I see the lion; I hear it moving through the bushes. According to Husserl analysis the intentional ratio between conscious act to an object in my consciousness is *constructed* in a way by which the background, that is, all that I know of lions at the time of the walk in the field creates certain content.

The content is 'the lion that I saw during my walk in the field'; the object of my conscious experiencing, the lion, enables an horizon of possibilities; this horizon is all the possibilities that can exist for the objects 'lion', 'sun' and 'field'.

The subject who is "I", in a conscious act, sees the lion visually which is an object in the consciousness while I have "at the background" information (all that I know...) on fields, lions, sun etc. and "at the front" there exist few open possibilities.

Husserl calls these possibilities "Horizon". The objects are always presented that way or the other. The objects are always more than we actually perceive.

For example, the lion that is walking in the field is perceived only from a certain perspective. I can see or remember or imagine it from the front or from the side and maybe I am positioned just under it and observe it from beneath. It may be that I have a perception of all of his side and when I approach it, I have a narrower perception on one hand but on the other hand I perceive more details. I suddenly notice, at close range, its mane, teeth, fur and ears. However, there is no possibility for the representation of the lion in its generality; I cannot perceive, at the same time, all of its sides and traits. The point being that I do have only partial perspective of the lion.

Husserl calls the different angles—perspectives from which an object can be perceived by us 'shadings' (Abschattungen).

If we examine the nature of these shadings from a phenomenological point of view, we can see that they have a complex intrinsic structure; the structure enables them to have an intrinsic relation to other descriptions which are not present. If we are thinking of a concrete experience of perception, let us say a visual experiencing of a lion, we are tempted to think, naively, that something is presented to us which is, more or less, stable, static, intrinsic and independent, something as a picture.

Every given perception holds in itself insinuation of past experiences and prospective experiences, in other words, my intentional object is a three dimensional, physical object with four sides, face, place and history.

For example, the lion is in a certain place in time-space and has a history from the time it was a young lion. When I watch the lion, my sight is directed and moving from one of its parts to the other. What I have seen, that is, the side of the lion, still leaves some impression in my consciousness, it is linked to the present and continues to define the object; moreover, the object which I perceive now leaves me with the impression of expectation of what I will see in the future, therefore, in a certain sense it was already determined or defined; seeing its golden mane, I expect to see it that way in the future.

Each description contains a structure of 'a memory from' and 'an expectation for' which are functions of memory, imagination, expectations and habits. A description, due to its sense, remains in an intrinsic relation to past or prospective descriptions which in return creates a system of cross references to experiences. There is intentional *horizon* of potential references to the consciousness.

The experiencing is what we have to focus on in a pure intentionality, that is, we have to focus on the conscious act and ignore anything else. The conscious act in itself is a state or a mental process; its object is different from the act itself, in our case, the lion toward which our conscious act is being intended.

To remind you, intentionality occurs always on or toward something external! The object of my experiencing is a lion walking in the field provided that such lion exists and is not a hallucination. All that I have is a consciousness of a lion but I am not confident that a lion exists external to my consciousness; there is always the possibility that the lion is a hallucination or fantasy in my head.

For you and for the psychotic, "lion" can be a synthesis of five senses. As I have contended at 09:15, hallucinations are defined as sensual perceptions *without external stimulus*, therefore the lion which I apparently see, smell, hear and touch is no more than a figment of the psychotic's imagination, without anything existing outside. The subject of the experience in our story is "I", the individual that has a conscious experience, in other words the ego.

To summarize, the conscious act is the content or *the intentional content;* the content is characterized by the answer to the question of what do I see or hear or imagine?

The description is simply a description of what I see and how do I see it. In our case as I have mentioned before, the content is *the assertion* 'the lion which I have seen while walking in the field on a sunny day'. The content represents the visual object, that is, the assertion 'the lion which I have seen while walking in the field on a sunny day' represents or stands for the visual object as I have been experiencing it.

The same object can be represented by different contents, for example, I can see the lion from a different physical point of view and then my description will be different. In the said experience the representation of the object will be by a visual content.

The content of a conscious act lays down the background of lions for the subject; they roar, they are mammals, they can be dangerous and that is why we must beware of them and so forth.

The background which we have on lions defines the possibilities of my experiencing. I know that I will not see, for example, the lion producing horns; on the other hand, I know that there is a chance that it will devour me should I not withdraw.

Husserl calls these possibilities "a horizon", but they exist only in the context of a certain background. The content lays down the background that I have on lions in general, that is, the knowledge that I have on lions which leaves possibilities open as to how the lion will behave in the future ("horizon"). All these traits are part of the intentional ratio between an act and my conscious object. That is, in my intentionality there is a link, as we have seen before, between the conscious act in itself, the conscious content and the object it represents.

## 14:00 Myself, others and interpersonal

Except for fruits, trees, tables and lions there are more objects that exist in relation to us. These objects have a mass like the fruit, but they have one more important property, they are also "mental"; there are other people near me, more "I"s.

I see around me other people, other "I", other beings which are subjects with their own consciousness that are part of the human race and are also organism of nature; however they are also "mental", members of my culture.

Therefore when I see things and objects in time-space around me, I understand these things as "exist for everybody", these things are being perceived by others (humans), that is, others are experiencing them also.

The world around me is an interpersonal world. The "interpersonal" is something that I am experiencing in a natural way, I look at objects, I think about them etc., we are social creatures that live in socialization with other people, that is with our family, our friends, our people and so forth.

I can experience myself as a subject, as a biological creature and as a social creature. I can experience in others (humans), other "I", the same way. As I have said, I can perceive others as another subject that sees what I see, hears what I hear and feels what I feel (by empathy). I perceive them as another living person, for example, as a worker when he plucks the fruit from the tree, as a human biological creature when he has a sore knee, I, also, perceive him as a member of my community. I can experience natural objects that are related to me thanks to our essential property, the intentional experiencing which materializes in social and cultural act.

When I see the fruit on the tree I am experiencing it while it is available to be experienced by others; the object of my perception is being formed as available to the experiences of others; especially that object is being formed as an interpersonal, physical thing which is identical by me and by you, the fruit is the same fruit for both of us.

The same thing is right also for other persons, I and others perceive the same person, for example, having the same emotions. That way, the object is being formed as an interpersonal thing, that is, I and others can perceive it the same way. An object is interpersonal as long it is accessible to an intentional conscious act by other subjects, by me, by you and by others. My experience of interpersonal objects places in my consciousness other subjects.

How am I aware to the others as others? My perception of the other is the formation of a material thing, a physical thing in nature but not only! Surely, the other is being formed as a living creature, in nature, but, in addition, it is perceived as a member of the human community.

According to Husserl, our first experiencing of others is by empathy. We are experiencing animals in nature as physical objects with mental life. I see the dog immediately and directly as a being which is a body full of life with its own experiences and passions.

Similarly, I am experiencing, by empathy, another human being as a being with body and soul. By experiencing through empathy, I am experiencing another person as someone with a body and with mental experiencing; I see in the other "a human being"!

Husserl contends that I transfer that term of body and mental experiencing from the other to me and vice versa. In "on the Problem of Empathy", Edith Stein, Husserl's student, contends that by empathy, the sense of the "I" (ego) is being transferred between the totality of my experience and that of the other, therefore empathy is a form of intuition or direct experiencing another "I", an experience through which I understand the experiencing by the other as if I am the one who is experiencing in his place. By intuition, I am experiencing the other "I"; when I am experiencing the other I am not only experiencing a physical thing but also you that is, something with a soul or consciousness.

The sense "I" is being transferred from me to the other. Husserl analyzes empathy as a productive form of the experience by the other as if I myself am living through it. When I see somebody else, the content of my seeing the other is actually another "I" that sees the object as if I was in his place.

My present consciousness presents in a productive manner (the type of experiencing, in which the sense of "I" is being transferred, is called by Husserl 'productive') what is being experienced by another "I" in his case, but while maintaining a certain *distance.*

I "relive" the other and the experience of the other from a certain distance exactly as I know that he is at a certain distance from me. That way the other "I" is experiencing by empathy which is being formed as if I would have lived by this way of experiencing in my flow of consciousness. From an ontological point of view the intentional content or the sense "I" is my unique awareness by the way by which I am aware of myself as "I" while the other is aware of himself also as "I".

In my flow of consciousness the sense "I" is characteristic of me; in your flow of consciousness the sense "I" is a characteristic of you. Empathy is being created out of common understanding of consciousness in the "first person" form. I understand, in a direct manner, that you see a thing in an identical manner more or less as I would have seen the thing if I was only in your shoes seeing the thing from your perspective. I understand that I see the fruit on the tree the same way as you see it if I would have been in your place and see it from your perspective.

Having said that empathy is being created out of common understanding of consciousness in the "first person", you do not understand the psychotic because you see him from the "third person", something is always hidden from your eye, that is, his intrinsic consciousness (the hallucinations and delusions);

However, and that is an important point, you can understand him by empathy and so understand the hallucinations or the vivid imagination as if it was yours; this understanding is possible only because the semantic language is ideal, it is objective.

You can understand the psychotic by empathy, you fantasize his fantasy and you "see" what he sees and thinks his delusions as if you are in his place; in Ideas II, Husserl analyzes empathy as an imagination that I develop when I supposedly am in the place of the other, I am supposedly imagining how is it to be in his place.


## 14:15 The development of phenomenology


Philosophy, according to Husserl, must start from logic that investigates ideal sense and gives account and analyzes the logical ratio and the analogies between assertions. Philosophy has to investigate semantics and ideal sense; it is what philosophers today call logic.

Semantics states that there is a match between sense and external objects where assertions represent state of things in the world. Objective knowing is the basis for assertions, which is if I say "it was raining" thus a state of events must exist that actually it was raining.

In Ideas I Husserl makes a transcendental change. Phenomenology is not a step between pure logic and objective knowledge, but is the basis of logic as well as the basis of objective knowledge. When we define logic (semantics), an objective knowledge (epistemology) and ontology (the theory of being, the basic study the basic things constituting the world; for example, electrons and protons, how they are linked, what is their essence, their properties, etc) we are doing so by the structure of the consciousness, that is, by intentionality. The intentionality is, therefore, a precondition to logic (semantics or the theory of the sense), epistemology (the theory of knowledge) and ontology (the theory of being). Every sense is based on consciousness and the mission of phenomenology is the analysis of the structures of consciousness as we are using them in conscious experiencing like seeing, imagination, emotions and feelings, desirability and thinking.

In Husserl opinion phenomenology is transcendental; it is the focusing of the consciousness on an object and particularly on the structure of an ideal sense or noema that represents such object in such a way. Transcendental phenomenology provides a basis for philosophy, science and art. In Ideas I, Husserl makes few distinctions which I will examine extensively later on in this essay; for now, he makes a distinction between consciousness, feelings, sensual perception, that is, I perceive the fruit using my five senses, intentionality and terms as "noesis" (real and concrete experience) and "noema" (the content of ideal sense). Husserl continues and distinguishes between logic, evidence which is intuitions and the objectivity of the knowledge.


## 14:15 The method of phenomenology, an initial discussion.


Phenomenology must investigate the way by which we are experiencing the different forms of consciousness and needs to characterize "how is it" to experience different states of consciousness. In Ideas I, Husserl presents the method for phenomenology; Husserl presents phenomenology as a new and criticizing science. He takes upon himself to investigate and examine all assertions and suppositions that the dogmatic and objective sciences are making in advance. However, it is not possible to start the revolutionary research if we accept in advance the assumptions of metaphysics and epistemology that characterize everyday life and are accepted by all sciences. The metaphysical assumptions discussed by Husserl are, primarily, the assumptions and the absolute belief in the existence of a world independently from a consciousness. Many commentators see Husserl, at this point, changing his mind and move from realism to idealism.

Our "natural standing" includes a complex system of beliefs interwoven and supportive of each other that regulate our everyday life and its understanding. We believe, for example, in the existence of things external to the consciousness; actual reality that extends in time-space and comprises of objects that have causal influence on each other.

Our system of beliefs include also the belief that the world is populated with other people with consciousness of their own, that enjoy feelings, emotions, perceptions, thoughts and emotions similar to those we have.

The natural standing includes also the belief that, generally, the world is similar to the one that is perceived by us. Moreover, we believe in the validity of logic and mathematics and the truth of science. Our commitment to the natural standing enables us not only to perform our everyday acts and think sensibly, but also enables us our yearning for the objective truth of the natural and human sciences.

The important trait of the natural standing is, for Husserl, the philosophical naivety; that is, naivety that is transferred to the natural and human sciences.

For David Bell[5] the commitments of natural standing are ontological commitments. They are commitments to the existence of physical objects, the existence of traits, of facts, of individuals with consciousness, of causal links, of space, namely of realism.

The realistic assumption is so rooted that in addition to being accepted by the sciences it is also being diffused into our views on everyday life. Therefore, Husserl calls this standing "the natural standing". It does not matter how obvious and natural it is to assume the "natural standing"; Husserl insists that, philosophically, we should not accept its validity as obvious. Our investigation should be criticizing and not dogmatic. It must be guided by what is actually given to us and not by what is expected by us to be found, given our theoretical commitment.

The investigation must focus on the way by which reality is given to us through *experiencing*. We should not let predesigned or guided theories create experiencing but let experiencing determine theory. We should let the original or initial intuition that is given to us to be the source of all knowledge, a source that no authority (not even the exact sciences) may raise questions about it. Groundwork should be done before the start of the investigation, that is methodological preparations.

[5] Proper disclosure, in some cases I have used text of three thinkers: David Bell, Dan Zahavi and David Wooddruff Smith. Following are the books:
David Bell, Husserl, Routledge 1990
David Woodruff Smith, Husserl, Routledge
Dan Zahavi, Husserl's Phenomenology, Stanford University Press (2003)

In order to avoid naive, reasoning assumptions (including metaphysical suppositions on the nature of reality), it is necessary to *suspend* the acceptance of "the natural standing". We keep the natural standing for research purposes but bracketing its validity. This procedure which requires the suspension of the realistic natural tendency is called by Husserl epochè. Further on, I will use the expressions "the reduction", "the phenomenological reduction", "the transcendental reduction" or the epochè in order to name the same procedure.

The central technique of the epochè is called "bracketing", in German "Einklammerung", i.e. we are bracketing the world around us; this is done in order to draw our attention to the sense of the object as we are experiencing it. Husserl characterizes the bracketing method as a change in our standing toward the world. I am drawing my attention to the sense that an object has for me through my visual experiencing it (visual and vocal). Following the bracketing I am not asking whether the lion does indeed exist in time-space, only focusing on my consciousness of the lion. So I focus on the lion by way of which I "see" or experience it as he appears in my consciousness without considering whether it exists indeed. If you wish, following the bracketing I avoid the question whether I have a hallucination, instead I am focusing on what appears befor me; I describe it and do not consider the question whether I am hallucinating.

In changing this standing I turn to the object as it is perceived in my consciousness. I turn toward the consciousness which I am experiencing as a consciousness of an external object. Using the "natural standing", I see the fruit as existing outside my consciousness. Following the bracketing I put a question mark on the existence of the fruit outside my consciousness, that is, I ask whether the fruit exists in the world objectively and not only in my consciousness. I focus on the way by which the object is represented in me seeing it, that is in my consciousness.

## 14:45 Bracketing

In the "natural standing", we accept the existence of a world around us as obvious, that is, I accept myself and the world existing in time-space as obvious; I am aware of the world that exist in time.

I am aware of the world around me by my senses. As far as I am concerned, physical objects are there. I am not dreaming.

The assumption that out there in "the outside", a world exists around me independently of my consciousness is called by Husserl "the general thesis of the natural standing".

So, I assume that here before me, my laptop exists and it is not part of a dream; this is a thesis of the common sense. Now, let us assume that I put the thesis of "the natural standing", a thesis of the common sense, in "brackets".

David Woodruff Smith, in his book "Husserl"[6] contends that we do not deny the thesis of the existence of the world around us, we continue to believe it, but we do not make use of it.

We do not perform the epochè in order to negate, abandon or doubt the reality that is being researched, but to suspend few dogmatic standings of reality, that is, in order to focus directly on what is given to us in phenomenology- the objects as they appear in a conscious experience.

---

[6] David Woodruff Smith, Husserl, Routledge.

By reduction, as said, I am not doubtful; I do not negate the existence of objects and the causal links between them and my consciousness. Following the reduction I suspend the thesis, I have a different ideal standing, I do not observe the world as I have seen it, that is, in a realistic way.

The epochè requires a radical change in our standing on reality but it does not require its invalidation; through this suspension we can approach reality in a way by which we can unravel its true sense. To talk about the sense of reality in this context does not mean that the being of reality, that is, the true existence of the world is somehow being negated from the field of research of phenomenology.

Through the epochè, we will discover a new way of experiencing (also in psychosis), of thinking and of theorizing that will be open for philosophers; a way that stands above the natural being and the natural world; the philosopher does not lose or negate the existence and the truths of the physical world. The world is not lost by the epochè.

When I look around me I am not focusing on the existence of things around me, if they exist at all, but I am turning my attention to their appearance in my consciousness. In other words, I turn my eyes or my attention away from the objects of my consciousness to my consciousness experiencing objects. By changing such standing which is called a phenomenological standing I apply phenomenology! I reflect or *look* at my consciousness as it is being intended on things while I am not considering the question of their existence in the world around me. The purpose of bracketing is the creation of a new field of research, the field of "the pure consciousness", "pure experiencing" and "pure I".

The aims of the bracketing method may be presented in the following way:

1) The thesis of our natural standing is that there is a world existing outside our consciousness, we also act within it.

2) In order to turn my attention from the things in the world around me I have to "bracket" the general thesis of the natural standing.

3) Now I turn my attention to how things are perceived in my consciousness, that is, how they are in my consciousness.

4) Now, that I have turned my attention away from the world around me to my consciousness, I give a phenomenological description of experiencing or of different states of consciousness as I am experiencing them from a "first person" point of view, I report how is my perception of the fruit for me.

Husserl, as said, calls this method "epochè", that is, I am avoiding the assumption that the world exists outside; "epochè" is a Greek word for avoiding. Moreover, Husserl also called this method phenomenological reduction i.e. I suspend certain theses about the existence of the physical world including scientific theses, theological and even logical. Thus, in a pure description of experience in my consciousness I suspend everything I know about physics, God, etc.

Husserl also uses the word annihilation (Vernichtung) of the world, that is, *annihilation* or emptying the world from its content and from its objects (Ideas I § 49).

Through the change of my standing toward the world I describe in a phenomenological way the different experiences exactly as I am experiencing them. These descriptions characterize the content or the sense of my experiences, i.e. the objects are the objects which are being experienced by me, irrespective whether the objects as they are represented by sense do exist!

David Woodruff Smith contends that in this account of the phenomenological method we use Husserl's intentional theory; a conscious act is being intended through sense toward an object, thus, phenomenology studies the experiencing and the content or the sense and not the objects themselves.

If I am experiencing rain, then the sense of "rain" is the rain itself (an external object, literally, water coming down from the sky), i.e. the term "falling rain" denotes a state in which water is coming down from the sky.

In phenomenology, on the other hand, I examine and describe the "rain" as I am experiencing it; I describe the experience of the rain as it appears in my consciousness, I am experiencing sense, "Rain" is a content of a certain feeling in my consciousness.

I walk in the field and I see before me a lion, therefore in phenomenology, I give a description of what I see and ignore the question whether it is a hallucination, I describe how I am experiencing the lion in my consciousness, that is, I "see" the lion before me. By the phenomenological reduction (epochè) I do not ask myself whether the assertion or the term "here is a lion" really represents a lion that exists before me, but "here is a lion" that exists in my consciousness and being compatible with a certain experience in my consciousness.

In order to understand the psychotic and the reduction in its purest form you have to experience his hallucinations through him by empathy, you are not supposed to ask whether he really sees a lion that may or may not exist in reality, you have to suspend the question whether he, the psychotic, have hallucination, in other words, you have to stop calling him psychotic; but you have to focus and turn your attention to what he sees in his consciousness and that is the intentional experiencing of content or the realization of the "lion"; he, the psychotic, has to describe to you his conscious experience of the lion. We have to understand psychosis as an epochè. Imagine yourselves as psychotics to enable the change of your natural standing.

The method for understanding the psychosis is, therefore, to make a phenomenological reduction and to intend on the experiencing of the psychotic. By making such reduction we do not ask whether his consciousness represents real things in the world (time-space) or whether it is a hallucination, but we focus on how the lion, for example, is being perceived in his consciousness.

Moreover, as for the delusions of the psychotic perceiving himself, for example, as the Messiah Ben David, you should not ask whether he is really the Messiah or it is a misbelief, try simply to understand how he is experiencing himself as a Messiah, how he sees himself, how he feels and what he wants as a Messiah.

I think that your entry into a psychotic state not only clarifies for you what it means to be psychotic but also will clarify for you what is a phenomenological reduction in its most authentic form.

The first step, therefore, toward the understanding of the psychotic's consciousness or the understanding of transcendental phenomenology is by empathy. Empathy, as I have said at 14:00, is a form of intuition or a direct experiencing of the other "I", an experience in which I understand the experiencing of the other as if I am the one that is experiencing his experience.

By intuition, I am experiencing or having an experience of the other "I". So, by empathy, put yourselves in the shoes of the psychotic, see the things from his subjective perspective and try to experience his experiences as he reports them from a "first person" point of view. I say, you have to ignore the question whether the mentally ill is experiencing a psychosis, that is, he has a hallucination; on the other hand you should not assume that there is a world out there; you should suspend your natural standing.

You have to assume seriously the phenomenological standing that a world may not exist outside your consciousness; the epochè of insanity is the true and the purest way to practice phenomenology; through the psychosis you practice phenomenology in its purest and most authentic form and are avoiding the thesis of the natural standing.

David Woodruff Smith contends that in Ideas I Husserl does not state explicitly the link between the phenomenological reduction method and intentionality. Such link is only implicit. When Husserl starts applying the method, he presents the consciousness as I am experiencing it.

The basic trait of the consciousness, of each conscious experience, is to be the consciousness of something, meaning the consciousness is being intended on something. While developing and laying out the structure of intentionality, he evaluates the way by which the consciousness presents its object, from a "first person" point of view; I see or imagine (fantasizing or hallucinating) or think (even delusions) or desire an object.

In order to characterize experience from a phenomenological point of view, we have to evaluate the content or the sense of the experience and its role in the representation of an object of the
85

consciousness as such. Through the phenomenological method, i.e. the phenomenological reduction, Husserl analyzes the content or the ideal sense of experiencing in comparison to the suitable object of experiencing (Ideas I §§ 80-90). He says: "inside" the perception, after undergoing reduction (in the phenomenology of the pure experience [Erlebnis]), we find, in a complex way, the essence of the perceived as it is, being expressed as "a physical thing", "plant", "tree", "blossoming" etc.

The quotation marks (Anfuhrungszeichen) are meaningful; they express the radical change in the sense of the words; the radical change is actually the entry into a psychotic state. The tree in nature can simply burn down, it can disintegrate to its chemical components etc., but the sense of this perception, something that necessarily belongs to its essence, cannot burn down; it does not have chemical components, no power and no real traits.

Real objects have temporal traits and they may change. On the other hand, ideal objects as noema are not temporal, they cannot cease to be or to be created as well as they cannot change. Therefore, when we say "fruit of the tree", we are describing ways of the tree in the consciousness and not the tree as a natural thing that exists in time-space. What I perceive in my experiencing through a phenomenological observation is not the material or the physical tree, but the sense "that tree which bears fruit" which is the content of my experiencing and carries the way by which the tree is being perceived as opposed to the physical tree.

Using this phenomenological analysis, in my experiencing, I find, in part, a vivid experiencing of the tree as I perceive it or of the tree being perceived by me. Husserl says that this is the perceptual sense of experiencing; while the object which I perceive is a physical object that can burn down, the sense of my perception is all together something else, it cannot burn down and it is not a physical object.

Such sense of an object as I perceive it is integrated in the perception, my perceptual experiencing. The fruit itself can rot but its sense does not comprise of biological cells thus the sense as perceived in my consciousness cannot be consumed.

What characterizes the description of my phenomenological experiencing is the sense of the experiencing and not the object of the experiencing; the object, as said, may not exist, this is the point of bracketing, to put in brackets the assumption that a tree exists; the tree that apparently exists before me and, in a causal form, reflects the light rays to my eyes so that I can see it; on the other hand in phenomenology I have to focus on the sense through which the tree is represented in my experiencing. That way I can evaluate the intentionality of the perceptual experiencing.

The bracketing, says David Woodruff Smith, is similar in a certain sense to a quotation. The quotation marks turn my attention away from the tree of which existence I presume to my assertion on it which is the sense.

Let us assume that I say "this is a fruit tree". You ask me "what did you say?" I quote myself and respond "I said 'this is a fruit tree'". When I said, the first time, "this is a fruit tree" I said that a certain tree is a fruit tree, that is, I have denoted a fact; however, when I have quoted myself and recited what I have said, I did not denote a fact but did recite my words by which I have expressed their sense, that is what I have said. Therefore, the quotation marks turn my attention away from the tree and its existence of which I only assume or suppose, toward my assertion, toward the words that I have expressed thus toward the sense of my sentence, the sense of my assertion. Husserl turns our sight away from the object to the sense of the object. In a phenomenological description, I recite "I see 'that fruit tree'". In a phenomenological standing I do not deal in the existence of the tree that I see, which is the tree itself; on the contrary, I am engaged in the visual experiencing itself (the seeing) of the tree.

In applying phenomenology, I make use of the quotation "that fruit tree" in order to focus directly on the sense, the *noetic* sense of my experiencing. In phenomenology, or in the noematic quotation, we focus on the sense of my words describing my experience. Therefore, a noematic quotation is moving through the words to the sense of the experience as I observe it. If we say that fruit tree and in addition we add quotation marks then we may say that this fruit tree is the noematic sense in my perceptual experience, the sense that is being expressed in my words "that fruit tree".

David Bell[7] contends that the reduction is not a theory or an assertion but a procedure; this is not something that Husserl would have wanted us to believe in; we have to *make* the reduction. Moreover it is not an assertion that supposed to be true, justified or logical but it is *imperative.*

The reduction is a procedure that supposed to introduce us into a certain conscious state, that is, to a pure, phenomenological world and, I say, the world of psychosis; without it, it is impossible to reach a certain place which Husserl considers as a starting point and through which we will see the world differently.

The value of the reduction is recognized only after it was performed. In his last work "The Crisis of the European Sciences and Transcendental Phenomenology"[8] Husserl writes "it may even

---

[7] David Bell, Husserl, Routledge 1990

be discovered that the phenomenological standing or the epochè that belongs to it was meant, in its essence, to bring about, initially, *a decisive personal change that is similar to a religious conversion"* (page 137, my underlining). Such an act "produces the biggest and most meaningful existential form change... that was given as purpose to the human race" (there).

You have to undergo such a metamorphosis not only for the understanding the psychotic but also to really understand what is phenomenology, it is an existential change due to the fact that the psychotic is in a certain state in relation to the world, to others and to the existential choice that awaits him in the future.

So, you have to undergo the metamorphosis or the changeover through me! Also the psychotic undergoes epochè while he passes from one conscious state to the other, a state that influences whole of his essence and which redefines him.

The reduction is taking me and you from one conscious state to the other, to the pure world of phenomenology.


## 15:00 The world in brackets


In Logical investigations (1900-1), Husserl still under the influence of Bolzano and Brentano took a standing style Aristotle: the world around us exists independently of us, things have properties, traits of their own, they exist and through experiencing, judgment and perception we can know their properties and their essence.

---

[8] Edmund Husserl, The Crisis of European Sciences and Transcendental Phenomenology, Translated by D.carr.

The thesis that the world around us, trees, animals, humans, electrons, protons and galaxies exists independently in our consciousness is called realism. On the other hand there are many who content that in Ideas I, Husserl changed his mind to some type of idealism. Idealism is a thesis which says that the world around us is dependent on our consciousness; it is the product of our consciousness i.e. the world gets its existence only in our consciousness. I tend to agree; the mentally ill is for all purposes an idealist but he is also, in a certain manner, a realist.

The logical investigations and Ideas I may be considered to be part of the same flow which I will explain in more detail further below. I read Husserl in view of the consciousness of the psychotic as someone who holds the kind of idealism as Bishop Berkeley.

George Berkeley holding his ideal Empiricism makes a reduction of objects to sensual ideas in the consciousness. In the 18th century, the Bishop contented that objects or material things exist only in our consciousness; "to be is to be perceived" was his mantra. That lion exists only as long as we perceive it! That is, according to idealism and to psychosis, objects do not exist "outside", there are no light and sound waves that have a causal influence on the eye or ear and cause the representation of a lion; there is no "Hyletic data". If the theses of the natural stand suspend casual relations, then the conclusion must be that the representation of the object, that is, the object "outside" cannot cause the mental picture in your minds. This means that there is no realism. So the conclusion must be idealism!


The voices that the psychotic hears are only in his head with no external stimulus. There is no lion outside the perception. The lion exists as long as it is made of simple ideas like shape, color, certain smell, certain texture etc.

The term synthesis or synthetic act of consciousness stands in the center of an ideal philosophy.

The consciousness stands on its own; it is pure and is not *dependent* on the existence of external objects. In light of this, consciousness is an independent being while the world in time-space and the physical objects are intentional only. The objects are relational beings and are secondary to the consciousness, its independence and explicitness. We can say that the objects are "a moment" suspended in our consciousness! The objects do not exist as such but are dependent on the existence of the psychotic's consciousness (See § 49 Ideas I).

David Woodruff Smith contends that the method of bracketing was actually not properly understood; those who were allegedly mistaken contend that the method is quasi a negation of the world or a matter of classical doubtfulness or idealism.

I think that David Woodruff Smith is mistaken in the matter of psychosis. The psychotic knows that his experience is knowledge and that is why he is not a skeptic but an idealist! Why the psychotic his both, realist and idealist? Hallucination originates in the past, that is, they were real objects in the past which were directly and normally perceived, but now, in the psychotic time they are an imitation or representation of objects that do not exist anymore but only in an ideal form in the psychotic's mind or consciousness. The psychotic was a realist in his past; only now since he became psychotic, he also became an idealist.

The psychotic creates a synthesis by collecting memory bits which are representative of past objects and through them he creates a

91

complete hallucination (sight, touch, smell, sound). The memory bits are imaginary elements that were real in the past, meaning they are imitation of real past objects (realism), but now, in psychotic time they become ideal (idealism), that is, they do not exist at this time before the psychotic (no external stimuli) because they are ideal creations.

There is no causal link between the representation in the psychotic's present and the object he has seen in the past or that existed in the past. What I am saying is that the past of the psychotic is a realistic one, however at the time of his being a psychotic he is a subjective idealist. The objects in his consciousness appear only before him, they are his private phenomenon (however he can, by language, let you participate).

David Woodruff Smith contends that from a phenomenological point of view we are not, ontologically, negating the world; the world was put in brackets in order for us to reflect on the consciousness of the world. David Woodruff Smith might be right about the "regular" person but he is mistaken about the psychotic, I say that the psychotic is an idealist from an ontological point of view; that is, there is nothing "outside" to his consciousness at the time of his insanity;

The hallucination is the product of his consciousness, which is the sense of being psychotic. In his case the noematic content does not represent anything "outside" but "inside". The sense "that lion" presents a content of a consciousness that does not represent anything in the "outside" but only represents memory! He is a realist in the sense that although he has hallucinations, the object does still exist out there, externally to the consciousness, independent of his perception and did exist transcendentally in his perception in the past. He is an idealist in the sense that the object which is present now in his consciousness is merely intrinsic, it is an ideal noematic content. It exists in the consciousness and in the perception as a memory being imagined and re-experienced and relived.

If the paranoid psychotic sees now a man in a black coat he has actually seen him in the past (at the time when he was not a paranoid) and now he reconstructs this memory by imagining in the present, his psychosis' time. It is clear that there is no symmetry or any fit between regular time and psychosis' time. The man is an image or an intrinsic term that actually existed in the past, real- transcendental.

To summarize, in a phenomenological observation I refer to the way by which I am experiencing the world in a conscious act; I therefore refer to the content or the sense in my experience.

We speak of the experiencing from the perspective of "first person", and we say that phenomenology supposed to describe the consciousness as I am experiencing it from a "first person" point of view, subjective and personal point of view. When I turn my look toward the structure of my experience, I describe a phenomenological and subjective account; the bracketing brings us to the intentional content through quotation marks that bear sense.

A phenomenological analysis leads us from the description of different ways of experiencing to the focusing on the content or the noema of experiencing and then to the analysis of the intentional content.

## 15:15 Noema

Sense is the measure of intentionality, the measure through which we are conscious of something. From a formal or an ontological point of view, the intentional relation between a conscious act and an object is being mediated by a noema or a noematic sense which is the ideal content of an act or conscious act and presents the intentionality toward the object in a certain manner.

In Ideas I, Husserl's approach is to start, by a "first person" point of view, an experience of pure consciousness toward the structure of intentionality while creating important distinctions between conscious act, object, noema or content and ego as they appear in the phenomenological analysis of different components of the consciousness. When we are bracketing the thesis on the existence of the natural world around us, we find ourselves observing the "pure" or "transcendental" consciousness (Ideas I §33). We find that we are focusing on the essence of the consciousness (Ideas I §34), a consciousness as we are experiencing it. A consciousness, we find, is mostly made of events of being conscious of something.

The property of experiences (Erlebnissen), that is, to be a consciousness of something is called, as I said earlier, by Husserl intentionality (Ideas I §84). Consciousness is part of a flow of experiences, a temporal structure that is characterized by unity; the experiencing in one united flow of consciousness which
94

belongs to one "I" or ego (Ich). A *conscious act*, therefore, is the way by which the consciousness is being intended from the ego to the object. In many cases the form of consciousness is a perceptual experiencing of sight, hearing and touching things in the context of daily life irrespective whether these things perceived by us actually exist. In the case of physical objects, *perception is an intentional experiencing that acts on the senses*. Perceptual experiencing is a temporal mental state with two interdepended parts "real" or temporal; one part is sensual or "sensual moment" and the other is an intentional part or "intentional moment" (Ideas I §85).

The sensual part that acts on the senses is called by Husserl *Hyle*. *Hyle* from Greek for matter, a primary material originating in chaos or is the primary product of chaos. The intentional part is called by Husserl *Morph* from Greek for form. For example, Aristotle contends that the bronze statue comprises of material and form. The material, the bronze, is designed in a certain manner and becomes a statue. In a similar way, Husserl says that a visual experiencing (visual perception) comprises of feeling (material or hyle) and interpretation or conceptualization (form or morph). According to Husserl's ontology, "moments" are dependent parts, that is, parts that cannot exist separately from the whole of which they are parts; the sensual part and the intentional part cannot exist one without the other, the two are interdependent therefore creating the whole.

I see a yellow fruit and in the background a green fruit tree. The experiencing by the visual sense of the yellow and green is at the same time a sensual and intentional experiencing of a fruit on the tree.

That part of the intentional experiencing is called by Husserl a *noetic moment* of experiencing or noesis; it characterizes the noesis by the experience of being a live basis which gives sense to the conscious act (Ideas I §85).

In order for the noesis to become noetic in its essence, it has to give sense. The sense that is given to a perceived object is the intentional content. We should remember that not all experiencing is a perceptual experiencing that acts on the senses; when I think I do not operate my visual sense, my vocal sense or my tactile sense.

In a pure thinking, my conscious act does not include a sensual component. My thinking does include a noetic component which is my thinking, a pure noesis; therefore, delusions are simply noesis.

With this noetic activity of the consciousness, Husserl presents a new term: noema. The noematic content or the noema of the conscious act is the ideal sense or the structure of the sense that fits the "real" or the active, temporal and noetic process (Ideas I §88).

The perception has noema which is a perceptual sense, that is, it is perceived in itself; in the same way, memory has the memories themselves as we remembered them; Judgment has what was judged; pleasure has what caused the pleasure etc.; generally, fitting the noema, that is, the sense is inside the experience of perception, judgment, imagination, pleasure, etc.

The sense or the noema which corresponds to the experience is the ideal noematic content; this sense presents an object in a certain manner and that same object can be presented in different ways through different structures of sense.

Following Husserl, David Woodruff Smith gives the example: let us assume that I am visiting a wax museum. I see a woman waving. In my perceptual experience, the object that I see is presented in two different ways; in the first case I see "a woman waving" and then in the second case I see "this wax figure".

The sense in my first perception is different and is separated from the perceptual sense in the second case. If I think "the victor of Jena" and then I think "the one who was defeated in waterloo", that is the same object, Napoleon, is presented through two different noematic senses in two experiences. The two senses denote Napoleon, that is, the same object but they denote him in a different way (Logical Investigation, Investigation I §12).

In a phenomenological observation we unravel the structure of relations of the intentionality; how an experience is being intended toward an object in the consciousness by a certain noematic sense.

In the consciousness I am aware of the object as it appears before me in the conscious act, that is, it appears through a certain noematic sense. We are aware of things, this is the central point in phenomenology; we know or are being intended on things only through a structure of sense that presents or denotes such things in different ways. However, we are not aware to a sense through which we are experiencing an object until we take a step back from the experience and outstrip its content.

Only through phenomenological observation we reach an awareness of the sense through which we are being intended toward an external object. Only through noesis and then through a fitting noematic sense, can the consciousness be intended toward external things. In Ideas I, Husserl contends that in phenomenology, sense or noema gives us an "intrinsic" viewpoint on how sense is representing the object in the consciousness; it is phenomenology from an "intrinsic" viewpoint of a consciousness that is being intended through the sense on an object as we have been experiencing it.

Gottlob Frege makes a distinction between sense and reference; the two expressions "the morning star" and "the evening star" denote the same object, Venus, but they have two different senses although they denote the same object in two different ways. Each expression expresses a certain sense that set a certain reference, but the two denote the same object by two different ways. The expression "the morning star" has the sense of the morning star which denotes Venus; the expression "the evening star" has the sense of the evening star which also denotes Venus; a different noema for both! Husserl and Frege had the same linguistic model, the model of representation; the relation of an expression to the object, which is represented by it, is being mediated by sense. When I think (thinking is a conscious act) "the morning star", my experiencing is being intended through sense or content which is the morning star toward the object Venus.

The sense presents the object in a certain manner; that is why Husserl characterizes sense "as an object which was intended by others". If, on the other hand, I would have been thinking "the evening star", my experiencing would have been intending toward the same object, Venus, however, by the sense of the evening star. Husserl made the distinction between noematic sense and noesis when an act or noesis is being intended through noematic sense toward a suitable object. The noesis is the act itself. Only through a phenomenological observation I am aware of the sense through which I am aware of the tree that I see. When I see "that tree", the sense of my experience is a perceptual content that denotes one certain object (that specific tree); on the other hand when I see "that fruit tree on the top of a hill" the sense of my experience is a content of a perceptual assertion that *denotes a state of things* around me. That is, a noema can represent a certain object but not only, the noema can also represent a fact or a state of things.

Although the noema or a noematic sense is an ideal "be" (extant) since it cannot burn down and it does not exist in time-space, Husserl still contends that the noema is "inside" the noesis in a very unique way, as a "moment" or a part depended on the conscious act. Husserl makes a very important distinction between the perceived object and the object as being perceived which is also called *the sense of perception.* These two "be" are categorically separated; they belong to different ontological categories. The tree itself is simply and naturally a thing in nature, a real object that exists in time-space, something that can burn down and disintegrate to atoms. On the other hand, the sense of perception cannot burn down, it does not have real properties; it does not exist in nature and is not a real object that exists in time space, but it is an ideal be, an object that does not exist in time-space.

By Husserl, a "thing" (Ding) is an object in nature, in time-space and sense is an *ideal content of an aware experience* that does not exist in time-space and is not in nature, the sense is "inside" the consciousness.

Meanwhile, we can sum up and say that a conscious act through a noematic sense ("the object as perceived") represents or denotes an object (if it exists at all). In Ideas I, Husserl underlines the method of "pure" consciousness. With the help of phenomenological reduction (epochè) we have to turn our sight away from the objects to the ways by which we are experiencing the objects (to the noematic sense).

## 15:20 The ontology of noesis and noema

A perceptual experiencing comprises of two parts; a sensual "moment" (a part depended on the whole that cannot exist without it) and a noetic moment (Noesis).

The sensual moment that is made of sensual data (as to see colors or forms and to hear sounds) or the "material" of the senses is what gives the experiencing its sensual trait; the noetic "moment" is what gives the experiencing its intentional trait, that is, the noema or the noematic sense that represents the object in the consciousness.

These two parts of experiencing, the feeling and noesis are not independent of each other; they cannot be separated from the experiencing as a whole and from each other. In experiencing pure thought there is no sensual part, only noesis (e.g. delusions).

Analyzing psychosis: Messianism, paranoia or megalomania are pure thoughts that do not include a sensual component; they come into being by the psychotic as a real and pure noesis. The psychotic is intendds in a conscious act on the object Messiah Ben David, or on the genius that he attributes to himself; but if he is a paranoid and he sees a man in the corner dressed in black coat then the man in black coat is the sensual component that together with the noesis is parallel to the noema, the sense, that is filled with an intuitive content.

The hallucination, that is, the sensual component is the product of the psychotic's consciousness; the sound that he hears is not external but "inside" his head. Husserl says that the sensual and noetic (noesis) "moments" in the perception are "real" parts (experiencing or a conscious act is a living mental process, experiencing is real (reell) or a temporal process, that is, happening in time) of experiencing while the noematic "moment" "is not real" in the experiencing. The feeling and the noesis in the experiencing are "real", that is, they are temporal components of perceptual experiencing. In experiencing, the noesis and the noema fit and are linked to each other. In perception, the noema i.e. the tree as perceived, "this fruit tree" is not something in nature, in time-space.

According to Husserl, the noema is not "real", does not exist in time, and not in the flow (temporal) of consciousness. The noema is an ideal being and it is also a "moment" in experiencing; therefore, the noema and the noesis are "moments", dependent parts of the experience, contents of the experience, beings that exist "inside" the experience, that is, they are parts depended on the experiencing. The noesis, on the other hand, is a "real" part, a temporal part but the noema is not real, a part which is not temporal.

But, how can an ideal part, not temporal, be a real "moment" in a temporal experience? The noesis as well as the noema are components, and by this sense are contents of the experience, however, they are contained in it in different ways. Husserl contends that the noematic sense in the perception is depended on the experiencing; the noema is a moment or a part dependent on the experiencing; nevertheless the noema is not a "real" component of the experience. We may consider a "real" being as a part depended on the experiencing, that is, is there and exists inside it and cannot be separated from it. But, how will we understand an ideal being, not temporal, as part of the experiencing? Well, it can be understood by the way of which Husserl conceptualizes for us the term "moment".

The ideal form 'white' exists "inside" the white paper as long as that white in the paper constitutes an event of the form 'white'; that is, the white in the paper is a special case of the general term white.

The ideal sense "that fruit tree" exists in the same way inside that perceptual experience while the noesis of the visual "that fruit tree" fits the noematic sense of "that fruit tree". Noematic senses are ideal beings that materialize in temporal experiences in a way parallel to the way by which ideal terms materialize in temporal objects; but senses materialize in such a way by which they are being intended by us in a temporal experiencing. Sense materializes in a certain way in temporal experiencing. Therefore, for Husserl, the noema is an ideal be, a "moment" or a dependent part of the experiencing; only sense exists that way. Ideal senses are "inside" temporal and real experiencing, they are ideal moments of lively experiencing. I know sense as "an intended object" by me in my experiencing.


## 15:30 Object X and the paradigms of the noema


When making contact with an object, for example, that fruit tree in the field, I see it from one side. When I approach it, I see it again from a different point of view. When I sit under its branches I see it from a different angle, I look at its trunk and

102

branches from under it. Notwithstanding these different angles of experiencing, I still see the same object; I see it sometimes continuously when, for example, I walk, and sometimes discontinuously when I turn my head away for a moment or close my eyes and open them again, but my perception of the tree is always intended on the same object.

In the noema, we make a distinction between two components: the sense of the object as was intended and the sense of the different properties that are attributed to it.

In a phenomenological description of experiencing, in the noema, we make a distinction between the sense of the object and the properties which we attribute to it. Being aware of an object, the noematic sense of experience is divided in two: the simple content of X and the sense of the attributed properties which are different properties that the object has.

I see a certain object and with it I see which properties it has (i.e. it is green) and which properties it could have. The sense of my experiencing "that green fruit tree" is divided in two; "that denotes a certain object before me ("X") and the sense of the object's properties, "tree", "fruits", "green" that link to "a green fruit tree". I can, for example, say "there is an object X so that I see X walking opposite me in the field, I think that X is an African predator, I also see that X has big teeth, I see that X runs, I judge that X is looking for prey, wild goats are the food of X. The variable X denotes for us the same object as was intended by different conscious acts, as we are experiencing it in seeing, thinking, judging etc.

The properties "mammal", "an African lion", "big teeth" and "predator" are properties that we attribute to the object while we are being intended on it through different conscious acts. In this phenomenological description of a complex conscious act that is being intended on the same object, we describe the noematic sense of the same object with the sense of different properties. Our experiencing is being intended on the same object through different conscious acts. The sense of X is to be intended in few ways. When I walk around the tree, away from it, sit near it, I see that same object X from different perspectives with different properties. My different experiences present the same object with different properties; the sense of X denotes for us a certain object and senses of its properties are added to it. X or the definition of X: a component in the noematic sense of the conscious act; the definition of X denotes the object itself outstripped of all traits or properties of the intended object.

## 15:45 Horizon and background in the sense

When I approach the tree, I see it from different points of view; when I turn my eyes to it at this moment, from this side, my present experiencing has more content than the visual perception of "that tree" or "this lion before me". Part of our understanding of things in nature is what Husserl calls "transcendence" which is the deviation from the present experiencing. There is always something above and beyond what is given to us now, above the thing or the perspective present before us now in the experiencing.

Such is, for example, a phenomenological description of the object and its properties: I see this tree, this tree is a fruit tree, this tree bears fruits now, it is located at the bottom of the mountain, its trunk is thick and so forth. "And so forth" is an important component in the phenomenological description and in the noematic sense. That component of the sense, "and so forth", is what Husserl calls "horizon" (Horizont), the intended object in the experiencing, or the range of possibilities of the not yet defined object, that is, the structure of the possibilities of that same object ("tree") that is not yet defined or in other words possibilities that remained open by the content of the sense (the noema) of a conscious act.

The horizon includes, for example, the description of how the object, which was perceived from a different point of view, will be seen from point of view (the other side of the tree) that is not present, at this moment, before us but does exist as an open possibility.

When I see the tree at this moment, I expect that if I will continue walking and move to the other side of the tree, I will continue to see that same object from the other side, I will see more fruit, more branches. When observing, we are forced by our previous understanding of things, however, my perception opens a "horizon" of possibilities on that same object. The range of future possibilities is defined by the noematic sense in my experience together with the background content for that object.

Therefore, one can define "horizon" of a conscious act as the range of the intended object's possibilities that remained open by the noematic sense of the act together with a preceding and relevant knowledge (background); for example, while I am walking in the field, in the wilderness in Africa, I know that there are predatory lions that might attack me and even cause my death. The fact of seeing that lion before I had some background knowledge on lions leaves a possibility open that the lion can be dangerous and if I will not undertake some precautions it might devour me. The possibility of being devoured is an open possibility that is linked to my background knowledge on dangerous lions.

One can also speak of *horizon* of possible and possible experiencing the same object together with additional properties, noematic senses which fit and become possible thanks to the sensual content's background of the object.

When I enter an unrecognized room, I see a table. I do not count the number of legs which, in part, are hidden from my point of view. I simply see the table. The number of legs this table has is my horizon i.e. the number of possibilities of the legs. Knowing tables (background), it has, probably, four legs; it may have six legs but, probably, it does not have ten legs; this possibility is thin given my background on tables.

A thing or a material object can appear before me at a given time only from one point of view or one angle; however, we understand that additional aspects of the same object can appear from different points of view. This understanding is part of the noematic sense of this object's perception; therefore, the sense of the experiencing outlines, in advance, for us a horizon of possibilities, a range of potential properties for that object. The range of the object's potential possibilities enables us additional perceptions from different angles that present the object. What is given to us inattentively is called by Husserl "background" (Hintergrund) or the horizon of the non-obvious background (i.e. what I learn inattentively and non-obviously about the object). The noematic content of the perception assumes or describes the horizon of the perceived object.

The sense of "and so forth" is a central component in the noema of the thing's perception (Ideas I § 149). This component of sense enables a horizon of possibilities of an intended object. Another part of horizon of what I see is not just physical but also temporal. The temporal flow of events (procedures) is part of that tree's horizon as I see it. The branches sway in the wind; I feel the wind and at the background, I know that the wind is swaying the branches and leafs so that the horizon of the tree remains open, i.e. I expect that the leafs will disperse or even the trunk will break. The perceived tree is present in time-space; we are experiencing things in nature as things in time-space.

The memory, the past, is part of my present perception. I see the tree swaying in the wind, the same tree which I saw one minute ago while I was walking toward it and the same tree I expect to see while proceeding with my walk. When I see "that fruit tree" as a temporal thing, the tree is part of the horizon of how I saw it and how I will see it in my perception.

An additional part of the horizon of what is present before me now is what I remember about the tree from my previous encounters with it; moreover, my flow of consciousness is also part of the horizon because my present perception is inside the flow of experiencing of which I am aware in my consciousness, in my intrinsic time.

## 16:00 Epistemology

Through his phenomenology, Husserl arrives at epistemology; he develops a phenomenological theory of knowledge. Watching the sciences develop, early philosophers have examined the intellect or the reason, the logic and the sensual perceptions in order to arrive to the theory of knowledge, epistemology. Epistemology is a theory of knowledge; what is knowledge?

When may I say that I know something? Under what conditions may I define a situation as being so? May we say that we know earth to be elliptical or maybe we believe in it and do not have any evidence? Plato, for example, contended that knowledge is justified, truthful belief. What do we know? Is our knowledge based on sensual data (e.g. observations, as I observe the moon through a telescope and discover that it is orbiting earth) or maybe knowledge is based on logic (logic and mathematics), or both? Epistemology deals in the answers to these questions.

In "Meditation on First Philosophy" (1641), Rene Descartes, a philosopher, mathematician and physician contented that if we want our knowledge to be true and certain, it must be based on reason. Descartes is the father of rationalism defining, as said, that knowledge begins in reason. At the beginning of the 18th century, John Locke, Bishop George Berkeley and David Hume contended, as opposed to rationalism, that our knowledge must be based on sensual perceptions, i.e. observations. Reason is built on testimony made by the sensual perception. Empiricism, therefore, contends that sensual experience is the basis for knowledge; for example, Galileo Galilei looked through the telescope and saw the moons orbiting Jupiter.

If science is a paradigm of knowledge, we can see that scientific and experimental investigations go through sensual observations resulting in complex logic and physical, chemical and biological theories based on mathematics. Empirical sciences start with inductive logic derived from subjective observations and the inclusion of same observations in a general rule as part of a mathematical theory. Empirical sciences also follow a deductive logic as in geometry and its axioms that are applied on observations i.e. the mathematical theory of Newton's gravitation. Therefore, what we call today scientific investigations is a synthesis of rationalism and empiricism. Where does Husserl stand? Husserl developed phenomenology as "pure logic" that has brought him to the theory of intentionality, a theory of evidence and from there to a phenomenological theory of knowledge.

Knowledge starts with simple experiencing or with other forms of intuition. Husserl's phenomenology tries to explain objective concepts like truth, being, knowledge, rationality and reality. He tries to explain the nature of these terms with the tools available to him: sensual intuitions. The purpose, in other words, is the phenomenological explanation of objectivity, or using Husserl's words "a phenomenological clarification of knowledge".

In Logical Investigations, Husserl tries to fill the gap between the subjectivity of knowledge and objectivity. The purpose for Husserl is to bridge the phenomenological analysis of subjectivity as presented in Investigations I-V (dealing mainly in phenomena of the conscious, intended, intuitive, abstractive, erroneous, and judgmental kind from the "first and second person" point of view) and the assertion that subjective and conscious phenomena can and must be characterized by objectivity, rationality, justifiability, validity and truthfulness.

The bridge between subjectivity and objectivity and the account of what is included in objectivity must be constructed by the subjective means at his disposal. Husserl tries to understand knowledge, justifications and truth based on the model of fulfilling. For Husserl, rationality is a function of availability of evidence; knowledge denotes the relation between a thinking act and intuitive fulfilling (Logical Investigations IV page 837). As long as we remain in the domain of semantics and language, meaning, as long as we make mere assertions, we deal in suppositions only.

However, these suppositions may be verified if the intentional and conscious act is fulfilled; for example, I do not remember what color is the fruit, but it seems to me that it is yellow, I think it is yellow; I look for it and when I found it, I have *discovered* that I was right. When I think that the fruit is yellow, I actually make the assertion "the fruit is yellow", or there is a thought in my consciousness and only by intuition (in this case, evidence by sensual perception) this assertion or belief is verified. Truth is the intended object being identical to the given object. My assertion is justified and *true* if the object (the fruit tree) is given to me by intuition as I was intended on it or thought of it; I have knowledge, I may tell myself "I know that the fruit is yellow". Therefore, knowledge may be characterized by the equivalence or synthesis of the intended object and the given object, i.e. the object is directly present before me, the object is given "in itself".

What makes Husserl's theory of knowledge phenomenological is the analysis of the experience's structure produced that is by knowledge. Knowledge is the product of two forms of experiencing: intentionality and intuition or evidentness.

These forms may also be called rationality and empiricism i.e. two "moments" in a cognizance experience.

Intentionality as well as intuition take part in the enabling of science; on one hand, intentionality provides representation of things in the world ("that fruit tree at the bottom of the hill") and intuition, on the other hand, provides *evidence* or proof of the existence of these things ("I see that fruit tree at the bottom of the hill"). The act of my seeing establishes the state of things or the fact that there is a fruit tree at the bottom of the hill. If I think that the fruit is yellow and then I see it, then I understand, through evidence, that my belief is *true*.

According to Husserl, evidence denotes the ideal of a full synthesis of fullness when a term or a linguistic mark (also an assertion on states of things) is adequately fulfilled by a suitable perception and, therefore, provides us with the given object. When an object is not only being intended by us but rather is given to us by intuition, it is given to us by evidence. Semantic intentionality denotes its object while intuitive intentionality gives it i.e. giving is the fulfillment of the object itself. The object fulfills our field of vision thus, for example, it is given to us by the visual sense.

The semantic intentionality does not give or present the object itself, rather denotes it by a linguistic expression. Husserl characterizes intuition (Anschauung) as an experience in which the object gives "itself" with "intuitive fullness" or "self evidence"; we see the object and not only think about it. If, for example, we stand at the bottom of the hill by the fruit tree and cover our eyes with a black ribbon and think about the fruit tree and then we take the ribbon off, then, the fruit tree in our thought is "fulfilled" with the help of our vision (sensual perception) by the fruit tree being external to the consciousness. One may say the tree fulfills itself; it is an evidence of it being seen, it proves its own existence. The fruit being outside my field of vision and being judged by me "it is green" is one act; being inside my field of vision and being judged by me "it is green" is another act; we deal in two judgment acts with the same material and the same quality. However, there is an important difference between the two judgment acts, a difference that is linked to something beyond the intentional essence.

In both cases I make a judgment ("it is green") on the same object, the fruit, but in the first case I have an empty intentionality that denotes nothing, whereas in the second case I have intuition or perceptual intentionality when the fruit appears or is given to us as itself. Only perception gives us the fruit directly. This is the only form of intentionality that presents us with the object itself in its physical presence. If I look for the fruit and then I find it, then we are dealing in a situation in which the fruit is here i.e. the fruit is given to us in a fulfilling or realizing perception of the intentionality. What was thought in the beginning is seen now.

The perceptual giving is identical to a self presentation of the object. Instead of speaking of the emptiness or the fullness of intentionality, one may speak of the absence or the presence of the intended object. In the imagination, the object is not given to us directly but by mediating intuition (mediation by memory) i.e. the object does not stand now before us rather in a mediating form by memory and imagination that represent it. Only the actual perception gives us the object directly and not by mediation.

According to Dan Zahavi[9], only intentionality of this kind gives us the object in its physical presence. Nevertheless, intuition is not only a sensual perception in which we see physical objects (or hear, touch, smell and taste in a case of a fruit), but we also "see" or we have insight on essence; for example, I see by intuition that the sum of the angles of a triangle is 180 degrees, this is the essence of a triangle or its truth. An intuition of this kind or such "seeing" include also an intuition of senses or intentional content.

In Logical Investigation (1900-1), Husserl starts to give an account on knowledge and in Ideas I he continues and describes in detail what he has previously started. In Ideas I, he focuses on the link between sensation and the sense of perception. In the chapter "phenomenology of reason" he denotes the conditions that enable knowledge using the phenomenological terminology of intuition together with intentionality. Knowledge in itself is not an act of consciousness but a collection of *beliefs* which are conscious states created by acts of judgment which stand in front of intuitive evidence, mainly, as we see things, think and judge them. If we assume intentional content then what we know is a body of knowledge that is made of a collection of assertions being supported by evidence i.e. assertions which are the content of past judgments based on observations (sensual perception) or another intuitive experiencing.

An act of perception (seeing the tree) is sensation merged with conceptualization; "Hyletic data" and noetic interpretation. Sensation is being seldom realized without conceptualization; sense is given to the inflow of informational sensation. Here, Husserl slightly deviates from empiricism and is following Kant.

---

[9] Husserl's Phenomenology, Dan Zahavi, Stanford University Press (2003)

Kant's theory of knowledge tries, among other things, to answer Davis Hume's skepticism. Kant made a distinction between a phenomenon and noumenon or things-as-they-appear and things-in-themselves; accordingly, we may know or recognize things-as-they-appear but not things-in-themselves. Husserl changed Kant's phenomenon to noema or the intended things i.e. to the ideal intentional perception. Accordingly, perception passes through the noema (that represent the 'perceived tree') until, finally, it refers to the existing thing (the tree in its simplicity in nature) provided, however, that a noematic perception is based on or "being fulfilled' by sensual information in an intuitive manner. As aforesaid, Husserl has developed a theory of intentionality on how the sense is being intended on our experiences of different things in the world. He used this theory for the analysis of perception and empirical judgment based on perception hence an empirical knowledge on nature.

In Husserl's epistemology, when we abstract and denote the essences of different things, we are making use of an ideal intuition or an insight of essences. Husserl goes beyond the classical empiricism and also beyond rationalism. In Husserl's epistemology, our knowledge of experiences of consciousness depends on direct subjective experience of consciousness. We may describe the intentional structure of the consciousness and focus on the senses of our experiences by phenomenological observation of our experiences and all this by using bracketing. In addition to the aforesaid, we describe formal essences like sates of things, thing and number by categorical intuition; in accordance, we perceive, by intuition, logical forms in assertions hence we "see" by conceptual intuition formal structures of objects in the world, structures which semantically conform to

114

logical forms of sense while observing terms of quantity, individual and states of things. Husserl extends the term intuition to include not only perceptual intuition but also conceptual and phenomenological intuition.

## 16:05 Hyletic data

The hyletic or the sensual components include the primary raw material of the consciousness; they differ from any noesis or intentional aspect because they are merely impressions i.e. the consciousness in this state is totally passive in receiving these primary materials; the primary material, a hyletic material, is given without the consciousness doing anything with it. Hence, the sensual material and the emotions we deal with do not refer to any object and are not in themselves an object; they are not intentional experiences or objects for intentional experience. Such primary material is only sensual i.e. it precedes terminological or intellectual expressions hence senseless. If we are not aware of them then they do not exist i.e. they do not survive lack of awareness, they are being created and annihilated quickly.

The hyletic material of psychosis is simple memory bits following a synthesis (representations of simple hallucinations like sound, form, texture, smell and taste which were captured in the past); i.e. I hear sounds, feel texture, smell smells, see color and form, all of which unite to one object in consciousness which is, for example, a hallucination of a person. That "person" (a complex hallucination) can speak, he has color, weight, etc., i.e. he is a noematic object with sense; the psychotic, for example, hears the

115

sounds and creates from them a voice with sense. The noesis is compatible and analogous to the noema.

The term 'noesis' denotes the parts and aspects responsible for the intentionality and the sense of the conscious act. The noetic elements in the intentional act are real intrinsic elements that bring to life or give sense to the hyletic material. The noesis in itself is not more than a concrete intentional act without its sensual data.

In delusions there is no external, sensual input hence they are noesis, pure thought without hyletic input.

In hallucination, there is no external input *now* but the input (hyletic material) was there in the past and now it exists as a memory of hyletic material perceived in the past. God as a thought is noesis; its compatible noema is "this which materialized before Moses by the burning bush". The noema gives sense to the synthesis of the hyletic material.

Husserl asks 'what do we really find in perception as pure experiencing? Are parts and moments included?' (Ideas I page 283). He answers that on one hand it has wild feelings, visual and sensual information which create an impression in my consciousness, on the other hand is the 'noetic component' turning the previous one to a coherent perception with sense.


## 16:10 Intuition and experiencing


In common language, intuition is being used to say that we have knowledge of something about to happen or one may say "I understood him even before he has spoken, I have an intuition about him' i.e. I know him through a direct intuition. However, in philosophy, mainly for Husserl, intuition is a technical term with a special role in phenomenology. Intuition (Anschauung) means "to see something". Intuition provides direct knowledge of an object without conclusions of other judgments. Therefore, intuition provides basic knowledge from which conclusions are being derived.

Visual perception is used as a paradigm or a founding example for intuition i.e. I see the tree in a direct and immediate way so that it stands before me in itself. Thereon, the theories of intuition change; Kant's intuition is a terminological and sensual representation of the phenomenon; for Husserl, intuition includes a scope of forms of experiencing which is self evident starting with seeing a physical object before me. Husserl says that in visual experiencing in which I see, touch, taste and smell, the fruit, object, is given in its corporeality (Ideas I §3). The trait of this originality denotes the knowledge originating in self evidentness. In sensual perception, the object which we experience is given to us "in itself", in its corporality, it, in itself, is present before us i.e. I am experiencing the fruit itself. I experience the fruit in itself which is being seen or is materialized in relation to me, in reference to me, for example, when I touch it.

Husserl extends this trait and generalizes it for all types of intuition, especially the intuition of essences as to see "the essence of the tree" or the essence of the triangle. The essence (Eidos) is the object in itself. As the intuition of the given of an individual object or an empirical object (Wesenserschauung) is an individual object, so the essential intuition is pure essence. "Seeing" of essence is intuition (Anschauung) as a conceptual object is an object. Empirical intuition, as sensual experience is a consciousness of a certain object that by intuition is given to us in

117

perception. Consciousness perceives the object in its originality as itself; the expression and the term really touch the object; the same way "seeing" essences is a consciousness about something or of something, of any type of "object" which is intended by the consciousness or the "seeing" hence "is given in itself" (Ideas I §3).

The central and important part of intuition is "evidence" (Evidenz) i.e. self seeing. In Logical Investigations, intuition is the fulfilling of a represented object i.e. it "is being fulfilled" in evidence just as hypothesis or expectation is being fulfilled or could be fulfilled by observation. In Ideas I, Husserl says that in intuition, the object is given in its originality, in its primary form as it is i.e. evidence justifies knowledge. We use evidence (assertions, for example, I think of the fruit and by observation I actually see it; "I was thinking of the fruit, now I see it") to be used as a basis or a justification for other assertions. Evidence has the status of experience.

As in David Woodruff Smith's example, if I think, hypothetically, that the suspect ran through the door, the thought in itself does not constitute evidence but if I actually see the suspect running through the door then I have evidence, in this case, of observation. Observation, therefore, is self evident, it does not necessitate any additional evidence for basing its truthfulness; in that sense it is the origin. Observation does not refer to other evidence, assertions or judgments. Intuition is such type of self evidence; evidence that was given to us as an origin, that does not need proof, it is primary and basic.

According to Husserl, an act of perception includes sensual "moment" and a noetic "moment" (noesis). The sensual part fulfills the noetic or intentional part hence fulfills the sense (noema) of the experience therefore, experience has a trait of intuition that is being fulfilled or *intuitive fullness*. The intuitive fullness of a perceptual act is characterized by evidence, "self evidently". In intuition, the object is "given" with evidence or fulfillment i.e. it is given intuitively, self evidently as such. The intuitive-perceptual sense represents the object as it is seen. In perception, Husserl contends that the object gives itself.

According to David Woodruff Smith, the experience is a direct representation of the object. When Husserl says that a given object gives "itself", "it" may be understood as being seen or touched by us; "this" object present itself before me; my experience denotes the object before me.

In Ideas I, Husserl gave up on realism in favor of idealism (so content most of his interpreters); the psychotic has authentic subjective knowledge i.e. he is idealist. The assertion or the thought is empty until it is being fulfilled by intuition; in this state, the psychotic "I" fulfills the assertion thought by the hallucination and unties with the hallucination's object.

There is no difference between the delusion and the hallucination because the two are the products of the psychotic's ideal consciousness i.e. if the hallucination and the delusion are intrinsic hence the identity of the ego. If, for example, I have a *paranoic* thought of a man in a black coat that stalks me and in my hallucination I see a man in a black coat at the corner, looking at me hence, the sensual data fulfills the thought, I have an intuitive vision in my delusions that is verified be sensual data. The "I" creates the thought (noesis) hence the hallucination fulfills such thought with reality; actually, there is no difference between the hallucinant and thought! The sensual component which fulfills the

119

noetic thought has noematic sense i.e. a sensual and intentional component. The noema is an ideal being, therefore not real, it does not exist as an external physical object (the man in a black coat) but exists inside the head of the psychotic.

The hallucination is a recycled imagination by memory! Unless the memory is being doubted which is an extreme skepticism, one may say that the memory touches the thing itself, the man in the black coat himself as was seen in the past. The psychotic is a realist in his past only now he is an idealist while being a psychotic. He is a realist in the sense of the object being there, transcendentally, outside of consciousness and independent of perception, he is idealist now, in psychotic time at the present, in the sense of the object being intrinsic in his consciousness; it exists in the consciousness and perception as imagined memory from the past.

Seeing now in his hallucination a man in a black coat means that the psychotic saw in the past a man in a black coat (innocent) and now he reconstructs such memory by imagining it. The man (not innocent) is an intrinsic image or a term in the psychotic's head in which it was itself in the past i.e. real and transcendental. The not innocent man is a present image in the consciousness, something intrinsic in the consciousness, "inside it", but the image stems from a real object from the past; in the past, while not being a psychotic patient, he saw men in black coats, only now he reconstructs (in hallucination) an imagination that was there before hence what is called memory.

In addition to the sensual component, there is also an interpretative component! Evidence can be strong or weak; weaker evidence may be replaced by a stronger one. As aforementioned, we have knowledge only if intuition is used as the fulfilling of semantic intentionality. Usually, the physical object is not given to us fully but only from a certain perspective. We do not perceive the object fully but always from a certain angle or perspective. I perceive the fruit from a certain side while other sides are hidden from me; nevertheless, we intend on the tree as a whole, or on the fruit as a whole. It remains always partially perceived i.e. we will perceive the fruit tree only from a certain perspective.

Although perception is defined as an intentional act which purpose is to give us a complete representation of the intentional object i.e. to let the object be shown in itself; such object remains ideal as long as we speak of a physical object i.e. some of his aspects were not given to us intuitively (intuition). Our perception of such objects will be forever insufficient or defect.

Husserl makes a distinction between two types of evidence, the indubitable and exhaustive and the inappropriate and inadequate, i.e. partial. As he denotes, it is illogical to pass requirements from one domain to the other, from one type of evidence to the other while it is clear that the requirements cannot be fulfilled. Whereas our insight on mathematical relations (2 is smaller than 3) may be considered as sufficient and indubitable, it is incorrect to apply these criteria on the perception of physical objects which remain experimental and correctable; therefore, we should not take a mathematical evidence and apply it on all types of evidence. The relational ability to be given of a physical object reflects the defects of our consciousness or the imperfection of its structure, however, it also reflects the imperfection of the physical objects themselves as opposed to, for example, numbers. As long as what is given to us intuitively fulfills the semantic intentionality, our knowledge on the object will grow if more of its perspectives or aspects will be given to us intuitively. Knowledge is not only a static reference between intentionality and intuition but a dynamic process which peaks when all the object's aspects are given to us intuitively; there may be different levels of fulfilling, the scope and clarity change. If I see a fruit tree from afar and then I bump into the tree itself then it is present before me by intuition but the tree is not given to me optimally. If I would stand near it and would see all the details, I would perceive more. It must be said that Husserl does not define the optimal terms as, for example, day light or a presence of a spaceship. It is best to see the stars at night and Husserl contends that the optimal ability to be given is the type which offers us the most information on the object.

**16:20 Imagination and seeing essences**

In "seeing" essences, I "see", for example, the essence of a triangle and I describe what I "see". I "see" that a triangle in its essence is a form; it is made of three straight lines that intersect each other, they meet in what is called an angle that may be of any size but the sum of all angles is 180 degrees.

I also "see" the essence of the table, not a certain table but generally an ideal table; I can describe what I "see"; I "see" that in its essence, the table has four legs that supports a vertical surface.

I "see" the essence of consciousness; I "see" that in its essence, consciousness carries sense or noema that intends to an object which is intended by a subject. Husserl's intuitive theory says that when I perceive "red", I use imagination for the distinction in it between different red objects, whereas each object carries with it the case red.

By abstracting different cases of red in different objects, I intuitively perceive the red itself. In Ideas I, Husserl characterizes the method of conceptual change; in order to perceive the essence red I use a form of imagination or a fantasy. I imagine different cases of red, I Imagine red objects with stronger or weaker shades and then by abstracting I perceive the essence which is common to the different red objects imagined as red.

Examining the triangle, I imagine few and different geometrical forms and judge which are triangles. I abstract from this imagined group (and judge) these traits which are common to all triangles. That way I create "insight", I "see" that the triangle, in its essence, is a form with three intersecting lines, creating angles summing up to 180 degrees; or, for example, the essence of the table, I imagine different objects, if i do not see that one of those object has four legs, horizontal surface, I judge them as not being tables and then I "see" the essence of the table, that it has four legs, horizontal surface. My judgments are based on evidence of intuition.

The pure essence may be given intuitively for an empirical experience of perception, memory, imagination etc., however, similarly, it may be given in fantasy (Phantasiegegebenheiten). Therefore, in order to catch the essence itself in its originality, we may start, by imaginative intuition, from the empirical intuition, but also from a non-empirical experience or non-existent evidence.

Husserl was in the opinion that knowledge of essences is not, necessarily, dependent on the knowledge of the facts preceding it. Obviously, our abilities to imagine objects under their relevant essence, usually starts in, really, experiencing same objects. Therefore, Husserl's assertion, according to David Woodruff Smith, must be that the moment we acquired knowledge, through facts, on objects under essence and we want to perceive the essence itself with the relevant intuition, then we may use fantasy or free imagination. Our perception of the essence depends on the changing cases of the imagined essence. The origin of the relevant intuition for the perception of essence stems from experiences of imagination. Husserl uses the example of the geometrician; by imagining different cases of triple without seeing actual triangles on the canvas, the geometrician obtains "evidence" of the triangle's essence. Therefore, phenomenological observation may exist by fantasy reflecting imaginative acts of consciousness. Since our knowledge of things in the domain nature is empirical, we do not fantasize freely while we are developing our intuitive perception of essence from the domain nature, for example, the essence of a tree. We see and touch trees every day, making distinctions between the traits of trees around us, a biologist, researching photosynthesis, cell activity etc., evolutionists researching how trees have developed in time. How does imagination play a role in our intuitive perception of the fruit tree's essence? When we organize the knowledge we have on fruit trees, we imagine different traits of trees and by judging our real observations on fruit trees, we decide that some of the properties characterize fruit trees and some do not. We have to be careful when we try to understand Husserl's assertion that memory alone provides intuitive support to the perception of essence. He assumes that we acquire knowledge on trees hence on their essence by empirical perception, however, following the acquiring of empirical knowledge, we fantasize, sort and perceive the tree's essence, but we cannot learn about the tree's essence by imagination alone. Intuition of essence is the experience of visual perception, how things are, given previous experiences and background beliefs.


## 16:30 Types of intuitions and evidence


Intuitions are divided into two types, an origin and a secondary creation. So far we have related to an original intuition. Intuition of origin is used as the origin of knowledge.

Intuition of secondary creation reconstructs experience structures which origin is in original intuitions. Intuition of origin includes perceptual experience, "seeing" essences and phenomenological "seeing".

Each type of these experiences presents its object in original form by intrinsic seeing. Perceptions present things in nature, "seeing" essences and phenomenological "seeing" presents conscious acts and their content. All these types of experiences present the object in its originality and its intrinsic seeing.

Intuition of secondary creation includes experience of memory, imagination and empathy. Memory presents events from the past, recreates what was perceived earlier by me or what was judged earlier based on perceptual evidence. Imagination presents events and possible objects that recreate what I will see or judge. Empathy presents experience of the other "as if" I was in his place; in that sense, empathy recreates in my experience the type of experience which, I think, another person has. The role imagination plays in seeing the essence is important, we rely upon imagination in knowing the object's essence or nature e.g. the fruit tree. We usually do not fantasize on a tree in order to judge that it is a fruit tree; however, we understand that it will not be a fruit tree if there are papers instead of fruit. Husserl's theory on "horizon" hints at our knowledge on known types of objects e.g. the fruit tree, depends on our ability to imagine i.e. we can imagine the tree's horizon.

## 16:40 Science and knowledge

'All natural sciences' are naive in relation to their starting point. The natural sciences (physics, chemistry, biology, neuro sciences etc.) and the human sciences (as history, psychology, anthropology and sociology) are philosophically naive; they accept for granted the truthfulness of the natural viewpoint according to which the truthfulness of the world may be founded by procedures and scientific method. As opposed to the naive perception of science there is a more rigorous science which is not philosophically naive i.e. it is not naive in its origin and questioning the assumptions on existence and the nature of reality, on the probability of objective knowledge and on the validity of procedures and accepted scientific methods.

At Husserl's time, the term "science" meant any systematical body of theory or knowledge on a specific domain of objects.

Today, sciences include physics, chemistry, biology, neurology, psychology etc. Also more abstract domains as geometry, arithmetic, logic and phenomenology (proper use assumed) are considered sciences.

The 'rigorous science' is such because it negates all accepted assumptions that are not critical hence it does not contain any assertions which are not based or absolutely justified. To contend that all assertions are 'absolutely justified' means that each assertion has to be justified, only such justification is not relational to a previously accepted assumption. The distinction between philosophy and any other theoretical system is not the method or the function, but the specific subjects that are being researched and described.

According to Husserl, science, basically, is descriptive, meaning that for a given scientific system there exists a domain of entities which nature is defined and independent. The purpose of the natural science is to research the said domain and describe what is discovered; therefore when Husserl contends that philosophy has to be a rigorous science, he also contends that it must be descriptive and its terms and methods will stem from the intrinsic nature of the objects it supposed to describe.

Its purpose is to exhaust the given ontological domain and to ensure that all properties are defined and independent. For Husserl, philosophy as a rigorous science is not different from transcendental phenomenology, the science of the ontological domain which is called transcendental subjectivity[10].

*If so, what makes theory to a body of knowledge and not just a theory of possible objects?*

---

[10] David Bell, Husserl, Routledge 1990.

The answer is that science is made of assertions based on evidence hence by intuition. Husserl says that basically, knowledge comprises of beliefs which are the product of judgments based on intuitive experiences. Our knowledge on objects and events in nature starts with sensual perception i.e. intuitive perception. We produce perceptual judgments (I see a green object in the forest and judging it to be a tree) on things that we see, hear, touch etc. and by making conclusions we produce additional conclusions i.e. I have judged that this is a tree; based on it having fruit and additional properties, I also remember it based on what I was taught when I saw these trees in the past. Here, we refer to knowledge which Husserl calls daily knowledge; physics, chemistry and biology originate in such knowledge.

I observe that an object that rises always falls down, I discover that one needs force for the object to rise etc.; sciences examine the behavior of physical objects (molecules, brain cells, volcanoes, stars, galaxies, etc) and events; then more abstract hypotheses are being created usually by the use of mathematics which characterizes the essence of the given phenomenon. Following a scientific investigation, a methodical body of assertions is created or a theory based on evidential observations i.e. I see how two objects with mass are being pulled to each other or meet.

Husserl suggested a complex theory on our knowledge of the consciousness. We "live" our subjective life, we experience in subjective conscious acts, we distinct our experiences as intentional, a consciousness of something; If we bracket the question of objects existing in our experiences then we turn our attention to experiences and their sense; then we "observe" the sense of the experiences hence their sense.

By using phenomenology, we develop a theory on the structure of consciousness which is based on intuitive evidence of our experiences of different conscious acts and the observations of them. That way we abstract and describe the essence of consciousness as the science of consciousness.

I have said that knowledge is created by rational judgment acts based on evidence or intuitive experience i.e. intuition. A systematical knowledge in a certain scientific domain is called theory; it is a system of assertions about a certain domain of objects that are bound to each other by deduction. The assertions are considered knowledge only when they are judged with supporting evidence or are intuitively fulfilled; such knowledge comes from experiences as perception. According to Husserl, intuition is composed of intentional conscious acts that are characterized by intuition or evidence i.e. intuition is composed of self evidence that is being intended on an object or state of things. A sensual perception is a paradigm of intuition. Visual perception is an intentional component merged with sensual component in an experience, noesis merged with sensual information (Hyle). The visual intentionality of an object is evidential or is being "fulfilled" intuitively thanks to the sensual component.

We can identify two components in knowledge: rational and empirical; also two aspects in experiencing: the terminological and the sensual e.g. while seeing the fruit tree (sensual) and judging (terminological) that such tree exists in a certain place. While the perception is a paradigm of intuition, Husserl recognizes additional types of intuitive experiencing: sensual perception, "seeing" essences, categorical "seeing" and phenomenological "seeing"; Husserl speaks of "seeing" although the different said experiences differ from each other.

Seeing essences or an ideal intuition comprises of "seeing" something that relates to a certain essence e.g. "seeing" the essence of a triangle or of a tree having a trunk.

Husserl contends that by using imagination (i.e. we imagine different and diversified objects) we reach such "seeing". I imagine a diversification of triangles or trees and by observing I change the objects' properties; then I "see" the triangle, essentially, having three internal angles (if not, then the said object is not a triangle), or the tree, essentially, having branches. By change of imagination I see the similarity of relevant cases of essences, a tree or a triangle. Categorical intuition is linked to seeing ontological category (formal essence) e.g. the category of state of things. Phenomenological intuition describes the structure of consciousness. Due to bracketing I turn my attention from the objects in the world around me to the structure of my consciousness of same objects. By making an ideal change, I observe a certain form of consciousness e.g. my seeing the fruit tree while considering its intentional essence. I reach the understanding of the experience's structure; I "see" that consciousness is consciousness of something, a sensual intentional perception, a visual representation of "that fruit tree" etc.

Phenomenologically, knowledge is being created by using observation or ideal phenomenological intuition. All our knowledge depends, in a certain way, on our daily experiencing the world around us; it is dependent on background knowledge originating in our daily life; Husserl calls it "the world of our daily life" or "life in the world" (Lebenswelt). "Life in the world" is a phenomenological structure; it is the world as we experience it daily i.e. life in the world is not a separate domain of objects but a scope of noematic sense which embraces types of sense representing the objects as experienced by us in our daily life.

Therefore, life in the world is a structure of sense that includes the idea of intuition. The world exists not only as a collection of facts or of all the actual state of things but also as a world of values, of taste, of goodness and a practical world. "That world" is the world in which I find myself and it is also the world around me. All my experiences take place in that world, the world around me, and all the objects in my consciousness exist "in the world around me"; the emphasis is on "my" or "my world" or "around me".

I experience objects as objective facts however, also, and in many cases, as valuable things and parts of my practical deeds; e.g. I see a fruit on the tree which is an objective state of things, yet, the fruit is nice and tasty, these are aesthetic matters.


**16:50 Ontology**


Formal ontology is a method investigating the being of an object. Formal ontology does not deal in the differences between different objects but in what is unconditionally true for any object, that is, the essence of triangles or tables.

The investigation of formal ontology is, therefore, the elucidation of categories such as quality, property, relation, identity, part and whole etc., as opposed to material investigation which examines
131

the essential structures that belong to a certain domain or type of object and looks to determine about each detail in the researched domain, whether it is, necessarily, considered true.

For example, the traits of mathematical beings as such, as opposed to mental processes or objects in time-space.

The domain of physics can also be divided to secondary domains as chemistry or biology.

As for consciousness, in addition to conscious acts being intended toward single objects, there are also conscious acts being intended on ideal or universal objects. While the investigation of the fruit's real traits is an empirical investigation of several traits that may have been different, it is not the case when we investigate the traits of the fruit as a physical object.

According to Husserl, the insight on the other may be acquired by what is called by Husserl a conceptual reduction (different from phenomenological reduction) or conceptual differentia.

Conceptual differentia is the terminological analysis performed when we try to imagine the object as being different from itself now. Sooner or later the imagining of this change will unravel certain properties that are unchangeable or may deviate without the object ceasing to exist as such.

The changing, therefore, causes us to distinct between the object's incidental properties i.e. the properties which could have been different (the fruit's color or size) and its essential properties without which it will not exist as a fruit. The essential properties are the unchanging structure that causes the object to be what it actually is. According to Husserl, I may, mentally, obtain the essential properties if I succeed, by conceptual reduction, to base or to create a horizon in which the object may change without losing its identity as a thing of the same type; in this case I will succeed to unravel the unchanging structure which is its essence.

## 17:00 Transcendental subjectivity

'Transcendental subjectivity', according to Husserl, precedes all concrete reality.[11] As aforesaid, the reduction is a step or a procedure which origin is 'the thesis of the natural standing' and which ends in what Husserl calls transcendental subjectivity and of which a central part is a suspension of all commitment or belief, explicit or implicit that appears as a natural standing.

The epochè takes us from one conscious state to another; therefore, Husserl says that instead of remaining in this position, we must change it in a revolutionary way (Ideas I page 107). The changing is actually the neutralization of the natural world's ontology; we are committed to its epistemology and ontology thus we must remove these commitments; the world remains as it is, we do not 'activate' it or 'avoiding' it, we rather bracket it. It is still there as the content which was bracketed... but we do not make use of it [the thesis of the natural world. We do not activate our ontological commitments (General thesis) which belong to the natural standing's essence, we rather bracket all that is included in relation to the being (Ideas I page 111). When I apply the reduction, while avoiding judgment of the world i.e. I avoid saying 'reality exists outside my consciousness', I do not negate the

---

[11] Edmund Husserl ,Formal and Transcendental Logic, Translated by D.Cains §65/ p.169

world by being skeptical; I rather perform phenomenological epochè which prevents me from passing judgment on everything that has to do with the existence in time- space.

It is clear that following the reduction, we may not speak again about the same world as if nothing happened; we may not speak or think of it as we did previously, moreover, we may not relate to it as we did prior to the reduction.

Then, one should ask whether any discussion of the world, following the reduction, has any sense; Husserl's response is positive. In "The Crisis of the European Sciences and Transcendental Phenomenology"[12] he says "it is really necessary to clarify the fact that we are not left with senselessness and natural abstention" (same, page 151). We remain with *the consciousness*! Hence, although the epochè is summed in the acceptance of a position of avoiding judgment of the world or we do not think about the natural world outside of consciousness, still remains a 'phenomenological residue', 'consciousness in itself' as a being on its own and due to its absolute essence remains uninfluenced by the phenomenological reduction.

The phenomenological epochè or the bracketing of the objective world... does not leave us with anything. On the contrary, we obtain ownership of something; what we obtain by it is our pure life with all the subjective processes that compose them together with everything intended by us...; i.e. the world of phenomenon (Cartesian Meditations page 20).[13]

The reduction leaves us with a residue, an absolute and pure transcendental consciousness. According to Husserl, following the

[12] Edmund Husserl, The Crisis of European Sciences and Transcendental Phenomenology, Translated by D.carr.

[13] Edmund Husserl, Cartesian Meditations, Translated by D.Cairns.

performance of the epochè I came to understand that "I, with my life (mental), remain... in my existential status, irrespective of whether the world exists or not... such ego, with its ego life... remains for me, necessarily, due to the epochè" (Cartesiam Meditations page 25). I am left with a reference to myself, with my acts of consciousness and their contents.

Husserl means that there are two actual domains of 'being', the one is the natural world which includes the empirical "I" and the other, the transcendental world and the transcendental subject which also includes my transcendental ego.

Two such ontological domains do not coincide, particularly, the transcendental ego is not part of the natural world and the empirical ego is not part of the transcendental world. The natural world, on one hand, is ontologically dependent i.e. it may exist only in relation to the transcendental "I".

Husserl writes, the domain 'transcendental consciousness' is an actual domain of absolute 'be' (Ideas I page 212). The cognizant and conscious acts of the ego 'are directed toward the world' and they are events that occur in the world. With the phenomenological epochè, the empirical ego which is part of the world is being bracketed. The thoughts and other conscious acts that occur following the reduction cannot be performed or be related to the daily and natural ego. The natural ego is a subject for research by the empirical science of psychology, while the absolute and transcendental ego is a subject for research by phenomenology.

*Why will the suspension of the natural standing lead us to a transcendental subject?*

Husserl suggests two ways to reach the transcendental reduction; the Cartesian way and ontological way. In Ideas I, Husserl turns our attention to the fact that there is a difference between the way by which objects of time-space are given to consciousness and the way by which consciousness is given to itself. While physical objects appear in perspectives i.e. never given as a whole but always through a limited angle, it is not true for the self appearance of consciousness. Objects are being given from a certain insufficient and partial point of view; it is necessary to pass through many perspectives for the perception of the complete object and actually to almost perceive the whole object; the experience itself appears directly and in full.

For Husserl, the radical change happening from the appearance of subjectivity to the appearance of objects shows that, phenomenologically, there is an essential difference between an object and a subject.

Instead of investigating consciousness as another object in the world, we must investigate it in different terms i.e. under its own conditions from a "first person" point of view. By making the distinction between two ways of appearance, Husserl suggests a distinction between a "first person" point of view and a "third person" point of view. Consciousness gets high priority.

While I investigate consciousness itself according to its own criteria, I investigate from a "first person" point of view; however, while I investigate and perceive it as another object in the world, I investigate it from a "third person" point of view. Being influenced by the Descartes' methodological doubt, Husserl contends that it is not possible to imagine a world without the existence of consciousness; the imagination assumes the existence of consciousness by giving some priority to subjectivity.

In paragraph 49 in Ideas I, it is contended that an unbiased investigation of the intentional relation between consciousness and the world must result in a complete consciousness that survives even an annihilation of the world. The objective world (as a rational and coherent structure being compatible with experiencing) assumes, necessarily, an experiencing subject; however, while the world can appear only in front of a subject, subjectivity does not necessitate the world for its being. This is the truth of psychosis.

In psychosis, I can hallucinate the world, we *imagine* the world from within ourselves i.e. there is no world outside the psychotic phenomenon; the psychotic consciousness is the founder and the creator of the world which relates to it. In the psychotic and transcendental subjectivity, the psychotic creates his reality; he creates the sights, sounds and smells.

The world and each type of transcendence is relational in the sense that the precondition of its appearance is external to it i.e. in the subject as compared with the subject, the intrinsic, which is complete and autonomous since its expression is only dependent on itself. Husserl tries to understand why the activation of the epochè will lead us to the discovery of the transcendental subjectivity. He draws our attention to the unique givenness and the autonomy of the "I" i.e. to subjectivity which cannot be investigated in the usual ways. The naturalistic standing which perceives consciousness as another object in the world cannot include everything i.e. to give a comprehensive account on the world because consciousness is transcendental. The consciousness goes beyond a scientific and empirical account. As said, the transcendental "I" (subject or ego) is being used as a precondition to appearance and expression. Husserl did not understand the transcendental "I" as an abstract and general thing or as a conscious state that exists beyond self identity; on the contrary, the transcendental "I" or my transcendental subjectivity is my individual and concrete subjectivity.

The transcendental subject is a founding subject. The empirical subject is the same subject that is understood and interpreted as an object in the world i.e. as an earthly "regular" object. In this context, Husserl denotes the fact that subjectivity may be interpreted in two different ways, by a naturalistic or psychological reflection and by a pure transcendental reflection; when I perform a psychological reflection, I interpret the conscious act as a mental process i.e. as a physical-mental being that exists in the world e.g. neurological acts in the brain; neurotransmitters being discharged in the synaptic region between the dendrite and the axon and cause me to think various thoughts or to see various things.

This type of self consciousness which Husserl often calls earthly cognizance, is an experience that belongs to this material earthly world just the same as a tree is an earthly thing. Husserl denotes that such earthly consciousness cannot grant us a complete understanding of subjectivity. Naturalistic reflection i.e. natural or regular, presents us with a subject which is perceived by us as a natural object. Pure transcendental reflection, however, presents us with a subject that is abstracted from any relation or an incidental interpretation. There is an empirical "I" that investigates the world and itself from a "third person" point of view and there is a transcendental "I" that investigates from a "first person" point of view; however, the way must be paved for that consciousness to be reached. The epochè paves the way for us; only by way of methodical suspension of the empirical "I" we can reach transcendental consciousness.

The ontological way by which the transcendental "I" is understood, does not begin with the immediate givenness of the subject rather with the analysis of the givenness of the subject in a certain ontological domain (the domain of the ideal objects or the domain of the physical objects).

The ontological description is used as a guideline for the transcendental analysis. When we face the appearance of the object i.e. the object as it is presented, perceived, judged or evaluated, we face an intentional and experimental structure with which these types of appearance are compatible. We reach an act of representation, perception, judgment and evaluation hence the subject with which the appearing object must be understood in the subject's context.

By the phenomenological standing, we are aware of the givenness of the object in the consciousness. However, we do not focus on the object precisely as it was given to us but we also focus on the subjective side of consciousness therefore, we become aware of the subjective achievement and the intentionality that acts so that the objects appear as they are.

The epochè does not cause us to focus away from the objects of the earthly world, but lets us examine them under a new light i.e. in their appearances and expression to a compatible consciousness. The attempt to reach a philosophical understanding of the world leads, by mediation, to the discovery of subjectivity because the phenomenological perspective on the world is being formed by the appearance of the world relating to subjectivity. However, the said subjectivity is not the empirical subject which is researched by sciences as psychology, psychiatrics, neurology, history and anthropology. The empirical subject is an object in the world and as all earthly objects it assumes a subject through which it appears hence unraveling the transcendental subject i.e. subjectivity which is the precondition to the appearance of the empirical subject and objects in the world.

While the Cartesian reduction emphasizes the different and distinct status of a subject e.g. when "I" think ("cogito") or when I imagine or hallucinate, the ontological form of reduction emphasizes the investigation of the subject being linked with the investigation of objects in the world. We understand the act of subjectivity through the epochè which is a focusing on the phenomenon i.e. the way by which objects are given to us (the subject). The world does not simply exist; the world appears and the structure of this appearance is conditioned and enabled by subjectivity.

The objects appear for the psychotic subject, the world exists as a phenomenon for the psychotic, i.e. by establishing and creating hallucinations or delusions. The psychotic subject creates the objects appearing before him by hallucination. In a psychotic state, the world does not exist as a separate and distinct thing i.e. a world that exists separately from any possible experience and terminological or semantical perspective.

Therefore, the psychotic is an authentic subjectivity in its purest form because he, more than anybody else, creates the world appearing before its subjective consciousness. As aforesaid, we must return to the things themselves i.e. we must found our theories on which is actually appearing and is present for the consciousness. As we have seen, a philosophical analysis of the object as a phenomenon i.e. as it appears, must, necessarily,

140

consider subjectivity. If we really want to understand reality, the physical objects, we must, ultimately, return to the conscious act which experiences physical objects; only there they appear as they are.

Shortly, subjectivity is a precondition to the possibility of the phenomenon (also presence) or its expression. Without subjectivity there are no authentic phenomena present.


## 17:10 Solipsism


Husserl struggles with the problem of solipsism as a challenge to phenomenology.

Solipsism (from Latin *solus* for solely and *ipse* for self) is the doctrine contending that there is only a perceiving consciousness, my own consciousness, the rest is a hallucination or illusion. By bracketing the world, it remains only one and isolated "I" i.e. my own consciousness hence phenomenology causes solipsism.

Husserl attempts to pass the solipsistic abyss inherited from his phenomenological position of the "first person" point of view; on the other hand he is still committed to a solipsistic position when he directly approaches the problem in Cartesian Meditation where he deals in subjectivity, privacy and solipsism.

"When I, the pondering I, reduce myself, by the phenomenological epochè to an absolute transcendental ego, am I not becoming a solus ipse? Am I not remaining that way as long as I continue the self interpretation under the name phenomenology? (Cartesian Meditations page 89).

If the answer is positive, then how can phenomenology solve the 'transcendental problem relating to the objective world'? Husserl considers his role, on one hand, to reconcile his commitment to the method of phenomenological reduction with the egocentric perspective it compels and on the other hand to continue with his commitment and purpose to explain the nature of the world and our knowledge of it.

Solipsism is the problem of our knowledge not only of the objective world but also of other "I's", their consciousness and mental state. Phenomenologically seen, I have direct access only to my consciousness, however, I do not know that others also have consciousness; I also do not have access to their consciousness by a "first person" point of view.

*How do I know that you have consciousness and not just body?*

There is an essential philosophical problem in the relation between my consciousness to its body and the behavior of the other and my consciousness or my cognizance to his mental states.

The theory of intentionality by Husserl, i.e. phenomenology, is egocentric; its concepts and terms relate, only, to the sensual information i.e. *my* conscious acts and mental states. Moreover, I have direct perception and I intend on other physical objects; I can experience, even if not perfectly, other objects however, as aforesaid, I do not experience the conscious state of others, the other "I". There is a domain which I do not have access to; I do not have experiences of things that are not physical, they are not given to me directly.

Phenomenology does not have the terminological tools to explain the consciousness of the other or his "I". Moreover, I am not sure that there are other "I" beside me.

The existence, the psychology and the subjective mental states of the other are not accessible to me. I never perceive or experience the consciousness of the other the same way as I experience the tree directly (which is, also, the product of the psychotic's consciousness).

Therefore, Husserl's purpose is to understand the nature of experiencing somebody by somebody else. My awareness (or the lack of it), not only of others having consciousness but also of my inaccessibility to it and to their mental state, is essential for such experiencing; nevertheless, Husserl contends that this fact is a necessary condition i.e. an assumption to the existence of additional consciousness in others. If the subjective state of the other was not inaccessible then whats belongs to somebody else, would have been given to me directly and it was indeed just a moment of my essence and ultimately he himself and I myself were the same person.

But this is exactly the problem. By the psychotic, and here I take an extreme solipsistic position, it is probable that the man I am talking to now is part of my consciousness, not only that i hallucinating his body but also hearing his voice.

I am, practically, talking to myself and he himself and his consciousness are part of my consciousness exactly as his body is a perceptual and visual hallucination. Husserl states that the fact that your conscious state and your thoughts are not given to me in their origin is what makes you somebody else initially. If your consciousness would have been given to me as my experience, I would have your thoughts, your emotions and feelings, then there would not have been two consciousnesses but one, mine, but this is what is enabled by psychosis.

Phenomenologically, there is a transcendental "I" and I do not know whether there are other "I's", moreover, I cannot know their conscious state which means a psychotic solipsism; "their" input/output is actually my projection on another object perceived by me.

The psychotic, for example, can hallucinate a body and hear a vocal hallucination originating in the same body; he, supposedly, hears the other however that other is actually the product of his consciousness and the voice he hears as coming from his mouth, is of his own creation. The psychotic does not only "hear it" but also attributes thoughts and his own conscious states to it. Simply said, I hallucinate his body and consciousness; his voice, odor and texture are actual "I". I create it and project my speaking on it so that whatever he says out loud are actually my thoughts.

*Is it possible to break out from the solipsistic jail?*

I think yes. A conscious act of expectation is intentionality toward the other. If, for example, I speak with somebody and I expect a certain behavior or a certain reaction from him provided that he is in a situation that is known to me from myself, then I expect a behavior or an account I am familiar with; i.e. since I am familiar with the situation from my case, I expect a physical and verbal behavior similar to mine; the other is a product of my consciousness hence I expect from him, who is myself, an identical reaction.

If I bring my hands close to the fire and I see him bringing his hands close to fire hence I expect his behavior and reaction to be similar to mine. If his reaction will, indeed, be identical to mine in the same situation it may be that he is a consciousness not

144

different from mine. It may be that I have created him and his behavior in my head hence being part of me. Surprise is senseless without having an initial expectation for something else to happen. If I am *surprised* from the account or from his behavior it means that I did not know or did not expect his mental states (thoughts, emotions, feelings and perceptions); hence the *surprise*, I do know that I face consciousness, an autonomic consciousness.

What I am saying is this: I speak with somebody that, assuming, I have created in my consciousness; this somebody, we assume, has consciousness which is actually mine i.e. as in psychosis when I duplicate my consciousness with that "other" who is actually me; if his physical or verbal behavior surprises me i.e. I expect a certain physical or verbal behavior (I expect *all* those reactions that I can think of) and then I discover that his behavior is different from my expectation, I then perceive an autonomous consciousness. I cannot surprise myself.

If I was alone in the world i.e. a single consciousness, I would be in a situation where the language and the behavior of the other are the product of my consciousness i.e. I would have known in advance how he would behave and what he would say exactly as if I was an engineer designing a robot (humanoid) which, given a certain input, in a certain situation, there will be a certain output (any physical or verbal behavior that I could think of), verbal behavior "P", but if his verbal behavior is "not P" hence I am surprised! Let us assume that the robot which is a perfect humanoid, surprises me with his physical and verbal behavior, then I would think to myself 'the machine received a life of its own', it has a consciousness separated from mine. There is another engineer, not me, who designed it (the humanoid robot).

145

My reasonable assumption is that I cannot surprise myself; therefore, when I am surprised from something, from a certain body, and by assuming that a body is being activated by a consciousness, I know that such body has a consciousness separated from mine!

Moreover, phenomenologically, I cannot be surprised from my own hallucination. I cannot be surprised from that which was created by me. If the reaction of the "other" (a complex hallucination of a person) surprised me meaning, I did not know of it in advance; since I cannot not know what I know hence, there is something here which is autonomous and not programmed (or programmed by another engineer).

Dialectically, once I know that I am not alone in the world; I can know his mental states also by expectation. in a certain situation I expect the other to act in a similar way as if I was in that situation; if his behavior confirms my expectations i.e. fulfills my noema then I may say that he has open a window for me to his mental states. While he reports to me about his mental states, I have access, however only *mediating*, by language to his mental states; he is giving me access to his consciousness.

Since I am familiar, from myself, which feelings, emotions, thoughts and perceptions I have in certain situations, I can enter his world and identify with him by empathy i.e. I now stand in his place, let us say, in his shoes. Due to the surprise I understand that I face a different consciousness than mine which, then, gives or invites me to enter and identify with it by empathy. I can understand the "not P" by identifying with, i.e. I put myself in his place by empathy. As aforesaid, if I have a complex hallucination of a person speaking with me (actually, I speak with myself because I put my consciousness in the hallucinated figure) and then "he" behaves unexpectedly (physically and verbally) I, immediately, understand that I have a phenomenon before me that was not created by me, something autonomous, separated and transcendental.

## 17:20 Body

In a certain sense, my body is a physical, material object existing in time-space; as any other object, it has weight, form, chemical components, history, etc.

Husserl calls the body, from a pure physical or material point of view, Der Koerper. However the body is given to me also by another way, I experience it, I know it in a way different from the way by which I am experiencing or knowing different physical objects e.g. a fruit; I know my body intimately, it is always there like a shadow which I cannot escape from, my relation to my body is, in a certain sense, not a relation at all since my body and me are not two separate things.

My body is a physical object and it is an intentional object in my perception and conceptualization i.e. I can see it, touch it and observe its behavior exactly the same way as I experience and perceive other physical objects but still, in a certain sense, it is a subject. My body may feel tired, pain, I feel fright, I can feel the heat when my hand is close to the fire.

According to Morris Marlo Ponti, my body is an object-subject or a body-subject which is, actually, a living body or a material "be" which also feels, a living thing (Der leib).

Phenomenologically, the living body and the physical body are two different things. The living body is, firstly, a "be" that expresses itself: when I am tired or feel pain, it is the living body that expresses pain or cries, this is our way to understand or to perceive the consciousness and the mental life of another person.

Secondly, it is also a "be" that feels; the living body can feel, I remove my hand from the fire because it hurts and burns.

Thirdly, the living body has the ability to move and act; Husserl calls it Kinesthesia. It is an organ obeying my will; it is the only object that moves as ordered by my will.

By intentionality, I communicate with other bodies through my living body i.e. I am linked to other objects not as a pure ego but as a physical thing. A fourth trait of the living body is its functioning as an absolute point of reference for all physical objects i.e. all physical objects are related to it in space.

Phenomenologically, the space in which I perceive and move, beneath or above me, left or right. It means that there is no pure point of view and there is no point of view from anywhere, there is only a certain point of view, from a certain position in relation to the body. I see the fruit in a certain angle from my eyes, which are in the center of my head which is a part of my body i.e. the body is a center through which we perceive physical objects. Every appearance from a certain perspective assumes that the experiencing subject is somewhere in space. Since the subject occupies space, the spatial objects can appear before a corporeal subject.

Husserl contends, therefore, that the body is a precondition to the ability to perceive and to the communication with spatial objects and every earthly experience is possible and being mediated by our body; even if I will seal all my senses i.e. my sensual perceptions, I will still feel my body. I know where my right hand is, I know it is the right hand and it is lateral to my body, the body is real and I perceive it directly without any mediation hence it is transcendental. I can describe the state of my body and the state of the body of others. While I open my eyes or, for example, touch my hand, thus, I verify its state by perceptual intuition, I know that I have a body and it is distinct and separate from my consciousness. The body is transcendental to consciousness, it is external to it i.e. precedes the visual intuition. Giving an existing body, hence, there is a world being distinct and separated from the consciousness; then, I know, there are other bodies. I know, by empathy, that if I see a hand close to the fire, a pain will be felt in the subject to which the body belongs; I put myself in its place.

## 17:30 Intersubjectivity and objectivity

Intersubjectivity is defined as the participation in conscious states by few individuals. According to Husserl, the perception of presenting me with an accessible intersubjective being i.e. a being that does not, exclusively, exist for me, but, publicly, for everybody else.

I am experiencing objects, events and acts as public things not private; i.e. the subject is one of many, he is a member of society or the community. All material or ideal objects have their sense and validity and exist thanks to a transcendental subject which exists ontologically. Husserl characterizes the transcendental
149

subject's society as the origin of all truths and objectivity. In Cartesian Meditations, he states that the transcendental intersubjectivity gives the world its objectivity. He was convinced that he has the key to the understanding and the establishment of a transcendental and objective reality; he considered intersubjectivity as a decisive factor in his views and philosophical development.

As I contended at 14:00, the way to subjects, other "I's" passes through empathy (Einfuehlung). Edit Stein in "on the problem of empathy" (*Zum Problem der Einfuehlung)* contends that the intersubjectivity is available to us by empathy; we put ourselves in the shoes of the other by way of our world is shared by different individuals. Through the intersubjectivity, we experience ourselves as different from the others and at the same time available to others. This component is a key for the establishment of my objective existence as a subject. In my experiencing the world, it is available not only to me but also to the other. The world and the objectively existing objects are being established by the intersubjectivity. Through intersubjectivity, the existence of others is also included; they are being established as I am, as objectively existing subjects. The question is whether empathy is indicative of direct or indirect accessibility to another subject and if this phenomenological account is logical.

In "The Crisis of the European Sciences and Transcendental Phenomenology: an introduction to phenomenological philosophy", Husserl contends that my experience and connection to another object as well as experiences that assume other subjects are worthy of the name "intersubjectivity". My experiencing the other is by his language (because language is being acquired by the history of the society in which he lives) and

150

his body hence the connection between subjects, intersubjective, is embodied by empathy. Husserl refers to empathy in order to assume a certain resemblance between another subject (another body and linguistic subject) who I meet and myself. But for being a body [and a linguistic subject] I could not identify other corporeal subjects. The fact that I am, actually, experiencing another i.e. other corporeal subject, does not mean that I can experience the other the same way by which he is experiencing himself as well as his consciousness is not accessible for me the same way by which my consciousness is accessible to me.

As Husserl emphasizes, if I would have accessibility to the other's consciousness, i.e. if I could know what the other is thinking, feeling, sensing and perceiving, the same way as I have immediate and direct accessibility to my consciousness, then the other ceases to be another and becomes an integral part of me and my consciousness.

The self givenness of the other is not open and is transcendental to me, however, I can experience the limit (Cartesian Meditation: An Introduction to Phenomenology). When I have an authentic experience of other subjects, I am experiencing the other, as opposed to objects, eluding me but, and it is an important but, he mediates for me by language; i.e. I know that the other's consciousness is eluding me and I do not have direct access to his consciousness, but it is mediating; he does not give himself to me the same way by which my consciousness is known to me.

Dan Zahavi argues that we deal with the relation between subject and object while the other eludes me, is not accessible for me; there is an asymmetry between me and him. There is a difference between the experiencing subject and the subject being experienced by us. The asymmetry is an essential part of my description of the intersubjectivity; without the asymmetry, there will not be intersubjectivity but a non distinct collective.

To speak of the other is to use terms of relation of which meaning assumes the ego as difference. The other is different from me, is stranger to me, he is another in relation to me, however, I know him by language. I contend that by expectation, the other is indeed an intentional object for me and that I have access to him. *Expectation* is an intentional act, I expect something to happen, I expect him behaving in a certain manner in a certain situation. If I was in a certain situation (e.g. my hand is close to the fire) and I would have said "it hurts" and then while I see the other in the same situation and he says "it hurts" then my expectations of him were strengthened; his *words* intuitively fulfill my expectation from him and that is exactly the evidence I need in order to know the states of his consciousness.

I know of myself how I would speak in a certain situation; if the other "puts himself in my shoes" or I put myself in his shoes i.e. he says what I would have been saying in a certain situation, hence, I consider him as a subject. He must say what I would have said in the same situation. In a certain situation we feel pain and show painful behavior. If we see other bodies in the same situation we say to ourselves "now he should cry out in pain".

If the sentence is in a language/thought being fulfilled intuitively i.e. that same other, indeed, cries out and say "it hurts", hence I am confirming his consciousness directly; not only I confirm his consciousness by the principle of *surprise*, I also know how he feels.

Now, by expectation, surprise and language, I know, in the sense of intuitive fulfillment, how are his mental states. The thought or his consciousness is compatible with mine should I have been in the same situation. I would like to contend that by the psychotic, the ego establishes the self givenness of the other, a self givenness that characterizes that same directness, absoluteness and immediateness that I have from my self-givenness. I invent or create the other's consciousness when I hallucinate him; the situation being as such, a negation of another subjectivity is deduced so that solipsism is unavoidable (i.e. I do not know whether others exist beside my consciousness); somewhat, the individuality of the other, actually, depends on me, I invent the consciousness of the other because I am psychotic and I create his subjectivity and his mental states, but, as I said, given the principal of surprise, the fulfillment of his speech serves as evidence for me of his distinct and conscious states; I *know* that he exists separately from me and I also *know* what are his mental states.


*Why is the other a precondition to my ability to experience an objective world?*
*Why my experience of objects is being changed radically when I experience another subject?*

Husserl's thesis is that my experiencing the validity of reality's objectivity is possible by a transcendental experience of other subjects and that such transcendentalism which in Husserl's opinion is the real difference, and therefore the origin of all types transcendental and real which gives the world its objective validity. The objective world is supported by the transcendence of the other subject.

*Why is the subjectivity of the other a precondition for the establishment of transcendental objects?*
153

*Why objects can appear as transcendental only through the other?*

Husserl response is that the objects appear also before the other. The intersubjective experiencing of objects ensures their transcendence i.e. if you and I can experience the same object e.g. the fruit, hence it has an objective existence independent from my consciousness.

*How "I", the psychotic, can be sure that there is a world out there; that the transcendental objects exist and i am not hallucinating? I.e. the objects are not private, only for me?*

By recognizing the other! I.e. now, that we, both, are subjects thus, if we see an object that is given to us by intuition then it exists as transcendental, it is present for me and him; it exists.

By the psychotic, there is a hallucination, of a lion for example, that does not appear by the other, they do not agree on the object that is given to the psychotic. They do not agree that the lion is really there; they are in a disagreement whtere it exists out side the psychotic mind. However, if there is an agreement it means that the psychotic is not hallucinating and there is an objective lion outside his consciousness.

Finally, the psychotic must choose to visit the physician and return to an agreement with the other. As long as I am experiencing that the other is experiencing the same object which I am experiencing, I am experiencing a real and objective object. Only then, the objects appear with a validity that makes them more than an intentional object. Now, they are given as real intentional objects (objective i.e. valid as intersubjective); an object which, principally, cannot be experienced by another, cannot be objective and transcendental.

Only at a time when I am experiencing others that are experiencing this fruit thus, the noematic assertion that "the green fruit on the tree" is being fulfilled by evidence expressed by language. I communicate with others that fulfill my intentional act; i.e. the fruit which exists now in my consciousness has existed as a real transcendental fruit through another intersubjective subject who speaks with me, i.e. his language is the evidence for the existence of the fruit. It is important that my experiencing the other will be an experiencing the other who is experiencing as well, i.e. a subject with experiences.

Husserl contends that the sense and the categories of transcendence, objectivity and reality are established by the intersubjective. These categories of validity are established by a subject who has experienced others. The subject may experience the world as long as he is a member of the community i.e. a part of social structure. If we accept Husserl's determination that reality is strengthened by the intersubjective, thus we have to seriously consider not only the consensus (general agreement) but also the disagreement.

Husserl referred repeatedly to the category of "normality". My normality "from home" is shaped by tradition and by generations preceding me and is, therefore, historical. Normality is a collective of agreements that usually originate in the history of such collective. Husserl contends that, basically, comprehension, perception and our experiences are shaped by typical and normal structures, models, examples and ideals that were established through experiences in the past. If what we perceive contradicts with previous experiences (being different) thus, we have experienced an abnormality (anomaly) following which we may change our expectation.

"Normal" is a state of agreement within a society of subjects; as for the psychotic, it is, ultimately, the standing of the one versus society i.e. the individual, the psychotic has to get in line with "those"; I have made an existential leap by going to the physician and agreed that something is wrong with me. If I would not go to the physician, I would be in a state of disagreement with others hence the lion which is a hallucination, would not be objective knowledge but subjective.

We and the others sign "a social and semantical treaty" that we will not change the sense of words and interpretations. The one who changes the accepted interpretations is expelled from the social circle and sent to "the ship of fools". Agreement is a matter between me and the members of my community; if there is no agreement in the matter of description and object, i.e. if I see an object, "a man in a black coat standing in the corner" and I describe and interpret him as an assassin and you in contrast, contend that he is innocent person, thus we disagree. In this case, a disagreement leads to misunderstanding.

The idea of the social and semantical treaty is based on people, members of the community, who have agreed to unite around a single semantic system and accept rules, laws and limitations relating to a certain dialogue. The treaty is actually the expression of an agreement between people to create a semantical framework that will ensure what is comprehended which ensures the community's existence. The semantic rules are agreed by all participants of the semantical framework. A person, actually, received the language and its rules from his parents and they have actually introduced him to the social and semantical treaty. Without the social and semantical treaty there will be chaos, literally a state of the tower of Babel following the punishment (Creation, 11, 1-9):

"And the whole earth was of one language, and of one speech. And it came to pass, as they journeyed from the east, that they found a plain in the land of Shinar; and they dwelt there. And they said one to another, let us make brick, and burn them thoroughly. And they had brick for stone, and slime had they for mortar. And they said, let us build us a city and a tower, whose top may reach unto heaven; and let us make us a name, lest we be scattered abroad upon the face of the whole earth. And God came down to see the city and the tower, which the children of men built. And God said, Behold, the people is one, and they have all one language; and this they begin to do; and now nothing will be restrained from them, which they have promoted to do. Let us go down, and there confound their language, that they may not understand one another's speech. So God scattered them abroad from thence upon the face of all the earth and they left off to build the city. Therefore is the name of it called Babel; because God did there confound the language of all the earth and from thence did God scatter them abroad upon the face of all the earth."

Humanity is characterized as one united figure that speaks a common language that reaches a decision and executes it. According to a story from the past, there was only one language and one society. As a result of the punishment, the languages mixed and with them many peoples were scattered.

The said existential leap is a leap over an abyss because the psychotic believes in his own story and he possesses intuitions and truth or subjective knowledge. His delusions or misbeliefs, from his point of view, are intuitions that were fulfilled by hallucinations therefore he possesses knowledge and subjective and intuitive truth.

If for example which was previously used, a paranoid believes and thinks that there is a person in the corner stalking him, thus the intuition (the perception of a man with a black coat) is self evident for the truth of his misbeliefs; now he *knows* that he is being stalked and that someone is trying to harm him. Therefore, the psychotic must irrationally leap to another system of beliefs.

In fact, the transition from one thought system to the other is irrational. The transition is bound by an existential leap. The intersubjective plays a key role in the category of "normality". As far as I remember, I live among people; my expectations are understood in the context of the intersubjective that was given to us by preceding generations. Normality is also norm, or a social convention, in which essence exceed the individual. I learn from others about what is agreed. I am involved in a certain culture, a certain language, a certain history and customs that were given to me by others from preceding generations.

As far as the establishment of objectivity depends on the security that the experiences of others are equal, or may be equal to mine, then a problem will arise, should they contend that they have a different experience. Every subject is part of other normal subjects and he is normal within and by the community. Only through him we mediate truth and falsehood.

For example, if I see a man in the corner and I address my friend and say "you see him there"; if he sees him, thus we have an agreement, he strengthens the validity of my experience and then I really perceive the man in the corner existing objectively. If he does not see or agree, thus the validity of my experience will undergo change; i.e. I, the psychotic, shall need to visit a psychiatrist, i.e. due to the disagreement I decide that something is wrong with me. I cannot continue to hold my belief of really experiencing the man in the corner if the object is not accessible to my fellow man; we have a disagreement.

Even if we negate hallucinations and say that the psychotic is only delusional, hence we could have disagreement as to the interpretation; the object is the same intentional object, same person, but once, we see it as an assassin and another time as an innocent man.

The object is the same, we intend on the same object i.e. the image or the impression remains as it is but we intend on it differently, i.e. interpreting it differently; according to the late Wittgenstein, interpretation is the description of something as something. In the transition from normality to psychosis, the innocent man is described and perceived as an assassin. The radical change is the transition from a normal state to a psychotic state i.e. by a radical change in consciousness. The radical change is a sudden change that takes place instantly. At one moment I see the man in the corner as an innocent man and at another moment, suddenly, I see an assassin.

## 17:40 The logic of psychosis, memory and essences

As I have said at 13:30, the intrinsic logic of hallucinations is such that the psychotic sees, touches, hears, smells and tastes objects that do not exist externally.

There is no external stimulus in hallucinations. However, by memory, he touches the real thing.

I, for example, hallucinate Van Gogh's painting "starry night', my hallucination is a recycled memory of the real painting seen by me in the past. Therefore, the hallucination is an object's representation, an intrinsic image without an external stimulus, it is actually a memory of a real object from the past, an object that existed in time-space but *now* (in psychosis) it is reconstructed to become an intrinsic image. The psychotic conscious act, in accordance with its intrinsic logic, intends on an external object that existed in the past but is absent now, in the present; it is intending on an intrinsic object (intrinsic image) which is a recycled memory of the external object that existed simply in nature.

Hallucinations are imagination i.e. an image or an imitation; this is the sense of psychosis. According to the realistic point of view in direct perception, there is an external object, i.e. transcendental and real which you touch immediately and directly; on the other hand the psychotic holds 'the representative perceptual theory'; in hallucination, which is an ideal act, there is an intrinsic object which is a picture, a picture of something seen in the past, which is, actually, an intentional content that mediates for a transcendental-external object. The representation is what is present in phenomenological consciousness of the psychotic but it is an image from the past.

"The man, there, in the corner" is a noematic content which is a representation (image) of the man in the corner that was there, outside, in the past; the image in Hallucinations mediates between the perceiving subject and the perceived external object. The image of the person that is being seen now does not exist in the present rather originates from the person who we have seen yesterday; this image suddenly emerges and appears in the present of the psychotic.

Using the metaphor of the movie which I have given before in which I contend that we are sitting in a movie theater and watch a figure in a movie; this figure is an original and authentic photography of a real person outside the movie, the actor (who was given to us as he is, in person); however while the movie is played, we do not see the real person, rather the figure that represents the real person (the actor). There is a gap of *temporality* between the figure and the real person. While we are watching, the figure is present however, the person (the actor) is not, and he is absent. I hear the person's voice through the figure, the voice of the figure is identical to the voice of the person (the actor) because they are identical, however, now, at the time of playback, I hear a voice that was recorded a day before. The figure in the movie does not "unite" with the person due to the time that passed from the filming to the screening. I.e. in the metaphor of the movie, the figure is a hallucination that was a real actor in the past. We can now give a semantic and noematic description of what we hallucinate! The psychotic is, therefore, a temporal idealist; I, as aforesaid, call this standing an idealism of temporality.

*However, one should ask frankly, does the memory really and truly represent the transcendental objects?*
*Is it not a fact that what is present in the psychotic's consciousness is actually a memory and therefore there is no authenticity between the memory of the fruit and the fruit in itself?*
*Is there a difference between the representation which is a memory by the psychotic and the object in itself?*

Husserl responds: "it is erroneous to distinct between 'just intrinsic' or 'an intentional' object, on one hand and "transcendental" and "real" objects that may be compatible with them on the other. ...it should be said and recognized that the intentional object of representation is the same thing as the real object... it is absurd to distinct between the two.

The transcendental object would not be the object of representation unless it was its intentional object" (Logical Investigations V, annex to §§11 f/20 page 595).

Many critics see in this paragraph the evidence to Husserl's realism. The intentional object of an act and the external, transcendental, actual and real object are one. If the psychotic is an idealist, but through his memory he touches the thing itself, in person, he stands before the objects themselves, then it seems, apparently, that in psychosis, the objects that mediate and that are given to us by memory, are authentic representations.

The intentional object of a conscious act and the external, transcendental, actual and real object are one! It seems that it is a confirmation to a realistic perception of intentionality. In intentionality, when someone intends an object or performs an act 'on something', thus there is sense in speaking of hitting the intended object or actually touch the intended object. With regard to perception, Husserl believed that the most important trait that makes the perception unique and distinct it from other intentional acts is the ability to present the object "in person".

However, Husserl contends that what distinct an authentic perception by memory or expectation or imagination, is that while acts which are not perceptual are, basically, bound by some kind of image, imagination or representation of objects, in authentic perception the object itself is present.

Perception is characterized by the fact that the object itself appears and not as an image. Imagination, as perfect as it is, is, still, not the same as direct perception, it does not present the object itself and it just gives us a representation or image which is not the thing itself, 'That we owe perception' (Logical Investigations page 761). Perception, therefore, gives us a direct and immediate contact with the object itself.

Through a direct, intentional and conscious act we reach a state through which we "touch" the object itself. In light of this, one should ask whether memory or intrinsic representation count while an imaging of something external takes place. The traits of representations in memory are events that were experienced in the past. The attention is drawn to them as second level remembrance by reflection. There is a perception; when we remember it by reflection, there are representations of the perception in the memory.

These representations are of the second order. So is in fantasy (hallucinations), we imagine a chain of events that took place in our consciousness and which are representative and we reconstruct them in representations of a higher order which are the hallucination itself. If we remember how we have remembered, yesterday, a childhood experience, hence, the noema "a childhood experience" in itself is with a characterization of something of the second order that we have remembered. The attention of the ego goes directly through the noema of the different order flows until it reaches the final object beyond which it is impossible to go and fixates on it. Husserl says that memory is a representation of the second order of perception itself. If the memory mediates between the perceiving subject and the perceived object in itself, it seems that every mediating base is taking us back to non-mediating base. The primary origin of all legitimacy lies in immediate and in original evidence (Ideas I page 338).

Every clean memory has, in a certain manner, a base and immediate legitimacy, it has certain weight; it does not matter how big or small, legitimacy weights something, but it has an uncompleted legitimacy. In regard to memory representing past event, it has a natural, intrinsic link to the present reality (same, page 338), i.e. to actual perceptions.

Memory is strengthened with any advancement from memory to memory and into a chain of events. To a certain limit, the strengthening is mutual, the weight of memories dependents on each other. Each memory in the chain of memories has more power. If the chaining of memories reaches, eventually, the present reality, hence the perception, its weight and its evidence illuminates the whole chain.

If we understand properly, then, only original evidence has a legitimate base and "originality", for example, rationality which we relate to memory, hence all reproductive acts, including also empathy, are not original but "derived".

Its seems, apparently, that memory by the psychotic is not original evidence, however it has weight, i.e. hallucination which is memory stands before the object and it has weight, but not the same weight that perception has in itself. Let us say that I have hallucination and I see a man in a black coat standing in the corner; Husserl says that it has weight however there is still an epistemological gap between the hallucination and the real man in the corner (innocent) seen by me in the past; Therefore, one may summarize that hallucination being a memory, cannot, authentically, give us the object in person but one should ask which type of authenticity we are talking about.

I have seen Van Gogh painting 'starry night' and now I hallucinate the painting, hence probably, the representation by memory does not give us the painting in itself but only a respectable image. However the psychotic's hallucinates, for example, a person in general; he hears a voice in general, not necessarily a real person's voice which he knew in the past.

As I have denoted at 16:20, according to Husserl's intuitive theory, "in seeing" essences, while perceiving "red" I use imagination in order to distinct the imagination of different red objects which carry, each one of them, the event red. By abstracting different events of red in different objects, I perceive intuitively the red itself.

In Ideas I, Husserl characterizes the method of *ideated change*, in order to perceive the essence red, I activate a form of imagination, I activate the imagination or fantasy (also hallucination). I imagine different events of red, I imagine objects which color is red in strong or weaker shades and then, by abstraction, I perceive the essence which is common to the different red objects which I imagined as red.

In §4, Husserl says that pure essence can be given intuitively for an empirical experience in perception, memory, imagination etc., however also and in a similar way it can be given in fantasy (Phantasiegegebenheiten). Fantasy is equal to hallucination. In order to perceive essence in itself and originality, we can start from empirical intuition; it is clear that our ability to imagine objects under the relevant essence starts, usually, in a real experience of same objects.

Therefore, Husserl's assertion has to be that in the moment we have, by facts, acquired knowledge on objects under, for example, a physical essence and we want to perceive the essence itself with the relevant intuition, then we can use fantasy or free imagination.

After we have acquired an empirical knowledge, we fantasize and sort and perceive the essence "person." Therefore, when the psychotic hallucinates a person, he starts from seeing real persons, factual persons from the past and then he abstracts from all the real persons whose essential properties he has seen (for example, he "sees" that all people have two legs which they use for walking, and the body rests on the legs, etc.) the essence in itself which is perceived in the hallucination. The psychotic perceives the essence-"person" in person and it is being realized in a concrete experience.

## 17:45 The evil demon

Rene Descartes, in his book 'Meditations on First Philosophy'[14], opens with a philosophical tractate in which he depicts his philosophical meditations from a "first person" point of view. The tractate was written as personal description of evolving thoughts by Descartes himself.

---

[14] Rene Descartes, Meditation on First Philosophy, translated by Yosef Or, published by Magness, The Hebrew University, 1996

A person in search of the truth, says Descartes, must doubt anything that is doubtable. Most of our beliefs originate in our childhood, in non-judgmental sensual perceptions, irrational impulses and in unreliable testimonies of educators and other authorities. Our system of beliefs is built on shaky foundations. The process of doubting supposed to set a screening mechanism for true beliefs. Any questionable opinion is an object for doubt. Certainty is a very rigorous criterion; it is a very high standard for accepting true beliefs.

A small doubt is enough to disqualify a belief or opinion. Descartes searches for a method to screen the untruthful beliefs and will provide us, exclusively, with true opinions. He wants to rebuild the system of knowledge and philosophy, to demolish the existing structure and to cast new foundations; therefore, he does not present doubtfulness for its own sake but for obtaining undisputable beliefs.

The process of doubting has to be methodical. Descartes uses the following metaphor, in order to remove the rotten apples from the basket we have to empty it completely, only then we may return the unspoiled apples.

The first assertion by Descartes is the sensual errors; it opposes assertions based on sensual perception. We know that when we look at things being far away from us, we may perceive them wrongly. I, for example, see from afar a quadrilateral tower which is, actually, round; the sun looks small to me while, actually, being huge.

The assertion's preface says that sometimes our senses mislead us; since we cannot distinct between reliable and unreliable sensual senses, we should doubt every belief based on sensual perception.

There are no criteria for the distinction between reliable and unreliable sensual perception. From there, Descartes continues with his assertions of casting doubt. In Meditations, Descartes refers to the assertion about insanity but does not develop it; instead, he develops the assertion about dreaming.

The assertion about dreaming supposed to achieve what the insanity's assertion would have. Sometimes, we could have sensual errors relating to objects from afar but we may not doubt objects which are very close; for example, I am here, typing at my laptop, sitting on a chair near the desk, etc. these opinions seem reliable and certain. However, I may dream that I sit in the chair near the desk typing on my laptop, while, actually, I am lying in my bad sleeping. I may dream that my body is made of plastic. The insanity and dream's assertion drive a wedge between the perceiving "I" and the external world; i.e. collapse the idea according to which the perception of the external world, by senses or by any other way, gives us some knowledge on true reality. When I dream about sitting in a chair near the desk while I am actually asleep in my bed constitutes a discrepancy between dream and reality. The dream does not reflect reality. The dreaming experience can be very clear and vital (sometimes, believing in it so strongly, we wake up dreadfully); such being very similar to reality, Descartes doubts the factual reality and contemplates whether it is only a dream.

*How do I know, i.e. what criterion do I have to distinct between dreaming and being awake? Could it be that I am daydreaming?*

Descartes complete assertion is: sometimes I dream; I cannot distinct (I do not have criteria) between dream and reality hence, I may be dreaming now or at all times.

Trying to develop the insanity assertion, let us assume that the insane has hallucinations and he cannot distinct between hallucination and reality (which actually happens), the hallucination seems full, clear and vital.

*What criterion does he have for the distinction between hallucination and reality?*

He may hallucinate something not fitting reality. In reality, outside from his hallucinating consciousness, in the external world of the insane, the true world is very different.

*What does it tells us about the laws of physics?*

If a mentally ill "sees" angels flying in the sky, does it not contradict the laws of physics e.g. Newton's gravitational force?

*Are the laws of physics valid by the psychotic?*

Following his assertion about dream, Descartes continues with an additional doubting assertion, the assertion about the cheating God or the assertion about the evil demon following the assertion about dream.

Not wishing to contend that God cheats, Descartes makes the assertion about the evil demon. Its purpose is to dissolve truths being immune to the assertion about dream, for example, dream contains real components; may be only theoretical assertions as arithmetic and geometry are real? 2+3=5 is always true because it is not based on senses and experience. Mathematics is real and certain without any link to a material and physical reality; we do not have to count two apples and three apples for knowing that they will always sum up to five apples. Assertions about numbers or geometrical shapes do not relate to the material world and are not dependant on it for their truthfulness. What is actually the assertion about the evil demon? Let us assume that there exist an omnipotent evil demon (strangely but possibly and logically) that undermines the rules and axioms of mathematics; whenever I add 2+3 in my head, the evil demon misleads me to think of 5 although, in reality, the result is a different number; or when I see triangles, he misleads me to calculate 180 degrees while in reality they have more than 180.

The evil demon is deceiving us. The intelligence system is doubted. It may be that our mathematics is different than the real or other mathematics that may exist. The notion that man in general can reach the truth is doubted; the whole structure of knowledge is built on paper foundations.

There is something very disturbing in Descartes' assertions, especially in the evil demon's assertion. I do not argue that Descartes was mentally ill but the assertion about the evil demon is a classical and paranoid psychotic thought. One should remember that the psychosis' content is depended on culture and time, e.g. today we think of the paranoia's content in terms of aliens or "the government" while in the past we have thought in terms of evil spirit or demons.

As I said at 09:25, paranoia is the thought or the belief that someone is persecuting you and conspires to cause you harm. In such situation, one is convinced that someone wants to hurt him e.g. the evil demon! The evil demon conspires to cause me harm and to deceive me.

In paranoia, the precondition of 'guilt' has to be fulfilled, i.e. there is always a guilty party; the deceiving evil demon is the guilty one! Why does he do it? Because "he is deceiving me"! He wishes to cast doubts so I will know nothing; this is his conspiration against me.

A special trait of schizophrenics is a delusion through which the patient believes that the processes of his thought, parts of his body, acts and passions are being controlled and dictated by external factors. The paranoid schizophrenic tends to fear that hostile elements wish to gain control of his mind by transmitting certain messages to him and by planting various chips under his skin or in other organs; in another case, these are aliens who control his thoughts. Patients might believe that other people control their minds and "transmit" thoughts to them. The evil demon tries, also, to gain control of our thoughts and thought processes, e.g. by planting in our consciousness the number 5 each time we add 2+3.

I am bothered by Descartes doubting, for centuries, the truth of mathematics and our logical thought processes just because, one day, he had a paranoic delusion like thought. It seems that Descartes was influenced by the mentally ill more than he was willing to admit; Descartes could not comprehend that his precious cogito is "I am insane", he did not develop the assertion about insanity because he got scared! It was nightmare for him; doubtfulness, therefore, is a type of insanity, in one word a scandal. Therefore, while the assertion about dream is hallucination, the evil and deceiving demon's assertion is a paranoic delusion.

If there is no criteria that differentiate between dream and hallucination, and there is no criteria of insanity maybe all of us are insane?

*What is Descartes' state at the end of the doubting process?*

He falls into the abyss of absolute skepticism, he needs an Archimedean point to extricate himself, i.e. he needs at least one certain truth. Indeed, Descartes discovers the one, certain truth, his existence.

Even if he doubts everything, he himself is the doubting being. Even if the evil demon deceives him, he still exists as the deceived. Even if everything is a dream or a hallucination, there, still, exists someone who dreams it. Descartes may say, I have all kinds of thoughts, thoughts which I doubt their truthfulness, however I cannot doubt their existence, there is someone who thinks, doubts, dreams and hallucinates.

Descartes defeats doubtfulness on its own turf in one kick, his discovery of "I think therefore I exist".

## The time 18:00 Depression

Major depression also known as clinical depression or unipolar depression is a continuous mental state characterized by a declining mood accompanied by sinking into deep sadness and despair and the loss of interest and pleasure, disrupting almost all aspects of life.

Depressed people experience mostly negative emotions, either in low self-esteem or toward others by feeling not loved and unwanted. By misunderstanding the distress of the depressive, one might think that they are "lazy" and simply, "should take themselves in their own hands". For the depressed, this criticism is yet another source for disappointment and self criticizing thoughts.

173

Clinical depression which is not transient or mild, is a mental disorder with which coping is very hard. At least two weeks of severe decline in mood are needed for the diagnosis of depression. Depression affects all aspects of life of the patient, family, friends, work or school, sleeping and general health. In the USA around 3.4% of patients commit suicide. The diagnosis of a person with major depression is based on the patient's reporting from a phenomenological point of view ("first person reporting") and on behavior reported by relatives or friends.

The most common time of onset is between the ages of 30 and 40 years, with a later peak between 50 and 60 years. Depression appears in women twice as much as in men; however men tend more than women to commit suicide. The course of the illness changes, from one episode lasting several months to a lifelong disorder with recurrent episodes.

The understanding of the nature and causes of depression has evolved over the centuries, though many aspects remain not understood. Proposed causes include psychological, psycho-social, hereditary, evolutionary and biological factors. Some wide scoped research show rates of depression increased in the last decades. Moreover, it appears in younger age groups. Researchers proposed many causes for these findings as changes in the family structure, urbanization, and substantial decline in cultural and religious influence [3].

Moreover, it was found that the phenomenon is more common in people living without a spouse. In the USA, clinical depression appears at least once in the life of 16% of the population. It is the primary factor for disability in the USA and other countries. The World Health Organization projects that by 2020, depression will become the major factor for disability worldwide, second only to heart diseases. 60% of suicide attempts are due to depression out of which 15% are successful. Most of those who suffer depression do not seek treatment, probably out of ignorance or shame. Nevertheless, most of them could be treated beneficially, drastically improving their condition.


## 18:10 History

Depression is a mental disorder that is well known since ancient times. In the bible days, it was believed that depression is caused by evil spirit that attacks a person from the outside. A famous biblical figure probably suffering depression was King Saul; music played on the harp, supposedly relieved his suffering.

The Greek physician Hippocrates, the father of western medicine, determined that all ailments are the result of imbalance one's temperaments and that it is stronger by the depressive, he named it "melancholia". One of the common treatments by the Greek was phlebotomy which supposed to have balanced the dosage of melancholia in one's body.

Hippocrates described a syndrome of melancholia as a distinct disease with particular mental and physical symptoms; he characterized all fears and despondencies, if they last a long time as being symptomatic of the ailment. It was a similar but far broader concept than today's depression; prominence was given to a clustering of the symptoms of sadness, dejection, and despondency, and often to fear, anger, delusions and obsessions.

The term *depression* itself was derived from the Latin verb *deprimere*, "to press down" or to bring down in spirits. Since

Aristotle, melancholia had been associated with men of learning and intellectual brilliance, contemplation and creativity. Claudius Galenus a Roman physician of Greek descent assumed, to the joy of his patients, that the treatment must be by way of releasing fluids during the act of love making. Later, during the Middle Ages, Christian people believed or have returned to the belief in a demon entering one's body and cause him sadness and apathy which was considered a major sin leading one to inherit hell.

Following in their footsteps, Dante Alighieri, in his Devine Comedy, described the location and state of those who sinned in self-indulgence (in the fifth circle, deep down in the river Sticks). Starting with this period until modern time, rituals of exorcism in Christianity formed an integral part of the treatment of the sinners in "self-indulgence".

The new concept of melancholia abandoned these traits and in the 19th century was associated with women. A German psychiatrist Emil Kraepelin coined it as depression.

Sigmund Freud likened the state of melancholia to mourning in his 1917 paper "Mourning and Melancholia". He theorized that objective loss, such as the loss of a parent or spouse through death or abandoning, results in subjective loss as well; the depressed individual has identified with the object of affection through an unconscious, narcissistic process called the libidinal cathexis (the energy of Libido) of the ego. Such loss results in severe melancholic symptoms more profound than mourning; not only is the outside world viewed negatively, but the ego itself is compromised. The patient's decline of self-perception is revealed in his belief of his own blame, inferiority, and unworthiness. I am of the opinion that the Freudian concept of loss as a cause of depression is a bit naive and definitely not satisfactory, don't you

176

think? One must distinct between mourning, the feeling of sadness resulting from loss and depression. As aforesaid, already in the middle of the 20<sup>th</sup> century, depression is attributed to a chemical imbalance in the brain.

## 18:20 Symptoms

Medicine cannot diagnose depression by simple tests. There is a need for a comprehensive, clinical psychiatric interview including information from family and friends as well as psycho-dynamic tests in order to diagnose depression, its type and severity. However, much research of the brain is being conducted with the help of MRI and fMRI; in the future, we may be able to diagnose depression by blood tests which enable to measure the level of neurotransmitters in the brain, e.g. Serotonin. The diagnosis of depression is mostly being determined by the appearance for more than two weeks of most of the following symptoms:

## 18:25 Physiological level

Eating disorder: decrease or substantial increase of appetite.

Sleeping disorder: insomnia, waking up early, hypersomnia and difficulties to wake up.

Change in body weight- increase or decrease.

The feeling of fatigue and weakness.

Digestive disorder: diarrhea or constipation.

Sometimes disruption in vision.

**18:30 Emotional level**

Lack of activity and energy.

Deep sadness, despair, anger, outbursts of crying, outbursts of rage, distress.

Extreme mood changes not typical in the past.

Social isolation and the severing of social contacts.

Indifference and the loss of interest in enjoyable activities (hobbies, sports).

Decline of sexual desire.

Self criticism and loathing.

The feeling of helplessness and hopelessness.

The feeling of emptiness and apathy.

**18:35 Cognitive level**

A somber and pessimistic world view.

Decline in concentration and memory, hesitance in making decisions.

Suicidal thoughts.

Impaired judgment of reality, especially of the self, low self-esteem.

The attribution of failures to one self and a gloomy outlook for the future and the world.

## 18:40 Causes for depression

Depression is caused by many factors among which are hereditary predisposition, childhood events, recent events, personal crisis and social- economical factors as poverty, drug abuse, personality structure, innutrition etc.

In most ethnical groups the occurrence among women is twice as among men. It seems that among Jews, the occurrence in men is as high as in women. Research shows higher occurrence of depression in families of patients. The rate of compatibility in identical twins is 50% and in non-identical twins between 10-25%. As of now, several depression related genes were identified, but not one can explain the development of depression without additional conditions.

The development of depression is often attributed to psycho-social factors as stress events or child abuse, acute traumatic events or a loss of a close person. Recent research show a link between hereditary predisposition and stress events, i.e. the risk of developing depression following stress events is also depended on the hereditary predisposition.

People, who suffer from attentive disorder or from personality disorder as borderline personality disorder, obsessive compulsive disorder or post-traumatic stress disorder, suffer from depression more frequently.

Several psychoanalytical theories on depression were suggested by Freud, Abrahms, Klein and others. In addition to psychological factors, depression may be caused, also, by physiological factors among which is the lack of vitamins (as B6 and B12), chemical imbalance in the brain (low levels of serotonin, noradrenalin and sometimes dopamine).

The psycho- biological model suggests that chemical- biological, psychological and sociological factors play a role of some level in the development of depression. It may well be that stress and anxiety in a stressful life constitute a catalyst to the illness of which the origin is genetic. It may also be that pessimistic views acquired in childhood constitute another factor of depression.

Most of the antidepressant drugs increase the level of neurotransmitters as dopamine, serotonin and norepinephrin. Norepinephrin so is suggested, can affect alertness, anxiety, vitality and interest in life. The lack of serotonin is attributed to anxiety, obsession and compulsiveness.

Dopamine is attributed to attentiveness, motivation, pleasure as well as interest in life. Changes in the brain's structure were discovered in brain scans of patients suffering from depression.

Various aspects of personality and its development are attributed to the appearance and lasting of depression. Notwithstanding depressive events are attributed to an acute event, the personality of the patient and his way of coping affect his recovery. Low self- esteem and distorted thinking are linked to depression.

Depression may appear less or vanish quickly in religious people. Poverty and social isolation combine into high risk of developing psychiatric illnesses in general and depression in particular.

Child abuse (physical, emotional, sexual and neglect) is also considered as risk factor of the development of depression later on in life. Disruption in the functioning of the family as one of the parents being depressive, divorce or the death of one of the parents constitute a factor of the development of the disease. In adulthood, stressful life is attributed as a catalyst for the development of major depression. In this context, acute events in life which are associated with social isolation seem to be, especially, linked to depression. An episode of major depression, as aforesaid, is characterized by low mood that lasts, at least, two weeks. The episodes may appear once or recurrently and may be categorized as mild, medium and acute depression. In case the patient had a manic episode or an extreme increase in mood, the diagnosis will change to bi polar disorder (manic- depressive). Therefore, depression without manic episode will also be called unipolar depression because its mood remains in one emotional pol.

## 18:50 Sub types

The DSM-IV-TR (Diagnostic and Statistical manual of mental Disorders) by the American Psychiatrists Association negates cases of which symptoms are the result of mourning; notwithstanding it is possible for mourning to cause depression should the situation persists and the traits of a major depression continue to develop.

The DSM-IV-TR recognizes two sub types of depression:

Melancholic depression which is characterized by the lack of feeling pleasure in most activities, the lack of reaction to a pleasing stimulus, law mood which is expressed stronger than mourning or loss, the deterioration in the condition in the mornings, early wake up, decrease in weight (not to confuse with anorexia) and guilt.

Untypical depression that is characterized by responsiveness i.e. the reaction to stimuli called also paradoxical anhedonia and positivity, fattening and healthy appetite (consolation in eating), sleepiness, the feeling of heaviness in the limbs and a social deficiency as a result of oversensitivity to interpersonal rejection.

Catatonic depression is rare but particularly acute which involves an acute deficiency in motoric abilities. The patient seems to be a silence statute.

Post natal depression relates to a deep, prolonged and sometimes paralyzing depression appearing in mothers after giving birth. The depression will hit at least 15% of young women and usually lasts three months.

Seasonal depression appears in autumn or winter and vanishes in spring.

Psychotic depression, a deep depression accompanied by psychotic traits, loss of contact with reality, delusions and hallucinations.

People suffering from depression do not, necessarily, experience the same symptoms. The severity, occurrence and duration may change from one individual to the other.

## 19:00 Bilogical mechanism

The two neurotransmitters most relevant to the development of depression are serotonin and noradrenalin (norepinephrin). Those two materials are also the focus for the activity of most of the popular antidepressants. Hormonal regulation is also linked to the development of depression, in particular, hormones in the axis of hypothalamus- hypophysis (pituitary gland) - adrenal gland (cortisol, DHEA and pregnenolone), and changes in the levels of hormones of the thyroid gland (thyroxin and Triiodothyronine). Moreover, the lack of vitamin B12 and/or vitamin B6 may cause depression.

The biological infrastructure of depression being not clear enough is extensively researched. The most accepted thesis deals in the lack of neurotransmitters noradrenalin and especially serotonin in the synaptic spans between brain cells as being a cause of depression. The lack of such neurotransmitters causes also a physical change i.e. the degeneration of dendrites that supposed to receive the neurotransmitters. The antidepressants act in several directions with the purpose of keeping a proper level of these neurotransmitters in the synaptic spans. Some antidepressants try to damage the process of absorption and reuptake of the neurotransmitters back to the axon and some are blocking receptors which prevent secretion of the neurotransmitters. The newest are effective two to three weeks from commencement of treatment as opposed to the older antidepressants as the Prozac family of drugs which peaks after five weeks.

## 19:15 Treatment

Following the negation of all physiological factors, one may assume that depression is caused by "mental" factors (i.e. "psychiatric disorders" which have also a biological factors relating to the brain). In that case, there are various methods for the treatment of depression; the principal methods are psychological treatment and treatment by drugs. Many use both and enjoy better results.

The method of cognitive treatment calls for the patient to think positively, to confront the depressive thoughts directly, to challenge them, to try and see reality differently, not in a saddened and depressive way. It was found that the depressive thinks in distorted thought patterns which relate all failures to himself and see the world in a gloomy way. Such treatment is mostly short-lived than the psycho- dynamic methods and according to many researches is more efficient. Although the psychological treatment may be efficient, in cases where the depression is "endogenous" (i.e. depression-disease, usually with

184

recurrent episodes) it is considered less efficient and treatment by medication is preferred because the problem apparently lies in the biochemical imbalance of the brain.

When the psychological treatment fails, it is recommended to visit a psychiatrist and receive medications designated for the relief of depression. Generally, the medications maybe categorized as follows:

"Old class" antidepressants, tricyclic, tetracyclic and other antidepressants

New generation antidepressants:

Serotonin reuptake inhibitors, SSRI

Serotonin-norepinephrine reuptake inhibitors, SNRI

Noradrenergic and specific serotonergic antidepressants, NaSSAs

Norepinephrine (noradrenalin) reuptake inhibitors, NRI

It should be noted that most of the "old class" antidepressants as tricyclic also act by serotonin and epinephrine (noradrenalin) reuptake but not specific. The most common drugs are of the group SSRI which include Fluoxetine (Prozac, Prizma, Afectin), Paroxetine (Paxil, Seroxet, Paxet), Sertraline (Zoloft, Lusteral), Citalopram (Celexa, Cipramil), Fluvoxamine (Luvox, Feboxil), Escitalopram (Cipralex) and more. These drugs raise the level of Serotonin in the inter-synaptic span by the inhibition of the reuptake in the cells. These drugs start to take effect of in two weeks to one month. Finding the suitable drug and dosage is a complex procedure which may take weeks or even months.

Findings show that in many cases of people suffering from depression, drugs improve the symptoms and daily functioning.

## 19:25 Electroconvulsive therapy

Findings show that in extreme cases of deep clinical depression not treatable with drugs or accompanied by extreme eating and drinking disorder, electroconvulsive therapy improves the state of the patients. Electroconvulsive therapy leads to improvement in mood probably due to enhancement of discharge of the neurotransmitter serotonin. This is a last resort treatment when all other treatments fail and there is eminent danger to life of the suicidal patient. The treatment is performed under mild anesthesia. Side effects of a recurrent electroconvulsive therapy are a temporary damage to short term memory. There are testimonies of permanent damage to the brain's frontal lob which causes memory loss; there is the risk of general anesthesia as in every chirurgical intervention. The treatment is controversial among physicians who, on one hand, prefer the efficiency in severe cases over possible side effects and the on the other hand fear permanent damage.

## 19:30 Innovative treatments

Transcranial magnetic stimulation (TMS, rTMS) applies powerful magnetic fields to the brain and cause change to the brain's cortex. It is similar to ECT in its effectiveness but does not require anesthesia.

Vagus nerve stimulation (VNS), in this treatment, an electrode connected to an external pacer is planted in the area of the Vagus nerve and generates electrical pulse. This treatment is being used also to treatment epilepsy.

Deep brain stimulation (DBS) is a treatment in which a pacer and electrodes are planted in certain areas in the brain. It is intended only for severe disorders such as Parkinson's disease since requires an intrusive and complex chirurgical intervention.

## 19:45 Personally coping with depression

Beyond the psychological and medical treatment, the patient's behavior may have a strong effect on his depression:

Distraction- during many years of psychodynamic treatment of depression, it was assumed that the understanding of its origin and causes will assist in its elimination or reduction, but new research conducted by Professor Suzan Nolen-Huxama indicates the danger in Rumination; Rumination performed in psychological treatments or independently of any treatment (mainly in women) may cause the amplification of depression. An alternative is the distraction by occupation and doing which enhance mood and is joyful.

- Social activity- going out and meeting people. Following a depression, the patient is usually isolated and secluded which strengthens his initial depression. Social contact is, therefore, important to break this circle.
- Sport activity- fast walking, bicycling, weights lifting. In sport activity, opiated substances are being discharged (endorphins and others) which improve the mood. Moreover, it improves health and raises energy levels and stamina and positively affects the production of hormones.
- Creative activity- painting and writing. The creation provides distraction and fills time as well as improves self esteem.
- Comforting activity- listening to music, reading books, watching movies, computer games and shopping.
- Emotional support from family and friends- depression stems, sometimes, from loneliness. The contact with other people may have positive effect, although, sometimes, the depressed lose their confidence in their surrounding and refuse to be comforted by others.
- Communal voluntary activity- a transition from self focusing to the focusing on the suffering of fellow men prevents the patient from dwelling on his own thoughts. It may give him a new meaning in life.
- Caring for animals- findings show that having contact with dogs or cats that create a meaningful relationship with humans, improve the state of the depressive.
- Auto- cognition- the study of depression and the understanding of its mechanisms as opposed to contemplation oneself which is not an efficient way to overcome depression.
- Sleep- depression causes difficulties to sleep; good sleeping habits, constant sleeping times and avoiding the

consumption of caffeine before sleeping improve the depressive state.


## 19:55 Prognosis


Major depressive episodes often resolve over time whether or not they are treated. The median duration of an episode has been estimated to be 23 weeks, with the highest rate of recovery in the first three months. General population studies indicate around half those who have an episode (whether treated or not) recover and remain well, while 35% will have at least one more, and around 15% of those experience chronic recurrence. Around 90% of those with severe or psychotic depression experience recurrence. Recurrence is more likely if symptoms have not fully resolved with treatment. Depressed individuals have a shorter life expectancy than those without depression, in part because depressed patients are at risk of dying by suicide. Moreover, they also have a higher rate of dying from other causes such as heart disease. Up to 60% of people who commit suicide have a mood disorder such as major depression. The risk of suicide associated with a diagnosis of major depression in the US is estimated at 3.4%. Suicide attempts are more frequent in women although men are more successful.


## 20:00 Depression in men and women

It is estimated that depression is frequent twice in women than in men. While the rate of depressive episodes in men rises with time, in women, it peaks at the age of 35-45. Depression is more frequent in women than in men. Causes unique to women (biological, life cycle, hormonal and psychological) may be related to higher frequency in woman compared with men. Research shows the female hormones affect the chemistry of the brain which controls mood; for example, women undergoing hormones' change following childbirth are vulnerable to depression as well as the responsibility toward the newborn being a psychological cause for the outbreak of the disease.

Men, sometimes, experience and cope with the disease differently than women. Men are willing to admit sadness, nervousness, lack of interest and sleeping disorder while women admit sadness, low self-esteem and guilt. Depressive men, more than women, might turn to alcohol and drugs or become frustrated, nervous, angry and sometimes rude to their surroundings; sometimes, they become workaholics or engage in dangerous activities in order to avoid the discussion of their state with family and friends. Notwithstanding more women try to commit suicide, men are more successful.

**20:15 Preliminary discussion and the question of being**

A depressed man is first of all a human being. He is depressed human being.


Being and Time[15] is the investigation of the sense of being (Sinn von Sein). Heidegger uses the German word ueberhaupt which sense is approximately the sense of being as itself.

Heidegger asks 'what is considered as being' or what do we mean when we say "to be"?

Sense, by Heidegger, is from which something is understood as it is. Although the definition is nearly correct, it is not sufficient.

Let us assume, says Magda King[16] that we are in a strange town and ask passers-by "what is this building"? They respond "it is a theatre". By this explanation, the building is understood by us as a theatre, i.e. as a thing in itself, as it is. However, let us assume that we do not know what a theatre is and then we will take the next step and ask for an explanation of what is a theatre; they will explain it as a building designed to host plays. With the assumption that we know what a play is, this specific building is being revealed as something in its essence. When we understand something as a being thing then we understood its being in its essence. Therefore, sense for Heidegger is something from which something is being understood as it is in itself.

A theatre may be understood only out of a world of human existence. To write, produce and value plays is something that is

[15] Being And Time, Martin Heidegger, translated by John Macquarrie & Edward Robinson, 1962 by Harper & Row.

[16] Magda King, A Guide to Heidegger's Being and Time, State University of New York Press, 2001. At some places I was close to her text.

unique and available only to humans. Only in the world of humans a thing may be understood as theatre. The thing that enables such human understanding is sense. The sense of theatre originates in the human world and only there it has sense. The world of our daily existence is the perspective from which our understanding comes; hence things we encounter become understandable to us only in relation to such perspective or from it, for example theatres, schools etc., i.e. things that are usable for a certain purpose; this building, being a school, exists for the purpose of acquiring education and values. Our world's perspective gives sense; this is the sense through which we live in the world.

One way to convert sense to something else than the daily understanding, is to refer to the scientific world e.g. theoretical physics. Things like theatres, buses and fruit become, at once, senseless. The perspective from which things are now being understood is primarily the essence of material. Why the sudden change? It is due to the physicist's change of perspective. The world of human existence is changed to a theoretical conceptualization of material reality which expresses itself in categories and terms like mass, motion and energy. Since such perspective gives sense to the physicist, each thing that is observed by him must show itself as a complex system of motion of physical objects. This perspective does not give anything that is usable for a certain cause or relevant to the human world. The only possibility (for these objects) is to show themselves as objects with material properties moving in the flow of time-space.

In summation of this stage, as aforesaid, sense is what gives us the understanding of things as they are themselves, i.e. essentially being relevant to a certain human purpose. Sense is not in words or things but in the structure of our understanding itself. We move a priory from the perspective of understanding from which and in relation to it, things that we encounter are being done or understood as such.

The world of our existence is the perspective from which we, primarily, understand things as relevant to a certain purpose. It can be changed to something like "nature"; from such perspective things are understood to us as objects in motion. The changes in the horizons of our understanding enable us to understand things by different ways.

What is the intention of Heidegger when he asks: how is it possible for man (Da- sein or "being here") to understand being? From which perspective does he understands being? What is the sense of existence or being in existence?

Magda King contends that all these questions are actually one. The perspective or the horizon, from which it is possible for us to understand the being as such, is the sense of the existence of being. What is this horizon? It is what "Being and Time" shows- time. Heidegger tells us that the interpretation of time is the possible horizon of all understanding of being. The two similar expressions of 'what and how' is the being and they are in a simpler way understandable when they are expressed as what is the thing and how is the thing.

The being of things that are revealed to us as what they are is called 'essence' and as how they are, i.e. if they really exist, they are revealed to us as a possibility or as necessity.

In a narrow and initial context, "things" are concrete things that are given to us through our senses and which may exist independently as, for example, mountains, stars, trees and animals. These things stand there as existant. Things in a wide context include almost everything; being as such and as a whole, these things are in the field of research of philosophy. Except for the field of concrete being, i.e. things that are given to senses and which played an important role in philosophy, also non-sensual phenomena as consciousness, knowledge and number were understood in comparison and as opposed to the preceding things.

In philosophical investigations, reality of one type of things is measured by the reality of the other type of things. However, the widest expression of the idea of being gives us the widest concept of being as such: they are being and not nothing. Hallucination, the sense of a song, God, hope, thinking, seemingness, formation etc. are something, they are not nothing notwithstanding not being concrete sensual things.

Heidegger's idea of being expresses the demand that ontology, i.e. the research of being, must begin with the widest and deepest distinction between something and nothing. Man (Da-sein) is something and not nothing.

Traditional metaphysics understood being as substantial. Heidegger formulates substantiality as "permanent presence" or "present in the present"; i.e. the property or the state of something as permanently and consistently present. This is the perspective from which traditional philosophy defines what things are real and not platonic shadows, for example a human soul present, existant, independent, persistent in time etc. it is not by chance that Greek- Western philosophy had respect for the formal sciences as logic and mathematics. The pure formal concepts and their connections are being studied by these sciences provide, primarily, the idea of persistence and unchanging presence which is the sense of substantiality, i.e. "permanently present" or "present in the present".

There are, for example, triangles in various sizes and angles, however, what is persisting and remains unchanged in all triangles is the fact that all of them have 180 degrees; this is the essence of a triangle, its substantiality.

How the concept of substantiality evolves with "being and time"?

How is it possible, at all, for a person to understand being?

How is it that time is the horizon or the perspective from which one needs to understand being?

How is time supposed to be interpreted?

The answesr demand an investigation into the being of man as "Da-sein" or "being here" (I will use these expressions alternately). The purpose of this investigation is to unravel all essential structures of human existence thus, explaining the way by which man understands his own being and the being of another being and things.

Magda King summarizes Heidegger question the following way: this is the question of the intrinsic possibilities of understanding the being and of the intrinsic sense that is folded into the idea of being as such or as itself.

Heidegger, sometimes, calls this question the question of being as being. The expression, however, is a bit problematic because the ontological tradition of philosophy expresses the same idea by the same expression; the problem of our understanding the being exists in all questions which philosophy may ask, moreover, the problem exists in such a way by which it is impossible to raise and solve it by tradition.

Why traditional ontology failed in the understanding of being? The traits and limits of western philosophy exist with the Greeks; the Greek philosophers have asked a similar question: what is being as being or what is the being of things? Despite minor deviations along history the question still remained the same.

Heidegger contends that that traditional ontology investigates the being of beings and not as should be, the investigation of being as such. The sense of the Greek term *Ta onta* could be being and also beings or things (absorbed into this expressions is the idea 'this exists'). The interpretation and criticism by Heidegger focuses on the beings in the traditional sense. The sense of *Ta onta* is that it is the things which are (exist); actually, the word beings is similar to *Ta onta*. When western philosophy speaks about to be, it thinks on the "is" of something that exists.

To what do we intend when we say that a thing exists?

We mean that it actually exists among other things, that it is happening, that it may be somewhere in the natural world. When we speak about reality or actuality, we speak of something that is actually present among other beings in the world. The actuality of the thing in a wider context is the main conceptualization of the being in traditional ontology.

As aforementioned, the main trait of reality is substantiality. In ancient philosophy substance was understood as material, as a material object, as the essence of an idea or form and as a combination thereof. No matter how philosophy understands the concept of substance, it always understands it as sufficient for itself, as self persisting or self maintenance with no need for the help of other things for its existence.

The essence of the concept is linked to an unchanging presence as an independent thing. Just for such independent and self sufficiency being the traits of substantiality, its materialization must be due to self causing, non-external causing, without an external reason and non-formation. Each thing being created is necessarily dependent, needs maintenance in the sense of being cared and it will disappear and be annihilated.

Final things, therefore, may not be considered substance (independent existence). Every problem raised by traditional ontology was understood primarily through the horizon of substantiality.

This idea of being, according to Heidegger, is too narrow in order to contain and explain all the ways by which it is possible to understand being. All things said and done, this sense of being cannot give a satisfactory account for the unique distinction of man as being. I.e. one must give an account for being human! The human exists as such and its being is unravels to him as his. As a result, every person has to say to himself: I exist or being (I am).

"Being and time" will show us that sense and the structure of our being which we express by I am, is different from the real existence of things. The tendency to interpret the being of humans (human beings) as the beings of things could be explained, basically, by the way of man as a "thing" among other things. Due to basic tendencies of man to let himself fall and spread himself among his deeds and the things he does and meet, man, actually, finds himself "there" between things that he is busy with hence he is perceived as they are. Therefore, there is the impression that the being remains indistinct and applied in the fuzziness of presence and occurrence in everything including man. Metaphysics develops the being by this way of understanding. The horizon from which the being is understood does not become interpreted and its possible distinction does not become problematic. What is distinct is not the being but the being of things. The philosophical tradition begins to distinct by starting from the being of things, defines them and divides them to categories in accordance with their essence as they are. Man himself enters the list of live beings, i.e. of "live be's" (animal) and stays there. Man is a speaking animal which has soul and consciousness, logic, self awareness and the ability to think.

The essence of man or the understanding of the essence of a "human being' underwent changes through generations of philosophy; but what has not been changed is that human existence is understood primarily as a real occurrence of a strange type among all other things (beings). A human being as was understood by tradition from Descartes onwards as 'I think therefore I exist' was understood as a subject of 'I think' with substance that is present, i.e. something sufficient for himself, persistent and independent.

According to Descartes, he has soul and this is the essence of the human being as thinking is (res cogitas). Heidegger in "being and time" analyzes the being of man (Da-sein or "being here") in a different way; he will see that his understanding is from temporary perspective. Being is not substance, i.e. it has no essence as other things have, according to the understanding of traditional philosophy, which are persistence, self sufficiency and self maintenance.

The "I think" of Descartes, who contends that substance is the essence of man, draws the conclusion that man's essence is eternal and understood in relation to certain time, i.e. in relation to the present 'moment'. However, Heidegger contends that being should be understood in a different way of time.

Heidegger asks how is it that the sense of "being" is to be substance?

Independent existence, unchanging presence, pesistance in identity, in all these there is a relation only to type of time that exists as real in one flow of moments: the present. The future is 'not yet now' the past is 'not now anymore', the real is the present.

Time is the horizon in which not only tradition but all understanding of being is understood. Time, specifically, turns our understanding of the being as possible upside down and until the phenomenon of time will be properly explained, the problem of the sense of being will stay unresolved.

Traditional ontology draws its main idea from only one way of time- the present, what is present right now before me. As much as something is present so it is more real. The God of philosophers conform to the requirement of being by being eternal, persisting in time, unchangeable, independent and always present in infinite moments. Such interpretation of time holds from the Greek days until now.

The assignment of "being and time" is to show that infinity of the moments at present, in which things become existent and transient, is, although a real phenomenon, but not the original.

According to Heidegger, time is not presented to us in its originality, in what and how things are, rather in our being and existence, the I (I am) and time are final, the final time of our existence. It seems that "being and time" is out to investigate what remains hidden from the ontological tradition, i.e. investigate not only the essence of man but also the way by which he exists. The end of existence is revealed only to man, he is aware of death and its finality, and that alone, as the "being and time" comes to show, enables it to understand also himself and other be's (beings).

The way of man, therefore, is to understand the being, thus every possible expression of the idea of being must unravel in the essential structure of human existence. This is the concrete way to understand being. The way for man to be is the understanding.

## The time 20:30 the changeover of Heidegger

Michael Galvin explains that when someone tries to understand revolution, if it is in art, politics or philosophy, one needs to first of all understand what the state was before the revolution. One needs to examine the domain before we can understand what does Heidegger. One needs to understand if only superficially what was before "being and time".

Heidegger rebelled against the metaphysical tradition. Therefore, in short, we can characterize the ontology which preceded Heidegger as the dealing with what things exist, i.e. the question that was asked by metaphysics is does something really exist? Does God exist?

Is there Liberty?

Is there a soul in addition to the body which is distinct from him and remains after it? Do things that are given to us in perception exist as material things or they are only mental be in our consciousness?

200

What justifications do we have in order for us to say that there are trees and stones externally and independent of consciousness?

All these questions are very important for philosophers to understand the world. However, all these questions are being raised in a strange manner because we ask them as if we already know the sense of existence and the important question is the between two possible answers: either it exists or not.

Aristotle, for example, as the one who thought about existence, tells us that what does exist is one of two, either a basic thing called prote ousia, "primary be" or a derived trait, i.e. a property dependent on basic existence as "primary be".

The sense of "Socrates is white" is that white is a trait while Socrates is a primary thing. Such analysis turned over the years to an absolute example. The investigation was conducted on things which exist and the basic definitions of existence of such type.

Heidegger as opposed to traditional philosophers contends that there is a more basic question: what is the sense of existence at all? The question is not whether a thing exists or how to characterize the existence of certain things like material or spiritual things, rather simply ask about the sense of being.
In asking a question of this type, one can observe the gentle change in what was asked. Dealing in beings like God, soul, body, earth and this computer, I actually ask two questions: do these things actually exist; if yes, what kind of things are they? But what can be asked about being at all? I can ask what the sense of it is. Contemplating the question, it seems that it is the only question one can ask. Heidegger identifies this question as very basic. To ask what is the sense of existence or of being is to deal with the

most basic question one may ask. Heidegger calls it 'die frage nach den sinn von sein,' "to ask about the sense of being" or more simply "the question of being". The question is not abstract, on the contrary, it is a concrete and immediate question, I, for example, exist.

Let us ask "what is a prison"? You answer "prison is the building down the road with bars on the windows and locks on the cell doors". In this case, the question is about an entity and the answer provides the traits which describe the entity, in this case, a prison.

Let us ask "what is the sense of being in prison"? You react and answer "to be in prison means to be guilty of a crime and be punished for it by suffering and the loss of liberty. To be in prison is, therefore, to be punished, reprimanded, to suffer, probably to be afraid, to live in solitude, to be outcast, etc.". the second question is answered by the relation to what is the sense of being in different ways, e.g. being guilty or without liberty. The question what is a prison is answered by describing other entities like bars on windows, locks on doors, guards, etc.; however, the question of the sense of something is answered by the relation to other senses. We, simply, recognize that there should be an analogy between the question and answer. Pushing for a distinction, I ask which question comes first. Contemplating it, I will conclude that the sense of being in prison is the cause or the justification for a prison being built that way (bars, locks etc.). In other words, the sense of being in prison precedes the definition of prison, i.e. the sense determines the entity. Understanding the sense of being in prison, I already know what should be done in order to build a prison. Formally, sense precedes entity, i.e. sense explains entity. I have to understand the sense of being in prison in order to build one.

I ask what soul is. This question is an example for a traditional metaphysical question; it calls for sorting and identification. I also ask if I have a soul which is more than the sum of all my chemical actions in my brain. Here the question is about the existence of something. Now, let us ask again the question which is of Heidegger's investigative type. What type of question may one ask? Well, *what is the sense of thinking*? By rephrasing the question to what is the sense of thinking I completely avoid the metaphysical tradition which asks whether this thing exists or not or of which type it is. However, at the same time the question investigates that which I actually want to know. It is, for example, possible to denote that the sense of thinking is a separate question from the sense of feeling and emotion. Therefore, I may ask what the sense of thinking is without asking whether a soul exists at all which makes this thing important. This is a big progress because the question about the problem of body-soul is avoided. Is there an external world? What is the product of the sense of being in the world? The example of prison was given in order for us to focus on what Heidegger does with the question of being.

By the same way by which we can ask about each entity the preceding question of its sense, we now ask about the being itself. We do not ask what the absolute type of a thing is. Or what things do really exist but what, at all, is the sense of being. This is the basic question; however, one may not simply raise it and answer. One should know how to approach such basic question; i.e. a preceding analysis and careful thinking is requires before asking. All the rephrased questions as what is the sense of being in prison contain the verb *"to be"*; we, for example, ask ourselves what is the sense of being in space? Or what is the sense of being with consciousness? What is the sense of being thoughtful? The point being that by all such ways, we exist or do or act upon ourselves; it is possible to phrase the question so that the source "to be" becomes the basic question, thus the method and technique become clear. What is the sense being as thinking becomes a fundamental and basic question about what, at all, is to be?

The question becomes accessible, firstly, by the analysis of the certain question; in other words, it is, exactly, because I can ask what is the sense of being a body thus partly answer the question of what , at all, is the sense of being. By investigating what is the sense of a body, I already investigate and give sense to what is the sense of being in a certain way. Therefore, it is possible to focus on what, at all, is the sense of being.

Regarding the main subject, I will not deal here with the question of what a depression is as if depression is some kind of entity, rather I will ask what is the sense of being depressive. How is it to be in depression; how is it to be in a certain way which is the sense of depression. How come a person is in depression!

Heidegger starts the investigation with different ways of existence (one of them may be depression) and then distinct the common sense which lies under such ways of existence. We do not ask initially, for example, what is a human being and then ponder on the sense, but we ask what the sense of being a human being is, then we decide what a human being is. The purpose of "being and time" is to base an essential or fundamental method by a phenomenological analysis of the transcendental sense of being. The German term "Sein" is "to be." The Seinfrage is the question what is the sense of being. Only a human being can ponder on the sense of being; thus, "to be" may be analyzed only by reflexive consciousness of human existence. Heidegger refuses to distinct and differentiate the investigation of being from the investigation of man. He provides a picture of what we are; the picture is of a person by terms of self awareness of his self existence. There is no possibility for the analysis of a human being without the consideration of how a human being is connected to the possibilities of his existence.

## 20:40 Heidegger's preface

In the preface to "Being and Time", Heidegger asks the question of being (Seinfrage) or in other words to ask "what is the sense of being". He also asks how one can clarify the fuzzy awareness of one's self existence.

According to Heidegger, the main barrier for the completion of a meaningful answer to the question is the natural tendency of the consciousness to relate to itself as an object. The question we ask is about the process or activity of existence and not about what is it that exists. We do not ask what type is being but what, at all, is the sense of being.

Since the usual way to investigate something is to relate to the research's subject as an entity (Das Seinende), the first and important task is for the reader to clarify for himself the difference between an investigation of entity and the investigation of sense of being. Should the distinction will not be clarified, Heidegger's investigation will remain fuzzy and unsatisfactory. The second purpose is for the reader to comprehend why the investigation of the sense of being is primary and therefore, constitutes or establishes the fundamental method of philosophy.

The investigation of the sense of being is called by Heidegger "ontological"; the research's subject is "being" (Sein). An investigation of entity (Das Seiende) is called "ontic". The terms which describe ontical investigation are called "categories", while the terms which are used for ontological investigation are called existential. Every scientific investigation of an entity is ontic; it uses categories and is factual. A philosophical investigation of what is the sense of being is ontological, uses existential terms and is factical. The whole purpose of developing these terms is to emphasize that it is impossible to successfully investigate the being in the usual way i.e. the ontic way. The investigation of the being by the said way will lead to the question about the sense of being to become senseless. Hence, being is not an entity like like tables!

There are three assumptions at the base of the attempt to relate to being in an ontical way. Heidegger develops them in order to reject them later.

1) "The being" is the most universal concept thus without content.
2) It is indefinable.
3) It is self-evident.

1) Just because being is the most universal concept does not mean that it may not be examined. If being was just "a generalized concept" and did not have any other sense beside the sense of the most abstract and generalized concept, then there will not be any sense and possibility to investigate it later on. However, Heidegger denotes that also Aristotle considered the concept as having sense and being primary; we will understand it sense later on.

2) The assumption of the indefinable enables Heidegger to shed light onto an important point. The assumption is that being cannot be defined because by defining something, we need other, more generalized and extended concepts and since being is the most generalized and extended concept, hence it cannot be defined. Heidegger rejects this technique of extended and generalized concepts needed for the definition of being.

"Human being" is defined under a more extended concept of "animal" and then, we relate the property of rationality to it. However, should we ask about the sense of "animal", we will need a more extended concept or definition to explain what is an animal according to more generalized concepts, for example, being. Since we do not have a more extended concept than being, we face a problem. If this super-concept is senseless then how it can be used as type and explain other concepts beneath it? However, if it has sense, then, how can it be defined? Heidegger's point is that, indeed, this extended concept does not have sense; however, it teaches us that the sense should be discovered by a different way of investigation, i.e. ontological and not by a regular investigation of definitions.

Being, I repeat, is not an entity; to be is not a thing or entity as an apple. There is not a thing to be. If the question is not about something, does it mean that it is senseless? It will be correct only if "sense" relates only to objects thus one should ask how the question about being should be asked. Let us leave it for now.

3) The third assumption of the ontical investigation says that being is self evident. It is safe to say that, factually, the theory of being is not self evident. If, therefore, we wish to continue investigating the sense of being but we cannot do it with definitions, how should we proceed?

At this point, Heidegger is similar to Plato in the Menno dialogue. Heidegger contends that we do know something, maybe fuzzy, on the subject of our research, but my investigation is an attempt to convert fuzziness into clarity. I, for example, am aware of my existence although I do not know completely the sense of such existence. What I do know, although fuzzily, has sense.

Heidegger's choice of human existence as the subject of his research does require consideration of the concept Da Sein.

The concept relates to human existence; it comprises of two parts: Da which means "here" and Sein which mean "to be", hence the exact translation is "being here". The whole point of Da-Sein is about human beings, he himself can ponder on his existence. As we will see, the sense of existence can be essential and important only for the one asking. We do not investigate the sense of a certain thing nor the humane as a thing, but the sense of being. In other words, Heidegger starts directly with the human state of which the life and existence as sense of the human being are being investigated.

We do not investigate an object but a process; we are ourselves a process, the process of our life and existence. An investigation into this process is valid because it is sensible.

Two points were clarified:

1)"being" may not be analyzed as entity; hence every ontical investigation which uses categories by which we describe an entity does not fit.

2) Nevertheless the abovementioned, it is sensible to investigate the sense of being, since there is a different type of investigation, ontological. By such a way, the Da-Sein (human being) ponders on itself as existant.

## 20:55 Heidegger's phenomenology

Heidegger used the concept of phenomenology to describe his method. The science of phenomenon deals in the perception of objects in a way by which each thing that is discussed about them has to be presented directly. The notion of "phenomenon" as perceived formally or the usual way, is such that each presentation of an entity as it shows itself from itself may be called "phenomenology".

However, phenomenology lets us see the thing as it is in itself from itself provided that the phenomenon hides itself, i.e. in a mask. Therefore, one must unravel what is hidden in the phenomenon; that which remains hidden is not only the entity but its being. The being may be so hidden as to become forgotten and no question will be raised about it and its sense.

We have to bring forward the entities themselves in order to unravel their being because the phenomenon as it is phenomenologically understood is what creates the being, while the being is, anyway, of entities and things.

Phenomenology is the science of the being of things, i.e. ontology. Heidegger's investigations will show that the sense of a phenomenological description as a method will be performed by interpretation.

The unraveling will be achieved by hermeneutic phenomenology. The phenomenology of Da-Sein is hermeneutic. By the unraveling of the sense of being as the basic structure of Da-Sein a horizon of research into entities or things that are not of a Da-Sein nature will be reached.

Heidegger dedicating his being and time to Husserl admits that his investigations would not have been possible if not the preparation of Husserl's phenomenology and logical investigation.

The father of modern phenomenology, as presented in the preceding chapter, is Edmond Husserl. For him, the purpose of the method is to achieve a description of consciousness without interpretation; his motto was to let the facts speak for themselves; the motto of his phenomenology is "to the facts themselves!" (Zu den sachen selbst!); however, Heidegger phenomenology was hermeneutic, i.e. interpretative. The term comes from Greek for hermeneuein, to interpret. If Heidegger's methodology is interpretative and phenomenology is about letting the facts speak for themselves, then in what way phenomenology is possible?

It seems that, this way, Heidegger is not Husserlian but, still, he can use phenomenology as a descriptive method. Heidegger, also, wishes to let the facts speak for themselves and at the same time to contend that there are no facts without interpretation which means that we have here some tension or dilemma if not a contradiction.

While investigating the structure of hermeneutic phenomenology, we should remember that the method was meant to be applied only to the question of existence (i.e. it was not meant to be applied to exact sciences). On the other hand, it is also true that Heidegger believed that the question about the sense of being can be discuss only by way of a methodology which in itself is being discussed by interpretative phenomenology of the direct awareness of existence, i.e. to apply a metaphysical method to the question of being is to ignore the nature of the existential question. Having the question of existence opened for discussion just for hermeneutic phenomenology and hermeneutic phenomenology is only applicable to the question of being makes any attempt to see similarity in other investigations doomed to fail.

By which way does the method reveal the question about the sense of being? How does the hermeneutic method tell us about existence? Among the many ways of my existence I search for the answer to the question about the sense of being. The concept which is provided there is temporality. What is it that my comprehension can tell me about the sense of existence?

In "being and time", Heidegger contends that only phenomenology is possible as ontology. Heidegger executes the analysis of being by hermeneutics and remains true to the two principals: to let facts speak for themselves and there are no facts without interpretation.

According to Heidegger's translation of the term, the sense of phenomenology is "to let that, that shows itself, to show itself in a way by which it shows itself from itself" (being and time page 58). Having understood how it is hermeneutically doable, the sense of

Heidegger's phenomenology becomes clear. In "phenomenology", Heidegger intends that same analysis in which the sense of the ways of our existence may be translated from the fuzzy language of daily existence to a clear understanding of the ontological language without destroying the way by which these senses express themselves to us in our daily life.[17] The decisive argument is that the sense of being can become known to us only through a certain method: a hermeneutical process.

## 21:10 The being as Da-Sein

Given that Heidegger says something sensible about the man as Da-Sein, the sense of the concept "exists" is the unique way by which a person is being; he is such being that understands himself as his being. To be in such state, i.e. to exist, is the sense of a human being. In "being and time", the terms to exist and existence are reserved for the human being.

The real existence of beings other than human beings are called by Heidegger "real being" or "objective presence" (Vorhandensein) and the structure of such being is called "reality" (Realitaet). The basic distinction in "being and time" is between the existence of Da-Sein and the reality of beings which are not Da-Sein.

"To exist" and "to be real" are the two main ways by which beings may be beings. A real thing like a stone exists in such a way by which it is a being that is hidden from itself. Its reality is

---

[17] A commentary on heidegger's Being and time, Michel Gelven, northern Illinois University Press 1989. At some places I was close to his text.

characterized by passiveness in the sense by which it is revealed only to us, not to itself. Therefore the stone is "impassive" or "indifferent" to the being of itself or, more precisely, it is in such a state in which it cannot even be indifferent. On the other hand, Da-Sein exists actively and revealed. The exposure relates to the Da-Sein itself which understands its being. Such understanding does not belong to the Da-Sein in general but to every Da-Sein separately and uniquely. Only through his self existence, can a person understand: "I, myself, am a human being; this entity is me". The individuality of Da-Sein in which everyone is being exposed to its own being, is a sense and as such it is universal.

I understand that I myself am the man who is manic depressives, I am in this group, that is my universality, i.e. human beings that are Da-Sein, however, individually, I am manic-depressive Da-Sein (Avshalom) and I have to investigate how is the Da-Sein of a manic depressive is for me, i.e. I have to understand how do I exist, as a manic-depressive or as a depressive. The sense of the Da-Sein is to understand its being as a unique and individual possibility of its own; therefore, that Da-Sein is I myself. The possibility cannot be revealed by every Da-Sein in general, but by a private Da-Sein for which its self being is at stake. Every Da-Sein, therefore, is the possibility of its being and it is unique to him. His ability to be Da-Sein is at stake (es geht um).

My ability to be Da-Sein is at stake, what is at stake is my being, I understand it. Being depressive or manic-depressive is at stake (es geht um). For the depressive Da-Sein what is at stake is his being alive. Our discussion may, therefore, begin from "for the purpose of" (for the) as a main trait of existence. What is implied in "for the"? It implies, without a doubt, something as purpose, or aim and end; not a partial purpose that can be a mean or a step to a

213

higher purpose, but what is called a final purpose or a purpose on its own. In order for us to understand concretely, let us think about the well known experience pursuing a final purpose and about what is necessarily needed for that pursue to be possible. According to known experiences, when a person sets a purpose for himself, it is "before him" or "precedes him" in time; when a person sets himself with a certain aim as the climbing Mount Everest, he perceives it as a possibility which he could may or may not reach in the future. All this for a possibility that may not be realized and in trying, he may risk his life.

The final purpose of the manic-depressive Da-Sein, so I will contend, is to teach the people, to be a teacher! The depressive should teach the people, but there is a possibility that he will not be successful. If not successful as a teacher, he will fail realizing his final purpose, "for the". That "for the" is to be a teacher, however, if he chooses wrongly, he might not succeed. His final purpose is at stake.

Da-Sein has to project itself toward the future; the projection toward the future of Da-Sein has to lead him to a state of recognizing the non-existence of things or events and of drawing his orientation from such things and events toward what has to be done "here and now". He has to understand not only what he is now, but also what he could be (e.g. mountain climber) and then nearing himself clad in his possibilities. In other words, a person should be able to exceed himself, i.e. go beyond himself towards his potential future.

Such unique way of being is called by Heidegger existence. If a person was only real in everything "here and now" and its existence comprising of a series of leaps from one moment to the other, he could not have revealed its potential, he could not understand himself and his own ability to be what he could have been, therefore, he could not perceive any purpose or aim. A person understands himself through his possibilities of being. Moreover, the marvelous way by which a person exists from his possibilities is the way by which the person, in its essence, understands himself.

To be always ahead of himself is the main trait of existence and it is enabled through the forward projection of the structure of understanding.
The "I" is understood as "I can be", for example, in my ability to be your teacher, to teach you. The person as a Da-Sein exists primarily in the future. In expressions like "what is at stake" and "for the", Heidegger implies how the Da-Sein is being revealed to itself in its possibilities to be (I can be), leading us to the heart of the concept "existence". To exist as itself is not just another possibility from many, but its biggest truth.

What is the philosophical sense of possibility? There is an empirical term of possibility, i.e. that something or another may happen or that such or another event can be. Such possibility is incidental and fits only things. It is possible that something will happen to the Da-Sein, however, only due to its being that is at stake, fortuity gets a new sense. Heidegger does not refer to fortuity as a possibility. There is also a logical and empty term of possibility, i.e. it is possible to think of something which is not bound by absurdity or contradiction. Moreover, Heidegger contends, a possibility is a way or a model of a category of being, as opposed to something that is necessary and actual. In this case, possibility means something that is exclusively possible; however, it does not have to be actual and never necessary. Traditionally, possibility is considered something "lower" than something actual or necessary. Actuality, according to the tradition of philosophy, is more "true" and real than possibility. However, Heidegger emphasizes the contrary, as an ontological trait of existence possibility is something "higher" than actuality. Possibilities, according to Heidegger, are called Ermoeglichung which means the fundamental ability to make possible. When Heidegger speaks about the essence (Wesen) of Da-Sein, he means a possibility in that sense.

For the depressive being or the manic-depressive being, possibility is the way to understand its existence; when I say that possibility is in the essence of Da-Sein which is manic-depressive or depressive, I wish to say that he understands himself according to the possibilities opened to him and as fulfilling himself by free choice. Possibility, as aforesaid, is not necessary or actual, it is "higher" than actuality because the manic-depressive, by free choice, turns into actual that way or another. The choice of the manic-depressive or the depressive is free; he has to choose between being and not being; to be or not to be in ownership of his life. Not to be or to be, either authentic or not authentic.

For the purpose of this discussion, to be not authentic is not to be yourself. Manic depressive Da-Sein or a depressive Da-Sein understands himself through his possibilities, i.e. he understands that he has the possibility of being the teacher and the possibility of not to be. I.e. as a rule, there is a possibility for him to be authentic or not authentic; moreover, there is another possibility due to the nature of the disease, in which he could become a teacher or fail. He could be authentic by choosing to be a master of himself or he could be non-authentic and assimilate in "those".

216

How is it possible that Da-Sein can understand the being of something by the way by which he is not? Only by way of the "non-" is the way, initially, revealed to the Da-Sein from being itself. The important term of "at stake" (es geht um) implies how the "non-" is initially being revealed to the Da-Sein from itself. Da-Sein exists, i.e. understands itself from being the permanent possibility of maybe not being. The "non-" is not merely negativity but also positivity. It enables the Da-Sein to understand the possibility of being itself and the being of others. It is the source of possibility: also not to be. Da-Sein is cared with his being. Da-Sein considers itself as being at stake, it has the ability to understand that the being it might lose is his and of the others. The "non-" which can end its being is a menace on it alone, on its ability to be at all, thus lead to the uniqueness of its end. Its ability to be itself is being revealed from its end (its death) of being Da-Sein. The possibility of its end does not reveal itself to the Da-Sein as a fact to which it is indifferent, however, this fact hits at the heart of his consciousness.

The existence of Da-Sein is the opposite from the realization of things which as such cannot "care" or are not caring about their own being. Not only does Da-Sein care about its being, moreover, Heidegger says, it is a "Care".

What does "to lead to the uniqueness of self end" tells us about the manic-depressives and the depressive?

A depressive being thinks about his end in a more authentic way than any 'just' Da-Sein; this is one of two possibilities for his existence and self understanding. He understands one of his possibilities as committing suicide; depressive Da-Sein is, primarily, a being that understands himself, he understands his possibilities in a more profound and authentic way from any 'just'

Da-Sein; he chooses from one of the two possibilities available to him; i.e. he can chooses not to live!

To be the end or he can choose to be as a teacher by living. That is a choice!

The possibility of the depressive Da-Sein's end heats him at the heart of his being. Depressive Da-Sein is "care" with how he exists, the way by which he exists and therefore, understands his possibilities: to be for an end. The end is in the future. However, to be depressive can be also a different future, a future in which he chooses to be a teacher.

When Heidegger contends that Da-Sein exists "for" itself, it does not mean that it is egoism. Its existence "for itself" means that, firstly, he can achieve some self purpose or authenticity, i.e. a connection to what he himself is. Da-Sein in general and manic-depressive in particular exist in time.

Three structures of manic-depressive Da-Sein are distinct: balanced, manic-psychotic and depressive. Each of the three is 'not yet' the next step.

Da-Sein, psychotic or depressive, is present now, however at the same time it has the possibility of being in the past or future. The existence of Da-Sein, psychotic or depressive, is always external beyond itself, he projects itself forward toward the future; he projects itself beyond the moment of now, the present. He projects itself toward what it is not now, i.e. the future.

The self understanding of a manic-depressive Da-Sein is of his temporal states. The temporal sense of "the self projection toward" or forward projection outside "this moment" is the future. Da-Sein can be "before it" or "beyond it" provided it is already now, in the present, in a certain situation. Depressive Da-Sein brings his possibilities to himself, he, always and necessarily, returns to himself as he actually and factually is being. Such factuality "I am such and I can be" is always present before him and looks into his eyes. I.e. the manic-depressive or the depressive Da-Sein has to see himself in the future as a teacher: "I am the manic-depressive (or depressive) and I have to be a teacher".

I demonstrate the existence of the three structures of the manic-depressive Da-Sein, how is their being! I.e. how is it to exist in the three states.

Manic-depressive Da-Sein is a temporal phenomena, its ontology reflects phenomenological temporality. Manic-depressive Da-Sein is a circled ontological structure. Manic-depressive is in a passed present; he is 'not yet' the depressive; the depressive is a future and he is 'not yet' balanced (by balanced, I mean the state of just Da-Sein as it is in daily life); in his balanced state the mentally ill is 'not yet' manic-psychotic.

The temporality is a circle divided to three parts each of which represents another time in the stages of the mentally ill. Time is circular and the mind "circles" repeatedly in the three circles of its existence! Every state is temporality until it turns to another state. Manic-depressive Da-Sein is depressive in the present, psychotic in the past (manic); now, in the present, he is depressive and was, previously, balanced; when he is balanced in the present, he was, previously, in the past, depressive and in the future, he will be manic; this is the ontological circling of the manic-depressive Da-Sein. Moreover, on the other hand and by the same dialectics, it is being in a depressive present and being toward a balanced future; that future arriving, he is balanced in the present and is being toward a psychotic future (manic); when he is in a psychotic present he is being toward a depressive future. As aforesaid, the sense of Da-Sein is to understand its being as the possibilities available to it today which are unique to it, in this case, me personally.

The possibility cannot be revealed by any Da-Sein or in particular by a manic-depressive Da-Sein or any other depressive Da-Sein, but by a single and personal for which its own being, its existence is at stake.

When I say: 'at stake', by all means, I refer to life or death. For each Da-Sein, there are its unique possibilities. Existentialistically seen, freedom is the ability to choose this path of action and not the other or to pursuit this cause instead of another. Every "free" act is one of will which aims to fulfill some purpose; in the case of the manic-depressive or the depressive, the choice is very sensible, it is at stake; the choice is between being toward death or being the teacher, both are states (authentic). To be the teacher is the "for the" (the final purpose itself...) of the depressive or manic-depressive Da-Sein. The existence of a depressive or a manic-depressive Da-Sein is actually the existence of a free choice of possibilities to act. The revealing of possibilities as such is an achievement of existential understanding; according to Heidegger's interpretation, understanding is not cognitive ability but a basic way of existence.

Da-Sein is final, thus its possibilities are final; two possibilities are available for it to be. The state with a depressive Da-Sein is similar but more complex even difficult, it is similar to the Shakespearian question having two possible answers: "to be or not to be, whether 'tis nobler in the mind to suffer the slings and arrows of outrageous fortune, or to take arms against a sea of troubles and by opposing end them".

By Shakespeare and by me and as opposed to Heidegger there is also an ethical command. It is common to think that Heidegger does not deal in any ethical doctrine. Manic-depressive or depressive Da-Sein may choose one of the two: being toward death, i.e. toward the end or to say no to the being toward death or at least, so I contend, to say no to the being toward the end and say yes to the being alive and a teacher; i.e. to confirm life and to choose "being toward life". By exceeding to its possibilities, Da-Sein becomes free. Da-Sein cannot exist in a fuzzy generality only in one of its possibilities. Each Da-Sein is one of its possibilities; the other possibility is not. Each possibility, every "can be" is preset, also, to "no"; the "no" shows the final possibilities of the Da-Sein. Da-Sein has to make a clear and unequivocal decision!

How it, the Da-Sein itself, is determined by the way by which it gives its being to be itself. Nobody has chosen its being; if asked, he could have not wanted to be himself, however he is what he is and he can take responsibility upon himself and let himself being revealed as a unique thing.

Manic-depressive or depressive Da-Sein did not choose to become as such however, he needs to be what he is, "this being is mine", he needs to recognize his states and possibilities as they are. There two possibilities in which Da-Sein can be: authenticity (Eigentlichkeit) or non-authenticity (Uneigentlichkeit). To recognize your situation, i.e. your possibilities and be as you can be is to be authentic to yourself as opposed to being non-authentic; Da-Sein can renounce its being and state and what it can be and it may, also, not let its being to be revealed as it is.

Authentic depressive Da-Sein is such that it is the owner of its state and possibilities, it has the ownership of itself, i.e. as far as I

221

am concerned, that it chooses to confirm life and be a teacher or, on the other hand, chooses to end life which is, also, an authentic state provided it does not make this possibility actual.

Authenticity is to be the owner of yourself and your life; on the other hand, Da-Sein that is non-authentic, does not control its life, it does not make decisions and does not accept responsibility upon himself and for himself, rather it sinks to a state of acceptance compelled upon it by the "others". It lets circumstances determine who and what it is. It avoids making an existential decision.

The investigation of the manic-depressive Da-Sein has to start with its basic possibilities. As I have said, there are for the mental patient in general and the manic-depressive in particular three states of existence:

1) manic-psychotic,
2) balanced,
3) depressive.

I would like to speak about the balanced state. In a balanced state, a mental patient is just Da-Sein as any other Da-Sein. Even if one speaks of psychosis, it does pass with time. Also in a state of depression, the patient recovers at some stage. In a balanced state, Da-Sein understands itself not from itself but from what other people think. Da-Sein exists as being publicly revealed, of which its publicity is kind of concealment of its ability to be itself. Mostly, in daily life, this is the way by which it is in itself. "Daily" is how Heidegger calls the average, the indistinct way by which Da-Sein exists most of its life, from day to day; it takes what the day brings with it, it lives from what is brought to it by daily circumstances. In its daily life, the Da-Sein is absolutely tuned to a world in which the possibility of self understanding from its own being remains fuzzy. When Heidegger speaks about daily indifference, he does not contend that Da-Sein, in its state, ceases to be concerned or that the Da-Sein does not live for itself, rather he means that in such state the difference between self ownership or authenticity and non-authenticity is not revealed, not being expressed. Therefore, in its balanced state the manic-depressive being is not being revealed as it is, as itself. The manic-depressive being is being revealed by the poles due to manic-depression being a bipolar disorder. In the existential analysis, until a certain moment, a manic-depressive Da-Sein in its balanced state is just a Da-Sein as any other. Its uniqueness is expressed at a later stage, i.e. at a stage in which it can be more authentic which is more than "just" a Da-Sein; its uniqueness is being expressed when it becomes depressive, then its possibilities are revealed which, in my opinion, are more authentic and urgent than the possibilities of the "just" Da-Sein.

## 21:25 Sayings from the being depressive

At this stage, I would like to clarify where my loyalty stands, my loyalty, according to the phenomenological tradition, is given, primarily, to myself and people like Van Gogh, only then to Heidegger. It is important for me to denote that Heidegger tends to describe the Da-Sein according to his tendency or opinion, and therefore he does not describe all the possibilities of the Da-Sein. Heidegger describes a series of existentials which relate to Da-Sein (man) and thereof One May asks whether Heidegger relates to the full scope of the existentials?

No. he does not speak about pleasure and happiness which are too existential, moreover, they are the important existentials and with much sense for the manic-depressive being; he does not suffer only sadness and sorrow while in depression, but also happiness and pleasure while in the state of mania. The manic-psychotic has sense and purpose but he is senseless while in depression. Heidegger does not relate to it and therefore, in my opinion, he does not characterize the full scope of ways by which Da-sein may at all exist. The manic-depressive being is care about its existential states and about the senselessness and purposelessness while being depressive.

The Da-Sein and particularly the manic-depressive or depressive Da-Sein does not own its own life while being non-authentic. The starting point is the completeness of the Da-Sein; it is a question about the extreme possibilities of the Da-Sein's existence as opposed to its daily existence. The question of completeness and ownership or an authentic existence is a possibility of having a free and final choice.

The primary aim is to find out whether it is possible, existentially, for the Da-Sein to be complete by its own way. The answer is yes. Da-Sein cannot experience its own death; however it can experience the "being toward the end".
How death as the way by which Da-Sein comes to an end, can be characterized existentially? This is the extreme possibility of the inability to be anymore; "I cannot anymore" it says. A depressive Da-Sein reveals its ontological character by being thrown toward death as its extreme possibility. The permanent threat of the Da-Sein's death, from which the depressive Da-Sein is not afraid, arises from its existence. The threat is being revealed by the

anxiety, the anxiety from "there is nothing for the"; at this stage I will just denote that "there is nothing for the" is the existential exposure of the Da-Sein to the senselessness and emptiness in its life and from which (from such an absurd existential truth) he escapes to daily life and others. Depressive Da-Sein, as aforesaid, recognizes and experiences the "there is nothing for the", in its most profound form, thus understands the possibility of "the inability to be here anymore" also in the most profound way by which "just" a Da-Sein cannot understand.

Van Gogh understood well that possibility and was not afraid to choose the extreme possibility of "being toward death"; Van Gogh, following the pain from senselessness, understood that he "cannot be here anymore" thus putting an end to his life. He was exposed to the existential anxiety of "there is nothing for the", looked it in the eyes, did not escape to "those" and chose the tranquility of eternal death.

Heidegger assumes a concept called "the voice of conscience" which means that such voice cannot be a fact or an objective thing in the world but it is an intrinsic call that cannot be proven "realistic" but is a true, original and existential phenomenon of consciousness. The call says to the Da-Sein: "what for"? I see here the ontological function of a consciousness exposing something, giving us something to understand, not the Da-Sein in general but the Da-Sein in a private and individual way. My interpretation of the manic-depressive or depressive Da-Sein's structure is phenomenological! I describe their consciousness and possibilities.

The "no" is the answer of the voice of conscience to the question of "for what" and the answer or the conclusion is "I cannot be here anymore". Through the possibility of "being toward death" a depressive Da-Sein says "no" to life and no to the possibility of existence or the sinking in the daily world with others. The "no" is annihilation. By that way, a depressive Da-Sein reveals itself authentically, i.e. it is the owner of its being. An absolute existence of "being toward the end" is the way by which a Da-Sein can be complete. Depressive or manic-depressive Da-Sein does toward the end which is a possibility being revealed in its future, i.e. it is a future possibility. The manic-depressive or depressive Da-Sein has, always, an additional future possibility, i.e. an alternate possibility to the "being toward the end" and it is the possibility of "being toward life"; this is the possibility to confirm life and its purpose of being a teacher. He needs to choose one of the two possibilities available in his future: life or death.

## 21:35 Essence and existence

Heidegger says that the Da-Sein's essence is in its existence; this saying is interlaced with another saying, the being of the learned thing is always mine. These two sayings are very important in the understanding of why is the analysis of the Da-Sein is not, principally, an ontic analysis, i.e. scientific, but has to be hermeneutic. The sense of Da-Sein is such that it ponders on its own existence. It means that I cannot think of the Da-Sein but in terms of possible ways of existence. I can know what is the sense of being, however incomplete, and as much as I can know this, I am Da-Sein. The traditional sense of existence says or implies something that occurs in the universe, or something we encounter in the world.

Heidegger uses presence as a trait of such type of existence. In German, existentia is the existence of things, while existenz is applied to Da-Sein. From now on, I will use "my existence" for the characterization of the second term of Existenz. We need not confuse ourselves with the philosophical genre of existentialism which is identified with Jean Paul Sartre. Heidegger opposed the similarity between his analysis and Sartre's. According to Heidegger, when Sartre contends that human existence precedes its essence, he remains attached to the metaphysical tradition which contends that the human being has nature or essence which precedes its existence and then he overturns it. The result is another metaphysical assertion which is not related to Heidegger's basic ontology.

What is, therefore, Heidegger's intention in the assertion that the existence of the Da-Sein is its essence?

Only Da-Sein can stand by or "externally" to its own occurrence in the world and observe itself. Only the Da-Sein has the ability to be aware and alert to its own occurrence, an ability which is its unique trait, thus it is its essence; i.e. the ability to observe yourself and ponder on the way of your existence is the essence of Da-Sein. Therefore, my existence does not relate to my life or its functionality but to the awareness to my being. The assertion about the essence of Da-Sein being in its existence is, primarily, a basic or fundamental ontology. Metaphysics contends what we are; basic or fundamental ontology examines how such assertions are possible. Therefore, Heidegger distinguishes himself from existentialism (mainly from Sartre) which tells us what a human being is, e.g. he is free, absurd etc., and instead, examines a priori ways of the being which enable us to be aware of metaphysics. Heidegger wishes to show us that we can examine and investigate our existence; this is our marvelous ability to ponder on our existence. Heidegger uses traits like anxiety and fear and contends that they are facts occurring in human beings and therefore can be analyzed as description of its existence, but not only anxiety and fear are facts of our existence, also joy and pleasure.


## 21:45 My Da-Sein


As aforementioned, the thing to be investigated is mine. The thing that we investigate is, in any event, mine. From the awareness of the self pondering on my existence, I discover the universal principals which, by their nature, are rational, and therefore are applied to every Da-Sein. In my case, I discover, out of self pondering, the same traits and principals existing in every depressive Da-Sein. Therefore, the sense of the assertion is that the Da-Sein is always mine or I, simply, denote the availability of the research's subject and emphasize that the method of analysis has to be hermeneutic self pondering. What is mine is owned by me, for example my existence, and therefore authentic.

The term "authentic" denotes the way by which a Da-Sein exists i.e. I am aware of my existence. The opposite term "non-authentic" is the same way by which I am not aware of my existence. Heidegger intends by "authenticity" the self awareness of the existence; by "non-authenticity" he intends the self awareness as others see it, or to see myself as one with sense or essence which precedes my existence.

It is important to denote that the whole idea of "mine" is the basis for Heidegger's analysis of the terms "being authentic" and "being non-authentic". The distinction between authenticity and non-authenticity provides the philosopher with a polar pair, i.e. opposites without which Heidegger's theory will become incidental and non-coherent insights.

In my view, the terms make the distinction between a human state in which the depressive being is the owner of its life and a state in which he is not the owner of its life and simply drowns in the surrounding daily life which is determined by the "they".

The distinction must be applied to every possibility in which we exist. For example, Michael Galvin says that if we accept the assertion that speech is a way of existence, thus we can speak authentically or not. By speaking authentically, we may reveal something on the sense of being in existence; by speaking non-authentically, we could not reach such a revelation. Actually, Heidegger, by this distinction, wishes to show that the ways by which we exist, can be a subject of our thinking.

To be or not to be, i.e. Hamlet's question, is an issue for the depressive Da-Sein, it cares with its existence and the way by which it exists. It ponders on its life, possibilities and purpose. It is caring with how it exists and whether it does it authentically or not. Heidegger's wish is to say that my existence is the subject of research and care; i.e. the ways by which I exist are my care. I care about these ways even if they are an issue of hope for pleasure and avoidance of pain. The manic-depressive being, I say, cares about its existence, it cares about how it, notwithstanding the pain and sorrow, may find comfort also while being depressive exactly as Sisyphus finds comfort and happiness in his destiny. It is possible to investigate existence because as an existential Da-Sein, it is of interest for me. In view of this, the question of existence is not a formal one but a real question about the fact of the human being pondering and wondering about its existence.

## 22:00 The a priori structure of existence

What is a priori knowledge? According to Emanuel Kant, a priori knowledge is what we know before any experience, thus enabling knowledge.

For example, Kant contended that categories (e.g. causal) are a priori; they are not derived from experience since experience is dependent upon and enabled by them. Mathematics and logic are a priori because none of them is needed for the verification of its lemmas.

For other philosophers, the term a priori denotes every knowledge derived from logic and thinking. The importance of a priori is that it provides universal validity and it is necessary. It is challenging to see how the structure of the Da-Sein's existence is a priori.

According to Kant, for example, the category of causality is a priori; i.e. to think of causality in natural events is a natural and essential skill of consciousness, by which the human being unites the seemingly unrelated information of experience. For example, if I, suddenly, hear a blast beyond the door, my primary and immediate reaction will be to ask what caused the blast. We will not consider saying "nothing". Each thing, so we tell ourselves, has a reason, a cause that caused the result. I cannot accept the answer "nothing", because if I do, then one way by which I organize events in the world will not be available to me; I will, simply, not be able to organize events which I experience. The essential and natural way by which I am extant in the world is such that I have to assume relationships of cause and result between events occurring in it.

Causality is, therefore, an interpretative tendency that precedes any experience; it is the way by which my consciousness necessarily works; without it the understanding of the world as it is presented to me will not be possible.

Now, one may ask what are the preconditions or the hermeneutic tendency of the consciousness and the necessary ways of thinking that enable me to be aware of my own existence?

Heidegger refers to the necessary ways for the enabling of seeing yourself as existential. As the categories, so is also the existential a priori and moreover, as the categories, the existentials are necessary ways by which consciousness acts. Categories are necessary ways by which consciousness compels order upon the world beside consciousness itself and by which it sees itself.

How one may analyze the existential? How do we arrive at knowing it?

Kant derived its categories from the structure of traditional logic. Since existentials, not as categories, are applicable to the ways of being and not to things, the procedure of analysis by which the existentials become accessible to each other is performed by hermeneutic phenomenology.

## 22:15 To be in the world

The first a priori existential is "being in the world". "To be in the world" is the first of a series of existentials being analyzed by Heidegger.

Heidegger starts with the widest existential term: the simple fact that I find myself in something, the world. World is not necessarily the world of science which describes earth as ellipse orbiting the sun in the universe's infinite space. "World" in its existential sense is the place in which we are extant. When the analysis of existentials turns more specific and unique, we see Heidegger moving from the different ways by which the world has sense, as for example "to be useful", to more intrinsic and personal ways of self existence as fear, anxiety, loyal existence, the awareness of possibilities etc. The possibility for the Da-Sein to link itself to other Da-Seins relates to its existence.

The subject of this analysis is: to be "being in the world" thus the world itself; and the world should be understood through the horizon of the daily average which is a type of being close to Da-Sein. We need to investigate "being in the world" in daily life. The daily life's world which is close to the Da-Sein is the surrounding.
We deal with entities which we meet and which are close to us in the daily life's world; not intending cognitive perception but our dealing with them as given on hand, i.e. it usage, it is a type of "knowledge". In our dealing with entities, we come in touch with writing tools; sawing, cutting, grinding, etc; a tool is always "something for". In a structure of "for" there is a task or a relation

of something to something. The tool belongs or relates always to another tool: ink, pen, stationary, table, lamp, furniture, window, door and room. Such 'things' never show themselves by themselves. We encounter the 'room' as close to us, we do not encounter it as something within four walls in a spatial geometrical sense but as a tool for dwelling; from such a state, every tool shows itself, i.e. from a collection of tools. If we observe a thing just theoretically, we do not understand the "on hand".

If we deal with them by usage, it is not a blind act; it has a perspective of its own. In work, for example, there is a relation to materials; the work on a coat depends on the leather, strings, needles etc. The leather is being taken from animals that were grown by someone. Animals are also extant in the world without someone raising them and they multiply by themselves. Therefore, there are entities in the surrounding that become accessible as "on hand"; a hammer, pliers, nails, steel, metals, minerals and wood in the sense that they are made of. In usable tools, nature is being revealed together with them by the usage, i.e. the 'nature' which we find in natural products. In this sense, 'nature' is not something that is only understood as "on hand", the river is the power of water, the wind is the wind blowing in sails.

When we discover the surrounding, 'nature' is revealed in the meeting with it. If such type of being "on hand" disappears, 'nature' itself is revealed and defined only as "present on hand" in its simplicity. But in this case 'nature' remains hidden; the botanist's flowers are not, anymore, the flowers of the hedge. In a watch, an account is given to a certain state of the celestial bodies. When we look at the watch we make use of the sun's position in accordance with the measurement of time. When we make use of the watch as a tool which is "on hand", the surrounding of nature is also "on hand".

Da-Sein is being attached to things so that its understanding of itself as "for" dictates its behavior in the world. It directs it to the things which it meets as means thanks to which something will be performed in order to reach a certain purpose.

These complex associations between Da-Sein and other be are the coherent structure of the world. The way by which the Da-Sein relates itself to, intends itself toward, is the condition for its factual existence in which it is never alone but among other things in the coherent whole which is the world.

"The world" is not the causal links between real things in the world but it is the way by which Da-Sein understand itself. The world is an existential ontological concept which does not give information on the ontic world of physics. Da-Sein, surely, "lives" in an ontic world, but not only, it is in "for" connections with other things, for example, with a hammer which it uses to nail a nail. It is in a connection with the room that gives him shelter.

Heidegger's first step is to relate through the widest concept to how the world presents itself to the Da-Sein. He continues the analysis of things being in the world: objects, other Da-Seins and finally the self in the world; Heidegger calls the self in the world as the awareness of "the here" in the world, i.e. Da (here) sein.

He distinguishes between the authentic awareness and the non-authentic of the self, and between the decisive characterization of our occurrence in the world and the free characterization thereof. Finally, Heidegger exposes the existential that mostly describes the way by which the Da-Sein exists: "care".

Heidegger describes the ontological sense of being in the world and shows that the existential is a priori. It is a priori in the sense that Da-sein is already extant in the world from the start. One should see the being in the world not by an ontic way rather by an ontological way. Heidegger values and explains the in-the, i.e. inside. The ontic sense is not a priori because the world is being revealed by experience.

Heidegger intention by in-the, ontologically, is what enables the feeling of knowing that we have with the world, such that makes the world our home. Scientifically, the fact that I am extant in the planet earth (the world) is not a priori; it is learned by experience. However the fact that as a Da-sein I need a world to live in (it can also be a village in which I feel "at home"), to dwell in, to call it my home, is in itself a priori. What Heidegger intends in being in-the, ontologically, is our a priori ability to connect to things and be cared about them, to care ourselves with them. The human being belongs to-. It does not mean that a human being does not have feelings of alienation and strangeness in the world; to be a stranger in a certain place means that there is another place at which you feel "at home" even if you do not find it at the moment.

Heidegger speaks about dwelling; we say to him that water live in a glass, only Da-sein can dwell. The real sense behind such existential is that the surrounding (Umwelt) is not simply there, but it affects me and I affect it. I cannot think of myself as a point in time-space, therefore, the categories that do explain such state do not suffice to explain my existence in the world. I require, in addition, an a priori explanation as to whether I feel alienated or at home. To say that being in the world is a priori is also to say that one may successfully think about the sense of being in the world without relying only on experimental-empirical evidence. In Michael Galvin's example, I can go to a show with a friend and due to its success, we will be seated separately. I, therefore, am seated beside a stranger but with a friend. The difference between being beside and being with cannot rely just on spatial location. This state of being with a friend who I love or beside a stranger, for whom I do not have feelings, precedes a spatial or empirical calculation and therefore, it is a priori.

The importance of the result in this example is that Heidegger's strategy by which it is possible to investigate the a priori as ways by which we exist, is justified.

For what reason will someone want to contend that being in the world, ontologically, is a priori?

As human beings, we have relationships with things as well as with other human beings. These are relationships which we are aware of and which are changing us. In this sense, objects do not have relationships. Let us assume that someone will ask: what is the ability thanks to which we have such relationships? There has to be such an ability within us which enables us to connect, to be in a relationship with something. This preliminary ability which enables us to connect is the a priori existential "to be in the world".

Michael Galvin contends that being in the world is the preceding assumption to knowledge. The basis of epistemology is the knower and the known. However, before making the distinction between knower and known (subject and object) we consider the fact that the subject can connect to the known, i.e. that the premise for the distinction between subject and object is already based on a system of relationships, i.e. the subject has a world in which the object can occur. Knowledge, therefore, is not created by itself from the surrounding world. It is not true that we simply know something. There is information that gives me happiness and joy or suffering and pain; and what seems also to be a pure fact is derived from some need or wish for objectivity, e.g. the need of the scientist.

As aforesaid, to be in the world is the a priori existential. Our preliminary relationship with the world means the usage of it, i.e. the world is available to us; it is ready to be used. Heidegger calls this property of "ready at hand" zuhanden. To think about the world as containing or composed of things independent from their functionality or their usage (i.e. to see the world as "present at hand", vorhanden) is not the preliminary relationship with the world, but derived.

Heidegger shows, for example, that I make use of a lock in the door before I consider its physical properties. The world's image which is given to us by science is a type of a container in which objects occur or reside. These objects are "simply there". They are seen by the scientist independently from their functionality, value or usage. Such viewpoint is, of course, necessary for science.

As a scientist, I am interested in an object as such; however, such viewpoint of the world is not primary. The person turned into scientist did not consider the world merely as objects but, as things to be used. When the scientist enters the laboratory, and picks up a test tube or a Petri dish, he does not consider them as research objects rather he is using them for his research. He may take interest in the microbes' properties in the Petri dish however, the dish itself or the test tube is a tool of which the scientist does not think.

The usage of things in the world is primary to the connection to the world, i.e. such way of usage is primary. I see the world as ready on hand when I do not think about it as a thing rather as usable. The practical world in which things are together as purpose and mean is very different from the world of causal relations, i.e. from a theoretical world. The ontological term of the world in which Da-sein "lives", i.e. the close by world of daily life (umwelt) is the one being used by Heidegger as a starting point. The complete structure (the world) which Heidegger shows to be a complex system of indicators, indicated things and relations, must enable the Da-sein to relate to other things by ambiguous ways as well as to relate to them by relevancy and their effect on his existence.

The daily world of concern is a grid of relations. The sense of the grid is that there is nothing which is the application of a single tool detached from the others. Each usage of a tool indicates or relates to another as, for example, a screwdriver which indicates screwing and both relate to two boards or more precisely, being fastened to become a shelf, etc. Such grid of relations with its dynamics establishes the immediate surrounding (Umwelt) of the being-here (Da-sein).

In this daily surrounding, in worldliness, things show themselves or are being revealed in terms of their purpose. I.e. Da-sein reveals them in their sense for it. However, this surrounding is so well known and reliable in which the certain things which we encounter and the dynamic mutual relations in it do not stand out, break out, i.e. the world is not "present on hand" rather "ready on hand". Something becomes outstanding when it stops functioning, only then it shows itself, makes itself present.

For example, when we drive a car, we do not pay attention to the breaks while using them, however, when they stop functioning, they stand out. The world exists prior to the things within it; it is always, already "here". A practical activity using tools is the main way by which daily existence deals or takes care of things. Even an absolute authentic existence necessarily comes into contact with assets, production, fixing and using things which it needs for its existence. Heidegger's first step is to shed light on the phenomenological trait of things with which we are busy, the things which we use as means to our practical ends. The decisive trait of Heidegger's phenomenological analysis of tools is not focusing on practical things in daily life in relation to indifferent entities rather on things already extant in the world. Notwithstanding the worldly trait is not explicitly perceived while we deal daily with things, it is implicitly understood. I.e. the whole world is already "there" (exposed). A single and isolated tool as a hammer is not possible. The hammer, to begin with, connects and relates to hammering something in order to fasten things together, e.g. to build a roof. The hammer can show itself as it is only from and within a set of complete equipment (tool) belonging to the working world of the carpenter or a mason. The being of the being a complex hammer by being connected and related to something beyond itself.

The relational structure from which tools show themselves in usable "is"s in the world is called, by Heidegger, Bewandtnis mit, the reason and relevancy of things or the reason for a thing in a certain state, e.g. the reason for a hammer for hammering.

The being of the tool resides in its being which is destined for a certain purpose. The purpose is to complete a certain task e.g. to built a house. It unites the whole complex system of relations from which every tool may be as it is- a tool relevant to a certain task in the whole. The completed task, the house, has also a trait of a tool; it is relevant (destined to-) dwelling. The house is meant to be a shelter, protection, which "destiny" is the taking care of the Da-sein. Da-sein notifies itself as to how it can be toward other things; i.e. how can it relate itself to them as opposed to them being able to affect it, relate to its ability to exist. The whole complex system preceding the relational exposure establishes the ontological structure of the daily world in which it enables thing within it to express themselves as relevant to complete a mission or to achieve a goal. Therefore, Da-sein as extant together with things makes things relevant (Bewendenlassen).

Seeing the object as a thing, as something that occurs in the world is to see the world as "present at hand" and it is not wrong. It is wrong to see the world exclusively as "present at hand"; having the opinion that the world has only one way to present itself, i.e. the way of "present at hand" stems from a certain interpretation of human existence. Da-sein is only one object among many. Heidegger contends that seeing the world as "present at hand" is only one way to relate to the world. The position of consciousness through which one sees the objects in the world as "present at hand" is, undoubtedly, the best and necessary position for the scientist; however it is not, necessarily, the best way for philosophers.

To use something and to see it as an object are two different ways by which consciousness acts. Moreover, Heidegger contends that it is not the primary way or position by which we, as human beings, relate to the world. If seeing the universe, exclusively, as "present at hand" is just derived and not primary, then, the sense of existence may not be explains just by such seeing. Moreover, if considerations of "present at hand" describe the world-object in a way which is not exhaustive of all the possible ways, hence the methodology of an investigation of such type may not be the one by which the ontological truth may be revealed. Philosophy demands more than such narrow way of observation.

In summary, one can see things in the world as usable objects, i.e. a world in which things are "ready at hand" which is one point of view; another is to see the world as "present at hand" through which we see things as objects, i.e. as existing separately from us. Finally, the seeing of the world as existential in which the ways of "ready at hand" and "present at hand" are two different and incomplete ways to see.

## 22:30 The who of the Da-sein

I will start with the analysis and the distinction between an authentic and non-authentic Da-sein and leading to question who Da-sein is. How the investigation of the self achieves its goal? I.e. how the self sheds light on the question of being?

We are aware, we have a consciousness. The knowledge or awareness of my existence leads to the sense of my being. The question is whether it is significant or important for me that I exist? I.e. the question is whether I am caring about my existence. Let us ponder on the question of the importance of the existence? How is it not to exist?
In one sense this question is absurd; I will never be able to know how it is not to be since if I do not exist, I cannot know anything.

Still, the question is not entirely insignificant since it arouses the pondering consciousness by the reality of my existence not being for granted.

Notwithstanding my inability to know what is not to exist (because it is senseless), I, still, know that it is possible to cease to exist. This is the realization of the possibility to cease to exist and not existence as such which is significant and important for me. I can ask: does it make any difference whether I am aware of the fact that I may cease to exist, or not?

Of course, the awareness of me ceasing to exist is of importance to the different ways by which I live (e.g. I can be careful while driving). But then another question arises: is it at all possible for me to be unaware of the possibility of me not existing? Or is it just a repression of the terrifying possibility? Answering this question, one needs to examine the ways of the self that are not clearly visible and that are aware of the possibility of not being. Not to be aware of the possibility of not existing is to cover or to sweep under the rug the sense and importance of existence. However, it is not only the awareness of my possibility not to exist which is important; it also essential to recognize that I may exist and still not be aware to the sense of my existence. This is also a type of negation in which the sense of existence may be lost or hidden. This is clearly a form of self cheating to ignore the understanding that it is possible for me to cease to exist. However it is more deceitful to exist in avoidance of the understanding of the meaning of my existence and this is the important one and should be analyzed.

Heidegger starts his analysis by way of covering or repressing self awareness. Heidegger will compare the non-authentic of them-self ("those" being those who I cannot separate myself from, that is, other people) and the authentic self which is the way of being by which I am aware to the importance and sense of the being.

To understand the concept of being is to be aware of my possibilities.

To be aware of the possibilities is to provide the basis for liberty and truth. Either being unaware of the sense of being, i.e. my possibilities, is actually to be defined as non-authentic or I, decisively, define my own being. Da-sein is, authentically, aware of its possibility not to be, it exposes its finality; such finality exposes the ontological base for the temporality of the Da-sein, hence the awareness of time. I contend that the depressive-being, in its decisiveness to be facing death, is aware, most authentically, of the practical possibility not to be, it is more aware than just a Da-sein to the finality of its life which is an awareness of its temporality, i.e. time.

According to Heidegger, one can have an authentic point of view of the self, i.e. his own self as opposed to himself being reflected through others. There is no distinction between the lonely I and the others, but between an authentic myself (that part of its sense is to be with others) and a non-authentic. The difference between the authentic and the non-authentic ways of the self is not that the later is lonely and the first is mingled; by the non-authentic way, I deal with others and loose the contact with myself; by the authentic way, I am aware of the others and myself and my possibilities.

Following the Da-sein and its primary dealing with the world as usage, i.e. "ready at hand", we find that the usage of the world as usable includes a primary relation to other Da-sein.

When I deal with the world as usable, I recognize that part of it is also other Da-seins that are also using it. Heidegger contends that even by simply walking in the field, I share it with others. I do not walk on the crop thus recognizing its value for the farmer. "To be with" is the a priori dimension in which the self considers the farmer's rights to his crop; I, primarily, have to have the ability to do so; such ability precedes any specific consideration of the farmer's right to his crop and that is the meaning of being with him in the world. I can be aware of another Da-sein using the world as a usable thing only because I, as a Da-sein in my essence, "am with" others. To say that "to be with" is a priori existential of Da-sein means that I cannot be myself unless I can make a unique contact with others. Therefore, to be a Da-sein means also the existential "be with". To "be with" is the possibility of the whole self. It is not a non-self trait but an existential of the self. Heidegger poses an important question: is it not possible that the "who" of the daily Da-sein is not "I myself"?

Heidegger responds positively. What is Heidegger's intention by saying that in daily life I am not myself? The answer is in the distinction between the authentic and non-authentic ways of the self. I do not lose myself to another Da-sein but to "those" (others) which is a way of the self.


## 22:40 Being in the world as "being with" and being yourself. "Those".


Da-sein is an entity which, in any case, is mine; its being is in any case mine ("Being and Time" page 150).

244

The question of "the who?" is answered in terms of "I" the subject itself. The "who is?" is what persists as something identical despite the changes in experience and behavior. Ontologically, we understand it as something that, in any case and always, is "present at hand". According to this perception, Da-sein is perceived, from the beginning, as something "present at hand". However, "present at hand" is a type of being that belongs to entities which traits are not as the traits of a Da-sein. In our clarification of the being in the world, we have shown that a pure subject does not exist without a world, it is not given. Moreover, a lonely subject without others is also afar from being given, the others are already with us in the world. If the "I" is an essential trait of Da-sein then it has to be existentially interpreted. In this state, "the who" is answered only by a phenomenological presentation of a certain type of a being held by a Da-sein. "The essence of a human being is not the synthesis of body and mind, but existence (Being and Time page 153).

The answer to "the who?" has to be found by the analysis of that certain type of being by which the Da-sein is extant. Our investigation starts with being in the world, by describing our nearest surrounding, the daily world of work; not only do we meet the hammer and nails, but also the carpenter who uses them. If the hammer is "ready at hand" then we will find a being that is linked to it, involved with it, a grid of relations of carpenters and various consumers; using material, we will find a supplier. The others who we meet at "ready at hand", at the associated environment of the instrumentation, are not, somehow, added in thought to a thing which is only "present at hand"; these things are met, to begin with, as "ready at hand" to others; this world is always mine to begin with. Therefore, the Da-sein's world reveals entities that do not only differ from instrumentation and things, but also in accordance with the type of being as Da-sein themselves. These entities are not "present at hand" or "ready at hand" but they are as they are being revealed by the Da-sein, they are "here" as well as "there" with it. The world is something that is shared by me with others. The Da-sein's world is a world-with (Mitwelt), to be in- is to be with others.

"To be with" is an existential property of Da-sein, even if, factually, no one is "present at hand" or perceived. Also being-alone of Da-sein is being-with in the world. The other may be absent only in- and for "being-with" (Being and Time page 156). Surely, the being toward others differs, ontologically, from being toward things that are "present at hand". The entity which is 'other' is a being of the same type as Da-sein. By being-with and toward others, there is reciprocation of being between Da-seins. Expressing such existential of being-one-with-another, we will see a property of distance. Such distance which belongs to being-with, is such that Da-sein as one-with-another represses the other; the being of Da-sein has been taken from it by others. The daily possibilities of Da-sein as being are repressed by the others as they see fit. The others are not specific others, anyone may represent them. Their "who" is not someone specific, not that one, not myself, not other specific persons, rather "who" is indefinite, the crowd, those (Das man, Being and Time page 164).

Everyone is similar to the one beside him, however, the being-one-with-another dissolves the self Da-sein into "those". We are joyful and happy embraced by "those", we read, see plays, judge literature and art as they see and judge as well as we retreat from the crowd the same way as they do, we are shocked the same way as they are; the "those" which is not a defined thing of everyone is the being of the daily life. "Those" have their ways of living. "Those" ease the burden and suffering of the specific Da-sein.

"Everyone is another and no one is himself". The "those" which provide the answer to "the who?" of the daily Da-sein is the "no one" to which every Da-sein has already surrendered by being-one-with-another" (Being and Time page 166).

The daily Da-sein's self is the those-self which we distinct from the authentic self, i.e. from the self going by its own way. As those-self, the specific Da-sein disperses into the "those" and it needs to find itself, i.e. to recognize itself as a self. That means that the "those" itself is the interpreter of the world and the being in the world. Da-sein is for the "those" by the daily way. Mostly, the Da-sein stays as "those", a state in which it misses and covers itself. Heidegger is not original in the idea that a human being has a tendency to lose himself inside the "those". Being honest, we will admit that daily life can distract us from the awareness of ourselves.

Being true, it means that someone expresses different ways of being, i.e. once with self awareness and once without it; i.e. I am authentic while being aware of myself and non-authentic while I lose my self awareness.

As we shall see later on, the awareness of the possibility of not being (death) is one of the most important instances in Heidegger's teachings; it is the instance of me becoming authentic. However, Heidegger wishes to show that the way by which I lose my "self" is still my way and not others'; hence we can only blame ourselves for losing our "selves" to non-authenticity. The sense of "those" is not the same as of "others". "Those" (das man) is a characterization of the self that defines a way of existence; "others" is the relations that occur in authentic and non-authentic states.

Heidegger analyzes the daily existence of someone as something authentic or non-authentic. The non-authentic way is characterized by losing the self awareness to their chatter, there is an abandoning of the self; however, as we shall see later on, this state is based on the actual. The authentic state is based on possibilities.

## 22:50 "Being with" others and yourself

Da-sein can relate to other persons due to its being, essentially to begin with, being revealed to it as "to be with" which is also a priori existential.
Da-sein, always, enters into different associations with other persons; it is not due to not being unique in the world, rather, on the contrary, it can identify others similar to it in the world and make contact with them because its being is revealed to itself as being with others. According to Heidegger, being lonely in the world i.e. no other human beings exist, Da-sein will not cease to be with others, meaning it seeks to be with others. Usually, we think and it seems logical that Da-sein can understand others as their being, also as its "self" and also as other than itself. Exactly as the Da-sein is never a subject without a world, rather relates to itself a priori as connected to objects in the world, so it is, never, a lonely being without other beings, it is not a lonely "I".
248

However, I would like to emphasize, at this point, that one of the essential traits of the depressive-being is that it is socially secluded, it secludes in its home and avoids coming into contact with others; it is, in my opinion to be detailed later on, a virtue of the depressive-being; due to its avoidance of others, it has the ability to listen to itself and not to "those"; it listens to a call of conscience which tells it something that it must hear to become authentic.

For the those-self is harder to hear its "self" since it is so deeply involved with "those" until it cannot silence their futile chatter. Leaving this point for the time being, Da-sein always understands itself initially as "I myself with" (other "I"). The "with" already relates to others with a separated "I". The other is someone with whom the Da-sein can live in the world. Da-sein does not have to find a way through to another Da-sein, rather its own revealing as someone with (others); the existence of others is already given to its understanding. It is true that in daily life while we are together with others, an initial understanding of the other as well as oneself is sometimes covered and distorted, thus the understanding of someone else means to learn to know him. "To be with another" is a basic structure of Da-sein. It exists for the others or rather a part of its essence is the need for other human beings, it is some basic need of it which does not exist in the depressive-being. It understands others, initially, as other "I"s, as subjects that live in the same world and by the same way by which it lives in it; their being, i.e. the others have the same way of "for" as it has. The Da-sein's world contains, to begin with, other partners; "it being in the world" is by itself to be with others in the world.

"Care" is a basic type of being of something such that what is at stake is its own being. Heidegger's concept also includes solicitude for others or "being with others". The world of the being-here is to be with others (Being and Time page 118).

The analogy between the daily worldliness and the "being with others" stands out. A person is not more alone in the world than being without a world. The "being with others" and the daily worldliness are basic; they compose the "being in the world". However, at the same time, the daily worldliness and being-with-others differ from each other. The world of care is always a world in which other human beings exist "here". I meet others as being together with me. To be one with another creates the different possibilities for society. As in the case of "ready at hand" of things as tools in the daily worldliness, the access to others is initially implied. As the non-present of a reliable tool is what makes it visible and usable in the daily worldliness in which it functions; so, also, the non-presence of others pungently exemplifies the originality of being-with-others and, indeed, the possibility of authentically being with them.

Being-with-others and being-one-with-another are not based on the fact that various subjects connect. It is possible to feel loneliness even among others or simply feel the absence of someone since being-one-with-another determines the sense of "being in the world".
Even if Da-sein is being-alone, then being-alone needs to be understood as the way of being-with-others in the world (Being and Time page 120). Heidegger is trying to say that being alone implies a priori the being-with-others. To be-with-others shows the possibility of being alone, i.e. there is a possibility to feel

loneliness if, beforehand, we were with others; in fact, loneliness shows that initially, we were with others in the world. As aforesaid, we meet others in the world, not as things which are tools or things in nature rather as their ways of being in the world. The involvement of people one with each other is a result of dependency. People are dependent on each other in a world of care and they understand each other on this basis even if they, intentionally, behave as strangers to each other or love or hate each other. Being-with-others is an integral property of Da-sein. As I said the depressive Da-sein Dou to its illness is a lonely creature, but he is alone only because yesterday he was as every other Da-sein with others; however this lonelyness can serve him. When he is alone he can be with himself, listen to his conscience which has something crucial to tell him. The conscience tells him "be authentic!" be aware of your possibilities.

Heidegger tries to give a positive account of how it is to be-with-others and be-here-with; it is an account that does not reduce the others to the way by which one tool is connected to another or that one natural object is with another.

The key to this account is in the determination of "being in the world". To be-one-with-another is always a matter of being together caring about the world. To be authentically with another comprises of a relation to the other as it truly is, i.e. not something that is "present at hand" or "ready at hand" but as being-here (Da-sein), i.e. someone whose being itself is at stake. Daniel Dahlstrom[18] contends that if someone, on the other hand, is not really "here" with others, thus the others are not here in

_____

[18] Daniel O.Dahlstrom Heidegger's Concept of Truth, Cambridge University Press 2001. At some places I was close to his text.

their own right but non-authentically, i.e. as something "present at hand" in the world. Being-one-with-another is a certain type of care. If, for example, Daniel Dahlstrom contends, someone is behaving toward somebody else in such a way by which he tries to take care of everything for him, i.e. to take responsibility on him, thus he shows his relation to him as unfit to take care of himself and therefore unfit to be himself in the world of care. If he agrees to such reciprocation then he becomes dependent and the way by which he (the first) cares for the other takes the form of taking control.

If, on the other hand, his way of being-with-him is such that he trusts him and lets him be Da-sein (being-here) as himself, then his caring about him will free him.

To be-with-someone, authentically or not, depends whether the caring for that person is liberating or controlling in the relating to who this person really is. In the daily worldliness of relating, people, usually, are, from the start, in controlling relations with others.

The rate of distancing that separates people in daily life is the important thing. By trying to control each other, people are trying to reduce or decrease the distance between them; those at the top are trying to dwarf those at the bottom. By this way, people do not relate to others by a real way which enables them to be themselves, rather they become more or less "ready at hand" willing to be used by others.

To be in the world is to be immersed, on a daily basis, in the worldliness of care which is common to me and the others. In other words, people know each other on a daily basis in a public world of care. This public world is composed of a common social practice.

Heidegger denotes such way of being one with another in daily life as "those" (das man, Being and Time page 126). The "those" denotes a certain way of being in the world. By publicity, public opinion and conformity, the "those" holds much stability and imperviousness. The stability of "those" is a certain way of being-with-others which, unseeingly, subordinates everybody; i.e. everybody has to unite under the social convention. The distance between people is based on the "average" of the "those". Being average means that the role of the one may be replaced by the role of the other since the "those" relieves the Da-sein from its purpose of really being-with-others i.e. to be with them in a way by which each one can be itself; i.e. the "those" reduces the distance between the being-here and the others so that the Da-sein has not the freedom and distance to stand out above the "others" and be itself. Such being-one-with-another subordinates the Da-sein to the way by which others are being. Being-here allows itself now to be part of those; by that way, the others and their uniqueness completely disappear. When Da-sein is part of the "those", all its differences and possibilities are absorbed.

Heidegger's analysis proceeds from the fact that being in the world determines itself, initially and at its origin, based on the daily way by which a being-one-with-another is nothing but the immersion, together with others, to a world of "present at hand". From this aspect, Da-sein in the sense of being-with-others is trapped living in a world surrounding it by way of public opinion. Such world is composed of the tendency of "those": the care for the distance between the "self" and the others, the self esteem according to conformal criterion.

The sense of the world is identified with the aims of the "those" and therefore describes and judges in advance the interpretation of the world and of being in the world.

As long as a human being is "here" and lives among "those", he turns himself to victim that shifts the responsibility on himself to the unidentified world of public opinion. The "those" relieves the Da-sein in his daily life of the burden of being responsible on himself and be all that he can be.

Da-sein, therefore has a certain tendency to use the "those" in order to renounce the burden, a tendency to which everyone somewhat succumb. As long as the being-here has the tendency to consider things lightly, such way of relieving from the burden (of be as you can be) of being which is designed by it as a way of being-with-others, is willingly accepted. This tendency to take things lightly is, according to Heidegger, part and parcel of the escape from oneself. Da-sein escapes itself. Not only the tendency but also the escape itself compose or are part of the Da-sein's components. Heidegger relates to this component of escape as a fall or deterioration of Da-sein. A fall or deterioration is translated as verfallen, i.e. as fall from-. Heidegger discovered a certain type of being that belongs to daily life; he calls it "the falling" (Verfallen) of Da-sein. The term denotes that Da-sein, mostly and nearly, lives beside or lateral to 'the world' of its care. Such absorption has the trait of getting lost in the publicness of the "those".

At the first instance, Da-sein falls from itself as an authentic "is" with the ability to be itself into 'the world'. A "fall" into such world is the absorption of being-one-with-another. The non-authenticity of the Da-sein may be better understood through the interpretation of a fall. "Non-authenticity" does not refer to anything as "being no more in the world", rather belongs to a distinct type of being in the world, the type that is entirely fascinated from 'the world' and from Da-sein with others as "those". Not to be oneself (Das nicht-es-selbst-sein) functions as a positive possibility of such entity that is, in its essence, being absorbed in the world. Such type of not-being has to be understood as such type of being which is similar to Da-sein and in which Da-sein is extant most of the time. By falling, Da-sein, in itself being a factual being which is being thrown as being in the world, is something from which Da-sein already fell. It did not fall into any entity into which he ran for the first time while being or even fall into something which it did not encounter at all; it fell into the world to which being it itself belongs.

A fall is a defined existential trait of the Da-sein itself. It does not define the Da-sein as something as "present at hand". A futile chatter and the ways by which things are being publicly interpreted are based on being-one-with-another. Futile chatter is not something "present at hand" in itself in the world separated from the being-one-with-another. It is far from letting itself to evaporate into something universal that, since it does not, essentially, belong to anybody, it is 'indeed' nothing and occurs as 'real' only in the speaking individual Da-sein.

A futile chatter is a type of being that belongs to being-one-with-another; it is not revealed in certain circumstances and affects the Da-sein from the outside. However, if the Da-sein itself, by futile chatter and by the way by which things are being interpreted, presents itself with the possibility of losing itself in them and fall to a state of non-basis,  it indicates us that Da-sein is always tempted toward a fall.

Being in this world is always, in itself, temptation (versucherisch). By the way of self confidence and resolve of the "them", a futile chatter is spreading which affects the Da-sein and convinces it that there is no need for authentic understanding and the conscious state accompanying it. The assumption of the "them" about the Da-sein living full, complete and authentic life brings the Da-sein to a calm in which everything is as it ought to be.

A fall of a being in the world, which is tempting, is at the same time calming (Beruhigend). However, this calmness in a non-authentic being does not tempt someone to become frozen and inactive, rather drives it into unrestraint activity. A fall into the 'world' does not, somehow, come to an end. The temptation of calmness enhances the fall. While being calm, the Da-sein is swept toward alienation in which the ability to be itself is hidden from it. Therefore, the fall is never only tempting and calming but also alienating. Such alienation seals the possibility of authenticity for the Da-sein. It does deliver the Da-sein to an entity which it is not, but rather forces it to its non-authenticity, i.e. into a type of being a possibility of itself.

On one hand the alienation and on the other the temptation and calmness, all created by the fall, drives the Da-sein to type of movement in which the Da-sein is entangled. This movement of a Da-sein is called "deterioration". Da-sein deteriorates from itself to itself, into lack of base and emptiness of the daily non-authenticity. However, such deterioration remains hidden from Da-sein in a way by which things were publicly interpreted. This deterioration into the non-basis of non-authentic being of "them" (the crowd), is a type of movement which always tears the understanding from the projection of authentic possibilities and into calmness. Since understanding is being torn up from authenticity and into "them", the movement is also characterized as vortex (Wirbel).

While in a fall, nothing from our ability to be in the world is the subject for us even if by way of non-authenticity. Da-sein can fall just because being in the world as an understanding and a conscious state is the subject for it.

In addition to the fact that Da-sein is being thrown to the world and throws its possibilities as part of a being in the world, being here deals with the world and with the things in it such that one may say it falls prey to the world.

Heidegger characterizes such existential or phenomenon as a type of fall or deterioration. Our tendency to be wrapped in the world of care characterizes our way of being-with-others, and additionally what and who is every one of us. In this process, individual possibilities of being in the world are given to "them". The daily world ensures that each individual can be itself; however it is a lose self immersing in the non-uniqueness or the non-truthfulness of the "them". The differentiation is straightened or even being absorbed while the Da-sein disappears inside "them", this is an act of disappearance and blurriness by accepting the conventions of the public opinion and the criteria of normality. As Heidegger contends, such deterioration is tempting, calming and alienating. It is, actually, an existential of free fall.

On one hand we have the tendency to fall, i.e. to avoid us being thrown out of our existence by finding refuge in the world and things. On the other hand, we assist in our own fall.

Therefore, Da-sein falls in the sense of falling easily with little resistance and eventually with intent. As aforesaid, a fall to the world is the sinking of the being in being-one-with-another as long as it is led by chatter (Being and Time page 175). Chatter, as aforesaid, is the deterioration that is expressed by understanding and the daily life. In the extreme form of chatter, what is being said literally, i.e. spoken in words and word combinations, precedes the sense and importance of what is being said, or the fact of who have said it. What is being said and passes onward is being done with high priority, as an average; i.e. interpretation which is self understood. On one hand the Da-sein is near to the 'world' but on the other hand it is detached from the real ways by which beings are attached to the world, to others and to itself, or more precisely from the Da-sein's way of being itself or as it could be.

What characterizes the fall or deterioration as a way of such exposure is, exactly, the way by which it closes from the basic openness of the Da-sein, i.e. the hiding of the exposure which defines the being-here.

The phenomenon of fall, therefore, denotes a tendency and impulse to run away from oneself. A "fall", as aforesaid, denotes the way by which a being-here is falling from itself, self alienated; it assimilates in the daily worldliness and the "them". The fall and escape of the Da-sein from itself is a fall to the world. The self understanding of the Da-sein that, by its nature, is seeking its possibilities, is seeking calmness, the calmness in the understanding of others and in their knowledge as if they know the secret of the serene life. The serenity inside the confidence does not put the Da-sein in heaven, rather it enhances the fall, i.e. not being authentic.

To be tempted to deviate from the road of true possibilities of the single Da-sein displaces it from itself, alienating itself and finds itself in a personal tangle. This state renders all authentic possibilities of Da-sein to self understand as unavailable. It believes that others have the secret of self understanding which brings it to a state of personal tangle. Initially, the world of care determines the way of being-with-others which exactly means that somebody is busy with others the same way as it is busy with tools and usable things or things "present at hand" (natural things).

The common world, being parallel to the world of care is interpreted by Heidegger in terms of "falling" to "them" and falling to the daily worldliness. That way, Heidegger outlines a way by which a care to being-with-others is by control.

Heidegger insists that a real care for others turns the relation to a world of care to a world of being-with-others. The "them" perceive the human being based on the daily worldliness thus as a worldly entity usable as a tool or as a natural thing. Such a daily way fails to distinct, or blurs the differences between the different ways of being (being in the world, being usable, being-with-others) and being as it can be. In the daily way of being-here, the pre ontological interpretation of the self is perceived as a way of being part of "them", i.e. the tendency to forget any diversity in the ways of being.

The "them" is a chatterer. A chatter is not only senseless speaking or not important, it is more, it is a phenomenon of being-here and is distinct from other forms of discussion (listening and silence) due to it being public and that it composes the understanding and the average tendency of the daily characterization. Exactly because chatter is formulated publicly from daily interests, it has the tendency to reduce speaking to something usable relating, as to any tool being used for any daily care, to other usable things. Chatter is definitely usable, especially by way of communicating the words of others, thus releasing the Da-sein from the responsibility and burden of self understanding and formulating.

This state is different with the depressive-Da-sein. The depressive-Da-sein, as aforesaid, in its state, is not interested to be with others. Notwithstanding existentially, it is also "being with", it withdraws from society and others, it does not feel their absence and is sufficient for itself. It releases itself from their grip; it does not listen to the noise and chatter.

Depressive-Da-sein is a weird bird, its "choice" is solitude, the possibility of "being-with-others" is not of interest to it, it is simply in no need, it does not want, is not interested. The being depressive is with itself and nothing more. We shall see that this trait of the being-depressive is being of use in the future. It is an important precondition of the depressive-Da-sein to return to itself as an authentic being, only for that ability to be distanced, it is silenced and listens which are authentic ways of speaking. For the time being I would just say that due to its solitude it is more attentive toward conscience then to the noise of "them


**23:05 Understanding**


A conscious state is one of the existential structures by which Da-Sein is extant.

That same originality with a conscious state is "understanding". Interpreting "understanding" as a basic existential, it means that this phenomenon is perceived as a basic way or as a basic conscious state of a Da-sein's being. On the other hand, understanding by meaning of one possibility from many of

260

cognition, as for example explanation, is interpreted as an existential that is derived from the first meaning of "understanding" which is one of the components of Da-Sein. In "understanding" of "for", i.e. for a purpose or aim, the sensibility is revealed. The revealing of "understanding", as the revealing of the "for" belongs to the completeness of being in the world.

Sensibility is the basis by which the world is revealed. To say that the "for" and the sensibility are being revealed in the Da-sein means that Da-sein is an entity which is someone being in the world, it is sensible to itself, i.e. it is an entity which its existence is of sensibility to it. The "for" is the same existential which implies on sensibility, we, for example, say "for what purpose are you doing it, what sense have your doings or you in your doings". The "for" and sensibility are linked to each other and are related to the Da-sein which ponders on its own existence. In "understanding" as an existential, in which we have ability, is not a "what" but a being as existence. The type of being of the Da-sein, as a possibility to be, is extant, existentially, in the "understanding". Da-sein is not something "present at hand" with the ability to do something as an addition; it is, essentially, a potential-possible being. In any event, Da-sein is what it can be.

The potentiality of Da-sein to be toward itself is for itself. The possibilities of being an existential are the most original and absolute way by which Da-sein is ontologically characterized. The basic phenomenon of seeing it as such is provided by the "understanding" as the ability to be.

In any event, Da-sein, in its essence as having a conscious state, has, already, positioned itself for defined possibilities. Da-sein is the possibility to be free for the potentiality of being which is its most. The possibility of its being is transparent for it in different

261

ways or levels. "Understanding" is the being of the potentiality of being' which is never 'not yet' "present at hand", it is never something "present at hand". In the "understanding", Da-sein 'knows' what it can be, i.e. what its potentiality to be is, what its ability is. The 'knowing' does not result from an intrinsic self perception, but belongs to the being in its essence, "understanding". By being in "understanding" it can get lost and fail in self understanding. I.e. because Da-sein is "understanding", and "understanding" is the ability of the Da-sein to be, it can fail in choosing its possibilities thus losing itself.

"Understanding" is the existential being of the potentiality to be a Da-sein, being in such a way that this being reveals to itself what it is able. As an ability to be, each being in- is a potentiality to be in the world. Not only the world as it is is being revealed as a significant possibility, but being inside the free world, this entity is free to its possibilities. "Understanding" projects the Da-sein's being also on the "for" as well as on its sensibility as a worldliness of its present world. Da-sein, as being thrown to its possibilities, is being thrown to a type of being which we call "projection". Each Da-sein as a Da-sein has already projected itself; and as long as it exists, Da-sein always and forever will understand itself in terms of possibilities. In projection, Da-sein is being thrown and projects forward its possibilities as its own. Due to the type of being which is established by the existential of the projection, Da-sein is always more than it actually is, as if someone will want to make an inventory list of himself with something in hand, writing the contents of its being, as if someone can do it. However, Da-sein is not more than what it is, the factually thrown being.

Heidegger tells us "be what you are", i.e. for the manic-depressive-being be a teacher. Michael Galvin emphasizes that "understanding" is authentic, evolved from oneself or not authentic. The non-authentic way is based on actuality, while the authentic state is based on possibilities or potentiality. Such authentic existence is to be aware to the sense of the worldliness'; such non-authentic existence is not to be aware to the sense of existence. The question should be: how such awareness is possible? To see oneself as having this ability, according to Heidegger, is the real way by which a one is aware of the self with sense. To see oneself only as an actual entity is always to see oneself as an object, hence something else than oneself. Therefore, the basis for authenticity is possibilities or potentiality, while the basis for non-authenticity is the actual. I am aware not only to what I am now but also to what I can be in the sense of being all that I am not. Although I understand that I am sitting now in front of my computer, I can imagine myself being in Jerusalem.

Let me ask, how is it that I can exist by way of having possibilities? And how is it different from my existence by way of being actual? How my actuality does make sense for me? And how my possibilities are making sense to me?

For a scientist, the facts are of interest to him and not the possibilities. A person committed an immoral act can understand that he had the possibility not to act as he did thus the bothering question on his part should be why did I do it? It is more real for him, than the simple fact of doing what he did. Shortly, my life has sense not only due to what it is but also, and primarily, due to what might have been and what may be. I am getting interested with the same mental qualifications that tell me only what is the possible, there is nothing in this mental activity to differentiate the possible from the actual.

Since a person lives a life in which actuality as well as possibilities is important, it seems obvious that a philosophy which gives accounts for both is important and thorough. One has to build a viewpoint that will take into account both realities. It is obvious that I have possible as well as actual life; in my life, the possibilities as well as the actuality are significant, one should show how the two are connected to each other, one has to describe the connections and relations between them.

Not only consciousness is aware of the two states but also our life is affected by such awareness. Heidegger describes it in a phenomenological way. Avoiding the negation of any of these states (actuality and possibilities), we should start our analysis by fully revealing their sense. Heidegger insists that the two states are primary (Being and Time page 133); meaning, that not one of them may be explained by the other, i.e. a reduction of one by other is not possible.

There is a need for a more generalized concept in order to explain the two. Such existential that unites them both is called "Care/ Sorge".

The "care" has to be exposed. The analysis has to begin with description of two ways of the being, the one being my actuality being exposed (State of mind: Befindlichkeit) and the other in which my possibilities are being exposed (Understanding: Verstehen); for Heidegger possibilities are more important than actuality; possibilities as well as actuality are equal and primary, still, possibility have higher priority over actuality.

Following the metaphysical tradition one has to say that actuality is more real or *concrete* than possibility. That is the base of metaphysics: it deals with "be"s (Seiende) and not with the sense of being (Sein). If a reality or actuality, in its narrow sense, is just the sum of all "be"s extant in the world, thus actuality is "more real" than possibilities. However, with Heidegger, possibilities, on the other hand, are more significant than actuality. It is important to remember that Heidegger investigates the sense of being, i.e. what is the sense of being. In such an investigation, possibilities are preferable to actuality. In his assertion that possibilities are preferable to actuality, Heidegger does not say that actuality does not matter, it does, in fact, to be aware to actuality is part from being authentic; we shall not want to contend that if someone is blind to reality then he is authentic. Actuality has the sense of the existential; it is also wrong to contend that the awareness to actuality creates non-authenticity. Actuality and possibilities are ways to explain Da-sein and its self awareness in the world.

## 23:20 A conscious state and actuality

Macquarrie and Robinson are the translators of "Being and Time" to English. They translate Befindlichkeit to something such as "conscious state"; perhaps it will be better to say "the state in which someone is".
I prefer the expression "a conscious state" which is, as aforesaid, is closer to my state. Heidegger says that this expression is a priori existential in which the Da-sein is always at a certain state or way.

What is the sense of the saying that I find myself in that or other state or way?

I find myself in the world without having been asked whether I would like to be in it; I did not choose to come into the world. I did not choose the circumstances under which I was born. I can even complain that it seems unfair that I was thrown to this world and that this situation is beyond my choosing. Therefore, I can complain about being manic-depressive and that it was beyond my choosing and that I did not want to be born under these circumstances of being manic-depressive-being; I have been, simply, thrown to the world under the circumstances of being sick. This is how destiny wanted it and I am in a situation which I did not choose. There is no choice; I am in a situation in which I exist. But I have to do my best under these circumstances, to get the best out of them. There are many things in my existence that cannot be changed; I can, in certain states, either to ignore them or to accept them in several ways; nevertheless, my actual state or my way is always there.

Heidegger denoted such way or state of consciousness as actuality, a conscious and actual state. He denotes three traits of this existential:

1) The exposure of my falling into the world or into certain conditions and circumstances which is beyond my control. This state suggests a position of someone in relation to the traits which restrict him in his existence.

2) The exposure of being in the world as a whole.

3) The revelation of the fact that whatever the Da-sein encounters in the world is important to it.

The term "disclosure" (Erchlossenheit) does not say "to be known as such thing or another". Therefore, when speak about disclosing the conscious and actual state of the Da-sein, we do not intend to these ways which disclose and unravel everything there is to know on the circumstances of Da-sein. A conscious state discloses or reveals the fact that Da-sein is in the world; but not what or what for. Therefore, there is always something unknown about my actual state in the world. Our states or ways disclose a lot about our position toward the inevitable in the world. I.e. for the depressive-being or the manic-depressive-being the fact that he is as such in the world exist or being revealed as well the position in which he can be in the world and the way by which he can exist. The disease is inevitable but what is indeed in our ability, is to choose to be in a certain position toward the world. Our ways never disclose the full sense of our existence. Often, our ways put us facing the inability to understand and comprehend the condition in which we exist.

Michael Galvin contends that terms as "destiny", "luck" etc. can never be understood by a rational investigation, but they are true positions of consciousness which we use for the saying the unspeakable or for the rational understanding. Notwithstanding destiny may not be with sense in terms of rational investigation of the causality, it can be of sense for us in the terms of what the sense of existence is. Destiny is significant as a trait of the way by which I exist.[19] One of the bothering questions one could ask oneself when we do not have control on circumstances and especially when we cannot understand, is: why me? One person

___

[19] A commentary on Heidegger's Being and Time, Michael Gelven, Northern Illinois University Press 1989. P.81

blessed with happy life and the other is cursed with an endless series of cruel fortunes. Ayub could have asked himself: why me? Why do I deserve all the blows hitting my head? On the other hand they say that Sophocles was blessed with happy life. If we cannot control the destiny of our life, how will we able to give them sense? The truth is that we cannot know why one person was blessed and the other cursed. The evil has it good and the just bad? We simply do not know why luck smiles to the happy and annoyed to the miserable. However, although we do not know the reasons for these things, we can and have to think about their sense. In order to do so, we have to understand that our sense of existing is understood only by the recognition that we are also free and given to the will of destiny. The way by which we exist in the world is characterized by how we adjust ourselves to the circumstances, easily or with difficulty. This is a kind of intentionality for the world. The understanding of how we adjust to the whole. Heidegger uses the word "Stimmung" (the way) also in a sense of "Gestimmtsein", i.e. he means that we should focus on the sense of being is to be, at least in part, without control on the circumstances, as I do not have control on the disease or on the fact that I got ill at all.

Ways, by Heidegger, are defined as independent from my choice and control.

The intention in "being by way of" is the way by which we find ourselves in a world which is not under our control. Therefore, we find ourselves already in ways or certain states; it is called Befindlichkeit, i.e. in a conscious state of how we find ourselves.

I found myself in New York in a state of manic-depressive. To ask "why me" is to confront the suffering inflicted by such understanding.

Heidegger contends that what makes the half-determined (for us), the free half-existence (ours) understood is the understanding that these ways or states are a priori, i.e. they are not available for accounting by any principle or power, but they are given basically by which we need to find the sense of us being in the world. It is their being not given to understanding which makes our existence understood.

To ask why me implies that there is a final answer as "God is trying you"; it is the wrong question to ask.

The right question is not why me, rather "how should I think about their sense". Heidegger gives us the basic principal to do just that, insisting that it is how we, already, find ourselves in the world (Befindlichkeit) and how we project our possibilities which are partly under our control; i.e. both are basically necessary to give sense to what we are. I find myself in a state in which I am a manic-depressive-being or similarly a depressive-being, this is, as aforesaid, a conscious state, i.e. I am aware to the state at which I was thrown; such a conscious state and the possibilities facing me give the sense to my being.

A conscious state and my possibilities are the way to be myself; i.e. the essential traits of my existence are mine. The manic-depressive disorder is mine and therefore it is mine or not, i.e. authentic or non-authentic. However, a conscious state is that same existential that exposes the Da-sein as accepting the authority of the world.

One of the aims of the analysis of a conscious act as an existential of a Da-sein is to show that when the Da-sein becomes aware of itself in the world (here), it is affected by unchangeable facts. Assuming that both, actuality and possibilities are of sense to the Da-sein, we have to account for how the Da-sein, in its existence, becomes aware of them.

The awareness of the Da-sein to an actual existence is due to the conscious state. The Da-sein's awareness of a possible existence or ways of existence is due to "understanding". Therefore, a conscious state is not only the way of being non-authentic, but it has to be, also, in an authentic state. The existential which establishes the sense of the world as it is, is a conscious state. Since each way or conscious state has to precede a fact, hence it is an existential and as such a priori. The existential conscious state does not only expose the Da-sein as it is in the world, but exposes it relating to the world.


## 23:35 Understanding and possibility


Heidegger's analysis of the "understanding" (Verstehen) is one of the most important analyses in "Being and Time".

"Being and Time" is an interpretation to the question of existence. "Understanding" is important because of:
1) It accounts for, out of the existential analysis, how the Da-sein is aware of its possibilities.
2) It provides the basis for Heidegger's theory of freedom.

In a preamble to everything, Heidegger contends that "understanding" is an existential. Therefore, as we have seen, it is a priori and exposes the way by which Da-sein exists. It does not tell us only, how we think, but also how we are.
270

"Understanding", primarily, exposes the Da-sein's structure of existence to itself, and only through such exposure, can the Da-sein use the existential as a cognitive function.

So, how "understanding" does expose to the Da-sein its way of existence?

It is by way of the Da-sein being able of "can be" or of "being what I can be". "To be what we can be" means that by my being as a human being, my ability to be is something of which I am aware.

My own existence is a possibility extended before me, which is present before me and precedes me, with which I am dealing and am interested in. I do not only exist, but my ability to exist as a possibility is part of the way of my existence.

Assuming that I am aware of my possibilities, how such awareness is possible?

Heidegger's answer is important: I know about possibilities because I have possibilities. According to Heidegger, the roots of the "understanding" are in "my ability to be" (Seinkoennen). The function of the "understanding" is in the projection, i.e. in being thrown forward. We, quasi, throw ourselves toward our possibilities.

In Heidegger's description of a Da-sein's awareness of how it is connected to the world, we shall remember that he describes such a connection as "ready at hand", i.e. something that is ready for use, meaning that Da-sein sees the world *for* its purpose.

"Seeing" the door as something for my use only at the instance of its opening reduces the door to something that exists for my sake. In order for the world to be at my service it has to be seen as presenting itself *for* the purpose of my doings. The world has sense as it presents itself available for my plans, my projects and my possibilities. Even seeing the world not as something "ready at hand" but as something "present at hand", it is still for my sake; this position is perceived, for example, for the increase of my knowledge. However, if Heidegger is right, then the world presents itself to us not as a simple and actual entity, rather as possible ways of usage.

The world is my project; in a certain sense, it is a type of a future world that has to be realized. By the same token, my disease is a fate fallen upon me, being my project; i.e. I have to see in which future world am I going to live. I need to realize one of my possibilities. So is also by me being manic-depressive, the "understanding" acts by projecting possibilities preceding Da-sein.

Da-sein is such because it has possibilities. The world presents the Da-sein with a series of service possibilities. Therefore, it does not present me only with actuality ("present at hand"). I consider possibilities since I am free. "Understanding" and it is important for me to emphasize again, acts by projecting possibilities. Projection is existential. Projecting forward the possibility of our existence is an essential trait of what we are. "Understanding" is like a flashlight illuminating the way ahead of us, ahead of the Da-sein. The metaphor of the flashlight has to be extended to include the "something" that is being illuminated and projected ahead of Da-sein is the Da-sein itself.

Husserl actually contends that Da-sein is merely its factuality, but it is merely "factually projected". "Factually projected" denotes its ontological state of the Da-sein having possibilities; the first term relates to its ontical existence of the Da-sein as "present at hand". Ontical presence at hand is limited to the actual, i.e. facts, which are observed separately from their possibilities, determine ontical cognition. However, ontological considerations must take possibilities into account.

For Heidegger, possibilities become accessible to the researcher not by pure cognition and not by experience, rather by the existential structure of the researcher himself. Possibilities are not something which we experience (we can experience only in actuality), they are also not pure thought (possibilities are not the result of a cognitive thinking, they rather enable it). Possibilities are part of the existence of the one who thinks. In order to be able to think about what can be, I have to be able to be.

Heidegger lays the foundations for his analysis of the sense of "understanding", he highlights the German use of "understanding" which means "being in control", I have control on my existence. Anyway, for me, the being-depressive has to be in control of its existence, it has to be the owner of its life and not to be dragged by its circumstances. It has control on its existence. We shall see that by Heidegger, "decisiveness" is an essential trait of an authentic existence. Now, we can also understand why Heidegger provides the seed for the interpretation of existentialism as "having courage to be".

The being-depressive is what it is since it has possibilities from which it is free to choose. It is courageous! It can wish to die, to be decisively ready for death, or and in particular, and here I, seemingly detaching from Heidegger, being a depressive-Da-sein, can, with the same decisiveness, confirm life and want to live thus being toward life. The depressive-being and the manic-depressive-being can choose the possibility to live and be a teacher!

I have said before that I am, seemingly, detaching from Heidegger because in my opinion, Heidegger finally confirms life because the Da-sein may not execute "it being toward death" and therefore says "yes" to life. We have determined, therefore, that cognitive capabilities of "understanding" are secondary to and based on the existential aspect.

"Understanding" functions through the projection of possibilities. The whole range of the Da-sein's possibilities was projected. I can think of possibilities since I have them a priori. Da-sein is "factically projected" more than being actual-factual. I am more my possibilities than my actuality. Let us go back, for a moment, to such an analysis in "Being and Time".


Heidegger explains how the Da-sein becomes aware of itself in the world. What has to be analyzed is the "here" (Da) in the Da-sein (Being here). Da-sein finds itself in the world in two ways:

1) By way of a conscious state, a way of existence which exposes for the Da-sein the fact of its existence as "factically projected". At such state, the Da-sein becomes aware of the world's givenness and its projection.

2) Through "understanding", a way of existence which exposes the Da-sein to its existence.

At this state the Da-sein becomes aware of its possibilities. These possibilities are always the possibilities of the Da-sein itself, or in our case of the being-depressive. Therefore, the existential sense of possibilities precedes the cognitive sense. Heidegger contends that the awareness of the Da-sein, through a conscious state, of its facticity and its awareness of it being through "understanding" are original or primary equally.

Me being in the world as it is and me existing by way of having possibilities are equally primary in my awareness of myself as a human being in the world. It is not possible for one to reduce the other. The extent of my freedom does not matter, nor the richness of my understanding of my ability to be in different ways, still, I was thrown onto the world and I am still facing the inevitable and the unchangeable (the fact of me being manic-depressive-being).

On the other hand, no matter the extent of me being determined by the facts and circumstances of me having been thrown onto the world, I cannot avoid my freedom or negating the reality of possibilities. What did Heidegger do when he has analyzed these two elements of the "here"? He described his interpretation of the way by which self awareness exposes the two ways of existence.

## 23:50 Anxiety

Being in the world is a structure which is basically complete. Let us ask how the totality of the complete structure which we have, thus far, investigated, will be defined in an ontological-existential way.

The answer is a uniting, basic and single phenomenon which is already extant in the whole or in the totality in such a way by which it provides the ontological basis for each element in the structure.

As a conscious state which will fulfill our methodological requirements, the phenomenon of anxiety will be a basis for the analysis. In our dealing with such conscious state and by the ontological characterization of what is being exposed in it, we will relate to the phenomenon of falling as our reference point.

Heidegger's research is about whether there is, existentially, an ontological unity or the being factual essentially belongs to an existential. Since the Da-sein, in its essence, is in a conscious state, it has a certain type of being by which it precedes itself being exposed to itself in its being thrown. However, being thrown, as a type of being, belongs to an entity which is, in any event, its own possibilities and it (Da-sein) exists in such a way by which it understands itself through its possibilities and their terms and projects itself toward them. To be at the side of the "ready at hand", i.e. at the side of other entities in the world, is, basically, to be in the world as well as being with others; and being in the world is, in any event, for itself. The self, anyway, is in approximation and mostly non-authentic, it is the "them-self".

Being in the world is always a fall. Therefore, the average daily of Da-sein may be defined as follows: "being in the world which is a fall and being exposed, thrown and projecting and for which the ability to be is the most for it and is of an interest for it, even if it is a being at the side of the 'world' and also being with others" (Being and Time page 225).

One possibility of being for a Da-sein is anxiety-together with Da-sein itself as being exposed to it and which provides the phenomenal basis to perceive the basic completeness of Da-sein.

The being of Da-sein exposes itself as "care" (Sorge). Should we investigate, so according to Heidegger, such basic phenomenon, we shall have to distinct it from another phenomenon of care as, for example, will, wish and urge. "Care" cannot be derived from such phenomena rather it establishes them.

"Care" (Sorge) is the existential that unites all the other existentials to one structure and therefore, provides the analysis for a basic ontology. In order to understand the importance of such unity, one needs to understand why it is essential to begin with. Moreover, one has to clarify why anxiety (Angst) is being used to the clarification of the function which unites the existential.

Why Heidegger, all the way up the end of the existential analysis, feels the need to base a single and uniting existential to be used as a base for the others?

There are two reasons for it; the first reason being that without a uniting existential, the analysis will be just a pile of incidental existentials. There is a need for a specific and unique existential that will focus on the Da-sein as Da-sein.

The second reason, which is more important, being that if there would not have been a unique and uniting existential, there would not be any reason for going beyond the list of existentials and there would not be any connection between the analysis of the daily life and its ontological base.

The ontological base of the Da-sein's existence, or, in our case, the existence of a manic-depressive-Da-sein, is *temporality*. Before we can expose the temporality as the being of the Da-sein, Da-sein has to be perceived in terms of its existence. There must be some trait of Da-sein that can be shown to be extant at the base of all existentials and as a single phenomenon may be exposed to the same type of investigation with other existentials.

All along the analysis, the investigations of the different existentials were expressed in a structure: what is the sense of being in such a way or another?

We have asked, for example, what is the sense of being in the world?

What is the sense of being with others?

If all of these different investigations have a common sense, if all of these different existentials have a sense beyond themselves, hence the important question is what the sense of being Da-sein is. The current task is to show that the previous analysis actually enables the consideration of what is the sense of being a Da-sein as Da-sein. The isolation of the uniting existential is of great importance for the matter of doing basic ontology.

How does Heidegger expose this term out from the other existentials? He, simply, examines the phenomenon of anxiety and shows that the uniting existential is "care".

Anxiety is interpreted as "escape from" and also "confront with" the self. What we would like to know is the sense of the self. Why examine the one phenomenon that leads us to escape from the very thing we want to understand, the self?

Heidegger answers that our escape reveals what we are escaping from. Taking an example by Michael Galvin, I am in a relationship which requires sacrifice from me, I am committed to my girlfriend and I recognize that I have to do something for her which I find hard to do. Let us assume that in a moment of weakness I distance myself, turn my back to my commitment.

This is a known human state. Now, let us assume that somebody will ask me to what I have turned my back, I would have known the answer. Actually, just for the reason of knowing to well what my commitments are, that I have fear from them. I do not turn my back to the commitments toward my girlfriend because I do not know them, rather because I do know them. Sometimes it is true that the authentic trait of something is surfacing only when

278

we are turning our back to it. As in every ontological analysis, the ontological interpretation of a Da-sein as "care", with all that we can earn from such interpretation, is far away from what is accessible to a pre ontological understanding of being or even from our authentic acquaintance with entities.

The Da-sein's analysis which continues on to the phenomenon of "care", has to prepare the way for the problematic of a basic ontology, i.e. for the question on the general sense of being. In order for us to turn our attention to it, in light of what we have earned from it, and go beyond the unique task of a priori, existential anthropology, we have to look back and get a penetrating look into the most authentic phenomenon which is linked to our leading question: the question of being.

One of the Da-sein's possibilities to be is to give authentic information on the Da-sein itself as an entity. Such information is possible by such exposure that belongs to the Da-sein and in which base there is a conscious state and understanding. The absorption of the Da-sein in "them" and in the 'world' shows something of an escape from oneself, from the self (of the Da-sein) as the authentic ability to be oneself. This phenomenon of the Da-sein of escape from itself and from its authenticity seems to be a suitable base for the continuation of our investigation. To bring yourself face to face with yourself is something which the Da-sein does not do when it escapes from itself. Only to the extent that Da-sein has brought itself ontologically before it through an exposure, it can escape from itself, i.e. from what it is escaping.

Anxiety works by way of existential examination which exposes the authentic structure of the self; this is the knowledge of the

279

self from which we escape; such escape or distancing is terrible. Therefore, such anxiety is, paradoxically, the turning back to ourselves; anxiety is exposing for us the initial and true view of unique trait of the self; through anxiety, we look ourselves straight in the eyes. At certain moments in our life, we can find strange feelings through which the familiar world loses it sense. At such moments, things which usually are familiar and related suddenly seem strange and weird. I live in Ramat Hasharon, a place in which I grew up and is well known to me and suddenly I can feel as a stranger, alienated, not at home. Most of us have felt at a certain time and in a certain place similar feelings. Sometimes, when we become aware of these experiences, we find ourselves pondering on our existence. We stop our daily activities and feel the need to ponder on our existence. We look at ourselves, suspend our consciousness from our daily life and feel as if we are strangers to ourselves. These experiences of weird feelings of strangeness, of not feeling at home, seem to have been always there with us, at the edge of our consciousness, ready to be expressed clearly. Even if we manage to put them to rest by other feelings, they are still there.

Heidegger considers such phenomenon as having an important sense for his analysis. This feeling is called "anxiety"; one may even say existential anxiety.

The reason for our interest in anxiety is for the shifting of our focus from our daily dealings, thus enabling us to ponder on our terrible existence.

By focusing our attention on our existence, we obtain valuable insight on the question of being, i.e. on the sense of being.

Heidegger will examine how the experience expresses itself. From the description of the phenomenon, Heidegger will obtain an existential and then will derive an ontological sense. Firstly, Heidegger examines the ontological description in order to see the way by which Da-sein exists. Later on, we could find out if such way of existence can enlighten us about the question of what is the sense of being. Having fear as opposed to anxiety is always from something specific, from some object, for example that dog in front of me.

Fear is "having fear from" which always reveals a specific threat approaching from a certain direction. The fear is from real things, something touchable, it can also be another Da-sein which is a part from the world in which the Da-sein lives. Somebody does not necessarily escape or turns his back from just a thing. One has to distinct fear from anxiety. We have fear from something specific in the world which arrives from a certain area which is near to us but can still keep its distance.

In a fall, Da-sein turns its back to itself, i.e. it is running away from itself by running to "them". Therefore, the self escaping in a fall is not an escape based on fear from entities in the world. The turning back on oneself is in the anxiety. To understand the idea of a Da-sein escaping from itself in a fall is to remember that to be in the world is a basic state of the Da-sein. The subject of the Da-sein's anxiety is being in the world as such.

The subject of our anxiety is not an entity in the world. We are anxious of something which is not defined. In such a state of non-definability it is not possible to decide which entity is threatening us; moreover, he also tells us that entities in the world are not relevant at all.

Nothing which is "present at hand" or "ready at hand" in the world is functioning as a thing of which we are anxious. Anxiety does not "see" that the threat is coming from a defined origin. The subject of our anxiety is characterized by the fact that the threat is not "located" anywhere. Anxiety does not know the subject of its anxiety. The subject of which someone is anxious expresses itself in nothing and from nowhere. The persistence on "nothing and nowhere in the world" is the phenomenon of the world as such is the subject of our anxiety. The worldliness of the world and the entities in the world are losing their sense. "Being in the world itself is the subject of our anxiety" ("Being and Time" page 232).

To be anxious reveals, basically and immediately, the world as a world. The world as a world is initially revealed by anxiety as a way of a conscious state.

Anxiety is not only of something, but as a conscious state, it is on something. With anxiety, the world cannot offer anything, it is senseless, the depressive-being can no longer get anything from the world, the world is senseless for him, i.e. it cannot offer him any sense, security or serenity; the depressive-being is anxious from the senseless world which reveals itself as impotent. Also, the "them" no longer offer him anything. Anxiety deprives the Da-sein of the authentic ability to be in the world. I.e. the Da-sein is anxious from being thrown, it is anxious to be authentic; it will rather fall into serenity and security which are offered by "them". Anxiety reveals to the Da-sein its being toward its most ability to be, i.e. it being free to choose to be itself and to take itself in its own hands.

Anxiety brings the Da-sein face to face with it being free, the authenticity of its being, and with such authenticity as its own possibility.

Anxiety turns the Da-sein into an individual that is capable of self understanding and of self throwing toward his possibilities. He is an individual since he feels the need to detach from "them".

As aforesaid, a conscious state expresses how someone is. With anxiety, someone feels not at home which also expresses the "nothing and nowhere". The "them" bring the Da-sein the serenity and the sense of security of being at home; however, when the Da-sein falls, anxiety brings it back from its fall in the 'world'. The daily acquaintance as whole is collapsing. "Being within" no longer brings with it an acquaintance with the world rather an existential state of "not being at home". Now, one can see phenomenologically the subject from which the fall as an escape is escaping. It does not escape from entities in the world; rather these are the subject to which the Da-sein is escaping.

In summary, in escaping there is a possibility of a different exposure since anxiety turns the Da-sein to an individual.

This phenomenon brings the Da-sein back from its fall and expresses the authenticity and non-authenticity as the possibilities of its being.

But of what am I anxious?

I cannot point on one object. In a case of fear, I know what will remove it. However, in a case of anxiety, I cannot point out exactly what it is that bothers me. What is the "nothingness" of which we are so anxious? What is the existential sense of "nothingness", "the not"?

The sense of the existential "nothingness" is that a human being by self pondering on his possibilities arrives to the insight of his end, i.e. he knows that he is going to die, not to be.

The strangeness of this feeling is not similar to any other human experience because all other forms of human experiences are understood by the continuous time in which the continuous existence plays a decisive role. But with death, or with the awareness of the senseless existence, we are aware of something different from any other experience.

The term "nothingness" means, therefore, something which has definitely an existential sense but it cannot be an object for any experience. A human being is suffering from some type of strange awareness when the possibility of the final end of his own consciousness comes to mind.

One has to understand that the term "death" is no replacement for "nothingness" because it is not the experience of death itself. Death is a type of experience thus one can have fear from, but to be aware of the possibility of not being anymore is something else all together which is more compatible with the meaning expressed by Heidegger.

Heidegger uses "nothingness" in order to represent an existential. "Nothingness" is exactly the awareness of being-able-to-not-being-anymore. I note that it is also the awareness of being insignificantly; so is the being-depressive becoming aware of him not having sense anymore.

The existential which causes us an awareness of nothingness is anxiety.

Anxiety is a conscious state; this means, as we have seen, that we are aware of an actual thing, of something which is actually, as

284

opposed to an understanding which causes awareness to what may be.

Due to anxiety, the Da-sein escapes from itself and deals with the daily "normal" life. The escape, which is a non-authentic existence, is a basic way of a Da-sein to be in the world.

Anxiety cannot be an incidental event, a single experience; rather it directs the Da-sein and exposes it to the anxiety of its existence.

Anxiety is a basic way extant at the base of the Da-sein's existence although it surfaces only seldom. However, the threat of anxiety is revealed and confirmed by the escape of the Da-sein from itself.

In a non-authentic existence, Da-sein is escaping from itself. The threat may not arrive from other beings in the world, since the Da-sein is, particularly, escaping to them, it escapes from itself to the daily life and to "them". The threat which is exposed by anxiety cannot hit the Da-sein from a certain direction or another, or from a certain thing or another, rather anxiety hits it only from within itself. Anxiety is from the final existence of the Da-sein in the world.


The senseless life of the being-depressive lack the "for", there is no purpose to his life, i.e. the world and life lack the "for" which is for a certain purpose, the world, in such state, loses its purpose and sense. However, as aforesaid, he has to find purpose for them.

Depressive-Da-sein feels senselessness in the world. He is frightened from the revelation that he has no "for what". He discovers the emptiness and senselessness as well as the feeling that there is no future. In anxiety, all the things in the world around it seem as irrelevant and senseless. The world seems as senseless. It seems that the frightful (death) cannot be something about which we can do anything. Each one of us feels, at such stage or another in life, the sense of impotency and helplessness of "I cannot do anything that will help me". The power of anxiety lies exactly at the place in which it brings things to insignificance and irrelevance and so expresses the fact that anxiety is not a thing, it is to be anxious of nothingness, of the negation or the senselessness and the absurdity of existenceIt is not possible to find the anxiety in the real world. The world cannot offer us anything; we also find that others cannot offer us anything. In anxiety, Da-sein feels discomfort in the world, it is not "at home" and said home is life, except for suddenly the recognition surfaces in the Da-sein of its finality. What seems earlier as familiar and with sense and relevance to our life is vanished; we, therefore, feel uncomfortable in the world in which, in the past, we have felt "at home".

Da-sein is anxious of its non-existence and therefore escapes from itself into the world of daily dealings and the sense which others give it. It deals with the daily life and its relations with others in order to escape the truth of the nothingness.

Da-sein is anxious of the emptiness and helplessness in its situation and therefore escapes to the daily world and others.

However, the depressive-Da-sein as an authentic being is not anxious of the "nothingness", of the "not", rather goes toward it, accepts it as it is, it is ready not to be here anymore.

I use the "nothingness" in two ways: firstly, a depressive-Da-sein discovers that its existence is absurd and that the world has *no* sense and secondly, the Da-sein in its depressive state does not have fear from going toward the possibility of *not* being anymore, i.e. to be nothing-*not*.

A depressive-Da-sein does not feel at home in the world, it feels uncomfortable to be in the world in which, in the past, it felt comfortable and which supposed to be its home in which he will find its serenity. It does not escape to the daily world; it does not escape from itself to the others.

A depressive-Da-sein as opposed to just Da-sein is, therefore, not anxious anymore of anxiety, it is not anxious not to be in the world and is not anxious of not being with others, i.e. it prefers to be in its solitude which is a social death.

It chooses to be authentic and not being anxious and by that return to itself as a depressive-Da-sein as it is. Van Gogh, as aforesaid, was anxious from the sadness that will last forever, there is nothing in the world that lasts forever, therefore, he is not anxious of a certain thing that is in the world; sadness is not something in the world but an intrinsic and natural structure for the Da-sein and particularly for the depressive-Da-sein.

If a Da-sein is anxious of its non-existence and escapes to the other, thus the depressive-Da-sein is not anxious, it overcame the anxiety of its existence and therefore, dialectically, it is not anxious of not being at all, it is not anxious of the "nothingness". It accepts it calmly.

The depressive-Da-sein is not anxious of being authentic as opposed to just a Da-sein that is anxious to look death in the eyes. Just a Da-sein is escaping the authenticity being expressed in death. It is afraid of the nothingness of the "not"; the depressive-Da-sein accepts it with open arms and even runs toward it.

Anxiety also has elements of understanding, but as long as we see anxiety as a conscious state it reveals us how we are in the world. How are we in the world?

We are being thrown to the world. Anxiety brings us face to face with this throw. Anxiety not only presents us as being actually in the world, rather, because the world exist while we are in a state of anxiety, it is alienated, we no longer feel at home. Anxiety, according to Heidegger, brings us to a state of individualism.

This awareness of my individualism reveals my possibilities to me. Actually, we understand now the subject of anxiety. We are anxious of our ability to be ourselves. Since anxiety brings us face to face with ourselves, we turn to be aware of the possibilities of what we can be or to the ways by which we can be: either be ourselves or lose ourselves in the consolation by "them".

We can get lost in the serenity and daily life, we can alienate ourselves, avoid the self confrontation, however with anxiety, we cannot avoid ourselves although we can distance from the confrontation which is always there. This is anxiety; it is the unpleasant awareness of the self to be authentic or non-authentic. Heidegger emphasizes that the primary sense of anxiety is the feeling of not being at home, i.e. I interpret it as being not at home with yourself as if you are a stranger to yourself.

As we have seen, the non-authenticity of them-self causes us to feel comfortable in the non-scrutinized, lacking awareness life of the "them", i.e. their world is where we feel at home. However, we lose that feeling of being at home with them while having anxiety. Now, while having my moments of anxiety and not feeling at home, I am forced to confront myself and look myself in the eyes. Due to the fact that more than any other existential, anxiety focuses on the state of my being, Heidegger considers it a tool for the exposure of the basic existential of the Da-sein. He shows that anxiety can reveal something that many other experiences cannot: awareness can turn into a self awareness as itself. The purpose of the existential analysis of anxiety is to show that the primary existential of Da-sein is "care" (Sorge).

## 00:05 Being caring

Anxiety as a conscious state is a way of being in the world; that, of which we are anxious and turn our eyes from it, is being in the world; that of which we are anxious is the potentiality of being in the world.

We have said that all the existentials which we discussed so far are united to become one which is "care"; now, we have to see how to characterize it. Da-sein is an entity which its being is of interest to it, i.e. it is interested in the way by which it is in the world and it cares about how it is in the world.
The term "interest" becomes clear in a state of understanding-of understanding as a self projection toward its potentiality to be. Such potentiality is what every Da-sein as it is, is for. In any event, Da-sein has already equalized itself, in its being, with its possibilities.

Being free for your potentiality which is your most to be, as well as the possibility to be authentic or non-authentic, seems, together with its originality, the state of being anxious.

Ontologically seen, to be toward the potentiality which is your most to be, means that in any event, Da-sein precedes itself already; i.e. forward, to itself in its being. Da-sein is always farther
289

from itself, beyond the-, as a being toward the potentiality of being as itself.

This structure of being which belongs to the essence "interest", is called "to precede yourself" of a Da-sein. "To precede yourself" denotes being in the world. To the being in the world belongs the fact that it is given to itself, i.e. in any event, Da-sein is already been thrown to the world. The desertion of the Da-sein of itself is seen in anxiety. Therefore, "to precede yourself" means "precedes yourself which is already a being in the world". This term, in simple words, means that to begin with, Da-sein finds itself already in the world; it is already a being in the world; now, it has possibilities that are potential for it, i.e. it is free to be as it can be; the potential possibilities are in front of it, i.e. it is free to be as it can be; the potential possibilities are there in front of it, i.e. in the future.

We have seen that the structure of worldliness in which there are relations of sense is linked to the "in order to" which in return is linked to the "for" of the Da-sein as "care" and therefore, this structure gives us the complete structure of the Da-sein. Existence is always a factual being as projected.

"Care" as "precedes itself which is already there (being) in the world beside other entities" includes also, in its essence, its fall and it being beside these things which are ready at hand (which are always in order to-) in a world which cares about them, it deals itself with them.

The formal and existential totality of the complete structure of the Da-sein has to be perceived as follows: the being of the Da-sein says that being by itself which is already in the world as being beside (entities which it meets in the world). Such being fills the sense of the term "care" (Sorge), which is used by an ontological-

290

existential way. Since being in the world is in its essence "care", the being beside "the ready at hand" can be understood from our previous analysis as care, i.e. the Da-sein cares about entities which are beside it in the world as well as it cares about being with others, it cares about others being beside it which such being is called by Heidegger solicitude.

To be beside something means to care because it is defined, by its structure of "care" as a way of being in-. I.e. concern is possible if there is "care". Not only does "Care" characterizes existential as detached from a fall or as factual being, on the contrary, it "embraces" their unity by which it is characterized.

The ontological-existential condition of the possibility to be free for your authentic possibilities is in preceding yourself as being toward the possibilities which is your most, i.e. toward your potentiality. To the extent of this being is toward its potentiality which is characterized by freedom, Da-sein can behave toward its possibilities non-volitionally or against its will; it can be non-authentic and factually, it is not authentic most of the time and in most cases.

The authenticity of the "for", i.e. for the realization of some purpose which is a possibility, can be taken away from it; the projection of your potentiality to be the most you was deserted in favor of "them". Therefore, when we talk about being ahead of yourself, the "yourself" whom we have in mind is, in any event, the self of the them-self. Also with the non-authenticity, Da-sein remains in its essence ahead of itself the same as a Da-sein that is escaping from itself while falling, still shows to be in a state of being of an entity for which such being is of interest.

"Care", therefore, is the being of the Da-sein. This is the understanding that everything being done by somebody can be

291

interpreted as expressing some kind of "care". When I self reflect, I discover that I am focused on my concern, my interests, my excitements, my fears, my disappointments etc.; all these things can be seen as a type of care. The depressive-being has self awareness of self care, he is concerned about his state, he is concerned about the senselessness in his situation, he is concerned about how he is, he is concerned about his being and in particular about his existence, he mourns himself. Mourning is a type of care for somebody who is no more. Such things strengthen his uniqueness and individuality.

The analysis of the fall has shown that the Da-sein turns its back to himself through the interests and the concerns in the non-authentic world of "them". Indirectly, the fall of the Da-sein reveals care of the Da-sein for itself. The fall revealed all of this through the recognition that the turning of the back to yourself is a type of involvement in the world of the them-self, i.e. the self is an integral part of them and their world. In such involvement of the Da-sein with "them", there is no possibility for the Da-sein to ponder on it. When the Da-sein enters a state or a certain way where such involvement is no longer simple, then it is forced to ponder on its role in the world.

The feeling of "at home" with "them" is lost. In such a state of alienation, the Da-sein is coming back to itself. Anxiety, as I have said, makes the Da-sein an individual by pushing it away from the non-authentic self and isolating it.

Under this context, for me, the depressive-Da-sein is pushed, due to its situation, into a state of loneliness and seclusion in which it draws away from the known world of "them" which no longer brings it solace and is forced to cope with itself; it does not have a choice, while in its loneliness, it is forced to look itself in the eyes

292

and examine itself and its possibilities; this is the way by which it ponders on it being in existence. The analysis of anxiety focuses our attention on the loneliness of the Da-sein, thus preparing the stage for the understanding of Da-sein as Da-sein. The analysis of the Da-sein is prepared.

The first series of existentials (to be in the world, to be with and to be yourself) deals with the way by which Da-sein is dealing with things which are not itself. When the analysis approaches the essence of the Da-sein as such, three existentials stand out above the others: a conscious state, understanding and fall.
The first which reveals the self is a conscious state; it expresses the way by which someone "is" actually (the way of the actual).
The second existential to reveal the self is "understanding", it expresses the ways by which we can be (the way of the possibilities).
The third existential is the fall which expresses the ways by which someone is hiding behind "them", the non-authentic existence.

"Understanding": in the analysis of understanding, I have said that its main trait is the projection of possibilities ahead of me, preceding the-, Da-sein. When applied to the sense of self, understanding projects ahead of the Da-sein the possibilities available to it.
Da-sein is aware of the state of authenticity in which my being is getting sense, or of a state of non-authenticity in which their being has sense, not mine. Heidegger calls such a structure in which the sense of being is of interest for the Da-sein, "to be ahead of itself".

A conscious state: the being which is ahead of itself is not an incidental freedom to live by anyway we wish. My world has limits. Actually, there are many things which I cannot overcome. Remembering the analysis of a conscious state, one needs to add to the aforementioned description that someone is already being projected to a world in which he has very little to do or say. The Da-sein's trait is, therefore, not the simplicity of being ahead of yourself, rather being ahead of yourself in the world.

The sense of all this is that not only do I have possibilities, but I also am aware of the limits of my actual. Existence is always a conscious state, this is how I was projected or thrown onto this world under set terms and conditions, hence "understanding" is always a conscious state.

Fall: in addition to the traits of understanding and conscious state, Da-sein as Da-sein is usually dealing with the daily world in which it lives non-authentically, this is the sense of falling; therefore, one must add it to the general trait of the Da-sein as Da-sein.

All of the above together characterize the Da-sein as 'being ahead of oneself already in the world as being beside entities which we meet in the world' which means "care". The "ahead of yourself" denotes the ontological characterization of existence in the sense of being projected toward possibilities; Da-sein is never here and now as a thing, rather always there in the outside ahead of itself or transcendental to itself linked as much as it can be, i.e. always linking itself to the possibilities of its existence. Since "care" can also be a non-authentic existence, thus in such case, it is projected to them-self.

How anxiety does show the "ahead of itself" of the "care" structure? What is the subject of its anxiety, i.e. the ability of the Da-sein to be its most?

At the same time, anxiety causes the ability to be enabled only to a being that has already been projected to the world. The frightened shows himself as being projected in the world. The "already" denotes the fact of it being projected; already living in the world. Da-sein in a state of "being beside entities which it meets in the world" is escaping by anxiety. It falls into a state in which it loses itself to things (also other Da-seins) beside it. All the existentials which are used to the description of the Da-sein itself converge or are based on "care".

## The time 00:15 Death

We use every protection and means of the mind to avoid the question of death; however, when it arrives we are forced to confront it.

In order for us to neutralize death and as part of the effort to avoid it we have invented Medicine, the next world and the written word. Every human being dies his own death. One cannot share death with somebody else. Death arrives very often, nevertheless, it meets a human being only once in a lifetime; its uniqueness makes it the subject of Heidegger's research. Actually, the perspective that is given by death to the human state is the perspective by which we evaluate and interpret life.

We, for example, ask: should we die today, what have we accomplished in our life, or we would say: we want to accomplish so and so until the day we die or we would wonder whether our life were worth living. We all know that a day would come and all of us will die. However, the complete sense of this knowing escapes our awareness so that even incidental insights on its true traits are shocking us. The terrible certainty of ceasing to be changes our consciousness. We know for certain that we will die, we simply do not know when. Why such ignorance of when death will come, releases us from the tragedy of death? Is it possible that such ignorance of the when death will come is cheating us into evading the inevitable?

Maybe the fact that we do not altogether understand that we are going to die; maybe the love of life or the comfort and serenity of self deceit is keeping us from understanding what it means to be something which, one day, will cease to exist.

The purpose of Heidegger's investigation is to find what the sense of being is (Sinn von sein: "the sense of being"). Since as human beings we will die someday, the sense of being is affected by our awareness of what it means not to be. Every human being dies his own death. However, it is not obvious that he lived his life. We often say that there are people maybe most of them that do not live their own life. On the other hand somebody cannot die the death of the other. It is clear that by dying, somebody is confronting his true authentic self, even if it is for a short moment, we find out that we are going to die alone.

The richness of the existential sense of death is what brings Heidegger to investigate the phenomenon in "Being and Time". As with the rest of the existentials, the analysis of death thrives to explain the ontological problem.

Therefore, the significant question asked by Heidegger is what death can tell us about the basic ontological investigation of the sense of being?

According to Heidegger, the most significant aspect of the phenomenon of death is that somebody's awareness of death can focus his attention on the self as belonging to the individual Da-sein, i.e. the authentic self. The existential analysis, as a preparation act, was the analysis of the non-authentic self or of the Da-sein which was not diagnosed, i.e. the traits of the self which are not authentic or non-authentic ways.

So far, we have learned, in a negative way, certain aspects of the authentic self, we have learned that the non-authenticity is characterized by the them-self. Before it will be possible to analyze the sense of being, the analysis of Da-sein has to be analyzed positively, i.e. what does it mean, positively, to be an authentic Da-sein. We will achieve this by exposing how the Da-sein abandoned its awareness of its own death by the them-self.

An authentic existence is characterized by the awareness of the sense of being. I.e. someone who exists authentically has to have ontological awareness. A non-authentic existence is a way by which someone has forgotten or is hiding what is the sense of being. In a non-authentic existence, the ontological awareness becomes fuzzy by "them". Also in death, the them-self are trying to evade the confrontation with the question of being.

The awareness of death, in any way, removes the cloud, then, there has to be something in the phenomenon which focuses our attention on the ontological question of what is on sense of being. Another significant point which Heidegger denotes is that death gives us a full or complete account of human existence because we see the human existence as starting with birth and ending with death, thus death is considered the aspect through which the complete human existence can be seen.

What is significant in Heidegger's analysis is not how someone actually feels at the moment of his death; rather what the sense of the arrival of death tells somebody about the completeness of his life. The fact that I, as somebody healthy, can understand that one day I shall die, provides me enough speculative material for the achievement of such insights.

Epicurus contended that death will never confront us because as long as we exist, it does not and when it does, then we do not. The dilemma is real. If only death could give us the complete aspect of human existence, then how it can, as an existential, be understood?

Heidegger puts it in these terms: as long as Da-sein exists, thus not all of its possibilities were understood as a whole. At the moment of its death, the Da-sein does not exist anymore. Therefore, it seems that a whole aspect of a Da-sein is not possible. The complete picture of what the sense of human being's existence is can be perceived only when all the possibilities including the ways of existence have been realized. It can be completed only when our life will end. However, at that time we can no longer ponder on the completeness of the picture.

One way to handle the dilemma is to analyze the death of others. We see others die, and assuming that others who have died are as we are, we simply "put ourselves" in their shoes. Such an experience is not acceptable by Heidegger. According to his analysis, someone cannot understand the sense of death by experiencing a death of another. Being and Time intends to show that such understanding of death by another is not possible.

According to Heidegger, the key to solving the dilemma is embedded in the understanding the nature of the "not yet" component which is linked to the Da-sein's existence. How should we understand the "not yet"? Part of the dilemma, as we have described it, is embedded in the fact that there is something in the Da-sein's existence which is unavoidable, i.e. something that did not yet happen but it will. Each one of us has a future which remains hidden and is not yet open for investigation. Heidegger contends that if such component of "not yet" is perceived as existential, then the dilemma will be solved and the Da-sein will be able to be perceived as a whole.

The question, therefore, is: how should the "not yet" component of the human being be interpreted?

The "not yet" component of the human existence is something that is already there. Da-sein, in its natural origin, is already "not yet". Although we have already examined this trait in our analysis of understanding as a projection of possibilities, Heidegger focuses his attention, in such case, on death. Da-sein is already "not yet". The aspect which we are looking for necessarily includes the end of Da-sein. We wish to understand the full existence, i.e. the complete, at its end.

The distinction which Heidegger makes which enables such completeness to be available for investigation is: somebody does not actually have to reach his end in order for him to understand that he will reach it. The aspect is not reached by being at end rather by "being toward end" (Sein zum Ende), which means that my awareness of me going to die suffice to enable me the aspect of completeness. I need not actually dying in order to see my end.

One will, for some reason, contend that someone has to actually die in order to perceive the aspect by which it is necessary to understand existence completely or fully. After all, we do not seek our actual life rather the fullness of its possibilities. We are not interested in experiences, also not in experiencing death, rather in the universal awareness of Da-sein of the possibility of not being anymore. It provides us the ultimate aspect, not because a death of someone puts an end to experiencing and by that actually limits the actual life of a particular Da-sein, but because the Da-sein's awareness of going to die means that the Da-sein's existence is limited as such. Actually, if someone could be, by some way, aware of the experience of death, such knowledge will not limit someone's way of existence more than someone's awareness of him going to die. Therefore, someone's awareness of him going toward the end provides the investigation with the full aspect which is necessary for the perception of the full Da-sein.

**00:20 Preliminary discussion on the ontological-existential structure of death.**

So far, I have tried and I will continue to try to show that the Da-sein's structure is similar to the being-depressive's structure and even realizes it in the most authentic way.

I suggest reading this part with the horizon of the depressive being. In this part, Heidegger wishes to interpret the phenomenon of death as being toward the end. We have seen that "care" is the basic state of Da-sein.
The ontological sense of the term "care" was set by the definition: "being already ahead (in front) of oneself in the world as being

beside entities which we meet in the world". In this term, the basic traits of the Da-sein's being are expressed: existence as ahead of itself, being factual, being already in-, falling in being beside. If indeed death uniquely belongs to being Da-sein, thus death (or being toward end) has to be defined in terms of these traits.

Firstly, so according to Heidegger, we have to clarify, initially, how the Da-sein's existence, the fact of it being projected and its fall are being revealed in the phenomenon of death. Being at end causes, existentially, being toward end. Death is something that stands or is in front of us, something that is threatened and imminent. However, there are many things that can be threatening for the Da-sein as being in the world.

The trait of a threat is not unique to death. On the contrary, such interpretation can even lead us to assume that death has to be understood under terms of any threatening event which we experience in our surrounding. For example, a storm, the renovation of the house or even the arrival of a friend can be threatened; such entities are something "present at hand", "ready at hand" and here with us. The threatening death is not a being of such type. Death is a possibility of being which Da-sein itself in any event has to take upon itself. With death, Da-sein is facing itself with the potentiality which is its most to be. This is a possibility of which the interest is not other than being of the Da-sein in the world.

The death of Da-sein is the possibility of not-able-to-be-here-anymore; in this context, the being-depressive, more than anybody else, can say to itself, in all honesty and authenticity, "I cannot be here anymore". If Da-sein faces itself with such possibility, it is committed fully to the potentiality which is its

301

most to be. While it faces itself in such a way, its links to other Da-seins are cancelled. Since the depressive-Da-sein secludes in its house thus it easier for it than it is for other "just" Da-seins to cancel its links with "them" and therefore be an individual and to look directly toward the potentiality which is its most to be. Such possibility which is its most to be and which is not linked to another Da-sein is also the superior one.

As the potentiality of being, Da-sein cannot bypass or overrun the possibility of death. Death is the absolute not enabled possibility of Da-sein. Death reveals itself as such possibility which you're the most which is not linked to others and which cannot be bypassed; as such, death is something threatening in a unique way. Its existential possibility is based on the fact that Da-sein in its essence is being exposed to itself toward itself. As a phenomenon, being toward the end becomes simpler more as being toward such unique possibility of Da-sein. Most of the time, Da-sein does not have theoretical or clear knowledge of the fact that it already has been delivered to death and that death, therefore, belongs to being in the world.

Being thrown to death reveals itself to Da-sein in an impressive and basic form through a conscious state of "anxiety". Anxiety from death is an anxiety from the potentiality of being yours the most which is not related and cannot be circumventable. This, of which we are anxious, is the being in the world itself. This, of which someone is anxious, is simply the potentiality of Da-sein to be. Such anxiety is not something incidental or a moment of weakness in a certain individual; but as a basic conscious state, it is equal to the exposure of the fact that Da-sein exists as a being which is being thrown toward the end. Therefore, the existential concept of death is revealed as a being which is being thrown toward the potentiality which is its most. Being toward end is not a momentary position; it belongs, in its essence, to the Da-sein's projection which reveals itself in a conscious state.

Most of the time, Da-sein hides its being toward death, escapes it. Factually, Da-sein is dying as long as it exists, however, most of the time it does by falling. In falling, and in escaping from the feeling "not at home", falling reveals itself which is escaping from the being toward your death. Existence, being thrown and falling characterize the being toward end, thus are fundamental to the existential perception of death. In regard to the ontological possibility, death is at the base of "care". "Care" as I have said, is a 'being preceding itself, already in the world beside things which we meet in the world', i.e. Da-sein is ahead of itself, in the possibility which precedes its death-self which is already in the world with possibilities to be toward death, toward the end. However, if death belongs, in its base and essence to it being a Da-sein, hence it has, also, to be presented in the daily life even if in a non-elegant way.

**00:25 Being toward death and the daily life of Da-sein.**

In being toward death, Da-sein brings itself toward itself in the uniqueness of the potentiality of being. However, the self of the daily life is "them". The "them" is established in the way by which things are publicly interpreted which expresses itself in a futile chatter. Futile chatter, therefore, has to express the way by which the daily Da-sein interprets it being toward death. The basis for any interpretation by an action of understanding is always accompanied by a conscious state. So now, one has to ask how being toward death is being revealed by a type of understanding which, in addition to a conscious state, is hidden in the futile chatter by the "them"; how "them" bring themselves to an understanding toward the possibility which is yours the most, which is not connected to others and which is not circumventable?

Publicly, while being one with another in the daily life, death is 'known' to be an incident and trouble that happens all the time. Somebody dies; he can be a neighbor or a stranger. We meet death as a known event which happens in the world. As such, it remains unrecognizable as something we meet in the daily life. It is unapparent. The "them" already arrange for interpretation of such event. "Them", for example, say "a day will come and also I will die but at this moment it is not relevant to me".

The analysis of 'somebody died' reveals unequivocally the type of being which belongs to the being toward the daily death. By such way of dialogue, death is understood as something undefined which, above all, must come sometime or another, however, it is not "present at hand" for me thus not being a threat. The expression "somebody died" spreads the opinion that what arrives through death is their death. In no event it is not me and that 'somebody' turns into nobody.

Death, certainly, is likened to an event arriving to Da-sein but it belongs to a certain 'nobody'. A futile chatter is always fuzzy, so is the talking about death is fuzzy. Death, which is principally mine

304

so that nobody can represent me by dying himself, is being met by somebody else, not me. It is an 'event' that always takes place. Death is being perceived as something actual and its possible characterization is hidden. By this fuzziness, Da-sein is in a position in which it losses itself to "them" in regard of its unique potentiality of being which belongs to itself.

The "them" grants its agreement and confirmation by which it strengthens the temptation of the Da-sein to hide from itself its ability to be toward death. The hiding from death controls the daily life by way of being-one-with-another, the neighbor speaks of the "he who died" and convinces himself that he will return immediately to the comforting serenity in his daily life. By such way, the "them" provides permanent serenity in front of death. It is well known that to think about death is a sign of cowardliness, weakness and escapism. The "them" does not give us the courage to think on death, and again under this context, one has to remind that the being-depressive which turn its back to "them" indeed thinks courageously about death. "Them" have already decided for the Da-sein in which conscious state it should be in order for it to think about death. The indifference of the "them" in front of death alienates the Da-sein from its ability to be toward death and from the fact that death is an unavoidable possibility for me.

However, temptation, indifference and alienation are signs of the being called by Heidegger as the "fall". In falling, the being toward the daily death is by constantly escaping it. The being toward end has the form of escaping from it, i.e. to give it new explanations, a non-understanding of it and hiding it. As a fact, the death of Da-sein is already done, i.e. it is already toward the end but it hides this fact from itself with their help. Also in the daily average life, the ability which is yours the most and which is not connected to

305

another is of interest to the Da-sein, but it is serene and indifferent as to its ability to be in its existence; to be toward such possibility, as an existing being, coming face to face with the absolute non-possibility of existence. As aforesaid, being toward death is based on "care". Da-sein as being thrown to the world had already been delivered to its death. In being toward death, Da-sein is factually and permanently dead as long as it did not yet arrive at its real death. When Heidegger says that Da-sein is factually dead, he also says that by being toward death, it made up its mind, i.e. chose a certain way or another. The daily fall as an escape from death is a non-authentic way to be toward death; however the non-authenticity is based on the possibility of authenticity.

**00:30 The ontological sense of death.**

The account which is given by Heidegger on the ontological viewpoint on death may be divided into four parts:
1) The analysis of death in terms of the three aspects of the Da-sein's exposure; existential, factual being as being thrown and fall.
2) An account on how the daily them-self keep us from a proper understanding of the importance of death.
3) An account on the "certainty" of death.
4) The sense of the authentic understanding of what it means to "going to die" or "being toward death".

In more detail:
1) How the existential which is the "I" being toward my death is ontological?

306

Heidegger follows the structure of the revealing; Da-sein is being revealed through its existential- its existence, a factual being as being thrown and fall.

A) What does the Da-sein's existential tell us about death?

As aforesaid, the existential is provided by the "understanding" which is the projection of possibilities. Death is certainly a possibility of Da-sein; indeed, as we have seen, it is a possibility which focuses on the being of Da-sein. We focus on the being of Da-sein in three ways:

1) We see that death is my death. Only I shall die my own death. If there is something which is totally mine, it is my death.

2) Being my death, it is impossible to be shared with another. Only I know the meaning of being toward my own death.

3) And finally, the projection of the possibility of death presents me with death as something from which I cannot escape. This is an unavoidable possibility.

B) The revealing of Da-sein, as we have seen, is never limited to what the understanding can project as a possibility. There is always also the component of a conscious state. What does the conscious state tell us about death?

First of all, since the main trait of a conscious state is the exposure of which cannot be changed in us, we arrive at the recognition that death is something not chosen by us, it is enforced upon us, or in existential terms, we are being thrown into it. The being thrown of the Da-sein reveals itself in our consciousness of us going to die. The way by which it is revealed to us is anxiety. It has to be clear that only because everyone dies it does not mean that everyone perceives the sense of going toward death or going to die. Moreover, it does not mean that the one who experienced being beside death, necessarily experienced anxiety as such conscious state which expresses the revealing of what it means to be toward death.

As previously mentioned, anxiety confronts us with ourselves. It is not the fear from death. Actually, the description given to such way suggests more alienation toward the existence of somebody in comparison with the known world. Anxiety is that same conscious state that reveals to the Da-sein that it is going to die. Only through a subtle awareness of anxiety, the sense of a factual being of death is being revealed.

C) Loyal to the structure of the revealing, the last trait of the sense of death is in the fall.

According to Heidegger, Da-sein tries to escape the confrontation with the sense of death. It does not say that the them-self pretend as if death does not exist, also not that someone is trying to avoid situations that may bring an incidental death. Fall relates to the Da-sein's tendency to exist non-authentically with the them-self. The them-self (the crowd) connive, by different ways, to avoid the true understanding of what the sense of dying is.

The central point of this interpretation is that the three aspects of the structure of exposure have shown that sense of Da-sein is "care". By that same interpretation, we have shown that the sense of death is also based on "care".

2) At 00:25, we have seen how the daily life of the Da-sein perceives death through "them", and how the non-authentic interprets death. Especially, the them-self interprets death in such

a form that will convince us that the death is not really ours. The them-self try to avoid any type of awareness or experience which cannot be joint with others. The technique by which the them-self tempt consciousness to believe that death is not something which is, mainly, ours, is to always relate to death as actual and not as a possibility: "he is actually dead, not you".

For Heidegger, as aforesaid, the possibility is more important than the actual. Relating to death only as an actual and never as a possibility, I will never be able to ponder on my own death. As long as I am conscious, the actual death belongs to someone else.

Only others actually died; therefore, for death to be of sense to me, it has to be a possibility. The them-self, on the other hand, always tend to consider the actual more than the possibility.

Death, from a non-authentic point of view, always seems as something actual, thus the feeling of inconvenience present in the awareness of death is such of fear of something, which is actually there.

The non-authentic way, which reveals death, is fear, while the authentic way focuses not on the fear from an actual event, rather on the possibility of a way of anxiety. Anxiety is not aware of something actual; on the contrary, it is something that focuses out attention on the possibility. Fear, on the other hand, has always a defined object. All this shows that I cannot fear from my own death. I have to have fear from something actual. My own death is not something actual, if it would be actual, I could not have fear, therefore, when I fear death, I fear somebody else's death.

To be anxious, on the other hand, is the inconvenient awareness of my possibility to die. The strategy of the them-self is their effort to cover the authentic understanding of death, i.e. to relate to death as an event or an object, which is feared from. The self, in its fear from death as an event, avoids the full understanding that it, itself, may not being or cease to be.

The Da-sein's fall reveals that non-authentic existence is escaping from death. By the description of the non-authentic way of the Da-sein as escaping from death, Heidegger does not determine that the natural and usual tendency of someone to avoid death is not authentic. Again, we do not speak of the circumstances or the conditions of an actual event of death, rather of the meaning to someone of knowing about death as a possibility. What is non-authentic is not to avoid the actual experience of death, rather to avoid the sense of our ability no to be.

3) Before we turn to the authentic account on death, something has to be said on Heidegger's interpretation of the certainty of death. The daily life interprets the certainty of death in an empiric way. We have an empiric certainty in death. However, what is empirically known is limited and being determined by "the when?" However "the when?" of death is unknown. Therefore, the rigidity of the unavoidable in death is softened by the uncertainty of "the when?" The them-self cover the full sense of an authentic understanding. The them-self is clever enough in its daring trial to negate the non-avoidance and the certainty of death; however, it covers the power of such awareness under the uncertainty on the timing of our death. The daily sentence "I will die someday" can become authentic only when the last word will be detached and the sentence becomes "I will die"! We have seen how someone avoids the awareness of the sense of death by using the daily point of view. Now it is possible to turn to the authentic way by which the sense of being toward death is.

4) The key to the understanding of Heidegger's interpretation of being toward an authentic death is to get to know the problem developed by him. As aforesaid, the authentic awareness of death not only emphasizes that we are those who die, i.e. the death is mine, and not of the them-self, it also emphasizes that we should not consider death as an actual event rather always as a possibility of us being. The difficulty is apparent: how can we be toward something, for example, how can we go and do something unless we look forward to an actualization of the event or the experience?

Heidegger emphasizes that to see death as an actual future is a non-authentic viewpoint of death. However, he described the authentic viewpoint as "to be toward the possibility"! Can such an expression be of sense only as a result of the interpretation of expecting an actualization of something?

The question may also be phrased as how do we interpret "going to die" as something which we do not want to become actual rather to keep it with sense as a possibility?

The answer lies with a proper understanding of what the sense of the term "to be toward a possibility". From the beginning, we know that to be toward a possibility cannot be interpreted as "being toward actuality" of something. What can it be? Heidegger makes a distinction of importance not only to his current discussion on death, rather also to his late development of time as being of a Da-sein.

There are two ways, he contends, of "being toward something" (i.e. there are two ways by which someone can go toward something). To expect something as actual, an even that will come, means expecting it (Erwarten); however to expect something as a possible way to be is Vorlaufen. The translation cannot give us the exact meaning. Vorlaufen carries in itself the sense of "running toward" or "running into", while Erwarten means to wait passively. The distinction arrived from the analysis of how someone is thinking about death.

Heidegger is right in contending that death has no sense for me in respect of how do I see life. There are two possibilities to be and not to be. To know that it is possible not to be focuses our attention on the possibility of a being that can be, i.e. to be. To expect (Vorlaufen) death, not as an actuality, rather as a possibility, is to focus our attention on being that can be. We may ask two questions: what is the sense of being? And what is the sense of not being? If by these questions we mean something actual then they are senseless. Why?

We will, firstly, examine the second question. If by this question I mean what is the actual sense of not to be? I can say that the question is senseless since if I do not exist thus the question is senseless to me. It seems right for the second question. However since the two questions have the same logical stand, the same thing can be said about the first question. If the question about the sense of being is about my actuality, hence it is senseless as the question about me not being actual. If the questions have sense at all, then they have to have sense as possibilities. The two questions provide us with the understanding of our finality. To know that I may not be reveals also that I may be. I am free to be or not to be, that means to be free to understand or not to understand that I can be or not be.

An authentic existence is to be aware of my ability to be. This is the reason for Heidegger to contend that Vorlaufen is the *possibility* of being authentic by observation, not of the actuality of existence or non-existence, rather the *possibility* of existence or non-existence.

What have we learned from Heidegger's analysis of death? Death focuses especially on the question of what is the sense of being, i.e. the question of being. Since the existential to be toward death means to be aware of the possibility of a human being not to be, such existential deals directly with the awareness of the being.

The awareness of death denotes an important thesis for Heidegger: possibility is considered more than an actual future. As a human being, I live in the reality of possibilities and such reality of possibilities is what causes the authentic existence to realize. Heidegger has shown that possibilities cannot be defined in simply non-actual terms. How can a possibility have sense without being actual? The answer is freedom.

Pondering on the possibility of not being (to be a being which is able not to be) reveals the possibility to be (to be a being which is able to be) in such a way by which a possibility is not being seen anymore only as an abstract and logical function of a not yet actual, rather it is seen as a basic way by which a human being exist; such an essential way is called by Heidegger freedom. What Heidegger tries to say is that we have the freedom to be in such state of pondering on our ability not to be.

**00:35 Expecting death as authenticity.**

Factually, Da-sein, usually, keeps itself in a state of non-authentic being toward death. How the ontological possibility of authentic being toward death can be characterized as being 'objective' if, at the end, Da-sein never behaves authentically
313

toward its end or if in accordance with its sense, the authentic being has to remain hidden from the others? Does the Da-sein give us instructions for authenticity? Does our analysis of the Da-sein, until now, gives us the recipe for the ontological task which we have set for ourselves? The existential term of death has been defined and with it we have defined what is it that the being toward the authentic end has to be able to do. Moreover, we have characterized the non-authentic being toward death and therefore noted how Da-sein should not be. Da-sein is established by exposure, i.e. by understanding and a conscious state. Authentic being toward death cannot allow itself to escape the possibility which is its most by escaping to "them".

In an existential projection of an authentic being toward death we need to investigate the being's details which establish it as an understanding of death and as such, the understanding of the possibilities without hiding them or escaping them. Firstly, one needs to characterize the being toward death as a being toward a possibility, a unique possibility for the Da-sein. "To be toward" the possibility, i.e. toward something possible may denote also the actualization of the possibility, i.e. the possibility is executable.

However, Heidegger negates it by saying that to execute a possibility means to bring someone to its end. Should it happen then Da-sein is denying itself the basis for existence as a being toward death (Being and time page 305). Da-sein leads itself toward something possible by way of priming or anticipation (Being and Time page 306). Through this phenomenon of priming we define the possibility and not the actualization.

The nearest Da-sein that can be toward death is not the actualization. Heidegger is full of hope and light for the depressive telling him not to execute the possibility of being toward death; do not commit suicide, get down from the roof. The depressive being *after* being toward death authentically, has to confirm life and choose, as a free being, the being toward life. Death, as a possibility, does not grant the Da-sein with actualization. This is the possibility of the impossible, of any way of existence by which you will lead yourself toward something.

Being toward death as the anticipation (readiness) of the possibility is what turns, in the first place, the possibility to be viable. Being toward death is the anticipation of the potentiality to be of an entity of which type of being is the anticipation itself. In exposing this anticipation to be in the potentiality, Da-sein is exposed to itself as the most authentic possibility. To throw yourself to the potentiality of your being means to be able to understand yourself as a being, i.e. in existence. Anticipation reveals itself as a possibility for self understanding of the potentiality of your being which is you're the most, i.e. the possibility for authentic existence. One has to remember that understanding is not the observation of meanings but the self understanding of the potentiality of your being which reveals itself in projection.

Death is the Da-sein's possibility which is it's the most. Being toward this possibility reveals to the Da-sein the potentiality to be which is its most when its being is of interest to it. Here, the Da-sein may find out that this unique possibility of it has been distorted by them. This possibility which is the most for you is not linked to others, i.e. anticipation enables the Da-sein to understand that the potentiality of being in it which is its own being is what is at stakes and therefore is of interest to it and should be considered by the Da-sein alone. This ability to be a being does not pertain to others.

Death is a potentiality of the Da-sein of its individuality. By this individuality, Da-sein gains authenticity, i.e. by self projection to its most potentiality and therefore it must distance itself from "them". In anticipation, Da-sein understands that it is impossible to by-pass or escape the possibility of death and that as opposed to being non-authentic which tries to deceive the Da-sein by convincing it the death does not pertain to it; Da-sein accepts the fact of its death. In view of this, one may say that Da-sein is sure in its death. The way to be sure is determined by a type of truth which is exposure. The possibility is being revealed because it is enabled by observation. By observation, Da-sein, for the first time, ensures its own being in its generality. Now, one may summarize what characterizes the authentic being toward death: anticipation reveals to the Da-sein the fact of it being lost in "them" and leads it to face the possibility of being itself, without "them" it can be itself relieved from "them".

## 00:40 Authentic existence and the call of conscience

Most of the time, I myself am not "the who" of the Da-sein; the "them" are "the who". The "them" even hide the way by which they made it easy for the Da-sein to relieve the burden and chose its possibility.

The choice remains fuzzy and is not defined pertaining to who had made it. Da-sein does not make any decisions; it is swept by the nobody and therefore is trapped in the non-authenticity.

316

However, this process may reverse only if the Da-sein returns to itself from the "them" who led it to loosing itself. In choosing to make a choice, the Da-sein enables, for the first time, its potentiality to be authentic. Since the Da-sein was lost in the "them", it needs to, primarily, find itself. In order to find itself, it has to "show" to itself its authentic possibility. This potentiality is being confirmed and enabled thanks to the voice of conscience (Stimme des Gewissen).

Conscience let us understand; it reveals. This revealing, as a basic state of an entity which is us, is based on a conscious state, understanding, falling and dialogue. Should we deeply analyze conscience, it is revealed as a call (Ruf). A call is a type of dialogue. The call of conscience has a trait of calling the Da-sein to return to the potentiality of being itself; that is being done by way of a summoning to the awareness of being guilty. The possibility of hearing is suitable for the call of conscience. Our understanding of the calling to the Da-sein as a request reveals itself as the will to have conscience. However, an existential choice, which we seek, resides in this phenomenon: the choice of being you which in accordance with the existential structure will be called "decisiveness".

Freedom has two components: the first, a heavy load is lying on the free human being, it, sometimes, forces him to seek any way to evade his full sense. And the second, it isolates the free human being from the comfort and security of an orderly existence.

Heidegger recognizes that the loss of freedom is in accordance with the loss one's authentic trait. The non-authentic human is sure that he solved all his problems by covering what he really is, something that can make a choice. The choices for the them-self have already been done, there are no more choices.

Heidegger starts the second chapter in section two with the most important component in authenticity: freedom. He emphasizes that by avoiding making choices one becomes non-authentic, and that the problem is to find the base from which choices can be made. Therefore, the purpose of chapter two is to find the authentic self. Should we accept the validity of the assertion that freedom is the determining factor in an authentic existence and should we accept that the authentic self has to be in place before we can begin to know the sense of freedom, then the question that should be asked is: how do we reveal the authentic self? The origin of authenticity must reside within the range of is already understood (even fuzzily). From the beginning, we have seen that the Da-sein possesses a basic understanding of being and the purpose of the existential analysis, by interpretation, is to turn the fuzzy into specific.

The origin of the freedom which we try to reveal is in the daily way. The origin from which one can focus on the authentic self, according to Heidegger, is the call of conscience or the voice of conscience. Conscience and guilt are, according to Heidegger, the big and human existentials which reveal an authentic self and the basis for freedom. When we seek an authentic self, we seek the exposure the reveals to us the "self" in me. One of the experiences which is in range of most of human experiences which focuses on the self is guilt. There is something authentic in the awareness by the self of its guilt. Let us assume that we are doing something immoral. If you ponder on the fact that you have done such a deed, you become aware of yourself being able to be responsible. You are guilty. At that moment of awareness there is a new decision to be made. You can try to renounce your guilt. You do that not by denial of the done deed but that it was done under circumstances and external reasons. You can also go as far as to deny that every action is free, that no one is guilty. On the other hand, you can choose to admit your guilt, to recognize that you are responsible for the deed and the denunciation accompanying it.

Heidegger contends that if you decide to ignore the importance of guilt, you also ignore your awareness. By the avoidance of guilt, you become non-self self (non-authentic); whereas you face the guilt, you are real self (authentic).

Heidegger contends that this is not the actual experiencing of feelings of guilt of a certain authentic act, but the desirability to have conscience, the desirability to feel guilt if it is based. I.e. Da-sein has to desire to be guilty in order to be redeemed later. An authentic self is such that it is willing to be open to the voice of conscience. Should a person be deaf to any voice of conscience, should he not feel guilt, one may say that he is unaware of the sense of being a human being. Therefore, the one seeking to live that way which is without the possibility of being at all guilty, is a human being that hides behind the self-them thus being non-authentic.

To what someone is being called when asked to? To itself. For only the self of the them-self is asked to or invited and arrives in order to listen, the "them" collapse. But the fact of the call skipping "them" and the way by which the Da-sein withdraws publicly does not mean that "them" is not a concept. Because of the skipping "them" the call turns it to senseless. However, the self, to which the call is directed and which deprived it from its hideout, returns to itself by the call.

When the them-self is asked to come, it is being called to return to itself. But how can we determine what was said in a speech that belongs to such type of dialogue? What does conscience say to the one to whom the call is meant?

Nothing. The call does not mean anything, it does not give any information on world events, it has nothing to say. 'Nothing' is not said in the call to me; however, it was summons to itself, i.e. to its potentiality of being. The call calls the Da-sein to move forward toward the possibilities which are it's the most, i.e. summoning the Da-sein to be itself. The call gives up any vocal expression, it does not bring itself to the expression by words; still it does not remain fuzzy and undefined.

The conscience speaks by being silent. While the content of the call is allegedly undefined, the direction is clear. The call does not demand of us to seek by groping to whom the call is made. The call is a request or a summon to the them-self itself; as such, the request summons the self to its potentiality to be it and therefore calls the Da-sein to its possibilities.

Heidegger's analysis of conscience is a phenomenological description. As long as we remember that all purpose in analyzing conscience is solely for the focusing on the final analysis of the authentic existence being decisiveness; the analysis is simple.

In previous discussions, Heidegger already established the structure of the Da-sein's exposure as based on existentials, a conscious state and falling; the exposure of conscience is usually parallel to such structure. The only deviation from this structure is that the fall cannot be one of the authentic Da-sein's traits. Therefore, Heidegger uses the talk (Rede) as the third component of exposure. This structure particularly fits because Heidegger's interpretation of conscience is a type of call or of a voice. The

320

essential trait of conscience is a call and the way which fits an authentic existence is being silent.

The point is that if we are not silent and listen to the call of conscience, we will never hear it. Since an authentic existence is an essential possibility of a Da-sein as a Da-sein and it cannot be the result of external circumstances, rather its own existence needs to call it to return to its self, thus the call comes out of a consciousness of conscience. The experiencing of conscience is a type of *a call* which has something to tell us: it reveals something; it gives us something to understand. Conscience, therefore, belongs to the phenomena that reveal to us where we stand, i.e. we stand here and listen. The fact of the conscience expressing itself as a voice denotes it as being a type of talk (Rede). As an existential component of Da-sein, talk expresses what is understood. It enable us to explicitly express an overall sense and therefore to explain it and turn it to be ours. An existential talk is being revealed as a language, it expresses itself by language. However, also silence is a type of talk and that is the outstanding way by which conscience calls us or talks to us, i.e. conscience is talking to us by silence. There is no conflict with the daily experiencing by us of the "voice" since we mean by "voice" without sound, but the conscience is a function of giving us something to understand. The daily self ("I") is he, the confused by the public noise, that conscience is calling him to return from. The conscience calls the Da-sein itself.

Precisely as anxiety turns the relevant thing to become irrelevant, so is conscience pushing your public position to become senseless. It, therefore, deprives the Da-sein, among others, of its usual hideout, and leads it to stand here and face itself. But what does the call "tell" the self? Heidegger says: nothing. The call does not give information on world events and it does not relate to objective facts. I, to whom the call is directed, am not given or being told anything, only it is being summoned to itself. The conscience's purpose is to tell how we supposed to be. As a summons, the conscience calls the Da-sein to stand here and now facing its possibilities to be. Therefore, the call does not have to be expresses as a real voice or in words; "conscience always talks only by way of silence" (Being and Time, page 273). It forces Da-sein to be in silence. Silence by which conscience is talking, is the most basic and original talk: this is the way by which Da-sein calls itself from the deeps of its existence.

Undoubtedly, each one of us is experiencing a call that comes from within us and not from anybody else that is within in the world. It shows that thing that is calling and the thing that is receiving the call may be the same one. At the same time, it denotes that they should, somehow, be different and distinct one from the other, i.e. the caller, somehow, has to be differentiated from the receiver of the call.

The summoning of the Da-sein to make the essential choice is not picked by the Da-sein itself. It seems that there is certain fuzziness. Da-sein as the caller is "here" by a different way from the Da-sein which is the receiver. The one (Da-sein) to whom the call is directed, which receives the call is "here" in the daily world and which loses itself to "them", which drowns in the world and in the daily things, is non-authentic. The one who calls is the same Da-sein but in such a way by which it feels not at home in the world and is anxious of the senselessness and the absurd in the world in which it exists, it calls the primary Da-sein to get out from its state in the daily world and from its non-authenticity and become authentic, it calls it to be as it can be, to realize its potential.

The caller does not feel at home with the Da-sein that is getting lost in the noise and the futile chatter of different things in the world. The call, as aforesaid, has nothing to tell the one receiving it pertaining to information about things or facts; this is a weird call that stems from itself being aware of the senselessness and absurd of existence. The call of conscience comes following the senselessness and emptiness in the depressive-Da-sein's world. The call has to talk in an unpleasant feeling of silence since it has nothing to report that can communicate with a public talk. On the contrary, the call calls the Da-sein to return from the public talk to itself, to a restrained silence or the silence of its existence. It is clear, therefore, that conscience in its essence does not reveal any existential ideal which universally fits everybody, rather reveals to any just Da-sein and in particular to the depressive Da-sein, in its uniqueness, in its concrete situation to which it was summoned by a call of conscience, to be what it can be. The call coming from the deeps calls the Da-sein in general and the depressive Da-sein in particular to be toward most of its ability to be, to realize its potential and to realize the possibilities of its existence. The call calls the Da-sein to extricate itself and be what it can be.

When a depressive Da-sein hears the call of conscience it walks decisively toward death. To relate to conscience as a type of a call reveals four dimensions in the traits of the conscience. These four dimensions of conscience are right for every type of call:

1) Someone who voices it, "the caller";

2) Someone that is being called;

3) The subject of the call, to call pertaining to something;

323

4) What for is the call.

This last point is what distinguishes the call from other forms of talk. In Heidegger's analysis of conscience, all four dimensions are the self. 1) Is the self which is calling. 2) Is the self to which the call is directed. 3) Is the self that is being called pertaining to something and finally 4) it is the self which is unique and authentic. All dimensions represent different aspects of the self. The self which calls the call is anxious and does not feel at "home". Therefore, the self who calls the call is the self which had lost the comfort of being part of "them". The self, to whom the call is directed, on the other hand, is precisely the self that got lost in the them-self and the call is the attempt to bring the self to leave the company of the them-self (the "them"). The call is to the self in the sense of the conscience arousing the awareness of the way of existence by which the self finds itself, i.e. authentic or non-authentic.

The call is being made to me to become authentic. Should it really be possible for someone to be guilty, then conscience becomes senseless.
Ontologically, since guilt focuses on the unique self, it does so in terms of the self's ability to avoid possibilities as to accept them. Every analysis wants to say that since conscience is interpreted as the call by the self to the self, there must be meaningful choices available to the Da-sein, to be or not to be you. The second possibility is based on in the Da-sein being the base for the "no" which is guilt. It is not sufficient to describe the conscience as a call. It has to be revealed in terms of it being an existential of a Da-sein, in terms of an existential, a conscious state and talk. An existential, as aforesaid, is the projection of possibilities. Its

function is "understanding". Ontologically, to understand is to project the Da-sein its possibilities.

What is projected in the conscience? Being guilty. I am guilty because I ran to "them". Although I have the ability to run from "them" and be toward the potentiality which is mine the most I need to recognize my guilt of not being authentic, thus recognizing the possibility of an authentic existence which I may reach. I am responsible for myself because I am such a type of being which is free to accept or to reject possibilities. I also understand that my guilt is unique to me. In guilt, I am no longer protected by their noise. The conscious states which reveals the conscience is anxiety. Anxiety makes the Da-sein individual by way of causing it to not feel at home with "them" and therefore is focusing on the possibilities of being or not being, i.e. to be or not be authentic. The form of talk which reveals the conscience is to keep silence. It is understood such that we should want to hear the call to be authentic, we need to keep quite. This certain trait emphasizes that one of the ways for such non-authentic talk is noise, when someone is yelling, he cannot listen.

"Decisiveness" (in German Entschlossenheit) denotes our ability to decide and be decisive because we are free. To be authentic is to be decisive, to be free to choose the way of your being. The term focuses on the unique saying by the free individual of his existence which is bound by responsibility and guilt. A conscience and guilt are an essential basis for the decisiveness which is an authentic existence. The decisive human being is guilty, he knows that he is guilty and he wants to have conscience.

## 00:45 A debt to itself

The term schuldig expresses, approximately, the word debt. To be indebted expresses, primarily, something that we have denied or withheld or avoided to let the Da-sein to be itself, i.e. in that sense, Da-sein is indebted to itself with something. In another sense, the debt expresses that the Da-sein itself is the base (the cause or the reason), not only for its actions and free decisions, but also for its being and what it can be. I.e. Da-sein has to be in accordance with its own base or be loyal to its base, meaning to who he is and to what it can be. The ability of the Da-sein has a foundation since it is for itself that the Da-sein is always ahead of itself. The "for itself" is the ability of the Da-sein to be determined by the "no" that reveals itself in the most extreme way to the possibility of "not being here anymore". Since conscience, in its essence, belongs to the Da-sein, not to hear it or not to listen to its call, is also a choice. The freedom of Da-sein to make a choice is necessarily a type of choice. Only a final freedom can convert something as necessity, duty or responsibility to understood terms. Only because Da-sein is the base for its own formation by understanding itself through its possibilities, it can demand from itself and oblige itself to exist by way of the existential roots of morality reach to the depth of the structure of revealing its possibilities.

The final freedom at the base of the Da-sein is the precondition for the possibility of a moral "good" and "bad". The Da-sein has a moral debt toward itself as it is in the world. The Da-sein is facing its own truth, i.e. its own truth which is its possibilities as it can be, as someone that has the freedom of choice to be or not to be.

To be as itself dictates "directions" which become rule. The base obliges it to choose a certain possibility. If conscience, for example, calls the Da-sein to return from its non-authenticity and take responsibility on its existence, it is not an abstract idea, but it is a call for a basic choice which the Da-sein can accept. As a result, one could understand why an authentic existence has to be considered a "higher" existence than a non-authentic existence.

However, if a depressive Da-sein does not choose to be toward death, it, actually, chooses to confirm life; he can teach how to say "yes" to life and not to the actuality of death. The depressive-Da-sein has to be authentic in loving life and return to its most basic possibilities and fulfill its existential purpose as a teacher. It is at the same "place" at which its possibilities are revealed, i.e. its concrete and basic truth.

It seems that with the calling of the conscience, the depressive-Da-sein is invited to make a decision on how it will be; the conscience gives it the primary duty to do so. The German word "sollen" expresses our debt. This is the justification for the translation "schuldig is" which follows the "soll" as its explanation "he owes to do this" as opposed to the more natural sense of "he is guilty"; i.e. should the depressive-Da-sein not hear the call and the duty of conscience, then it is guilty.

The conscience, therefore, leads the Da-sein to face its original "duty" for two reasons: the conscience does not only notify the Da-sein of its duty, but summons it, not to say demand of it, to take it upon itself. In this demand of the conscience lies the duty; secondly, since a correct understanding of the call does not lie only in consciousness or logic of its saying but also in a decision. The decision enables the Da-sein to exist primarily as a being thus the duty stems from it. One should remember, however, that the Da-sein has two duties which cannot combine one with the other.

A depressive-Da-sein has to make a decision whether to be toward death, toward the end meaning "I cannot be here anymore", or to be indebted to life and tell itself "I have a duty to be here longer". As I have said, while conscience calls to run toward death, there is another voice or another choice which the Da-sein can accept and this is the call to be toward life, to suspend the run toward death for being toward life and fulfill its purpose and sense; to be or not to be, this is the question.

The depressive-Da-sein has a duty not only to itself, but also to society and fellow human beings, he ought to be a teacher.

## 00:50 The understanding of transferal and guilt

The transferal to them-self denotes the summoning of the Da-sein to be itself with its potentiality to be and, of course, as care Da-sein as being in the world and being with others. In our thesis where the call says 'nothing' that can be talked about and does not give any information on events, the call marks the Da-sein's ability of being ahead of itself and does it as a call which comes from the "not at home" from where the caller is calling; "the not at home" of an individual who was thrown - 'is being called to' in a call, i.e. even if it is revealed. In calling forward to something, the where of the call is to a place to which we are being called to return. When the call gives us the ability to be in understanding, it does not give us something ideal or universal; it is being revealed as something individual and as belonging to a private and certain Da-sein. We will not be completed with the traits of the call as an exposure until we will understand it as such which is calling us to return by a call forward. The call is directed to a guilty Da-sein! All the ways, by which we experience conscience, they all point at a guilty Da-sein! If a Da-sein treats itself as guilty, how can it arrive at this idea of its interpretation of its being? The question may be asked differently: who says how we are guilty and what does the guilt denote? All ontological investigations of the phenomenon of guilt, conscience and death have to begin with what the daily interpretation of the Da-sein says about them.

Since the Da-sein fell, the way by which the Da-sein is interpreted, in most cases, does not reach the essence. So how do we arrive at the criteria of the sense of 'guilt'?

The answer being: from the fact that 'gilt' is a property of the "I". The daily logic perceives the 'being guilty' in the sense of a debt, 'something on account', something which is not yet settled. Someone has to return to the other what he demands. Being indebted is a way of being with others in the field of involvement as someone who provides something or brings it along with him. Other ways of being involved as such in the daily world are: to negate or to prevent, to lend, to hold, to take and failure of the doubt, in this way or another, these are the demands other claim to be theirs. Such a type of being involved is linked to something which somebody may be concerned with. Being guilty also denotes 'being responsible for-'. In this sense of 'having responsibility' for something, someone can be guilty of something

329

without having something which will oblige him to somebody. The ordinary sense of 'being guilty' as 'being indebted to someone' and 'being responsible for something' can go together hand in hand and define a type of behavior which Heidegger calls it 'make yourself responsible'; i.e. to have responsibility to be indebted; someone, for example, break the law and make himself punishable. To 'make yourself responsible' by breaking the law, as we have defined, can be also characterized by 'being indebted to someone else', i.e. being responsible that the other will face the danger of extinction of his existence, that he took the wrong road, or to destruction. Therefore, the formal perception of being guilty in the sense of being indebted to another may defined as follows: to be the reason for the absence of something in the Da-sein of the other in such a way that the latter being, as a base, defines itself as 'lacking in a certain way'. This type of shortage is the failure to supply these or other demands which relate to our existence as being with another. Being guilty is a type of being belonging to the Da-sein. This being is valid, of course, also as a punishable being and as an indebted and responsible being; the Da-sein behaves also in such ways.

The idea of 'guilt' includes also the trait "no". If 'guilt' is something which relates to existence, thus the ontological problem arises of the clarification of the existential of the "no" as "no".

Moreover, to the idea of 'guilt' belongs also the term of guilt as 'being responsible for-', i.e. being the reason for-. Therefore, we have defined the formal and existential idea of 'guilt!' as being the reason (basis) of a being which was defined by the "no", i.e. "being the reason for nothingness". Being guilty is not, primarily, a result of a debt, on the contrary, a debt becomes possible only as a base of an original being guilty.

The being of the Da-sein itself, as we have said, is "care". It contains existence, projection and fall. As a being, Da-sein is something being projected; it is projected to "here" but not on its own terms. In being the base, i.e. existing as being thrown, Da-sein is always behind its possibilities. It never exists ahead of its base, rather away from it. The base being means that you will never have power on yourself from the base up. The "no" belongs to the existential sense of "being thrown". It itself, the base being is the nothingness of yourself. "Nothingness" does not denote anything as not-being-present-at-hand; but "no" which constitutes the being of the Da-sein as being thrown. The trait of "no" is that "no" can be defined as existential: by being yourself, Da-sein as itself, is the entity that has been thrown. It was released from its base, not through itself, rather to itself. As being itself it is being its base.

Da-sein is its base existential, i.e. in such a way by which it understand itself in terms of its possibilities and as it understands itself, it is the same entity which has been thrown. However it implies that when it has the ability to be always itself, it stands facing this possibility or the other: it is always not the other possibilities from which it has chosen, it gives them up by its existential projection. Not only the projection (being thrown) is defined by the nothingness of the base being; as a projection, it is, in its essence nothingness. The nothingness belongs to the Da-sein as a free entity with possibilities. Freedom is the choice of one possibility, i.e. the endurance of us not choosing another possibility and the lack of our ability to choose them.

In a structure of projection, as in a transferal, lies the nothingness. Such nothingness is the base for a Da-sein which is not authentic in its fall; and in falling, any Da-sein which is non-authentic exists factually.

The nothingness diffuses in the essence of "care". Therefore "care", the being of Da-sein, means the base being of nothingness (and such base being is by itself nothingness). This means that Da-sein as such is guilty! Existential nothingness does not have the traits of shortage, as if something is missing as compared to an ideal, rather the Da-sein's being is already nothingness by projection. The call is a call of "care". Being guilty establishes the being which the name "care" was given to it. In "not at home", the Da-sein stands with itself in its originality. This "not at home" brings this entity to face its revealed nothingness which belongs to the possibility of its ability of being. In the case of the Da-sein, as a care, its being is what at stake, i.e. it is of interest to it; it summons itself as "them" which is, actually, a fall, and summons itself from the "not at home" toward its ability to be as it is. The request or the application calls back by calling forward: it calls the Da-sein to go ahead of its possibilities, to be in self ownership, i.e. authentic; it calls the Da-sein to return to it being thrown, to understand this being thrown as the base for nothingness which it has to take. This calling back in which the conscience is calling forward means to return yourself to yourself from the self loss to "them"; and that means that it is guilty (i.e. the Da-sein is guilty of losing itself to them and it is called to return to itself). Correct hearing of the call is equal to being with the understanding of yourself in your potentiality to be, i.e. to project yourself toward your authentic potentiality of being guilty. When a Da-sein, in its understanding, lets itself to be called forward toward this possibility, it means that it becomes free for a call, its readiness for its ability to be called. In understanding the call, the Da-sein is enslaved to the possibility of its existence which is it's the most. It has chosen itself.

In this choice, Da-sein enables its guilt which remains blocked for "them". What is chosen is the conscientious being as a free being able of being guilty. "Understanding the call means to wish to be conscientious" (Being and Time page 334).
It means that someone is ready to be called. To wish being conscientious is the assumption in advance which is the most existential and original for the possibility to be indebted of something. In understanding the call, the Da-sein lets itself to act in terms of the potentiality to be what it has chosen to be.

Conscience, in summation, is the call of "care" from the "not at home " of the being in the world; the call summons the Da-sein to its potentiality which is its most to be guilty; and in accordance with the call, the will to be conscientious is revealed as a way by which the request or the application is understood. To want to be conscientious is, as the understanding of yourself in the potentiality which is yours the most to be, a way by which the Da-sein is being revealed. This exposure is made by the dialogue and a conscious state as well as by understanding. To understand existentially denotes a self projection toward your possibilities to have the potentiality of being in the world. But the potentiality to be is only understood by existence in this possibility. Which conscious way is suitable for this understanding?

The understanding of the call exposes your Da-sein in "not at home" as your individuality. The "not at home" which is revealed in the understanding and with it being exposed, is really becoming exposed by a conscious state of anxiety which belongs to understanding. The fact of the anxiety of conscience gives us a phenomenal confirmation that in the understanding of the call, the Da-sein is brought face to face with the "not at home" of itself. To want being conscientious becomes the readiness for anxiety. Everyone who keeps silence when he wants to let us understand something must "have something to say".

In the application to conscience, the Da-sein lets itself understand its potentiality to be. This calling is, therefore, 'keeping silence'. The talk of the conscience is always non verbal. The call comes from the silence of the "not at home" and the Da-sein which is called, is called back to restrain and silence. It takes the words away from the futile chatter of the "them". The exposure of the Da-sein in its will to be conscientious is, therefore, based on anxiety as a conscious state, by the understanding as a projection of yourself toward you being guilty and by a talk as silence. This unique and authentic exposure, which is made by this silence-conscience of a projection toward you being guilty, in which somebody is ready for anxiety is called by Heidegger decisiveness. In decisiveness, we have come to the truth of Da-sein in its originality because it is authentic. Every time the "there" (of the Da-sein) is being exposed so is the completeness of being in the world, i.e. the world, being in-, and the self as "I". In light of the "for" of yourself as choosing the potentiality to be, a decisive Da-sein releases itself to the world.

The Da-sein's decisiveness toward itself is what enables others to be what they can be, i.e. by way of the Da-sein's decisiveness, it releases others. When a Da-sein is decisive, it can be the voice of conscience for others. Only by being an authentic being in decisiveness, people can be one-with-the-other authentically. The decisiveness 'exists' only as a decision which projects itself in understanding. In decisiveness, the interest of the Da-sein is its potentiality to be which as something that is being projected, can project itself toward defined possibilities. Decisiveness reveals what is possible within "them".

## 00:55 The potentiality of the Da-sein to be authentically complete and temporality as the ontological sense of "care".

We have discovered that an authentic being toward death is expectation. We have also discovered that the potentiality of authentically being from an existential point of view is decisiveness. How the two join together? And furthermore, does the decisiveness denote toward decisive expectation as an authentic possibility?

Ontologically, Da-sein is principally different from anything which is "present at hand", its essence of the self is the existence of the self which being was understood as "care". The phenomenon of the self, a phenomenon which is included in "care" has to be existentially defined in an original and authentic way as opposed to the non-authentic "them".

We experience temporality in an original phenomenological way in which the Da-sein is a complete and authentic being by decisive expectation. The temporality of the decisive expectation is a unique way of temporality.

Temporality has various possibilities and various ways of self temporality. The basic possibilities of existence, the authenticity or the non-authenticity of the Da-sein are based, ontologically, on

335

the possibilities of temporary temporality. Expectation reveals this possibility as a possibility. Therefore, only when it is defined as a being toward death, decisiveness understands the possibility of its potentiality to be guilty.

Being guilty belongs to the Da-sein's being and denotes the nothingness, the base being of nothingness. 'The guilt!' which belongs to the being of Da-sein is something which cannot increase or decrease. It comes ahead before any quantities. Da-sein, in its essence, is guilty, not only in certain cases. To want to be conscientious means to be guilty. To project yourself on being guilty means that Da-sein as long as it is, belongs to deep sense of decisiveness. The existential way to decisively recognize guilt is achieved by authenticity only when such decisiveness, in the revealing of the Da-sein, becomes so transparent so that being guilty is understood as something permanent. However, this understanding is enabled only as long as the Da-sein reveals to itself the potentiality of being and reveals it until the end.

Existentially, Da-sein as a being finally denotes being toward the end, i.e. toward the future. Decisiveness has not only a 'contact' with expectation as if it is other than it. It is based in the authenticity of being toward death, i.e. in the expectation for death.


In "decisiveness" we mean "to let yourself be called forward toward the self as being guilty". Being guilty belongs to the Da-sein itself and we have defined it as the potentiality to be. Therefore, since a guilty being belongs to the Da-sein's being, it has to be understood as the potentiality to be guilty. Decisiveness projects itself toward the potentiality to be, i.e. understands itself through it.

When a Da-sein is decisive, it authentically accepts the fact that it is the nothingness base of its nothingness. We have understood death existentially as what was characterized as a possibility of the non possibility of existence, i.e., the definite nothingness of the Da-sein. Da-sein as a "care" is that which is projected, in its base ("nothingness"), to its death.

The nothingness which controls the Da-sein is being revealed to the Da-sein while being toward an authentic death. Only on the base of this completeness of the Da-sein, expectation is clearly turning the being to be guilty.

Only by decisive expectation, the potentiality to be guilty is authentically and completely understood. Decisiveness brings the Da-sein back to the potentiality which is its best to be itself. When we will understand the being toward death as the possibility which is ours the most, i.e. the potentiality to be becomes authentic and complete and it is transparent.

To wish to be conscientious denotes that someone is ready for the call to be which is its most, i.e. to be guilty. The phenomenon of decisiveness has brought us in front of the original truth of existence. Since in decisiveness, we are sure in our death, or in other words, expecting it (in the future), decisiveness achieves certainty which is authentic and complete. However, at the same time, Da-sein is without truth. Decisive expectation gives the Da-sein the certainty that it is closed. In decisive expectation, Da-sein leaves itself to its permanent un-decisive deprivation to "them"-deprivation which is possible from the Da-sein's base.

The non-definiteness of the potentiality of someone to be, even if the potentiality becomes certain by decisiveness, is becoming

337

firstly complete in being toward death. Expectation brings the Da-sein face to face with the possibility which is always certain however at any moment remains undefined in relation to the moment at which the possibility will become non-possibility.

The "nothingness" which is brought by anxiety brings us face to face and reveals the nothingness which is defined at the base of the Da-sein; and that same base is being projected toward death. The authentic thinking on death is to want to be conscientious which becomes transparent to itself existentialistically. Decisive expectation stems from the understanding of what are the actual possibilities of the Da-sein. Together with anxiety, which brings us face to face with our individual potentiality to be, there are also happiness and joy in this possibility because the Da-sein becomes free.

## 01:00 Time

The title of "Being and Time" implies that time is an important factor in Heidegger's thinking. Along the analysis of division 1 and also in the two first chapters of division 2, time seems as the same point toward which the existential analysis is directed. Notwithstanding the hints and the comments, the importance of time remains tense. The full analysis of time is revealed only in the last parts of "Being and Time".

The main subject of "Being and Time" is to show that for a human being as Da-sein, "to be" is always to be temporary, i.e. the ontological sense of being is time. What Heidegger means when he says that being is time?

338

Which evidence is brought by him to support this assertion?

In a discussion beforehand, we have seen that two terms are determinant: decisiveness and expectation which were analyzed existentially.

Decisiveness was observed as free consciousness, being aware of its responsibility and guilt and the emphasis is on its possibilities.

Expectation is the view of the no-more (possibility) of death. The analyses of both were determinant in giving the whole picture of the human existence.

How decisiveness and expectation connect?

This is the purpose of this chapter: to obtain an ontological base, a source of unification from which these two aspects of authentic existence can unite. By this way, the question of what is the intention to exist becomes the question of what is the true intention to exist.

The first is being answered by self pondering on the ways by which someone is actually dealing in existence. The second question, however, has to seek a deeper base in order to provide support for the ways of existence.

The first question: what is the sense of existing is being answered by the rich understanding of us as being decisive.

The second question: what is the sense of being is being answered by going beyond the simple ways of existence toward the absolute relation which gives these ways sense. This is temporality.

The absolute base through which the two aspects of an authentic existence (decisiveness and expectation) can be understood is that they cannot remain on a level of the simple existentials. On the other hand, the understanding of the ontological base may not be arbitrary; it has to be based and revealed in an existential analysis. The answer to question of the sense of an authentic existence opens, for the first time, the door to the ontological structure.

In part 62 Heidegger deals in the unification of expectation and decisiveness. The key to the understanding of this part is in the understanding that Heidegger speaks of existentiell unification of expectation and decisiveness. According to Heidegger the unification of expectation and decisiveness will be achieved firstly by the level of existentiell analysis in addition to the ontological analysis since the Da-sein is not only an "ontological" entity.

Heidegger makes a distinction between two types of awareness of existence, existentiellic awareness as compared with authentic awareness.

On the other hand, existentialistic awareness is the understanding of the structure of existence and as such it draws near an ontological awareness, notwithstanding the inability, as we have seen, to make a complete comparison.

By the use of the term existentiell, it is impossible to understand Heidegger as intending the awareness of an entity or a thing.

To be aware of existence as existence, i.e. not as a thing, is having existential awareness.

The link between decisiveness and expectation is base on the level of an existentiell awareness of the self. Should it be achieved, then the trait of the mutuality can reveal the ontological aspects. Heidegger begins with the lowest level of ontology, i.e. with the existentialistic awareness and from there raises to an existential awareness. Moreover, all existential analysis starts from the daily non-authentic existence which is

340

considered a lower level of being. If so, how does Heidegger show the reciprocation between decisiveness and expectation on the existentiell level?

Should we examine the traits of an authentic expectation, even if on an existentiell level, we will see that decisiveness is an important component of expectation. Moreover, meticulously examining expectation, we will see that it is part of decisiveness. The reciprocation between them shows the link to each other, they contain each other.

Decisiveness reveals to the Da-sein that it is guilty all the time and therefore the idea of decisiveness contains the term "as long as he" or "until he is finished". To be guilty means to be responsible or free for responsibility as long as we are alive. But "as long as we are alive" implies the awareness of death. Since being guilty is a way of an authentic existence, the awareness of being may not be, which is contained in it, must also be authentic and being authentic toward death is expectation. By a similar way, the investigation of expectation will reveal that existential decisiveness is implied by it.

## 01:05 Being-depressive as complete and authentic

A depressive Da-sein is being thrown to the world and into a destiny not chosen by him. He did not choose to be mentally ill. However, he has the ability to be what he is. I.e. he has the potentiality to be what he can be.

341

He has the potentiality to be toward the end, i.e. toward death or alternately he can have the potentiality to be! He can be "I cannot be here anymore" or he can tell himself in silence "I cannot be here anymore and yet I shall be". The senseless life of the depressive-being is missing "for what", there is no purpose to his life, i.e. the world and life are missing the "for" which is for a certain purpose; the world, in this state, loses its purpose and sense. However, as aforesaid, he has to find purpose for them. Depressive Da-sein feels and reveals the senselessness in the world. By anxiety, the world cannot offer him anything; it is senseless, he feels uncomfortable and not "at home".

The depressive-being can no longer receive anything from the world and from "them"; the world is senseless for him, i.e. it cannot offer him anything like serenity and security from the "them"; the depressive-being is anxious of the senseless world which is being revealed as impotent. He discovers the emptiness and the senselessness and the feeling that there is no future, there is nothing worth living. As the Da-sein, a just depressive-Da-sein falls prey to "them" and the world, but as a result of his illness and falling into depression, he is in social solitude through which he returns to himself from the "them" into his internal world where he has no choice but to confront himself and be aware of his being and to choose from the possibilities available to him; he can no longer console himself with "them" from whom he draws away. He stands face to face with his future- with the possibility of his death and has no fear from it. He understands that he is strange and alienated to this world and that he does not feel at home since the world is defined and determined and publicly interpreted by "them". Since he is in social solitude, he hears the call of conscience which tells him to return to himself from "them".

Conscience "speaks" to him in silence and does it by isolating the Da-sein from it surrounding and confronts him with the choosing of how to be. Since the depressive-Da-sein is socially withdrawn, i.e. drawing away from "them" into his internal world, he has no choice but to confront himself and be aware of his being and the choices and the possibilities available to him; he can no longer console himself with the "them" from whom he is drawing away. He does not speak to them; he has nothing to say at this *stage*, he keeps silence which is a type of a different talk than their futile chatter. To keep this silence is the essential possibility of a talk. By talking to each other, the person keeping silence can make the other one understand, i.e. he can develop by his counterpart an understanding and he can do so in a more authentic way than the one who does not stop talking.

To talk much about something is to hide that same thing and to bring what was understood to pseudo or fake clarity - the non-intelligibility of the trivial.

However, to keep silence does not mean stupidity; and it is particularly true for the mentally ill which is perceived throughout history as a fool. On the contrary, if a person is stupid he still has the tendency to 'talk'. Such a person did not prove that he can keep silence; indeed, he lacks the ability to prove anything. The person who is, by nature, used to speak measurably cannot show that he, indeed, is keeping silence or that he is the same type of person who can do it. To authentically keep silence is only possible through a real dialogue. By being able to keep silence, the depressive-Da-sein has to have something to say, i.e. he may be in a state of revealing himself authentically and he has to have something to tell "them".

At this state, the silence of the depressive-Da-sein expresses something by which it overcomes the futile chatter. As a way of talk, silence expresses the givenness of the Da-sein for the basic understanding which is the potentiality to listen truly and be-one-with-the-other which is transparent and clear.

The being-depressive keeps silent because nobody can understand it in its situation, thus it is saying something, it says I am empty, I feel emptiness. This emptiness is the senselessness of existence, the senselessness of the sayings of others. However, it, as aforesaid, says to itself and to "them" to confirm life.

Because the being-depressive is in the state of solitude, he is silent and can listen; he listens to its conscience. This self is a being with the potentiality to be toward the end or being toward death. However, while having the potentiality of being toward death, his conscience is also calling him to choose to be toward life. The being-depressive can be, at the same time, not being and being toward death; both dwell together under the same roof of the depressive-Da-sein. We are free to choose.

We have already said that just a Da-sein particularly the depressive-Da-sein face the possibilities above actuality. The possibilities are to be toward death or being toward life. The being-depressive can choose between being toward authentic death but not to carry it out; in this choice 'not to carry out' the end, the depressive-Da-sein chooses to be toward life. It should be emphasized that by Heidegger the possibility is what is important and not actuality and therefore, I think that in the end, the depressive-Da-sein has to confirm life. Being toward death is being toward the end, but being toward death which is not actualization is being toward potentiality which is not the end but being is a state of being in the potentiality for infinity. Being toward infinite potentiality is the choice of the manic-depressive-being to be a teacher for "them".

We, the being-depressive, feel guilty for being a being which can be not being, i.e. that we are toward death and therefore we are responsible for our being. We are responsible for what we are, i.e. to ourselves; ourselves is of interest for us. We are expecting to be toward the future which, by the Da-sein is the end and decisively we walk toward it. However, at the same time, we can be toward life and expect to be teachers. We have to decisively confirm life and teach "them". He chooses life because he feels guilty of temporarily choosing to be toward death. Being decisive and expecting to be able to be or being toward life, we are aware of this possibility of existence, i.e. being toward life. The being-depressive and the being-manic-depressive have to listen to the call of conscience which tells them to turn away from "them" on one hand, and on the other hand to withdraw from their choice of being toward their death; i.e. the call to return to yourself from being toward death to being toward life and with it the instruction which is an ethical imperative. One should remember that being authentic means being able to perceive the sense of existence, but existence is also living and therefore also being toward life is the perception of the sense of existence and it is also authentic; to be non-authentic means not to be aware of the sense of existence.

In the end, Heidegger prohibits the actualization of being toward death thus confirming life. Therefore, the depressive-Da-sein or the manic-depressive-Da-sein is authentic in any state: surely when it is toward death but also, and in my opinion Heidegger would have confirmed it, when it is toward life.

In the end, only when the depressive-Da-sein has the potentiality which is his the most not to be or to be and when he is free to choose initially the first one and then to elevate himself, dialectically, to the other, i.e. to be, then and only then, he becomes complete and authentic.

Once it, the being-manic-depressive or the being-depressive, returns to itself and becomes complete, he returns to "them" but this time for the purpose of teaching them. A depressive-Da-sein is also authentic in the sense of manic-depression being, meaning its nature, a return or a recurrence; then, to exist as such means to be in recurrence, i.e. temporality. The being toward death is only one stage in recurrence; the second stage is to excel yourself and be actually a being toward life and that means to be what you can be.

The being-manic-depressive expects to be toward the future which is an ethical imperative and it chooses and walks decisively toward it otherwise it might reverse the potentiality of the possibility of being toward death to be actual thus becoming guilty! The sense of temporality by the being-depressive or the manic-depressive-being is to look to the future and decisively walk toward it, i.e. to listen to its conscience and project itself toward the possibilities that are its most − teaching the crowd about saying "yes" to life.

## 01:10 Real temporality: five aspects

Being here decisively means to listen to your conscience and project yourself to the possibility which is yours the most: your death. Being decisive and true in expecting this possibility (the end of your possibilities), Da-sein can be described as arriving at the ability which is its most and in this sense to arrive at the authenticity and in other words to the truthfulness of joining yourself.

Future (in German zukunft) is composed of 'to' (zu) and arrival (kunft) so that together the term means 'arriving at' or arriving to-(yourself); from there Heidegger arrives at the original phenomenon of the future. This authenticity expresses the Da-sein by decisiveness.

To be decisive is to expect (death); this is a way of being toward the potential of being which is extraordinary and is yours the most. This is only possible if the Da-sein can arrive at itself as its own possibility and to hold the possibility in such a way by which it allows itself to arrive at itself as a possibility. To hold this extraordinary possibility and to allow yourself to arrive at yourself is the true phenomenon of the future (Being and Time page 325).

The true phenomenon of the future is composed of someone who accept the possibility of its death and who enables this potentiality which is his most to be accessible. Actually, he becomes existential. As far as someone allows himself, which is the original way of being himself, to arrive at himself in such way thus he is expecting it.

Heidegger calls such "true future" expectation or advancement-running forward. Such expectation is possible only because the

Da-sein is "always already ahead of itself", i.e. preceding it, he runs passing himself by the running forward death, something that cannot be said on something which is a tool or usable or "present at hand". The way of "arriving at yourself" is the true and original phenomenon of the future, in other words, whatever we will say about the future, in the end, it is a formation and a being authentic by decisively expecting death. The future as a formation is the basic sense of Da-sein.

The fact of Da-Sein is always being ahead of ourselves, to be advanced, something of which importance we know before any theory or practice and which, in any case, was projected and as long as we exist we continue to project ourselves in an non-theoretical way toward possibilities and that our existence is the projection of Da-Sein; such scope of understanding is, in the end, based on the fact that such Da-sein is "to arrive at" or to be formed yourself, to be yourself, and by this way to be, primarily, futuristic. To be here decisively is to take command and expose ourselves as anyone of us is already exposed. "To be originally ahead of yourself" and to project yourself to the possibility which yours the most (death), is to return to the possibility in which someone is already projected. As long as being here in general is as I was, only then it can return to itself in a futuristic sense so that it returns to itself (Being and Time page 326).

To be here authentically is to be one who already was; someone can be "already" originally as long as someone projects or expects that it, actually, already is not.

In expectation, Da-sein returns to itself or retrieves the ability to be as it is. To arrive at yourself (the authentic sense of the future) means, at the same time, to return to whoever is already you. Being here is really with itself, it does really exist if it holds itself in such expectation.

In decisive expectation, Da-sein is ahead of itself authentically and really returns to its being projected, its permanent death in such a way by which it primarily finds itself in a real situation. The real or original way of being-already (retrieving or returning) and the real way of being "at the moment" (to be present in the world and let it present itself) are linked to the real future (expectation) without being entirely depended on it.

All dimensions of time which are depended on each other are untied as a whole which enables temporality. The real and original future has the priority. From this priority, Heidegger derives the finality of the future. The real future is not a simple possibility of another not "present at hand" which leaps forward at certain moment out of a chain of moments in time.

Death is the unavoidable possibility, not of something "present at hand", but of the impossibility of the Da-sein (Being and Time page 262).

"The real and original future" is the way of the Da-sein by which it enables this possibility to arrive at it, "to exist as a possibility of nothingness, a possibility that cannot be passed" (Being and Time page 330).

Another dimension of real temporality deals in the link between temporality and Da-sein. Real "care" is an expression of real temporality or, in other words, temporality is the precondition to the possibility of "care", i.e. original and real temporality provides the meaning of a real "care". To be here in originality becomes understood in the aspect of temporality as a type of expectation which returns me to myself and by this process it overturns my situation to a formative moment. From one perspective, real temporality provides the horizon for a real and complete "care" thus the meaning for a real human existence; from another perspective, similar to the first one, any way of real temporality which Heidegger calls ecstatic or in other words to exist beyond yourself in expectation of the return and the moment that has its relative horizon.

Real temporality contains the horizon of the "care" and therefore the meaning of existence by combining the horizons of the ecstatic expectation, the return and the moment which together compose the real future, past and present respectively. Real temporality is a projection (i.e. expectation) from which a real way of "I was already" (return) and a real way of caring for things (at the moment) are stemming. Being here (being in the world, care for others and yourself) is beyond itself. The original being beyond itself is the temporality by which Da-sein is here.

**01:20 Temporality as the ontological sense of care.**

Da-sein is becoming in its essence a Da-sein by an authentic existence which composes itself as a decisive expectation. Such expectation as an authentic way of "care" contains the completeness and the original self stability of Da-sein.

What are we seeking ontologically in the sense of "care"? What does "sense" specify?

We have seen previously, according to our analysis, that sense is something by which the understanding of something exists even if it is something which is not revealed to the eye. Sense specifies the basic projection in terms of which something can be perceived in its possibilities as it is. Projection reveals possibilities, i.e. it reveals a type of a possible thing. When we investigate the sense of "care", we ask what enables (the preconditions) the totality of the complete structure of "care". Meticulously, sense specifies the fundamental projection of the understanding of being. When being in the world is being revealed to itself and understands the being of this entity which it is it, it understands equally the being of the entities which are being revealed in the world even if it does not wonder and the fundamental way of existence and actuality is not yet diagnosed.

The sense of the being of a Da-sein is not something abstract which is something different and beyond itself, rather it is the self understanding of the Da-sein itself. I.e. the understanding by the Da-sein of itself is what grants it its sense. The one that was projected in the original and existential projection of existence was revealed to itself as a decisive expectation. "A decisive expectation is the being toward the potentiality which is yours the most and yours the most unique. Such type of thing is possible only by way of the Da-sein can arrive toward itself in the possibility which its most and it can offer such possibility as a possibility thus giving itself to come toward itself, in other words, that it exists. The letting itself to come toward itself in this unique possibility which it offers, is the original phenomenon of the *future* as coming toward. Should the authenticity or the non-authenticity of the being toward death belong to the being of the Da-sein, then the being toward death is only possible as something futuristic... we view the arrival (in the sense of arriving toward something as to arrive toward death) as something by which Da-sein in the potentiality of being, which is its the most, arrives at itself. Expectation makes the Da-sein authentic for the futuristic and in such a way by which that expectation itself is only possible as long as the Da-sein, as being, always arrives toward itself, i.e. as far as it is futuristic at all" (Being and Time page 373).

Decisive expectation understands the Da-sein in its essence as being guilty. The sense of this understanding is that in his existence, someone is taking command of his guilt. To take command on the being thrown specifies the being Da-sein as authentic as it was. To take command on the being thrown is only possible in such a way by which the futuristic Da-sein can be 'as it already was'. Only as far as it is futuristic, the Da-sein can be authentically as it was. The characterization of the term "as it was" stems, in a certain way, from the future.

"Being beside" decisively, which is "ready at hand" in a situation, i.e. to act in a way of coming against what is present in the surrounding, is possible only by returning this extant to be present in the present. To act is the ecstasies of the present. Only as present in the sense of doing, decisiveness can be what it is. By returning to yourself futuristically, decisiveness brings itself to a situation of action in the present. The characterization of "as I was" stems from the future and by way of which the future would have released the present from itself. This phenomenon of uniting the three ecstasies, a future which acts (present) in a process of as already has been (the past), is called by Heidegger temporality.

As much as Da-sein has a defined way of temporality, the potential authenticity of being complete of a decisive expectation is enabled to the Da-sein itself. Temporality reveals itself as a sense of authentic "care". "Care", as aforesaid, has three traits in the ontological structure of the Da-sein:

1) It is ahead of itself in terms of its awareness of the possibilities;
2) It is already in the world;
3) It is beside the entities which it discovered, whether by concern for other Da-seins or by dealing with other entities than Da-sein.
The original unification of the structure of "care" is in temporality. The advancement itself as ahead of itself which is aware of its possibilities is based on the future. In "being already in- (the world)", i.e. the characterization of "as it was" expresses the past and "being beside" expresses itself as possible by acting, i.e. an action performed on something which is "ready at hand" which is the present. The three of them should not be taken in the sense of the simple time. The "before" and "advancement" implies a future of such a type which will enable the Da-sein to be such which its potentiality to be is of interest to it.


A self projection toward "for yourself" is based in the future and it is an essential trait in the existential. The primary and original sense of the existential is the future.

With the "already" we look at the temporary and existential sense of the being of the entity of-, as far as it is, it is already something that has been projected. Only because "care" is based on the trait of "I was", Da-sein can exist as an entity which was projected as it is. As long as Da-sein factually exists, it is never the past rather it is always "already was" in the sense of "I am as I was"; and as long as Da-sein exists, it can be "I was". Da-sein never 'finds itself' except for being factually projected. In the conscious state in which it finds itself, Da-sein storms itself as an entity which it is still being and as it was, i.e. that it always is "I was".

The original and existential sense of factually being as being thrown is in the trait of "I was". In drafting the structure of "care", the temporally sense of the existential and the factually being as being thrown are specified by the expressions 'before' and 'already'. Temporality enables the unification of existence, a factual being as being thrown and a fall and by this way composes the complete structure of "care".

Temporality is not an entity at all. Temporality is various possibilities of time. It enables the variety of the ways of the Da-sein as being and particularly the basic possibilities of authenticity or non-authenticity. Temporality is the beyond itself as itself. The main and original phenomenon of authentic temporality is the future. "Care" is being toward death. We have defined "decisive expectation" as being authentic toward the possibility which was characterized as non-possibility of the Da-sein.

By being toward such end, Da-sein exists by way of which it is authentic as an entity which can be when it is being thrown toward its death. It is important to remember and to remind that Heidegger produced the analysis of temporality from the trait of the authentic existence as a decisive expectation.

The form of question which is used to extricate the interpretation of temporality from the existential account is this: how is it possible that there will be a decisive expectation?

And the answer: because there is a future and not only because there will be a future.

In part 65 of "Being and Time", the temporary base of the authentic existence is being revealed and the three components of time, i.e. the past, present and future are being ontologically analyzed.

Time is being revealed as a being of Da-sein, i.e. the sense of Da-sein of being is always to be temporal, thus the headline of "Being and Time" (Sein und Zeit). In part 66 it becomes clear that if time is the being of Da-sein, then all analysis of the existential structure of Da-sein has to repeat itself while emphasizing and interpreting in terms of structure of temporality.

All that we have learned on the existence of the Da-sein was just an existential discovery; in order to convert it into an ontological discovery one has to re-interpret the existence of the Da-sein in terms of time: past, present and future. Therefore, in chapter IV (temporality and every day), Heidegger re-evaluates all existentials from the perspective of temporality. Heidegger's analysis of time and temporality begins, as aforesaid, from an account, based in ontology, of "care" (sorge).

The simple intuition is that the assertion that the human existence is based in time in not difficult to be accepted. All that we do is temporal; particularly when we ponder on existence, we, often, think of it in terms of transition of events, or of hope, fear and we wonder what the future holds for us. But this intuition through which we accept time as the base for the human existence is failing in spotting how, exactly, someone has to perceive time as a basis for existence. To say that all human events are taking place in time is not saying that time is the basis for existence since, among other things, we do not know the sense of "basis". When someone seeks the deep sense or even the ontological sense, we will ask how this thing or that thing is possible. This is what Heidegger intends by the definition of sense. When I ask about the sense of something, I actually ask what makes it possible.

Kant's question about the sense of science is, of course, answered by the consideration of how science is possible.

The answer: by categorization. Heidegger intends it by the ontological sense. The question is formulized as follows: what is the sense of care??

And this question gets the form of: how is it possible that something like "care" exists?

We have answered it previously. Now, one has to ask how care (and decisive expectation is an authentic care) is possible?

What makes the being of the Da-sein possible?

We have seen that decisive expectation is the authentic way in which Da-sein is a possibility of being. Therefore, when we ask on the basis or the possibility of the existence of the Da-sein, we have to formulize the investigation in terms of decisive expectation. Decisive expectation was revealed as being toward your possibilities. However, how is it possible to be toward something at all?

The answer is: only because there is a future. What does it mean that there is a future?

The future, in its simplicity, is not something which "is not yet" or "still not" and now awaits our arrival on the path of time as if time is a road on which the objects of future occurrences await its arrival, rather the future is meaningful to someone since it is going toward him, running to him. To have a future is to expect, to be ahead and to look forward. Therefore the future is meaningful. Should the future not be more than "not yet", it would not have any meaning for us at all. I look forward to finishing my book; I expect a certain measure of satisfaction from a completed work.

The future is not meaningful to *me* in an abstract way of moments in the present of "not yet".

The future is meaningful for me because it is one of the ways by which I exist. For Heidegger, the future, as a way of existence, turns into the definite premise of an authentic existence. What Heidegger does in this part is profound; he gives an ontological account of sense of being in time.

One needs to pay attention that the question Heidegger asks himself is: what is the sense of being in time? And not what is time?

We are all in time. Surely, we can ponder on the sense of being in time. Heidegger described a future "as to arrive toward" or to "arrive to"; in this term he intends our existence as expectants, to look toward, to feel yourself going toward, etc. the most sophisticated form of this is the understanding that someone is going toward not being, i.e. going to die, which has already been analyzed by us in the discussion of being toward death.

Going toward death is an authentic form of the Da-sein's existence. A similar state and the most authentic, i.e. that realizes authenticity exists by the being-depressive; as far as I am concerned, it is sufficient that the being-depressive seriously considers the possibility of death in order to become authentic. It must not execute the expectation and it must not be decisive all the through and make it actual. It is decisive, i.e. feels guilty in its mind and expects death which means that it is considering very seriously and definitely its ability to be no more; i.e. it is enough for it to see death as a possibility which remains non-actual to make it authentic. However, at the same time, while it considers the going toward death, there is another human factor which causes it to consider another possibility. The other possibility is to make a decision to expect and to be toward life. It needs to listen to such factor which commands it with life, such voice is, as in the case of death, the voice of conscience, i.e. the conscience calls it to listen to itself and be decisive in its decision to be toward life and to realize such possibility which is available to it. The being-depressive is decisive because it is guilty! It is guilty because it has chosen to go toward death. The being-depressive and the being-manic-depressive have to listen to the voice of conscience which expresses life. Instead of realizing the possibility of being toward death and make it actual, it has to think about the "no" of toward death; this "no", this possibility, is a confirmation for life, for rebirth.

When a depressive-Da-sein chooses to be toward life it is more complete. In order for the being toward death to have sense, there has to be another possibility which is also authentic for the being-depressive which is the running toward my life; one has to have to opposite of death in order to give death sense, its other possibility which precedes it, i.e. to be toward death gives sense to life-being.

There is no sense to life without the possibility of not being and there is no sense for death without the possibility to live.

By Heidegger, one of the three ecstasies of time, i.e. the future is the most important. It is not the present which leades the existence, but the future, i.e. for Heidegger, the future is more important than the present. It should be emphasized in terms of priority or the primary possibility. The second in importance to the future is the past. The present is the last in importance for Heidegger. In the interpretation of how the past is of sense to the Da-sein, Heidegger has chosen the term "Ich bin gewesen" which is usually interpreted as "I have been".

Macquarrie and Robinson who translated "Being and Time" to English have translated this term to "I am as having been".

Let us assume that I contend that the past, since it is no more, cannot be of sense for me since to have sense means that something has to actually exist and the past is something that does not exist anymore. The promise of yesterday is senseless since the day of yesterday does not exist anymore. Still, by refuting this naïve position, something is being revealed which is there to begin with, i.e. the past has sense. Neither the past nor the future can be described in an abstract way as not yet or not anymore. The past and the future are meaningful, they have sense and as such they have to be seen as linked to the *human existence.*

From these considerations, we can now raise the question: what has to be there in the past, to begin with, in order to consider the past as having sense for us? Similarly, one can raise the previous question: what has to be there, in advance, in the future in order for it to have sense for us?

The answer to both questions lies in the understanding that the two ecstasies of time, the past and the future, have to be interpreted in terms of human existence. The future is meaningful for us in term of "I am as going toward"; the past is meaningful for us in term of "I am as having been".

But what about the present? In the traditional theories of time, it is usually considered as the significant focal point in which reality and existence have received their sense. However, also in such traditional theories, a difficulty arises pertaining to the ecstasy of the present.

When is the present? If the future is the position of reality, how, by broadening, one should perceive the present?

Is a fraction of a second, passing for a moment in consciousness, fading into the "no more" of the traditional past or is an imminent fraction of a second not yet fading from any ontological status because it is not been yet realized? Or is the present only a link between the imminent moment and the one that had passed?

Such questions make it difficult for those who consider the present as the significant focal point. Heidegger, as opposed to them, turned the future to the significant focal point thus avoiding these difficulties. But the present is still the real ecstasy of time and therefore should be described existentially.

The same way, by which we have answered the question of the sense of the future and the past, we will answer the question of the sense of the present.

We have asked how the past and the future are meaningful for the Da-sein. We, now, ask the same question about the present.

Heidegger's answer to the question how the present is meaningful for us moves the investigation from considering the present as such in which something is happening, to the real execution of an action.

Ontologically, the present is to perform the present. Therefore it is the execution of an actual act which turns the present into a meaningful present. Surely, this is what we are actually doing at every moment which is being turned into a meaningful moment in the present.

The primeval sense of each moment in the present is in the fact that someone is directly aware to his activity as an act. Therefore, to perceive time as a geometrical series of isolated "moments" is completely alienated to our existential experience. For this reason, the present as the last of the three ecstasies of time and not the first, is interpreted as leading to; leading to an action. In summation, this interpretation of the analysis of temporality should be simplified: as a human being, I have a future. That means that the future has meaning for me. It is because of my possibilities that the future has sense for me; actually, in the end, my ability to be with possibilities to be is the sense of the future. On the other hand, I perform acts and find myself creating situations. This way, the present is meaningful to me. The sense of being in the present is, for me, to perform acts and create situations. Finally, the base on which the past is meaningful to me is the forgetfulness and memory. The past would not have been of sense to me unless I would exist in such a way of being able to remember and forget how "I was". I have used the term ecstasy; contextually, the term was clarified in this way or another. Nevertheless, the term ecstasy comes from Greek for protrude, to stand against something. The focusing on the past, present and future is to "stand by" the general flow of time and existence, i.e. we stand by in the sense of something outstanding against the background. Only while interpreting temporality in terms of the ecstasy, one can ontologically view time correctly.

Heidegger draws these ecstasies from the structure of the authentic existence. One should remember that, in the previous chapters, I have dealt in the authentic existence as "care" in which the structure of "care" is bound by the projection of possibilities together with the being already in the world beside the entities which we have met in the world.

The Da-sein's care has three traits: 1) It is ahead of itself in terms of the care's awareness to possibilities; 2) it is already in the world; 3) it is beside the entities which it discovered whether in concern for other Da-seins or in dealing with other entities than the Da-sein.

Heidegger asks about the base of these existential traits or them definitely becoming possible which is ontological. Because of its ontological future, it is possible for the Da-sein to be ahead of itself; it is possible for the Da-sein to be already in the world because of the ontological past; and it is possible for the Da-sein to be beside entities because of the ontological present.

The basic structure of Heidegger's analysis is this: given the authenticity of the account of the structure of "being concerned", what has to be there, to begin with, on order for this structure to become possible?

The answer: a form of a temporary existence with a structure compatible with a structure of "care". The three traits of authentic existence are based on the three ecstasies of time. Heidegger is avoiding the formulating of a metaphysical time as if time is an entity or an essence. He is avoiding the ontic description of time in order to enable the ontological description. One objection that may be raised against him has already been answered by Heidegger.

Should we understand time in terms of the ecstasy of temporality, we will see that time is limited by the final existence of someone. However, surely, I can imagine a time before my birth, i.e. prior to my existence and after my death, i.e. time that will continue after my demise. Does the fact of the continuity of time which is really meaningful to me, harm Heidegger's account?

Heidegger contends that these possibilities do not harm the finality and temporality of time. Even if I can imagine events which will take place, time is still temporary and limiting, hence time is finite. Since authentic time is finite, non-authentic time is indefinite. The real ecstasies of temporality have been seen as a basis of someone's existential understanding of himself as finite.

Describing time in any other way is to describe it as based on something other than the self, i.e. as based on the non-self, the non-authentic. Should such thing as an indefinite time was possible metaphysically, it would not be available to us existentially. May be it would be only abstract, the creation of consciousness which will not be based on any human activity. In order for time to be of sense, it has to be the time based on our finite existence as temporal. To perceive time as objective, i.e. as something external and independent of consciousness, or as subjective, i.e. as a form of consciousness, is to ignore the essential and existential trait of how to view time. Time and temporality are not objective in the sense that they can be termed as independent entities or entities which have sense external to the human existence; they are also not subjective in terms of they are the pure forms of intuitive experience.

Time and temporality exist as long as human beings exist; temporality is being revealed as an ontological and necessary condition for the ways by which we exist. In part 66, Heidegger explains that if the ontological base of an authentic human existence is temporality, then the whole structure of the existential analysis has to be reviewed in light of the temporal characterization of Da-sein. The important existentials have to be more deeply researched in order to reveal the ontological structure of time. This is the de facto performance of the reconstruction in order for Heidegger assertion to become understood. As I have said, the structure of care is temporality.

The review of Heidegger of the existentials, this time from the point of view of temporality has to show that the different traits of care, i.e. understanding, a conscious state and fall are, all of them, based on temporality. The important existential components of Da-sein have to be evaluated now ontologically. Heidegger interprets each one of the components of the care's structure in terms of ecstasies of time. It is important to remember all the time that Heidegger is trying to reveal the temporality of the ontological base of each of the components of care. Shortly, he wishes to show that temporality is the base for all components of "care".

## 01:25 Understanding as temporal

Since the existential sense of understanding is a projection of possibilities, the main ecstasy of this existential is the future. In the case of a conscious state, the main ecstasy is the past. For a fall, the main ecstasy is the present. One has to remember, as aforesaid, that all ecstasies have sense and saying that the future is the most representative of the temporality of understanding does not say that the past and the present are not meaningful for understanding. The same thing is right for a conscious state and fall. Understanding in its existential meaning as a projection of possibilities is not initially a type of cognition.

The cognitive aspect of understanding is derived from the existential aspect. How understanding as a projection of possibilities can be interpreted revealing its temporal base?
Understanding has sense not only in terms of each of the three ecstasies of time but also in terms of the distinction between authenticity and non authenticity.

364

Let us be reminded that understanding is playing a major role in the distinction between authenticity and non authenticity because it is the projection of the possibility of not being which the Da-sein is becoming aware of as having the ability of authenticity by going toward death.

Together with the three ecstasies of time, the distinction between authenticity and non-authenticity, which takes place in each of the ecstasies, creates six ways of understanding. I.e. Da-sein projects its possibilities authentically or non-authentically in each of the ecstasies of time.

Since the future is the most important ecstasy of understanding, the distinction between the authentic and non-authentic futuristic ways of projection has to be clarified.

Anticipation (vorlaufen) is an authentic futuristic understanding in which the Da-sein exists authentically, i.e. lets itself to come toward itself as far as it can "be or not to be". It means that in anticipation, the Da-sein sees the future as being composed of its own possibilities; the future has sense as long as I am aware of- and can be in different possibilities.

The non-authentic future, on the other hand, does not see possibilities in terms of Da-sein but in terms of circumstances and events surrounding the daily activity. The non authentic future, which is characterized by waiting, projects possibilities only in terms of day to day life in which it is busy. The non-authentic in waiting for a future as opposed to an authentic anticipation for it manifest in the way by which the projection (of possibilities) of the future becomes meaningful. The non-authentic projects possibilities on objects which can only be related by us.

The authentic way, on the other hand, projects on the Da-sein not only the possibilities which are of our interests but also our decisions on the matter, i.e. projects our possibilities. An authentic futuristic projection, which is aware of our finality and our responsibility, enables not only the awareness of possibilities but also the role which the Da-sein plays and takes part in them. One may say that an authentic understanding (anticipation) exists in the Da-sein when it walks toward the future while the non-authentic understanding (waiting) exists in the future when it arrives for the Da-sein; i.e. non-authenticity is to sit and wait for the future to arrive for the Da-sein while authenticity is to walk toward it. These are the two ways of understanding: to sit and wait or to rise up and walk toward the future.

The past as the future, is important for the projection of the Da-sein. According to Heidegger, the factor that establishes a non-authentic being is the existential trait of forgetfulness while the authentic past is repetitiveness. Only because forgetfulness and repetitiveness are real ways of human existence in which temporality can provide an ontological base for a projection through understanding.

## 01:30 Conscious state as temporal

Heidegger chooses two forms of conscious state which were analyzed as existential: the non-authentic way of fear and the essential trait of authentic existence in anxiety.

The task of showing the temporality of a conscious state will be successful only if it is possible to show that conscious state reflects an authentic or non-authentic existence, anxiety and fear respectively, having a temporal base.

The question is how fear and anxiety can be interpreted as being temporal. Heidegger says that the main ecstasy of a conscious state is not the future but the past. In light of the fact that fear looks always as fear of something in the future, it seems, initially, as a dubious effort to hold such interpretation. However, in a deeper consideration of what it means to have fear or to be anxious, it seems that Heidegger insight penetrates deeper than the achievement of symmetry between the two.

The ways which constitute the structure of a conscious state reveal how the Da-sein turns its back to its being.

The fact of "I have been" is the base of someone's way and therefore a conscious state. Heidegger explains it by a conscious state returning someone to something. I.e. a conscious state returns us to a perspective or a status which in its essence is "I have been" (Gewesenheit).

It should be emphasized that also the future and the present belong to a conscious state. Heidegger just intends to say that the past is the special ecstasy of a conscious state. What is the meaning of fear not being futuristic but is meaningful in the "I have been" (in the past)?

When someone has fear it is the future he is retreating from. Fear freezes you, takes you back. The existential meaning of having fear, I take my place from my being as I have been. The future threatening me is the reason for me basing the focus of my attention to the type of my being as I have been. The safe harbor of the past stands against the threat of the future. Fear sees the threat in the future but the one who is threatened is the one as I have been.

Fear is a type of being forgetful of yourself; it is big confusion. Forgetfulness, as we have seen, is the non-authentic trait of the past. Fear, the way of forgetting your being, draws your attention away from the question of the being. Forgetfulness, the non-authentic way of the past is an essential component of fear. If non-authentic fear is a temporality of forgetfulness, which is the non-authentic way of the past, then authentic anxiety has to be temporal by the authentic way of the past, i.e. repetitiveness.

Repetitiveness, the authentic way of I have been, is the ontological base of anxiety. Anxiety, as aforesaid, is the awareness of nothing of the "no", a feeling of alienation from the known world. The involvement of someone in the world reveals a certain type of repetitiveness of possibilities. The focal point to be kept in mind is the similarity between fear and anxiety, i.e. both have to be present in the ecstasy of the past of I have been. Anxiety, which is an authentic way, has to be revealed in terms of authentic ecstasy: repetitiveness, knowing in advance and anticipation. Fear, the non-authentic way has to be revealed in terms of non-authentic ecstasy: forgetfulness and waiting.

## 01:35 Temporality of falling

Not as understanding and conscious state, falling cannot be with authentic ecstasy. In its nature, falling is non-authentic. Moreover, the trait of the fall's ecstasy is the present which, as we have seen, is considered the lesser ontologically.

368

Fall, in its essence, turn us away from the ontological sense. The daily perception of time is, usually, such that the present seems as the location of sense and reality. Such an opinion on the present turns the experiences of events to series of actual facts which can be observed.

Each understanding of time emphasizing the actual has to consider the present as the main trait of time. The temporality of a fall is easy to understand: such interpretations of time, which focus on the actual and not on a possibility, provide the ontological base of falling. Therefore, the ontological base of the present is, in terms of falling, the same present which comprises of actual entities; the authentic present sees the present in terms of possibilities which were willingly selected and set. The ontological base of the past in terms of falling is, similarly, the same view on the past which was seen in terms of a series of not just actual events (forgetfulness) instead of authenticity as, still, meaningful possibilities (repetitiveness).

The ontological base of a future fall is limited to not-yet actual events (waiting) instead of possible projections of its ability to be a being of someone (anticipating the future).

## 01:45 World time and clock time

Da-sein is a temporal entity by its own existence and it is busy with time. Da-sein calculates time and organizes itself accordingly. As opposed to anything as "ready at hand" and "present at hand" which exist in the world, Da-sein is not present in time; rather it is time to begin with.

What is important is the way by which Da-sein calculates time prior to using any measuring devices. Such calculation is not incidental; rather it is necessary ontologically and existentially for the basic state of the Da-sein as "care".

Due to the Da-sein, in its essence, falling as something being projected, it interprets its time by its calculation. In its calculation of time, Da-sein itself, ontologically and existentially and according to its own criteria, is the place at which time is interpreted.

As opposed to Da-sein, all other entities not having the same character are inside time. The calculation precedes any device and it is actually the factor enabling the use of a clock at all. Da-sein needs not carrying a watch with it; by a certain sense, it is a clock itself.

The same way by which a being "ready at hand" shares few traits with a being "present at hand", so is time of "world time" provides the clues to the way by which what is called the perception of public time (the objective) is derived from- but also covers an ecstasy's time. While the usual public perception of time (vulgar) appears from the looking at a clock time, "world time" comes from the use of a clock and generally from the calculation of time.

Time is public and is pertaining to everything existential of a being in the world. I.e. since Da-sein, as a temporal entity, has already been revealed, and since understanding and hermeneutics belong to its existence, time becomes public.

We tune ourselves according to it so it has to be something available to anybody. Someone can deal with time in a way of dating surrounding events meeting the Da-sein in the world; it is always happening inside the horizon of a type of dealing with time which is annual and astronomic i.e. by calculability.

'Public time' is the same type of time in which the "ready at hand" and the "present at hand" in the world meet the Da-sein. It seems that the public perception of time is verified by the phenomenon of measuring time. Clock and yearly calendars manifest a series of measurable units which are interpreted as parallel to the appearance and disappearance of "moments" in various time spans. Otherwise, how can months, days, hours and seconds be explained?

However, nobody will contend that the series of appearing and disappearing moments of the clock or the yearly calendar is identical with time. The measurement of movement by movement is a way to tell time however it is not the definition of time.

Nevertheless, to be able to tell time in such a way reveals the properties of time. There is an understandable tendency to look at the clock for the definition of time or at least for the distinction of the properties of time. The clock gives us the image of time being a continuum of "moments" which is composed of "moments" not existing anymore, the moment which is now at present and moments yet to come. Thanks to the clock it seems that time can be counted as a chain of moments accessible to anybody thus being public. The fact of that time can be counted means that time can be broken to units. Surely, one hour can be seemed to be longer than the other but these experiences, it seems, are depended on states and certain circumstances of the subject; he can, for example, say "time flies when I am having fun" or "time goes by slowly when I do not feel well".

With the manic-depressive, time is, in this sense, subjective since in the "spring", i.e. in a manic state, time passes quickly because he feels good and is happy as opposed to "autumn" while in depressive state, time passes slowly because he suffers, each day seem to last forever; according to such logic, sufferance is a blessing for longevity.

As opposed to such subjective time, an objective time is public, accessible to all, everybody can count the seconds and measure it by units.

In Heidegger's analysis of time, the term "to bring to the public's attention" (veroffentlichung) or publicity is not, directly, part of what is usually understood as time; rather publicity characterizes time of care or "world time".

In it being thrown, Da-sein gives in to the changes of day and night. It also understands itself in terms of work day, one works during the day and rests at night. In this understanding, Da-sein formulizes for itself the term "when", i.e. when there will be night, when I will go to work during the day, when, in the evening, I will eat a dinner, etc.

The "when" with which Da-sein is dealing is turning into a date in the sense of something environmental, i.e. the sunrise. "When the sun will rise, it will be the time to do this and that", therefore Da-sein dates the needed time in term of something it meets in the world. The sun dates time which is interpreted by a daily relating. In this sense of dating, the most trait of time is being revealed - the day. Since the temporality of that same Da-sein which takes time (and makes use of it) is final, its days are already numbered. The dating of things in terms of celestial body which distributes light and heat is a way of dating time which is agreed upon by you and me, i.e. the being with each other in the world which everybody can agree upon. The public dating of time upon which everybody can agree upon means that everybody can calculate it at the same time; we use the same measurement device. The dating calculates time in terms of time measurement; this measurement requires something by which the clock-time will be measures. However, precisely due to the success of the public time measurement, and of course due to the need for it, it is usually right to relate to time as something which is "present at hand", thus available to be used as a "scale" or as capable of being measured.

In short, time seems as a present dimension in the present, i.e. something that always is present at hand and is countable. By the use of a clock and a calendar, time is measured or at least a continuum or a movement of something which is understood as a movement of natural objects which always seem as something "present at hand". As the natural clock that supposes to measure time, time itself is perceived as something natural "present at hand". Moreover, it is comprehensive and includes all natural things that are present at hand and that exist in it. He is, therefore, worldly. Any usable thing (device - "ready at hand") or "present at hand" which we meet in the world is present in time or inside time (innerzeitig, Being and Time page 412).

Nature itself, so it is being said, unifies everything in time, i.e. such time encloses anything and everything is inside it. According to Heidegger, this trait of time of "enclosing everything" or "contain everything" is another facet of the usual perception of time. The permanent and constant movement of the second indicator in the clock reveals to us another trait in the usual perception of time.

It is difficult if not impossible to imagine time being stopped, i.e. that there will be a "moment" which will not be replaced by another "moment". The units of time follow each other in such a way by which time appears as a persistent and stable flow. Each "moment" is, in its essence, not anymore and already not and each "moment" is also shortly. Therefore, each "moment" has a passing trait, such that time which is composed of "moments" is indefinite in few senses. The continuum of "moments" is seen as being stretched backwards and forwards indefinitely when time moves from the past through the present to the future.

There is no limit to the rate in which every moment becomes more accurate. Time, in this sense, seems as more complex than being and not being, i.e. what is not anymore "present at hand" and what is not yet "present at hand". Time can be imagined as a unified, stable one way stream. The metaphoric expression of "forward" and "backward" specifies another trait of time in the usual perception which also can be read off the clock: the asymmetry (irreversibility or one way) of time. The seconds' indicator moving always one way shows the irreversibility.

Each "moment" in the infinite continuum of "moments" is passing. Daniel O. Dahlstrom[20] defines the clock as follows: a device for the measurement of passing movement and time. It is clear that there is a different between the definition of a clock and the definition of time; however this definition shows a tide link between movement and time. According to this definition, time as well as movement comprise of processes which are countable and measurable thus time, as compared to a clock, is something countable and measurable. However, what are the

---

[20] Daniel O.Dahlstrom, Heidegger's Concept of Truth, Cambridge University Press 2001, p.364

processes which according to the definition are counted and measured? The logical answer is given by the clock itself, i.e. the hours, minutes and the second during the whole day. However, this answer is not really suitable since the hours, minutes and seconds are being realized by measurement of time and therefore should not be compared to time itself.

Artificial and natural clocks count and measure "moments" which can be defined more precisely depending on the given time unit (millennium, year, month, second, nano second, etc.). That way, the definition of a clock is parallel to the term of time as an infinite continuum (and even a replacement of one passing "moment" by another "moment", i.e. which comes in its place) which contains all natural things or events as well as being accessible to all.

This definition of the clock includes traits which, in Heidegger's view, seals what is called by him the usual perception of time: countable, accessible to all, enclosing all, and an exchange of series of "moments". Of course, one should not forget the irreversibility or unidirectional. The usual understanding of time only includes the time which is revealed by counting and by the continuum of "moments". Out of this understanding rises the term of time as a series of "moments" which are measurable more or less in a precise and unidirectional manner, an irreversible of one "moment" after the other.

Heidegger makes specifies another form of time which he calls "worldly time": "therefore we will call time which is public by its temporality, worldly time. We will specify as such not due to its objective presence as an intrinsic worldly entity..., but due to its belonging to the world in terms which were existentially and ontologically interpreted... only now, the dealing in time is characterized in its entirety through its structure: it is dated, continuous and public and having such structure it belongs to the world (Being and Time page 414-15).

'Worldly time' does not stem from the analysis of the clock, rather from the use of it; it is about the term of "telling the time". In telling or reading the time, neither the clock nor time are the subjects of my intentionality. Surely, we calculate time, however not according to the clock and not by measuring time units and movement according to common perception. In such calculation of time, it has sense (in worldliness).

If, for example, I study at school and the bell is ringing, I know that this is the time to have a break and the next lesson will follow it; in this case, I do not need to read time from a clock. I conclude by calculation that the next lesson will begin following the break. Here, I do not consider the usual perception of time with all its traits. I know that with the ring of the bell, I will, for example, have something to eat and drink. I do not need a clock to tell me my options; the ring of the bell performs this function. We are using the ring of the bell as a clock. When a student hears the bell and says "now", he does not mean 4 o'clock rather a break and rest. The teacher may understand from the bell that this is the time to go to another class or to the teacher's room. The bell tells the teacher and the student two different things: the teacher - to go to the teacher's room and the student - to go and have something to eat and drink. Such example shows that time with which the teacher and the student are dealing is also public because they are with-each-other. This is the time with which we are dealing and to which we relate and in the same time we are with-each-other, i.e. we both hear (read) the same time but the meaning is different: on one hand to go to the teacher's room and on the other hand, for the student, to go and have something to eat and drink. Heidegger calls it also 'time of care' or more precisely "the time with which they are dealing" as well as worldly time (Weltzeit).

"Worldly time" is a term for the time which we are considering. The original giving of time is defined, i.e. dated from the worldly and daily occurrences without and before the calculation of a date from the calendar. At such time, we use the clock (the bell) as a usable device and not the theory of time as something which is "present at hand".

The time at school, the time of care, is having sense (worldly), it is dated, continuous and public (Being and Time page 406-411). It is public in the sense that the ring of the bell in our scenario is heard by all teachers and students; time is seen (heard) by everybody. Since all of us live under the sky, the most natural measure is the course of the sun which is open for all; with sunrise we go to school and with sunset we return home.

**01:50 Insanity time**

There is no public time for the being-manic-depressive, rather an intrinsic phenomenological-subjective time; he cannot share the recurrence, i.e. ascending to mania and descending to his depression with anybody else.

This is the trait which, in his private phenomenological time, is different from the objective time of the clock. The being-manic-depressive reads time from himself, he is a clock: while in mania, it is time to take anti psychotic pills as opposed while in depression, it is time to take pills to raise his mood; he "reads" time through his states, he does not look at the clock or at the calendar in order to know the time. He has an intrinsic clock.

The intrinsic clock is similar to the "worldly time" except for the fact that it is not publicly accessible and measurable. His consciousness is the device for the measurement of time.

This is what I call phenomenology time or insanity time, i.e. something private which is still being considered by the being-manic-depressive; it is being calculated (to take pills) and of course it is very significant for him, i.e. the pills become very important in the life of the being-manic-depressive. He takes pills because he is concerned about his state, i.e. he is concerned about how he is. From the horizon of the being-manic-depressive who, now at the present, is manic-psychotic, he is "not yet" in depression; in this sense, the present of the being-manic-depressive, while in manic-psychosis, has sense. While being depressive in the present, he was manic-psychotic in the past and he is "not yet" balanced, he is toward a balanced future, he is anticipating it. When he reaches a balanced state, he was, in the past, in depression, in the present he is balanced and he is "not yet" psychotic but he anticipates a manic-depressive future.

This recurrence is a recurrence of "not yet" and anticipation the future. One can see that there is an anomaly between the objective time of the clock and the phenomenological-insane time of the Da-sein-manic-depressive.

On a higher level, the mentally ill are temporal, however psychosis and depression are anomaly. Being-depressive or depression is an anomaly because it emphasizes the future and psychosis is anomaly because it emphasizes the past. Time has three dimensions, an objective clock time, a worldly time and an insane-subjective phenomenological time in which the clock is private and not public which is an anomaly of the objective clock time.

The being-manic-depressive and the being-depressive in the worldly time cares for himself and therefore takes antipsychotic pills while in a psychosis state and antidepressant pills while in depressive state. He understands the time at which he has to take pills. There is a discrepancy between clock time and the anomaly of an insane-phenomenological time.

A mentally ill does not exist in an objective time, he has a subjective time. In a state of psychosis, the past is present in the present, i.e. hallucination is, as I have said in the preceding volume, a memory of what the psychotic has seen in the past only now he had "jumped" forward to the present, i.e. the past is still here continuing and arrives at the present and at the same time the hallucinating present returns back (goes back) to the past, i.e. the psychotic is "I have been".

Hallucination of a man in a black coat standing at the cornet means that, in the past, I have seen a man in a black coat standing at the corner. The man from the past returns and "visits" the psychotic in his present. Therefore, the past is still in the present. Your objective past is no more, ours is still here, it is the present. The past did not pass but is in the present which is the state of the psychotic. The past is what is present in the consciousness but not in the reality of the present and therefore the present is no more; but still. What is present, i.e. the presence in the hallucinating consciousness of the psychotic is the man in the black coat standing at the corner however, he is not actually present at the objective time external to the psychosis, he was in the past, in the reality and now he is absent at the objective time, therefore, "the man in the black coat standing at the corner" in the hallucination does not denote anything in reality but in the past.

The man who is present now in the hallucination is a man who was present in the real past at the objective time, therefore now, the past which was real "jumps" to the hallucination, it is, still, present in the hallucination in the present although now, in the reality, it is absent, not present.

This is the sense of detachment from the reality by presence. In fact, the psychotic, for a short moment, succeeds to detach himself from the metaphysics of the presence. In the philosophical tradition, the treatment of the sense of being was, until now, as Ousia or Parousia, i.e. something which denotes presence in ontological temporal terms (presence or appearance). Beings are perceived as presence in the present. They are understood in relation to a defined time - the present. The present had always the precedence in western philosophy. The present had always been perceived which persists, near and available, exposed to be seen and given at hand, i.e. "present at hand".

These entities which shows themselves are perceived as present (Ousia). From Parmenides until Husserl the precedence of the present was not questioned, it cannot be "having been"; it is self evident and thinking cannot go beyond it. The being is the parallel of persistence in presence.

Despite all that, the one who succeeds to detach himself from the traits of presence and persistence is the psychotic. The presence is the past and the past jumped forward to the presence which is actually the past - "I have been".

The object, which is present in the present in the consciousness, was there in the reality but still it is present in the consciousness although, in reality, it is "nothingness".

This anomaly is the subduing of reality by the present which is present. Moreover, continuum and the directionality of time are broken with the psychotic; i.e. "moment" had passed and then it jumps (that same "moment") forward to the future which appears as a present which is past. While in objective time, we consider continuous and unidirectional time as moments spreading from the present toward the past and the future; i.e. as a continuous line on which the points are before and after a given point.

A continuous unidirectional time will look like this:

| 1 | 2 | 3 | 4 | 5 | 6 | 7 | 8 | 9 | 10 |
|---|---|---|---|---|---|---|---|---|----|
|   |   |   |   |   |   |   |   |   |    |

As opposed, psychotic time or a dream will look like:

| 1 | 2 | 3 | 4 | 5 | 6 | 1 | 7 | 8 | 9 |
|---|---|---|---|---|---|---|---|---|---|
|   |   |   |   |   |   |   |   |   |   |

Time will start from moment 1 and will be continuous until moment 6 and then moment 1 will jump forward and will reappear in the future as a passed present. Moment 1 will carry with it an image of a man with a black coat standing at the corner (in reality) and then will pass; afterwards, at the beginning of the hallucination of psychosis 1 "he will jump to the future" carrying with it "the man with the black coat standing at the corner" however, this time, he will reappear as a hallucination in the present which he had passed, i.e. the present of the hallucination reverses and returns to the past.

The irreversibility of time is reversed. You must bracket the world in order to understand the psychotic consciousness. I would like to clarify that we do not doubt the existence of the world, but doubt its existence *now* which is present before the psychotic at *this moment, at the present.*
We do not ask does the lion exist or not, it exists even for the psychotic however, it exists as a memory of a lion which was really perceived in the past. We ask, does the lion exist or is present before the consciousness of the psychotic now, right at this moment.
While having hallucinations, the psychotic is: "seeing", "hearing", "touching", "smelling" the directionality of time, i.e. its irreversibility, i.e. the fact that objective time moves continuously from the past through the present toward the future turns out to be untrue, there is a rupture in the world or in its time, i.e. since the origin of hallucinations is in the past, thus they are exists in his present despite the fact that at an objective clock time, they exist in the past.
The psychotic actually sees the present in his past; his past and present are mixed, the present is past and the past is present; as a result, the directionality and irreversibility of time are ruptured. This "rupture" in time is the moment at which the psychotic detaches himself from reality being the main trait of hallucination. With you, the present is always the present which is happening in
382

a defined directionality, with you, there is a simultaneous compatibility between the image and the object or between the noema and the object which it intends.

From time immemorial, the assumption at the base of philosophy, which I call the metaphysics of the moment, is that perception includes synchronization between perception and its subject. This is the basic assumption for the philosophy of the image or the representation.

There is a compatibility of temporality between the perceiving ego and the perceived object and it does not matter, according to Husserl, if we talk about a representative image or a direct perception.

The perception and the object are compatible and have to exist concurrently for the compatibility to be actual because the lack of actuality leads to the image or the representation not reflecting the actual reality but reflecting the reality which is no more! Reality being no more strips the idea of representation from its sense.

Through fantasy and in parallel to hallucinations, you can detach from the reality of the moment. You can overcome the metaphysics by imagination and fantasy.

While you imagine, the image arrives from the past and is present before you in the present, one can close his eyes for that purpose. The content of the dream is not present now in the actual reality as a thing external to consciousness but exist in it, the content is an image of something having been present before you in the past however, right now, the image or the dream is a passed present in the consciousness although it does not exist out there outside the consciousness; this your way to detach from the metaphysics of the present.

Subjectivity, by the psychotic, is therefore a temporal state, a rupture between reality and ego. We have to think about philosophy without the prejudice as if there is no phenomenon in which time is not unidirectional, i.e. as if time moves always in a certain direction, i.e. from the past to the present and from the present to the future. There is an authentic phenomenon, as I have described, of time of what has happened and is not present, jumping forward toward the future and appearing as a present which is actually a past; this is a reversible time in which the present denotes the past.

## Being manic-depressive

**"All signs of the overman nature appear in a human being as an illness or insanity"**

Nietzsche, unpublished texts dated from November 1882 to February 1883

**The time 02:00, introduction to manic depression[21]**

Everybody knows depression, but few know that depression has a manic side to it. The bipolar disorder, previously known as manic

---

[21] from "Manic Depression" by Professor Avraham Weizmann, Dr. Micahel Phoyerovsky and Dr. Vered Tal, Prolog publishing

depression, is a mental disorder under which the patient suffers from extreme and cyclic fluctuations of mood. What is mood? It is a well known phenomenon but difficult to define. One may consider mood as a color, the way by which we see and feel ourselves and the world around us in a given moment. Everybody has a wide variety of moods as well as a variety of physical and verbal expressions suitable for every mood. When we are joyful, our internal world is lighted, we fell good and see the world in a bright light. We express our feelings externally by smiling and laughing, our talk is swift and our body becomes vigorous. Similarly, while being sad, we feel distress, hopelessness, lack of energy which express itself in saddened face, lowered look and a sense of heavy limbs. A bipolar disorder manifests in the existence of manic states, i.e. elated mood and hyper activity alternating with depression. The disorder is a state in which people, patients, experience an elated mood (hypo mania) and even an extreme elated mood (mania) and on the other hand depressive states for a certain period of time which disrupt their functionality and the "normal" way of life. The book of psychiatric diagnoses DSM IV had changed the definition of the disorder from a manic depressive mental illness to a mood disorder, a bipolar disorder. This is an affective disorder, i.e. mood dependent. During the episode, the patient's mood fluctuates between mania - an extreme elated mood and depression. The disorder is characterized by the aggressive and cyclic fluctuation between the two poles. The episode can occur after years of balanced mood. People experiencing manic episode will usually experience also depressive episodes and symptoms or mixed states in which manic and depressive traits appear concurrently. A "normal" mood may exist between episodes however in cases of an acute manic depression the states of depression and manic will alternate quickly; this state is called rapid cycling. A state of acute manic episode may lead to a full psychosis. The illness is classified to sub categories according to nature, frequency and acuteness of the disorder: bipolar I, bipolar II, hypomania (moderate mania), Cyclothymia and other types. The distribution of the disorder is estimated at 1 percent of the population in western countries. The most common disease in the world is depression which is defined by repeating episodes of depression or in medical terms, unipolar depression which is not accompanied by the development of manic states; however, the bipolar disorder or the manic depressive, is a separate disease which is characterized by depressive states alternating with manic states. Notwithstanding the similarity in some of the manifestations, it is a different disease. It is characterized by lower incidence and infliction of different population. While the unipolar depression is more common in adult women (age 40 -50) of a relative higher socio-economic level, the bipolar disease is equally hitting men and women of younger age and does not distinct different populations. A substantial part of the patients develop their first depressive or manic episode before their 20th birthday. The incidence of the bipolar disorder in the population is at 1 percent, similarly to the incidence of schizophrenia. In Israel, about 65,000 people suffer from manic depression. There are claims that additional 2-5% is on the verge of suffering under the disorder. A worldwide research performed by Myrna Weismann, an American researcher and her colleagues, had thoroughly surveyed the rate of the disorder's incidence and its traits throughout various regions including the USA, Europe, Australia and even Israel; the researchers have come to the conclusion that the maximal risk for the appearance of the disorder is at young age and that the incidence is equal in every surveyed region without any connection to culture, race, religion or a socioeconomic state. There was no connection to urban living as opposed to schizophrenia which is more common in urban areas. The diagnosis is based on the report of the patient and people surrounding him, i.e. by phenomenology, however, the disease is hard to diagnose. Nowadays, it is estimated that the disease is caused by an imbalance of chemicals in the brain. The outbreak usually occurs in adolescence. Many celebrities, musicians, writers and leaders have suffered from a bipolar disorder (the painter Vincent Van Gogh, the writer Virginia Wolf, the write Edgar Allen Po, the poet Helderline, my poet, Byron, Abraham Lincoln and many others) and many of them and their physicians were troubled by the possibility that medical treatment controlling the mood might reduce their creativity. Anyway, there exist many testimonies that people with such disorder is indeed more creative when they are being effectively treated. Only the early stages of mania (hypo mania) contribute to creativity. The full blown mania (with psychotic symptoms) disrupts creativity and the entire course of life. While in its peak, the disease heavily disrupts creativity. The disease is fatal, i.e. patients may commit suicide mainly during the depressive stages. In certain cases, the disorder can be destructive for life while in other cases it can cause creativity, genius quality, ambitiousness and ambition. In the following parts, I will describe the bipolar disorder, how the diagnosis is done, what are its traits and causes and, of course, which way are available for treatment.

## 02:05 Historic background

During the years, the definition of insanity had changed its form many times until it became crystallized in today's form. Depression and manic cases have been documented in early times but the precise definitions of each one of them as well as the connection between them have developed throughout hundreds of years until the common perception of the bipolar disorder was formed. The Greek, before Christ, have described states of depression and mania; their definition was very wide and included almost all mental illnesses. In old times, insanity was considered as stemming from divine powers, inspiration or godly curse. Later on, the medical profession had developed from roots planted in philosophy; the philosophers of that era have tried to comprehend and learn about the causes of mental illnesses. Insanity states were related, then, to the diaphragm, a muscle tissue which separates between the chest and the lower torso. The mind, so claimed the thinkers back then, is located under the diaphragm. With time, the mind "climbed" up and claimed by Aristotle to be located at the heart. The father of medicine, Hippocrates, was the first to determine that insanity has to be related to a biological disorder in the brain which is also the source for feelings and thoughts. This determination has been scientifically founded during the years and is valid until today. Hippocrates has described in the scriptures: "people suffering under melancholy (depression) have fear from light and are deterred from others. They are full of concern and fears. It is common for them to complain about various pains, for example, strong stomach ache like thousand sharp needles. Sometimes, they will describe wild dreams or insomnia". He adds that in most cases "the sadness states will lead to seclusion, rejection of life and recurring thoughts on the angle of death". The explanation of melancholy which survived until the renaissance, relates most of the illnesses to imbalance between four elements: blood, yellow bile, black bile and saliva; according to Hippocrates and his students, a surplus in black bile causes melancholy which is also the literal meaning of the word as opposed to mania which, in their opinion, is caused by surplus of yellow bile; any state of retardation was interpreted back then, in Hellenic times, as melancholy and a state of hyper activity and unrest as mania; this a reason for various states as high fever or convulsions to have been diagnosed as mania. Nowadays, the term "psychosis" replaces the mania from back then and the definition of mania became more focused and narrow. Aristotle surely related the disease to a heart's disorder but he was the first to relate the idea of "tendency" to being depressive and genius. He gave as examples the fathers of philosophy Plato and Socrates who had melancholy and were known as geniuses in their field.

The first to describe the mania and its relation to depression was the Greek philosopher Aretaeus. He classified, differed and described the term precisely and vividly, a description which is useful until today: "laughter, the tendency for adventures and games. It is amazing how old forgotten memories return and become vivid. In this state, ordinary people start to deal in astronomy and philosophy, feel the muse and write poetry. Sometimes they will move constantly with no direction passing many kilometers without any purpose or awareness". Aretaeus was one of the first to observe that the disease outbreaks at a young age usually adolescence. He also observed that manic states happen before or after melancholy (depression) and concluded that the two states are connected and causing each other thus being actually one process. In the middle of the 19<sup>th</sup> century, French psychiatrics have arrived at the same conclusion: mania and depression are two sides of the same coin; the Frenchman Jean Pierre Falret called it a circular insanity (Folie Circulaire) fluctuating between two poles.

An additional breakthrough in the understanding of the disease occurred in 1896 when Emil Kraeplin, the father of contemporary psychiatrics, published the results of his life's work, a very long and comprehensive observation of 1,000 patients. He subdivided the psychotic diseases to two major groups: manic-depressive and schizophrenia; he had found that manic-depression is characterized in time limited episodes of change in mood, prolonged relapses in which the patient returns to function normally and better prognosis. Following Kraeplin, Eugene Bleuler called the collection of the manic and depressive states as affective diseases i.e. illnesses of feeling. Later on, a distinction between unipolar states, i.e. solely recurring depressions and bipolar states including mania and depressions was formed. This distinction opened up many research possibilities and with every additional piece of information it became clear that this definition was justified. During the 20<sup>th</sup> century and especially during the last two decades, a breakthrough occurred in the research of the brain and mental illnesses, neurotransmitters were discovered which communicate between brain cells playing a major role in the creation of mental illnesses. Contemporary genetic research tries to locate the gene or genes contributing to the creation of the illness and sophisticated imaging devices enable the measurement of different materials and the activity zones in the brain. Nowadays, we have very precise diagnostic definitions for the affective diseases as well as precise and sophisticated research tools. It seems that in following years, additional causal biological factors will be revealed and more effective treatment of the bipolar disorder will be developed.


## 02:10 Mania


Manic and depressive states appear differently in different patients because they are dependent on the patient's character, his thoughts and feelings. In this chapter, I will describe the common and the typical. The name manic-depressive describes the two poles of the disease. Actually, it is more complex including the zone between the poles. I will describe the extreme states as well as the intermediary and transient states. Mania is a mental disorder classified as a mood disorder and characterized by a feeling of extreme elation, euphoria, the feeling of being a superman and hyper activity; the patients experience increase of energy and do not need sleep, "thoughts race" (the thought is faster than speech not able to catch up with it), fast thoughts, and speech may be very fast (logo mania) leading the patient to drop sentences or parts thereof making him incomprehensible. He may seem rational at a certain moment and without control the next; his mind is easily distracted. The patient's behavior may be aggressive and unbearable; they experience increase in their libido. In a severe manic state, the patient may develop psychotic symptoms and think that he was "chosen" and that he has to fulfill a "task" or mat think other megalomaniacal thoughts. A person suffering from a manic episode tends to make new plans.

Many patients in a manic state experience acute anxiety reaching even bad and hot temper while others experience serenity and euphoria. The patient's behavior during an episode is characterized in rash deeds which he, later on, may regret (such as heavy money spending, purchasing expensive and redundant things, quitting his job and even a spouse or having relationship with a stranger). The mania is usually characterized by impatience reaching even bad temper and in extreme cases it might even lead to violence. The lack of need for sleep and the increase of the libido might jeopardize relationship with a spouse. All of these reflect a defect sense of reality. There are patients who, while talking about sexual subjects, loose their inhibitions. A key trait of a manic episode is the different between manic behavior and the ordinary personality of a patient. The appearance of the disorder may be gradual over a period of several weeks or months before the full outbreak of the syndrome. In the lack of treatment, a manic episode might prolong for months or years. Following the episode, the patient usually returns to his previous state. In a bipolar disorder, the patient goes through, at least, one manic episode followed by the opposite state of depression. There are patients who have had one manic episode during their youth and later on suffered only from depression while others will have alternating yearly episodes of mania and depression; others will have one manic episode in few years and will not have depressive episodes at all. The difference between bipolar disorder and unipolar major disorder is that the latter does not include elation and euphoria. In an extreme mania there are psychotic symptoms of delusions and hallucinations. Acute mania is an emergency medical situation. Should the patient suffering from an acute mania not be treated quickly and effectively, he might jeopardize his marriage, his job, his socio economic level and even his life. The identification of behavioral risks, verbal expressions of hallucinations or delusions (psychosis) as well as violence is a cause for forced hospitalization. People suffering from a bipolar disorder are often identified as schizophrenia patients although it is not the case. Manic state has three stages.


**First stage:** the patient seems elated and is slightly more active than usual, speaking quickly, his words out bursting, feeling happiness, increased abilities, experiencing fast and sharp thoughts, sharp memory and the ability to create without stopping. Patients describe it as a feeling of "high". At this stage the ability to function in daily life is not yet disrupted and the productivity may even increase. For example, a painter, poet or a salesman will experience it as especially productive period.

**Second stage:** the elated mood turns unpleasant for the patients and the people surrounding him. The patient becomes impatient and bad tempered. The fast talk progresses and becomes a flow of sentences and words. One can no longer follow the words and the patient who used to be vigorous, charismatic and funny turns into incomprehensible, rude and grotesque. Plans turn grandiose and incompatible with the patient's capabilities. While in the first stage it was difficult to determine the start of the disease, now, it is easy for the surrounding to identify a pathological state.

**Third stage:** in some cases the situation will deteriorate to an unorganized speech and uncontrolled and unrestrained behavior. The grandiose plans become unrealistic thoughts (delusions) of grandeur and even paranoia. The fast passage from one thought to another creates a flow of detached words, a state defined in professional terms as thoughts' race. These people seem often as disoriented, lacking control of reality, lacking judgment and might perform destructive acts upon themselves and their surroundings. This stage is defined as a psychotic stage, i.e. the ability to perceive and evaluate reality does not exist anymore.

At this stage the hospitalization is usually unavoidable and it is the only way to avoid severe results. There endless stories about people whose life was collapsed during these few hours. for example, a businessman who invested carelessly and lost tens of thousands of dollars within less than 24 hours; the owner of a huge collection of rare books decided to give them for education purposes and had spread them on the sidewalks of his town; or a high-tech developing new technologies suddenly busy day and night in grotesque inventions not fitting his level and corresponding with government authorities asking them to recognize his inventions. One can easily loose life savings, personal and professional reputation, harming relatives and close friends or even loose his life. A psychiatric hospitalization in extreme cases is justified and even essential. The cases described here are a flow of events usually happening without medical intervention. The identification and early treatment can stop the process returning to the previous state.

Since the state of the disease is characterized by so many signs, basic criteria were created enabling to unify the way by which a manic state is being diagnosed. According to current classification by the American Psychiatric Association, the diagnosis of a manic state requires the following:

1.  A defined period of at least one week in which the patient is in an irregular elated or bad tempered mood. Should this situation seem acute and requiring hospitalization, it may be diagnosed within a period shorter than a week.

2.  During such period, three of the following traits have to be identified:

    - Exaggerated or grandiose self esteem

    - Decrease in the need for sleep

    - Over speaking or the need to continue speaking

    - Fast changing of subjects or the feeling of "rampaging" thoughts

    - Distraction - attention is easily distracted to unimportant stimulus from the environment

    - Increase in activity or restlessness

    - An exaggerated dealing in pleasing activities resulting in long term damage, e.g. exaggerated shopping, high risk investments or uncontrolled sexual activity

3.  The disorder is severe so that there is a risk of harming the professional, social or personal functions or that there is a risk for the patient or his surroundings thus hospitalization becomes necessary.

One should not diagnose a bipolar disorder, should these signs originate in the abuse of drugs, medicines or a physical illness.

**Hippomanic state** - a more common state than mania is "moderate mania". The mania is classified according to its severity. Relative moderate episodes, without the psychotic symptoms or these which are risky for the patient and his surrounding are called hippomania. The syndrome of major depressive episodes along with the hippomanic episodes is called bipolar disorder II as opposed from the major diagnosis of bipolar disorder I. all traits of mania (elated mood and optimism, increase in energy, increased libido, the lack of need of sleep) exist also here but last between one and four days, the daily functioning is not harmed and creativity is increased. Therefore, in diagnosing hippomania one should not rely solely on the patient's account rather rely also on an objective third party testimony from a person knowing the basic nature of the patient and observing the change.


**02:15 State of depression**


Similarly to mania, depression may exist in varying strengths starting from physical and mental sluggishness and ending with extreme states of helplessness which are typical of decreased level of mood; depression may be considered as harming in three major levels - mood, thought process and physical activity. The depressive patient has a typical look, he is bent, moving slowly, sitting down sluggishly, his shoulders are bowed, and his head is dropped, his face expression is impervious and his eyes are astray. While having a depressive episode, patients often look ten years older. The depressed person suffers from decreased mood, from senselessness and lack of pleasure from activities which gave him pleasure in the past, from low esteem and helplessness, guilt or hopelessness. Many report difficulties to concentrate on simple tasks, lack of interest and difficulties making mundane decisions. Physical sluggishness and the lack of energy lead to the reduction in functionality and difficulties in carrying out necessary tasks. The patients suffering from depression have difficulties falling asleep and once they do, it is disrupted and with bad dreams. They usually wake up early, 2 or 3 o'clock in the morning without the ability to fall asleep again. The lack of appetite leads to loss of weight but sometimes the opposite is happening - increased appetite leading to increase in weight (a state called untypical depression and manifests also in prolonged unsatisfying sleep). In more severe states, the patients have suicidal thoughts and even plan how to do it. There are patients who write fare well letters or a will and meticulously plan their death; sometimes the decision to die provides them with a temporary relief from their miseries. The depressive patient is desperate, feels hard feelings of helplessness, hopelessness and lack of purpose in life and has difficulties to believe that this situation is going to change sometimes in the future. In conversations with patients, they always raise their feeling that the depression will never end even of some of them have experienced its finality in the past. The ability to remember positive things is disappeared. Depression may be accompanied by anxiety with all its physical signs as increased heart beat, the feeling of distress in the chest, mouth dryness and repeating thoughts of concern, hypochondriac fears and fears from severe illnesses of physical sufferings. Often it is accompanied by complaints about pains or a problem in the functioning of a certain organ without having a real physical problem. Sometimes the depression is complicated by additional phenomena. A psychotic depression is a more severe state which includes delusions or hallucinations. Psychosis usually has a frightening and threatening content. The psychiatric Eugene Bleuler describes: "the hallucinations - the devil appears at his window, grimaced at the face of the patient. He hears how he is condemned to die, the closing of the coffin cover and his relatives grieving the fate inflicted upon them". And delusions - thoughts about economic, physical and mental destruction which cannot be reputed even if reality shows otherwise, fears from losing control, the loss of sanity and inflicting harm upon their loved ones and more. The psychotic depression can be accompanied with restlessness and periods of hyperactivity alternating with periods of slowing down and freezing. The diagnosis of a depressive state has clear criteria according to the classification method of the American Psychiatric Association:

Five or more from the following signs which exists for at least two weeks differ from the basic mood of the patient:

- Reduced mood most during most of the day almost every day. A feeling of sadness or emptiness may be experienced. Emptiness is a feeling of senselessness of the daily existence. Nothing is exciting, challenging, of interest which is worthwhile waking up for.

- Minimum sleep or much sleep.

- Lack of movement or restless movement.

- Exaggerated feelings of low self esteem or guilt (not the guilt for being ill).

- Reduction in the capabilities of thought and concentration, difficulties making decisions. Repeating thoughts about death, planning suicide or even carrying it out.

1. These signs create distress or disfunctioning, professional or otherwise.

2. The state is not a result of a physical illness or substance abuse as drugs.

3. The signs are not a result of mourning - a reaction to the death of a loved one in the last two months - or their strength is stronger than in regular mourning situations. As I have said in the first chapter, Freud was little naïve contending that depression is a result of a loss. My experience is that the reasons for depression are more diverse.

Depression being part of a bipolar disorder has few traits which are not typical of regular depression (unipolar) such as relative frequent episodes which develop quickly already at young age or even earlier. Also depressions with non typical components as restlessness, the need for movement or increased appetite and sleep raise the suspicion of bipolar disorder. A patient in a depressive state who already experienced manic states in the past, the diagnosis is clearer. But when the disease manifests initially in depression, it is important to distinct between the various processes of the disease because the treatment is different. Sometimes the non typical components are so prominent overshadowing the possibility of depression. Therefore, the awareness of the existence of two types of depression is vital for a correct diagnosis.

**02:20 Mixed state**

The definition includes the concurrent existence of depressive symptoms with manic symptoms. Actually, the matter is more complex and the existence of these states exemplifies the complexness of the disease. They are common in half of the patients. The criteria for the diagnosis of mixed states include very quick fluctuations between the two poles and a prolonged state which includes traits from the two poles. The predominant trait in mixed states is a "dejected" mood (dysphoria), bad tempered person, speaks loudly, reacts angrily to any stimulus, keeps complaining and feels degraded. Mostly, the patients speak continuously, quickly and under pressure, they are restless and anxious. Their appearance is different that of the depressive, they demand attention, write complaints and move restlessly. Their vigorous but purposeless activity can arrive at extreme states to complete insomnia and confusion. Already at the beginning of the twentieth century, the father of psychiatry, Emil Kreplin, had described the types of mixed states. He described depression and mania according to three components: mobility - increased in mania and decreased in depression; mood, increased in mania and decreased in depression; and the pace of thinking - accelerated in mania and decelerated I depression. For example, the existence of one depressive and two manic components will create a mixed picture. An example is the description of restless patients running around purposelessly, touching everything, changing their cloth frequently and sometimes outburst in anger. Mostly they are desperate and under suffering but sometimes burst in laughter and immediately retreat to bad temper. The suffering in mixed states is particularly hard and therefore it is not surprising that a mixed state leads to high frequency of suicidal thoughts even to actual attempts.

## 02:25 Cyclothymia

Cyclothymia is a disorder manifesting in changing moods but as opposed to manic-depression, the moods are not as intense as by depression or mania in their extreme form. The relatives of the patients relate it, usually, to a personality subdued to changing moods. The mood exchanges can be fast, within days or hours or the present mood lasts for weeks before returning to norm or reversing itself. These people experience periods of good mood, low need for sleep, a feeling of vigor and achievability, a feeling that "everything goes" socially, professionally and personally. During these periods, the self confidence increases, there is interest and need for the surrounding people; sometimes it reaches exaggerated feelings of romance and sex or having relationship outside their marriage. Money is easily spent, productivity and creativity increase and world looks pink. And then, one day, they wake up in the morning with bad mood followed by days when they feel lack of energy, prolonged sleep, sometimes increase in appetite, seclusion and the avoidance of people, difficulty carrying daily tasks, difficulty in concentration and the decrease in production. Sometimes they sick solace in alcohol and indeed addictions to drug and alcohol are very common and problematic. Generally, one may describe these patients as unstable. Their social connections manifest in periods of investment and periods of avoidance, their achievements at work increase and decrease alternately, they show changing interest in various fields. It is typical for them to get excited by a new activity, to deal with intensely and suddenly cease, being disappointed or just indifferent. Cyclothymiacs talk about the difficulty in planning. For example, they do not know whether they will be energetic over the weekend (e.g. an actor having difficulties because 'he committed himself to a future show'). There are cyclothymiacs, who seem to be in a normal mood, there are those who fluctuate constantly; there are those who are mainly hypo manic and those who are mainly depressed (hypothemiac). There are those who suffer from moods only in transient seasons and those who do not recall being in normal mood. Cyclothymia is an easy manifestation of bipolar disorder and both have a common mechanism. A person having Cyclothymia will not be hospitalized because this disorder does not significantly harm his functions, but as it progresses, suffering increases. Many apply, at this stage, for medical treatment making the professional intervention even by medication. The right treatment will ease the suffering and therefore the disorder should not be considered as having no way out.

The criteria for the diagnosis of a Cyclothymia disorder exist only in part of the classification systems because there is still disagreement about the classification of it as a standalone disorder.

1.     At least two years of instability in mood including depressive states and Hypomania states among which exists a period of normal mood.

2.     During that same period, the moods were not extreme until the diagnosis of a medium or severe depression or of mania. Major depressive states or real mania may happen before or following said period.

3.  At least three of the following signs must exist during the period of decreased mood:

- Decrease in energy and activity

- Difficulties to sleep

- The loss of self confidence

- Difficulties in concentration

- Social withdrawal

- The loss of interest in sex and other pleasing activities

- Being silent

- Pessimism for the future or agonizing searching through the past


4.  At least three of the following signs exist during the period of elated mmod:

- Increase in energy and activity

- Decreased need for sleep

- Exaggerated self esteem

- Extra sharp and creative thinking

- Exaggerated sociability

- Chattiness

- Increased dealing in sex and other pleasing activities

- Over optimism or exaggeration in the description of past successes


## 02:30 The course of the disease


Generally, the bipolar disease outbreaks in the second or third decade in the patient's life and continues in depressive or manic episodes with remissions between them. There are patients by whom the pattern is constant - a depressive wave followed by mania or vice versa and there are others by whom the course is unpredictable at all; mostly it outbreaks as a depression and sometimes as a mania. It is important when medication is being chosen for treatment because both versions have different reaction to different medication. The lucky ones will suffer from just few episodes during the cause of their life and others, while not treated, may fluctuate between mania and depression almost incessantly. As a rule, with the increase in age, the waves multiply in numbers and last longer. The age in which the disease is out breaking is decreasing in recent years probably die to the increase in drug abuse. Relatives who suffer under the disorder show an increasing age at which the disease is out breaking.

**The frequency of the episodes;** it is a known fact that the remission time between the first, second and third episode is much longer than the remission time of future episodes. The intervals between the waves tend to reduce with the increase of age. Few of the patients, the ones having frequent and prolonged episodes may develop a situation in which they cannot maintain a balance and normal mood. There is even a biological theory contending that changes are taking place in the brain because it is being exposed to so many waves and these changes making it more susceptible to instability. This is why it is recommended to keep the treatment with medication and avoiding this complication because the first years are important for establishment of the future course of the disease. About one fifth of the patients develop alternating and frequent episodes. This course is called "fast cycling". Sometimes the exchange is so fast, within less than 24 hours, and then it is called ultra radiant cycling. As opposed to a periodical course of the disease, this patient enjoys no remission at all; he is in an infinite cycle and is being controlled by acute fluctuations of mood.

## 02:40 Diagnosis and classification

As deducted from the aforesaid, the diagnosis of the disease requires the presence of two polar states - depressive and manic. Reality is more complex and the disease has many forms of manifestation. A contemporary method of classification was developed which classifies the various forms.

**Bi-polar disease type I** - this is the classic type according to which the disease was defined. It is characterized by repeating and changing waves of mania and depression in their complete clinical form.

**Bi-polar disease type 2** - is diagnosed in half of the patients and is more common in women, in these cases the periods of depression alternate with hypomania states which do not develop into actual mania. Also the depression differs a bit from the classical depression and is characterized with "untypical" types. The patients often describe an unstable mood not, in fact, a prolonged depressive mood, they report over eating, prolonged sleep, restlessness and tension. Even though feelings as sadness and distress are less common, the general feeling is painted in colors related by experts to depression.

**Bi-polar disease type 3 -** this group includes a collection of states in which the diagnosis is particularly hard to reach. These are patients having a bipolar disease who, until now, have suffered from depressive states only and the other pole of their disease is still hidden and not being yet manifested but appeared following a treatment with antidepressants, hence the assumption that the mania might outbreak sometimes in the future. It is important to classify them in the bipolar disease's group defining the anticipation for a certain course for the disease and the treatment deriving from it. A relative common scenario is of a patient suffering apparently from depression, receiving anti depressants to which he reacts very quickly and already at early stages of the treatment the signs of the depression disappear. But this stability is not maintained. The mood continues to "climb" becoming elation and a feeling of happiness and joy. It may be that joy is a natural reaction to getting healed from depression but sometimes it is hypomania. How can we differentiate? A too quick reaction, over vigorousness and exaggerated joy which are not characterized by the usual personality of the patient indicate a bipolar disease. Should we not change the treatment, the situation will worsen. In another case, a depressive patient has relatives who suffer from a bipolar disease; this patient has the risk of developing fully blown bipolar disease. Also depressive patients who fundamentally suffer from changing moods and alternate between black days and happy days (Cyclothymia mood) belong to this group and might be suffering from bipolar disease.

From the aforesaid in this chapter, one may understand that psychiatry still does not possess the objective tools as roentgen or blood test for the diagnosis of this disease. The diagnosis is based on a flow of multiple events and may not be diagnosed always at the start of the process. A precise diagnosis materializes from detailed and reliable information from the past and the present, thus enabling the patient and his family to assist the physicians in the identification of the disease.

## 02:45 Distinctive diagnosis

The diagnosis of a bi-polar disorder is a complex task because as in most psychiatric states, we do not have a marker or a unique test for the disease. The psychiatrist's tools are, for the time being, despite the projection for the eminent discovery of the disorder source, the receipt of precise and detailed information on the history of the disease and a comprehensive check. Prior to the final diagnosis, it is important to negate factors and physical diseases which might cause the same appearance as bi polar disease. The correct identification and treatment will lead to improvement and even cure. The use of drugs is a spreading social affliction. We meet more cases of which the cause for the disruption in moos is the prolong abuse of drugs. Using cocaine, LSD, morphine and ecstasy create chemical changes in the brain similar to those taking place during the disease and may "deteriorate" the use into deep depression or stormy mania. The disruption of balance in the neuro transmitters as dopamine, noradrenalin and serotonin is related both, to drug abuse and bi polar disorder. Also alcohol abuse is a know factor for major disruptions of mood. Extreme bad temper, anger, stress and hard depressions leading even to suicide are the typical for alcohol addicts. Even if a physical problem was not identified which explains the development of the disorder, still, one should distinct between it and other psychiatric diseases. Often, we are asked whether the mental disorder is schizophrenia. These diseases indeed have common traits: both start at young age, compose of repeating waves and at the peak of the acute episode, the patient looses any logical touch with reality. But these diseases are separate. In schizophrenia, the course of the disease deteriorates very often and functionalities are harmed severely. The damage on the emotional level is different and characterized mainly by unwillingness, seclusion and non functionality and less by distress and sadness or by hyper activity and vigorousness characteristic of manic-depression. There are differences between the two diseases also on the level of thoughts' flow: the schizophrenics display a more disrupted and split thoughts' flow. A major difference is in the treatment methods: schizophrenia requires the treatment anti psychosis medication as opposed to manic-depressive which reacts to medication from a different group called mood stabilizers although, lately, non-typical anti psychotic drugs have been tested successfully.

## 03:00 (early morning) bipolar disease and additional syndromes

Double morbidity is very common with patient suffering from bi polar disease. About 60% from them suffer also from an anxiety disorder (as anxiety episodes and panics) or from drug and alcohol abuse. The alcohol consumption and drugs on a level of addiction and dependency is common among manic-depressive patients. Experience teaches us that a person suffering from bi polar disease is trying to relieve the suffering (when treatment is absent) using the means available to him. Some drink alcohol to feel pleasure, to dim the feeling of depression and to moderate the fluctuations in his mood. Some, for different reasons, abuse other drugs. Often, a random use turns into addiction, into another disease. Sometimes, this situation occurs during the course of the disease and sometimes precedes it. It is hard to know if this is the cause for the appearance of the disease or it is a failing attempt to cope with it and seek shelter. Depressive or manic persons describe how the thought about a drink "draws" them to it as the person walking in the dessert hoping for a drop of water. Experience shows that the alcohol or marihuana user will suffer from a more severe disease course, more waves, more severe disruption of daily life and from a lesser reaction to medication. The most severe is suicide. The combination of manic-depressive disorder and alcohol or drug addiction is lethal and unfortunately also common. An early diagnosis and intervention through suitable treatment can prevent the development and addiction and save lives.

## 03:10 Causal factors

The causes for mood diseases are not detailed clearly. Despite many efforts, there is still no identifiable biological or environmental (mental or social) direct cause for the disease. It is customary to classify the found causes to genetic, biological and psychosocial although such classification is artificial and different variables are interconnected and influence each other.

**Genetic factors;** the bipolar disorder is clearly hereditary. This is a disease with hereditary components. About half of the patients suffering from manic-depressive disorder have a history of outbreaks in their family. Should someone in the family suffer from the disease, there is high probability that an additional relative will suffer from it. According to statistics, in relatives in the immediate family, the risk is tenfold than in general population. The risk reduces in accordance with the decrease in relations' level, for example, a nephew as opposed to a brother. Children suffering from the disease are at high risk also when adopted and raised by healthy parents thus the conclusion that heredity plays a major role in the creation of the disease.

By identical twins, with identical genetic structure, the risk of suffering from the disease reaches 60-80% as opposed to 10-20% in non identical twins; the correlation is not 100% thus the importance of environmental causes. The combination between

411

certain genetic factors and environmental factors leads to the development of the disease. By genetic factors, we mean genes, that hereditary material present in every cell in which defects are causing the disease. Tens of thousands of genes were identified conduction the mapping of the human genome. The search after the genes responsible for the tendency to mental illnesses in general and bipolar disease in particular still continues. It is of importance because, firstly, the identification of the gene or a group of genes may lead to find a test for the diagnosis of the disease. Although we posses tremendous amount of knowledge, we still do not have a test enabling a certain diagnosis. In the future, we hope to create a diagnosis test for the disease; should a way be found to diagnose the disease prior to its outbreak, we may take preventive measures and decrease its severity. The discovery of a physical flaw directly responsible for the creation of the disease, will, once and for all, remove the stigma off the patients suffering from the disease. No more a character flaw or a mystery, no more "bad education" or insanity but a legitimate physiological brain disease treatable exactly as heart disease or excessive blood pressure. The discovery of the gene responsible for the disease and the identification of the product of that same gene will result in the ability to treat the disease "from the root". Having various types of flaws causing the disease, it will be possible to match each one a treatment according to the type of the problem. Having mapped most of the human genes in the genome venture, we are close as ever to the root of the disease. Should it become clear in the future that the bipolar disorder stems from a gene flaw, it may be possible to change it with an alternate gene. However, should it be made clear that the disease is caused by an increased activity of a flawed gene, we may depress and balance it. This is not science fiction because these procedures have already been used, for example in cases of disruption in the activity of the growth hormone. Many researchers have tried and are trying to find genes connected directly to the development of the disease or at least the region in the chromosome where these genes are located. Out of the 23 chromosomes in the human cell, the researchers have narrowed the suspicious regions and identified four chromosomes with particularly high probability for the location of the required genes; the chance to locate a gene increases with the number of the tested families because the test are conducted on patients and healthy members of the family trying to find a genetic common denominator; the comparison is more reliable as there are more patients in the family; these families can contribute their share by participating in this research.

**Biological factors;** an accepted supposition for the creation of the disease speaks about the "Kindling" phenomenon. It is about a nerve cell receiving very small repetitive stimuli, each one of them not sufficient to initiate it but their repetitive occurrences brings about the operation of the cell. Occurring repetitively in certain regions of the brain, it might cause the development of a center for the creation of spasm episode. There are contenders that a similar phenomenon leads to a bipolar disease. The source of the hypothesis is the similarity of the aggressive nature of the two diseases. This theory was created in light of the well known findings that anti spasm medications have relieving effect and indeed are used for the treatment of bipolar disorder. Another research is directed at the testing of receptors and carriers of the molecules' transporters detaching from one cell and attaching to another thus constituting communication between cells. The disruption of the balance particularly the activity of neural transporters, Serotonin, and the change in the sensitivity of the receptors identifying it, is linked to depression states. We assume also that the excessive activity of additional neural transporters as dopamine and adrenalin is related more to the other pole, the mania. The further strengthening for their involvement is the effectiveness of the use of effective preparations on these neural transporters. Recently, the research focuses not particularly on neural transporters, rather on the investigation of the process, signaling and the transport within the cell of the reacting system. A secondary messenger is the material created in the crust region of the cell in reaction to a stimulus acting on the cell and its movement within the cell toward the nucleus in which the productive activity is taking place (the creation of proteins according to molds made from genetic material) enabling the cell a proper reaction to the stimulus to which it is being exposed. Examples for secondary transporters are CAMP and phosphor-Insoretol derivatives. Corroboration to their importance in the development of the disease was received, among others, thanks to an Israeli research group headed by Professor Blemker from the Ben Gurion University which had conducted tests in the usage of a material called Inozitol for the treatment of depression and anxiety disorders.

**Psychosocial factors;** genetic factors, alone, cannot explain the development of the disease and it is clear that environmental factors influence it as well. Stressful life events often precede the first episodes. Later on their importance and influence are decreased. It is common that a patient arrives initially following special life events. For example, a patient arriving in a severe manic state about one month after receiving a big inheritance or others, being hospitalized following marriage or birth. Researchers assume that it is a primary stress state pushing toward the outbreak of the disease leaving its mark I the brain activity or in its composition in a way which exposes it to further episodes. In later stages, the disease does not need a "catalyst" for its development. Nowadays, there is a tide in the research of biological and genetic factors. Prior to this period, many psychological theories have flourished and also today they have their place in the explanation of the disease and its implications. These theories consider the manic state the protection of human being from the feeling of depression. Corroboration for this can be found in many patients where during the manic episode there are moments of reduced mood, ill feelings and discomfort. These moments are the fractures in that manic defense wall trying to close and push back the feelings of depression. Important stress factors are these which "settle" on sensitive points in that same person able to cause instability and the outbreak of the disease. These theories are instrumental in the understanding of the environmental stress factors and the understanding of the special sense of various life events to various patients. Nowadays, more than 100 years of researching the disease, we know that the key to a successful deciphering is in the overall view of a mechanism interacting between genetic and environmental factors.

## 03:20 Bipolar disorder and creativity

During many years, human beings linked extreme mood states to the "ends" of the human experience - insanity, creativity, despair, ecstasy, romance, charisma and destructiveness and saw in them traits of great creators and artists of the past. As early as in Greek mythology, the name of Dionysus, the wine god, was related with madness, violence, ecstasy and creation. Crazy drinking and dancing parties mixed with sacrificing animals or humans immediately followed by an outburst of creativity in cyclic circles parallel to life and death during the seasons of the year. In Aristotle and Plato times, creativity was related to exceptional conscious states as fainting or obsession and talent was considered a result of Godly inspiration, melancholy or insanity. During the period of renaissance a first distinction was made between "sane melancholic persons" who arrive at great achievements and those whose insanity prevented the use of their talents. The romantic poet Lord Byron is the prototype for genius related to crazy mood states as well as many other poets. Toward the end of the 19th century and the beginning of the 20th century, the founders of psychiatrics as Emil Kreplin gave names and classifications to the extreme and destructive states of the disease: psychosis or deep depression and described them at the edge of the range. The write Edgar Allen Poe, my poet, the composer Schuman, the poet Helderlein, Lincoln and many more, all of whom were describes as manic-depressive. However, it is important to clarify one un-doubtful fact, while the disease is raging, there is no creativity. Even if the transient states accelerate the creativity process, should the disease progress,

416

creativity will not last. Moreover, the right treatment will not extinguish the spark of genius and will not end the creation process rather will enable to save it in the long run.


## 03:25 Bipolar disease and being suicidal


A bipolar disease is a mental disease accompanied with a high rate of suicides. Unfortunately, 10-15% from the patients suffering from the disease will out an end to their lives. This fact urges us to investigate the risk factors and define the preceding symptoms to suicide. The suicidal rate is high particularly in patients who had tried it before and in those suffering from alcohol addiction. According to statistics, between one quarter and one half of the patients suffering from bipolar disease will attempt suicide. As a rule, various suicidal attempts are different than successful attempts because they are characteristic more of women, involve less lethal means, take place usually in the presence of people and accompanied with a notice of intent. Women tend more to admit previous attempts while man tend to conceal them or simply take concealed measures such as dangerous and reckless driving. Suicidal tendency may stem out of any of the disease states; out of despair, hopelessness of the depression, out of the beginning of the improvement of the situation when the strength of the depressed begin returning to him, out of returning to cope with the stress in life and daily demands; a suicidal deed may stem also from manic state; out of chaotic and reckless behavior, lack of sleep and alcohol abuse; also while exiting the manic state, a person might consider the destruction such a manic state leaves behind it and try to attempt suicide. Suicide is also common in mixed states in which restlessness is so hard and violent until it becomes insufferable and only the one experiencing it or observing it may understand it. Mixed states are particularly common in transient periods between depression and mania when the mania sends its arms into the depressive blackness filling it with energy, tension and uncontrollable impulsiveness.

## 03:35 The principals of treatment with medication

A treatment by medication; medications are the basis for the block treatment of bipolar disease. A treatment may moderate the symptoms and erase them until remission. The purposes of the treatment are also to treat the components of the disease, the mania and the depression and to prevent deteriorations since it is a disease with recurrent pattern. Unfortunately, there is no treatment leading to full recovery thus the need for taking medications regularly for life. A psychotherapeutic treatment is an integral part of the intervention in bipolar disease. In extreme states of the disease, it is common to treat with medication, but when the situation is calmed, one should learn to save the "mood hygiene". Similarly to a cardiologist instructing to keep the right life style, e.g. physical activity, non-smoking, eating habits; so is recommended to learn the right life style protecting from the recurrence of the disease. Daily agenda, regular sleeping routine, eating and dieting habits and physical activity and more; reconciliation with the disease, realistic consideration of its implications, coping with crises and hospitalization; the right relation to the medical treatment - something that was forced upon me or a too handed to me for controlling the disease, these are the main subjects dealt with by the psychological treatment.

**First principal** - experience teaches us that a separate consideration of each pole, without seeing the overall picture, does not cover all folds of the disease. The treatment of depression by antidepressants might cause mania and vice versa, anti manic medications might cause depression. Such treatment will not solve the problem, it will rather aggravate it. Therefore, the primary principal of treatment is the administering of medication with moderating and stabilizing effect on both poles. Such medications are called mood stabilizers. Lithium is the first medication from this family. We thrive to reach a state in which a treatment with mood stabilizer will lead to the moderation of the disease but unfortunately, such state is not common and often there is a need for the addition of more medications.

**Second principal** - a long term prolonged treatment, usually for years. Similarly to medications prescribed for Diabetes or excessive blood pressure, also in this case, medications have to be taken long term. An erroneous common assumption is that following the acute state is a complete recovery and there is no need of medications anymore. However the disease does not disappear even following the disappearance of the symptoms, rather staying dormant and might return with the cessation of medications. We should emphasize again, this is a recurring disease and one should avoided being tempted to cease taking medications.

**Third principal:** Even though we deal with a prolonged treatment, there is no one treatment formula that is fit for all. The treatment is custom fitted to every patient according to his state and the long term undulance of the disease. The mood stabilizers constitute the "spine" of the treatment. Nevertheless, in periods of deep depression or raging mania this treatment is not enough and an addition of anti depressants is needed (in a state of depression) or anti psychosis medications (in a manic state). Nowadays we are trying to use "assisting" medications for short periods of time only and stop taking them after the ending of the current wave of the disease.

**Fourth principal:** exactly as the bipolar disease being a complex disease with many faces, so is the treatment often needing a combination of several mood stabilizers with complementing activity mechanisms. The integration of several medications is a more common situation as opposed to the treatment with single medication and therefore, one should not conclude the severity of the disease from the number of medications needed for the balancing of it.

The application of the treatments principals to the bipolar disease is fine and complex. It is not enough to posses the skills and wide knowledge, sensitivity for nuances is need, flexibility and intuition for the choosing of the right treatment. Exactly as the choosing of a color by the painter creating an art, so is a successful treatment taking into consideration action mechanisms and side effects profiles becoming very close of being an artistic act itself.

**Hospitalization:** the bipolar disease is treatable also by hospitalization. The question of its timing is often asked. The stigma that comes with hospitalization is a hindering factor.

Notwithstanding the stigma, one should consider the professional recommendation because the hospitalization protects and removes stress factors enabling a quick and effective medical treatment accelerating recovery. Hospitalization may save life. It is required in a state of deep depression accompanied with suicidal tendencies or in a state of raging mania which was not successfully treated at home.

**The time 03:45 Nietzsche: the disease**

As of today, Nietzsche was not diagnosed! Nietzsche, who became a living legend, was born in Rocken, Prussia, October 15th, 1844. His father lost his mind; Nietzsche wrote, in an early autobiographical essay, "In September 1848 my beloved father suddenly became mentally ill." In 1889, at the age of 45, Nietzsche, as well, lost his mind. In the beginning of January 1889 he collapsed in the middle of the street in Turin. Before collapsing, he threw his hands around a mare beaten by its owner and screamed; this was the moment of the mental collapse. People had to drag him home. Later on, his friend took him to Basel for treatment; on the train, he sang a song from "Ecce Homo". In Basel, Nietzsche was taken to a clinic and from there to an institution in Gena. He passed away 11 years later in 1900.

Walter Kaufman contends that Nietzsche was probably paralyzed as a result of Syphilis; it may have caused his mental collapse since the third stage of Syphilis is known to cause psychosis in some of the cases. However, I do not agree with the prejudice that Nietzsche collapsed because of Syphilis since the best way to diagnose the disease, the Wasserman test was discovered in much later time in 1906, that is after the incident. Therefore, I consider the possibility that the physicians have diagnosed Nietzsche wrongly. My alternate diagnosis is that Nietzsche was manic-depressive! He was sick all his life with mild or medium depression and hypomania (mild or medium mania) and only at the final stage, in January 1889, it "upgraded" to acute manic-depression and was hospitalized for eleven years and ceased creating. In the interim, there were long periods in which he was mentally balanced. He must have inherited the disease from his father since he, too, was mentally ill and today we know that genetics play an important role in mental illnesses. Mental illnesses do not outbreak just like that, in the middle of life at 45, rather in early ages; thus Nietzsche was sick much earlier in his life. He was sick at least 20 years earlier during most of adult life; therefore, we should interpret his work under my assumption that he was manic-depressive. One should understand Nietzsche and his works by this interpretation and reveal them from under their wraps.

Nietzsche insists that his books will not be understood if read hastily; he asked that his works should be taught not only cautiously but also through the view of what comes first and what later, in a close sensitive look. Whether he was "really" a syphilis patient being in its final stage of psychosis or a manic-depressive for all his life, it is less interesting than the "truth"; "there are many kinds of eyes. Even the sphinx has eyes—and consequently there are many kinds of "truths," and consequently there is notruth". (the will to power 540[22]). I wish to tell and interpret Nietzsche under the reasonable assumption that he was manic-depressive most of his adult life - this is the perspective offered by me in this chapter. I will show that classical traits of manic-depression are accordant with term and ideas in the philosophy of Nietzsche. His philosophy was influenced from his personality: his moods, urges and feelings; i.e. his psychology is realized or translated into his ideas. His soul had revealed itself even vaguely through his philosophy. I will show how the properties of a manic-depressive appear as ideas in the philosophy of Nietzsche; terms like "the will to power", "Uebermensch", "Apollonian and Dionysian", "the eternal recurrence", "Self overcoming", "Zarathustra" are at the heart of his philosophy will be demonstrated as mental expressions of the manic-depressive.

---

[22] The Will to Power, Friedrich Nietzsche, Translated by Walter Kaufmann and R.G. Hollingdale Random House, Inc 1968.

## 04:00 Let the evidence show itself

In mid December of 1883, Nietzsche wrote Lou, a close friend with whom he later broke ties, a letter indicating his mental state at the time: "my dear ones, Loe and Ree: do not be too upset about the outbreak of my "megalomania" or "my heart vanity—and even if, prompted by some feelings, I should accidentally take my life, some day, that too, would not be reason for too much sorrow. What are my fantasies to you! (Even my "truths" were nothing to you hithreto). By all means, take into due considerations between the two of you that at the end, I am half-madman who suffers in the head whom long solitude had confused completely"[23].

Beyond his open talk of death and megalomania which are indicative of depression and mania, it is important for me to note that also loneliness and introversion (social seclusion) are traits of depression; the next section shows the loneliness and introversion of Nietzsche.

In Christmas, Nietzsche wrote: "this last bite of life was, until now, the hardest I have chewed yet, and it is still possible that I may suffocate on it. I have suffered of the ignominious and tormenting memories of this summer as of a madnes... I tense every fiber of my self-overcoming but have lived in solitude too long, living off my "own fat", so that now, more than anyone else, I am being

[23] Nietzche Philosopher, Psychologist, Antichrist, Walter Kaufmann, Fourth Edition, Princeton University Press 1974. P.58

broken on the wheel of my own feelings. If only I could sleep! But the strongest doses of my opiates help me no more than six to eight hours marches. If I not discover the alchemists' trick of turning even this destiny filth into gold - I am lost.--thus I have the most beautiful opportunity to prove that for me 'all experiences I are useful, all days holy, and all human beings divine!!! (Kaufman page 59). An additional trait of mental illness in the abovementioned section is the problems of sleep, particularly difficulties of falling asleep.

At the end of the "Anti Christ" and in most of Ecce Homo, another phenomenon becomes clear which characterizes mania, i.e. a state of promiscuity (with manic, it manifests in an unconventional behavior as money spending casual sex, etc.), inhibition and megalomania; a "strange" inhibition is eminent including un normal assertions pertaining to Nietzsche self importance, i.e. his megalomania which shows the first signs of his insanity. Research into his early essays, prior to the writing of his first book reveals many similar comments which are explicitly inhibitive.

However, Kaufman contends that the conclusion about them being the first symptoms of his disease is not self evident; However, for reasons previously explained about the disease the out breaking is at early age. Obviously, Nietzsche had a strong feeling of being under a "task" and mission (being sort of messianic or prophetic manifesting in his "alter ego", i.e. as Zarathustra appearing as a prophet in his writings). In 1888, the inhibition deteriorated quickly to a point of which he writes freely about these subjects not only in his letters but also in his books which, in my view, shows the evolvement of an acute psychotic state at the beginning of January 1889.

Kaufman asks "what seems important today is mainly whether any of his books can be discounted as the fabrications of a madman. To this the answer is an unreserved no." (Kaufman page 70). Kaufman contends that "in his later works we find a steady decrease in tact and a rapidly mounting lack of inhibition, and the form of expression shows signs of the coming madness" (same page) . But, at the bottom line Kaufman says that he loosed his mind only after the breake in the street. Well, I am very reserved, Nietzsche was manic-depressive and as such he had well balanced period between medium depressive periods and mild ones. I.e. we do not have to look for his insanity through all of his writings; in some he will be arrogant or, in other words, megalomaniac, and in others, he will perceived as mentally exhausted which indicates depression; we will identify in other parts more traits of mental illness. In his later works, we find an increased inhibition and the form of expression shows signs of imminent insanity. "There is a decided breakin Nietzsche's sanity which comes only later, after his collapse in the street. From then on, there is no startling lucidity, no great vision, but only a steadi increasing and unrelievedly dullness of mind, a spreading darkness surrounding Nietzsche's mind in a hopeless night" (Kaufman page 70). I can agree with Kaufman as to the last stage of Nietzsche's life, i.e. from 1889 onwards; it may well be that in acute manic-depressive episodes he was not productive; however in hippomanic and mild depressive stages, the manic-depressive is a very productive and creative person. Only in a stage of acute psychosis, the patient cannot think clearly and lucidly.

## 04:15 Ecce Homo[24]

The book "Ecce Homo" which was written in 1888, one year prior to his collapse, is sort of a biography of his life and a summation of his creation to date. I wish to quote some paragraphs evidencing his mental and existential states in different periods of his life and interpret them from my perspective, i.e. his manic-depression. The book contains chapters of which three I call, megalomaniacal, "why am I so clever', 'why am I so wise' and 'why I write such good books'; my answer is that Nietzsche was very creative, so creative as only a manic-depressive can be. Not to mention there megalomanic characterization.

- "this dual descent, as it were, both from the highest and the lowest rung of the ladder of life, at the same time a decadent and a beginning—this, if anything, explains that neutrality, that freedom from all partiality in relation to the total problem of life, that perhaps distinguishes me. I have a subtler sense of smell for the signs of ascent and decline than any other human being before me; I am the teacher par excellence for this—I know both, I am both"[25]. This paragraph indicates his mood, 'sunrise and sunset', i.e. "high" and "down"; the manic-depressive states.

---

[24] Friedrich Nietzsche, Ecce Homo, translated by Walter Kaufman.

-nobody has ever discovered any fever in me. A physician who treated me  for some time as if  my nerves were sich finally said: "its not your nerves, it is rather I am that nervous." There is altogheter no sign of any local degeneration; no organically conditioned stomach complaint, however profound the weakness of my gastric system may be as a consequences of all over exhaustion…"[26] Nietzsche did not suffer from an organic disease, i.e. physical; therefore he did not have had syphilis. 60% of the patients suffering from depression complain about psychosomatic pains as headaches, neck and back pains, abdominal paracentesis, etc. Nietzsche himself complained about headache. A 'recurring disease' is the manifestation of manic-depression.

- "looking from the perspective of the sick toward healthier concepts and values and, conversely, looking again from the fullness and self-assurance of the rich life down into the secret work of the instinct of decadence—in this I have had the longest training, my truest experience; if in anything, I became master in this. Now I know how, have the know-how, to revers the perspectives: the first reason why a "revaluation of values" is perhaps possible for me alone".[27] 'The heights of life' are the heights of his mental state and mood; 'down' is the mental state in which he is down, i.e. a poor and depressive mood; the self confidence which Nietzsche is talking about characterizes the megalomania and self confidence in a manic state; 'this is his unique experience', i.e. he, differing from anybody else,

---

[25] Same, page 222

[26] Same, page 223

[27] Same, page 223

"ordinary", knows what are moods; Nietzsche "knew to change" moods - perspectives.

- "Agreed that I am a decadent, I am also the very reverse. Among other things there is this proof: I always instinctively select the proper remedy in preference to harmful ones; whereas the decadent, as such, invariably chooses those remedies which are bad for him. As a whole I was healthy, but in certain details I was a decadent. The energy with which I forced myself to absolute solitude, and to an alienation from my customary habits of life; the self-discipline that forbade me to be pampered, waited on, and doctored-all this betrays the absolute certainty of my instincts in regard to what at that time was most needful to me. I placed myself in my own hands, I restored myself to health: to do this, the first condition of success, as every physiologist will admit, is that the man be basically sound. A typically morbid nature cannot become healthy at all, much less by his own efforts. On the other hand, to an intrinsically sound nature, illness may even act as a powerful stimulus to life, to an abundance of life. It is thus that I now regard my long period of illness: it seemed then as if I had discovered life afresh, my own self included. I tasted all/ good and even trifling things in a way in which others could not very well taste them-out of my Will to Health and to Life I made my philosophy. . . . For I wish this to be understood; it was during those, years of most lowered vitality that I ceased from being a pessimist: the instinct of self-recovery bade a philosophy of poverty and desperation. Now, how are we to recognize Nature's most excellent human products? They are recognized by the fact that an excellent man of this sort gladdens our senses; he is carved from a single block, which is hard, sweet, and fragrant. He enjoys only what is good for him; his pleasure, his desire, ceases

429

when the limits of what is good for him are overstepped. He divines remedies against injuries; he knows how to turn serious accidents to his own advantage; whatever does not kill him makes him stronger."[28] This paragraph speaks for itself!

- "for I come from heights that no one bird ever reached in its flight, I know abysses into which no foot ever strayed"[29].

- "versus a formula for the hieghst affirmation, born of fullness, of overfullness, a Yes-saying without reservation, even to suffering, even to guilt, even to everything that is questionable and strange in existence"[30]. Also the guilt which Nietzsche talks about is a well known symptom in depression where a person feels guilty. In this place as well as in other places throughout his writings, Nietzsche manifests the idea of the "confirmation of life" and the saying "yes" despite the decline, i.e. despite the depressive abysses; notwithstanding the depression, Nietzsche had decided, as opposed to Virginia Wolf who committed suicide in 1941 suffering manic depression, not to give in to life rather live them despite of everything and confirm them.


## 04:30 Health and sickness: Nietzsche's thought development


Nietzsche claims that it will be absurd to say that the artistic creation of the healthy artist will be beautiful while the art

[28] Same, page 224

[29] Same, page 263, my emphasis

[30] Same, page 272

of the ill artist will be ugly. Homer was blind and Beethoven was deaf when he wrote the ninth symphony. The artist creates his work of art by some deprivation or shortage, by suffering and not by good health -illness is an incentive for his life. "...it is exceptional state that conditioned the artist—all of them propoundly related to and interrelated with morbid phenomena—so it seems impossible to be an artist and not to be sick" (The will to power 811). Nietzsche knew something about suffering! He experienced depression and it was, as we will see later on, the incentive for his creations and ideas on the "self overcoming", "the Uebermensch", "the eternal recurrence" and "Apollonian and Dionysian". "Apart from the fact that I am a decadent, I am also the opposite. My proof for this is, among other things, that I have always instinctively chosen the right means against wretched states; while the decadent typically chooses means that are disadvantageous for him. As *summa summarum*, I was healthy; as an angle, as aspeciality, I was decadent. The energy to choose absolute solitude and leave the life to which I had become accustomed; the insistence on not allowing myself any longer to be cared for, waited on, and doctored—that betrayed an absolute instinctive certainty about what was needed above all at that time. I took myself in hand, I made myself healty again: the condition for this—every physiologist would admit that—is that one be healthy at bottom. A typically morbid being cannot become healthy, much less make itself healthy. For a typically healthy person, conversely, being sick can even become an energetic *stimulus* for life, for living more. This, in fact, is how that long period of sickness appears to me *now*: as it were, I discovered life anew, including myself; I tasted all good and even little things, as others cannot easily taste them—I turned my will to health, to life, into a philosophy." (Ecce Homo page 224). The Greek tragedies, so Nietzsche says in "the birth of a tragedy"[31] (Die geburt der Tragoedie 1844 - 1900) were created out of a need for something absent: to be able to live, the Greek had to create the gods out of deep need. The tragedies represent for Nietzsche an answer to the suffering in life, a victory over torments and the celebration of life. A tragic art was the solace which was created by the Greek for them out of need because they were, as all humans, capable of troubles and much suffering. He respects the Greek for looking with open eyes on the destructive and horrific nature and history. The Greek confirmed life by the creation of art. One can withstand bravely the historical terror and the "natural" and say "yes" to life. In health terms: Nietzsche considered health not as an incident of absent illness but as the overcoming of it. Therefore, the depressive, notwithstanding his illness, has to overcome himself and say a big "yes" to life and not only to life but also for the purpose of teaching. Goethe's health is the product of victory and overcoming of every illness that could have attacked him. Goethe overcame illness after illness in his life, sometimes even acute illness however, he overcame and recovered. Kaufman comments and asks whether Goethe's artistic career, is his vitality which sometimes seems to be butted by deep despair and still elevates itself to new creations (Kaufman page 131). It was well known that Goethe left deep impression on Nietzsche who was influenced by him. Those who have never faced disease and suffering do not have the need to create beauty; in "the birth of tragedy" in the final paragraph, Nietzsche says "how much did

---

[31] Friedrich Nitzsche, the birth of a tragedy or Hellenism and pessimism, translated by Israel Eldad, published by Shoken 1985.

theses people have to suffer to be able to become many such people have to become beautiful". Nietzsche says that what does not kill you strengthens you. For "the healthy", a disease can be a source of energy for life. Kaufman also comments the Nietzsche's theory is also compatible with empirical information in particular with the close link between artistic genius and a physical or mental disease. An example of the empirical connection between genius and mental illness shows that manic-depressives are very creative, e.g. Vincent Van Gogh, Virginia Wolf and Friedrich Helderlein. Van Gogh had suffered tremendously; he was in a major depression but also due his manic productiveness his illness became a fertile land for his artistic creations; for example, his painting "on the verge of eternity". Helderlein and Nietzsche have managed to overcome the illness and confirm life and teach us something; unfortunately, Vincent Van Gogh and Virginia Wolf said no to life. They did not mange to overcome their illness and chose to end life; they were not victorious in the battle of life but life had won a victory against them.

## 04:40 Perspective and interpretation

"Gradually, it became clear to me what every great philosophy so far has been: namely, the personal confession of its author and a kind of involuntary and unconscious memoir." (Beyond good and evil #6 page 13). In this way, Nietzsche discovers how the hidden history of philosophers, their psychology was revealed to him. Nietzsche's philosophy is "the personal confession of its writer" whether or not it was volitional and aware. His philosophy is not just a seeming confession but it is personal, he speaks from the blood of his heart. In this light I would like you to consider my interpatation. Nietzsche considers philosophy, according to citation, as an interpretative matter. Nietzsche holds the position that our psychology is interpreting the world, i.e. our impulses, passions and feelings are interpreting the "reality", what is present in our mind is interpreting life, the world and existence. The thinking of philosophers, no less than the thinking of most people, in particular the mentally ill's consciousness, is design and reflected by their impulses, tendencies and feelings. These factors have to be taken into account in order to understand Nietzsche (and any other philosopher) and the standings, the assumptions and starting points adopted by him. This is Nietzsche's psychology, i.e. his manic-depressive's psychology which I am trying to understand. Nietzsche claims that assertions and justifications for a certain philosophy of one philosopher or the other have to be given based on his psychology. And therefore, his answer to the question of "what interprets" is actually our emotions; and therefore, the emotions or Nietzsche's psychology is the secret based on which I shall interpret his philosophy.

Nietzsche considers very much the 'urges' and the 'emotions' manifesting themselves in different interpretations. The urge for knowledge itself, Nietzsche contends, is motivated by our urges and emotions thus making knowledge subjective and certainly not universal. Nietzsche suggests the philosophers to stand guard against the dangerous old perceptual fiction which presents a standing of 'super temporal knowledgeable subject, without pain, non volitional and pure'; "let us be on guard against the dangerous old conceptual fiction that posited a "pure, will-less, painless, timeless knowing subject"; let us guard against the

434

snares of such contradictory concepts of "pure reason," "absolute spirituality," "knoeledge in itself": theses always demand that we should think of an eye that is completely unthinkable, an eye turned in no particular direction, in which the active and interpretating forces, through which alone seeing becomes seeing something, are supposed to be lacking: theses always demand of the eye an absurdity and nonsense. There is only a perspective seeing, only a perspective "knowing"; and the more affects we allow to speak about one thing, the more eyes, different eyes, we can use to observe one thing, the more complete will our "concept" of this thing, our "objectivity," be."" (The genealogy of moral III:12). This which applies to philosophers referred to by Nietzsche applies also to Nietzsche's philosophy therefore, we have to interpret Nietzsche's philosophy in view of his emotional/affective disease, i.e. his manic-depression and not from objective interpataion (which is senseless).

Nietzsche's philosophy has more than one perspective, i.e. more than one interpretation; the more interpretations the merrier. In my opinion, one of the interpretations of Nietzsche's philosophy is to read it through his emotional disease. His emotional disease motivated him to write his works. I.e. we have to understand the main terms used by Nietzsche: 'the will to power'. 'ueber mensch', 'eternal recurrence', 'interpretation' and his obsession with pleasure and suffering as the products of his bipolar emotional disease. Nietzsche insists that there is "only perspective knowing' as opposed to an absolute knowing independent of any perspective; he insists that such a point of view may be achieved, i.e. interpretation but this is an interpretation with some objectivity. The emotional and perspective interpretations collide and result in objectivity, i.e.

435

objectivity is a situation in which we are not trapped with one interpretation but it is a perspective from which we may review different agendas of interpretations. More points of view and more perspectives will result in a more true, complete and objective philosophy. That is why I offer more "truth" of Nietzsche's philosophy.

The psychotic interprete the reality by his psychology. Imagine a case in which a psychotic thinks himself to be a messiah; as such he has a role in the world, to bring change, to bring about moral, ideological or political revolution. Our messiah also knows that he will have enemies, those who fear changes about to be brought by him and will want to stop him thus preserving the current situation. When the messiah understands that he has enemies fearing him and try to stop him, he may develop paranoia. He sees 'a man in a black coat standing at the corner', he perceives him as real and interprets him as an assassin since he experiences fear and persecution resulting in the man at the corner as the realization of fear. Then he sees the man at the corner as assassinating agent. Actually I am making a hermeneutic interpretative move which does not contradict with Husserl's motto: "for the facts themselves" since the fact of "the man in the black coat standing in the corner" is a hermeneutic psychology. I.e. I keep Husserl's motto only interpreting it based on the psychotic's psychology. The psychotic's consciousness and emotions which are an integral part thereof create reality - consciousness precedes and creates reality. Emotion, fear are the motives of perceiving the man at the corner as an assassin; on the other hand when there is no fear and feeling of persecution, there is no reason to perceive the man at the corner as an assassin but to perceive him as an innocent man. The point of view and interpretation belong to the interpreter and he interprets through his urges, passions and emotions.

Nietzsche suggests that future philosophers will be called "attempters" (Beyond good and evil 42), i.e. persons of experience and he calls the philosophy as he perceives it "experimental" (The will to power 1041). "Experimental" need not be understood as an empirical experiment but as different ways of looking at things and experience them and different ways of life where the experiences have to be efficient and productive. For Nietzsche, all perspective assessments are, in essence, "the perspective of life" and their proportional value is a matter of degree. The interpretations and assessments depend on an analysis of a variety of perspectives. The assessment and the adoption of different perspectives is the experimental philosophy by Nietzsche. The new philosopher according to Nietzsche has to experience many points of view, meanings and implications in different human lives. The experimenting philosophers and the experimental philosophy will be creative in the sense of being linked to a new development of interpreting things and unconventional models of human existence and therefore to perceptions and new systems of values. The philosophers should not, anymore, receive ideas and concepts from pure consciousness and polish them, rather create, present and convince others of their value. What is requested from a philosopher is active interpretation and not just the acceptance of conventions. The new philosopher has to consider every tool and means available to him. These tools may be psychological, social, physiological, historical, linguistic and scientific. All these tools are relevant to philosophical matters.

Many philosophers have somehow recognized that irrational factors as passions, urges, natural tendencies, etc., play an important role in human life. However Nietzsche contends that they were not treated according to their importance and influence. In the past, philosophers were not aware to the influence of psychology on their work. Only if these psychological, social, historical and linguistic factors will be taken into account properly, we could better understand their teachings. And therefore he asks: "who amongst the philosophers was a psychologist at all before me and not rather the opposite, a "higher swindler" and an "idealist"." (Ecce Homo IV: 6) The psychology and particularly Nietzsche's psychology is the way to understand him. "There are many types of eyes... and consequencly there are many types of 'truths' and consequencly there is no truth." (The will to power page 540) Nietzsche emphasizes that interpretation in general also basically defines the terms connected with our emotions. "one may not ask:" who then interprets?" for the interpretation itself is a form of the will to power, exist (but not as a "being" but as a process, a becoming) as an affect." (The will to power 556). And therefore the answer to who the interpreter is is our emotions: "who interpretate?— our affects." (The will to power 254). The emotions, the urges and feelings motivate our judgments and perspectives on the world. We refer interpretations to the interpreter as we relate thoughts and intentions to people. It is necessary to assume an interpreter behind interpretation. These are our needs that interpret the world; these are our urges and our "for and against" that interpret. We always consider different perspectives when we interpret something and the "for and against" in order to get the "right" perspective or the "wrong" one. Therefore, Nietzsche says that "each one has its perspective that it would like to compel all the other drives to accept as a norm." (The will to power  481).

What is knowledge and truth? There is no 'pure knowledge' or a pure knowledgeable subject from a divine point of view, i.e. an objective point of view. As many motives (urges, passions and emotions) we relate to one thing the more complete and rich it becomes. I.e., as many point of views we have on one thing, the more complete it gets and knowledge of it richer. By looking at things differently and wanting to look at them differently, we will achieve better objectivity and truth. This 'objectivity' should be understood as the ability to control the "for and against' and their value so that someone will know to use a wide variety of perspectives and interpretations motivated under the authorization of knowledge. It is because we seek and wish knowledge, Nietzsche draws out attention to the possibility of this 'objectivity' and the roles played by our motives. Our psychology plays a crucial role 'in knowledge and objectivity'. He calls others to dive into the deeps and dangers of such an interpretative way. Nietzsche emphasizes that he is 'a man of knowledge' by way of being a self interpreter, he interprets his own emotions and urges. In Nietzsche's opinion all perceptions are about interpretation; and 'truth' is a property that, properly, may be verified by nothing else than the justified assertions on interpretation.

If it is true, and since there are no stand alone interpretations rather interpretations related to interpreters, as we are, then truth and knowing exist only in relation to interpreters confronted with each other and particularly, they exist only as human truths and 'truths and human knowledge' and inseparable from the condition and the nature of our human existence. If the interpretative process leads to a state in which everything that is thought and said on the world (and on Nietzsche's himself) by a person (or particularly a manic-depressive) and not by definite and independent formulas, then this is also our way in to Nietzsche (and his consciousness). The many motives enabling to discuss something, the many eyes, different eyes there are, which we can use to distinct one thing; the more complete our 'concept' of the thing, so will our 'objectivity'. "But to eliminate the will altogether, to suspend each and every affect, supposing we were capable of this—what would that mean but to castrate the intellect?" (Genealogy of moral III: 12).

As a result, there is no objective, universal and certain knowledge. Philosophies value, necessity and universality are unavoidably related to a specific incidence of a person (psychological analysis) or a certain society. Nietzsche was suspicious of necessary and universal assertions always preferring an illuminating psychological insight on a complete comprehensive philosophical method. He believed that all doctrines are opinions and are partial and limited by a certain point of view, i.e. all doctrines and big methods are perspectives and a type of interpretation. There is a significant link between the thought and the thinker; the value and quality of an idea is in the person and the context which we discuss. The person, the thinker, is connected to an idea as being, for example, a Jew or he believes in God or being a socialist or atheist, male or female, Israeli or German. In other words, the person is connected to the thesis or assertion by being part of a community, the community is what spreads the thesis and assertion. In religion, the community is made of religious people despite the fact that the type of the community will depend on the matter on hand. If, for example, I as a Jew deals in the question "who is a Jew?" thus assertions or answers in relation to the relevant matter will be of interest to any Jew, Israeli, politician, philosopher and anti-Semite. Questions about the sanctity of Jesus will interest Christians, maybe also Jews. Nietzsche's declaration of atheism, "by instinct", is a perspective contradictory to religious dogma. All questions relating to something depend on the membership of a community and a certain culture from which perspectives are being expressed. If rules or universal principals are of any meaning, it is because we share the common link, the context in which we are all humans and we are all members of the human community and in this case, particularly the members of the mentally insane community. Another example is the questions about moral; are there different answers to the question what moral is. This will depend on the type of community seeking answers to moral questions, but any community asking the questions is eventually a human community and therefore it is possible at all to discuss considerations for and against relating to possible answers. Moral is a matter of human beings as well as questions about the sense of life. Only humans ask about the sense of their existence.

The scientific search after the 'truth' is an attempt to categorize all phenomena; there may be different categories through which we will understand reality; for example, categories of "causality", "quantitative" and "qualitative". And again, the search after certain categories depends on certain perspective. The search after the truth in philosophy depends on a person's abilities, attitudes and point of view. The perpetual search by the philosopher after a "method" reflects the indefinite desire for the final, the defined and for the direct approach to the relevant subject, however the prosperity in methods (for example phenomenology or linguistic analysis) only emphasizes the factual evidence that to philosophize differs from different people having different perspectives. We know something from impressions and environmental contexts, influences, ideas which perceived through language and community and eventually things are determined by everything related to you as well as your personality's psychological structure and history.

There is no free perspective, universal eye, a divine point of view, just perspectives. Moreover, there is no external base for comparison or adjustment which can be adhered to or any truth or belief in "the thing itself" only by comparison, competition and qualitative change between different perspectives. The metaphor of perspective leaves open the question if there is or could be a "truth itself" which is the final object of every perspective. Nietzsche contends: "there are no facts, only interpretations", and "There are no moral facts". There are some assertions and misunderstanding pertaining to interpretations and perspectives; for example, that interpretation does not have a comparable basis with another perspective and therefore cannot be evaluated compared with another and that no perspective can be evaluated on its own, thus: "one interpretation is good as the other". It is important to emphasize that to interpret does not mean to say something untrue. The perspective is always a perspective of something; it is always possible to speak of perspective and the interpretation of "something" and compare perspective in terms of that 'something', for example, is the atom a particle of a wave. The question that remains open is is that 'something' the same in both interpretations. There are always questions pertaining to a matter of practice leading to preferring of one interpretation on the other. Perspectives and interpretations are always a matter of measure, not of adjustment and comparison with an external "truth", but an evaluation in their contexts and according to their own target. Assertions about perspectives, as if their nothing but potential points of view, do not consider the criticizing view of Nietzsche's perspectivism. We can always be critics toward one perspective while the other will be protected from that objection. This is not a matter of the potentiality of points of view but a matter of interpreters' assessment as to how one can ask about the potentiality of the observer.

Inside the perspective itself, there is no distinction between the specific interpreter and the perspective itself. Interpretation is formulated and adopted by someone and the quality or their values depend on our opinion of the interpreter. If, for example, we believe that Nietzsche was manic-depressive thus we can understand, assess and adopt (or not) his philosophy; it does not mean, of course, that it is not "true" or "correct" but only if it is useful, that is is it may be useful to understand him in a different light? Or may it be used to understand the manic-depressive's consciousness? Or for example, that there is logic in insanity. Is it possible to understand anything from it on people in general, for example that may be all people share something common with the mentally ill, for example times of pleasure and suffering, of "high" and "down" or is it not correct to say that we all feel the senselessness of existence or can the psychotic tell us something about Descartes and maybe the psychotic can teach about phenomenology. The important point being, should we wish, from a moral point of view, to treat the mentally ill as we would treat Nietzsche himself or Van Gogh, with respect or as a fool?

Interpretation, therefore, is not only a matter of an abstract possibility; it is something that materializes in a realistic manner, sometimes as perspective excited by urges and interests. It is integrated in collision with cold, passionless logic lacking interests. Behind interpretation there is a human being and while we are willing to admit that a human being may have few opinions on a certain subject, there is real life that logic will not take into consideration. Is it logical to suggest that any interpretation and perspective is as good as the other? If interpretations and perspectives will be structured in an abstract form separated from any context, only then, they can be assessed. But this is exactly what Nietzsche negates. There is always a link and it is defined, more or less, according to its nature and circumstances in which the interpreter who holds them is present. There are interpretations and circumstances better than others which are more valuable because they are, for example, more interesting; the interest is not some "objective" truth, but we have to ask ourselves is the interpretation interesting; is there something to learn from; is it reach in details, explanations and examples; is it challenging, i.e. leaving place for doubts, wandering and questions demanding further investigation. For example, the advantage of science is that it is useful for life, i.e. it may be used to create technology. It is only degenerating to think that anyone has a perspective as good as another perspective, that all interpretations and perspectives are equal because all people are equal no matter what is true about them. For Nietzsche, not all people are equal; this is a truth that must be accepted even if it is not pleasant to the common liberal. There is a living human between the animal and the Super Man. What defines the context which is of interest to us is the unavoidability of the "confrontation fact". I.e. the confrontation between two perspectives pertaining to knowledge and values is unavoidable.

Usually, we understand that we have perspective in which we believe only in interpretation as we meet different perspectives or are confronted by alternative interpretations, for example, my interpretation of Nietzsche who was bipolar as opposed to other perspectives. We meet someone or enter the community and find ourselves strangers. We enter into a conversation and find ourselves not in agreement, not on the "facts" provided they were not determined by interpretation but by their importance and value. Two assertions about knowledge can be contradictory; two sets of values can collide and turn into an ideological war, think, for example, about Marxism. However, interpretations collide because they are interpretations of the same phenomenon, because they claim a common context despite having different applications in our life. Perspectives are identified as such only because they collide, being the interpretations of the same phenomenon. We, therefore, seek criteria by which we may assess the disagreement. We will use the "facts", should we be able to find them, but in most problems in philosophy, we will stand on our own and our conventions and collect assertions on order to justify our standings versus the competing stand particularly because there are ours. "'my judgment is my judgment": no one else is easily entitled to it—that is what such a philosopher of the future may perhaps say to himself." (Beyond good and evil 43) Nietzsche contends that philosophy expresses the philosopher's point of view and defines him as being in the world with others. Therefore the criticism on philosophy means the criticism on the philosopher and vice versa.

Nietzsche insisted that a philosopher, first and foremost, has to serve as an example and therefore, it will be fair to ask about Nietzsche himself; is Nietzsche is being used as an example? I think that Nietzsche will serve as an example and needs to be used as an example, for example, to the mentally ill. He has to teach them how to behave while being in manic-depressive states. Van Gogh, despite his genius, is a bad example which should not be admired by the mentally ill. Van Gogh committed suicide, he said no to life; he was a being toward death and executed it. Nietzsche did not commit suicide; he said yes to life and confirmed them. On one hand there is Nietzsche the manic-depressive, being in depression, speaking about suicide, the lonely, secluded and distanced and on the other hand, Nietzsche celebrating and loving life. "The love of fate" Amor Fati, is, despite his cruel fate, Nietzsche's love for life. Nietzsche had an ironic sense of humor. He did not want another life but the life he had. I believe that Nietzsche lived as he wanted to and did not cry over his bad fate. Nietzsche converted his flaws and disadvantages to beauty; he created philosophy doing exactly as the Greek have done by converting suffering into beauty. Nietzsche assumes a fundamental "I" who cannot be separated from his traits, standings and ideas, and holding the same opinion pertaining to ideas and assertions not as abstract assertions but as part of the personality distributing them. Therefore, with Nietzsche, the personal voice is not, as Descartes "I", only a display tool, a rhetoric anchor for a chain of thoughts. Nietzsche emphasizes his own uniqueness in his ideas and style manifesting the personality behind the thoughts, words and books. Therefore, philosophy, for Nietzsche, is first and foremost a personal involvement, not assertions and their rebuttal. The terms of philosophy do not stand on their own; they cannot exist without their thinker who is also a part of culture and a community. They have sense only in the aspect of being first and foremost personal.

## 04:55 The development of "the will to power"

The basic difference between the early and later theories by Nietzsche lies in his intellectual adulthood during which he was basing on the assumption of one basic principle. When Nietzsche present the will to power, all dual tendencies of his young thought are reduced to one motivating expression: the will to power. Therefore there is reconciliation between Dionysus and Apollo, nature and value, incidence and aim, empiricism and true self and physics and culture. Kaufman contends, for example, that Nietzsche is trying to prove his hypothesis that psychological phenomena can be explained by two basic terms: fear and power. After finding in his early works that many types of behavior can be explained in a similar way, Nietzsche tries to see how far he can go with the terms of fear and power.

"The Dawn" therefore can be understood as a final experiment prior to "The Will to Power". Indeed, in "The Dawn" Nietzsche does not mention the will to power, however one may consider the book as a type of introduction to following work. He tries to see how far he can go reducing complex phenomena to fear and power. Only later, the power of the results will be revealed to him. In his following work, "The Gay Science", Nietzsche still conducts an experiment with the term of power and still does not explain any monism or a systematical psychological theory. The book includes also an experimental study of the "Eternal Recurrence" idea. And then, suddenly, the "The Will to Power" and "Eternal Recurrence" ideas hit Nietzsche (Kaufman page 188); and is Zarathustra, he applied both ideas. In "The Dawn", power, not less than fear, is a psychological phenomenon. First and foremost, fear is our standing toward power or in Nietzsche's words: "is the negative aspect of our will to power. Prevention of power results fear and a will to power. Fear is the negative motive which will make us avoid something. We, for example, have fear from something, thus distancing ourselves from it. Nietzsche still does not conclude that where there is fear there is also a will to be powerful and cope with our fear. The two are applied as two different principals. Fear leads to unfortunate but ethical results; fear explains not only the acceptance of conventions of other people's behavior but also the adoption of their values. First and foremost, people behave as if these values belong to them because they are afraid not to obey; so they get used to the pretence and obedience becomes their second nature (Kaufman page 190). As children, we do not obey because the adults' judgments are more rational than ours, rather, according to Nietzsche, because of our impotence and fears ("The Dawn" page 104). Fear is also a great teacher: the mother of knowledge on human beings. Not as love, which has an hidden urge to see the other, as far as we can, the beautiful, and which in falsely willing to accept the other person's true nature, fear "wishes to speculate", to solve its riddle; it encourages us to find out what it can do, what it wants: to be deceived is to be in danger. Therefore, "fear motivates the general insight on man more than love" ("The Dawn" page 309).

The sense of "Power" is wrongly understood. It is enough to give some examples. "There is, first and foremost, the person's desire to find a scapegoat, the search by the weak and incompetent to find someone who they can oppress and condescend" ("The Dawn" page 140) thus feeling superior. Therefore, you, the sane, the weak and illiterate are seeking us the insane to make you feel potent, superior and good with yourselves. It gives you a sense of power. During centuries, you have oppressed us, incarcerated us, despised and expelled us from human society and all so you may condescend as if truth and rationality belong to you. You exercise violence against us because we are weak and you wish to feel powerful and oppress us out of your will to power and control over the fool; you are afraid of us since we are your alternative. You are barbarians, an illiterate mob! But even us, the impotent, the weak and oppressed, are trying to find power and empowering. We can be your teachers; we want the respect and recognition given by you to your greatest teachers.

In light of the will to power idea, Nietzsche considers the Greek differently; suddenly, it is clear to him that the basic motive of the Greek culture is also the will to power. The Greek preferred power over the "beneficial" and even over reputation ("The Dawn" page 360). The second comment on "The Will to Power" can be found in the records of that period in which Nietzsche contends that ancient Greeks frankly admitted their will to power. The linking of the will to power with the Greek was one of the decisive moves in the development of his perception pertaining to the embracing monism. Previously, Nietzsche considered the competition as the most important term in the analysis of the Greek culture. He considered not only the rivalry between playwright wanting the highest reward but also the Olympic games; Plato's efforts to defeat the Sophists and poets and to write prettier myths and deeper dialogues; and the Socrates' dialectics stating that thinking is a mental competition. Nietzsche, therefore, thought that competitiveness itself is the expression of the will to power. The will to power, therefore, is not only Satan leading men away from achieving culture or the psychological urge helping to explain different types of human behavior; rather it is also the image of Greek culture that Nietzsche considered as the peak of humanity. Instead of linking to neurotics expecting pity, the modern human's lust for money, the burning of the infidels and good books, the will to power is now perceived as a basic urge behind all human behavior. A philosophical study, the ancient tragedies, the comedies, the platonic dialogues and the Greek statues are now understood in terms of the Greek wishing to excel, to rise in their power beyond others. Not only Sparta and Athens and all the state cities but also Aeschylus (an ancient Greek playwright and poet 456-525 B.C.) and Sophocles (the greatest Greek playwright, "Antigone" and "Oedipus the King" 406-495 B.C.), Plato and Aristotle and all those who spoke at the banquet were competitors, and everyone wished to outdo one another and be powerful. Politics and cultural achievements, art and philosophy have to be explained by the will to power.

Only in Zarathustra, the will to power is declared as a basic force behind all human behavior. The psychological studies which brought Nietzsche to the perception of the will to power offer the possibility of a new experience to show how nature can create values. Before the account of "The Dawn" ends, several additional points should be clarified. First and foremost, Nietzsche suggests more comments pertaining to the connection between power and the will to power. The will to power can be a mean and cruel force

450

whereas power itself does not corrupt, rather tenderizes the mind. The powerful, as Nietzsche emphasizes, need not prove their power not to themselves or to others by their oppression and harm; they may harm others unintentionally by the process of using their power creatively; they hurt others without thinking about it. Only the weak man "wish`es to hurt and see the signs of sufferings" ("The Dawn" page 371). Surely, Nietzsche does not say that the powerful need cause pain to others; he only points out that should they hurt others, they are not moved by the will to cause pain. It implies that impotence is dangerous to the human nature: a person depressing his passions can be cruel and may be desirous to cause pain. Impotency can be the root of all evil and therefore to be powerful is a blessed thing. The assumption is that the powerful and potent are full of will to power and that extreme and long oppression and frustration can easily distort such passion and caused the oppressed to seek less valuable opportunities to confirm their will to power by being cruel to others.

Moreover, "The Dawn" is the culture's history having to be explained in terms of a person wishing to rise, excel and be more powerful than the other. The barbarians do it by being cruel to their neighbors. Power, therefore, has to be understood as a criterion for values. It attaches to Nietzsche's perception of health as the ability to overcome the illness. Health is exchanged for power. The artist's power is composed of his ability to rise above the sufferings in his life. In Zarathustra's words, it seems that Dionysus defeats Apollo; the demon of darkness is more powerful then the restraining power of the sun's God; wisdom is no more recognized as the supreme principal and ethical criterion. This interpretation, according to Kaufman, is partially true. It is certain that Dionysus' style in the song of glory to Zarathustra symbolizes the abandoning of Apollo. It is also true that Nietzsche declares the will to power being the motivating principal of the universe. Man is also a micro universe! Therefore, there is no difference between "nature" and human nature. Nietzsche's basic perception pertaining to the final theory of value becomes clear: a qualitative difference between different ways of power reduces to more basic quantitative differences; rationality is considered as a sign for great power; however, the quantitative measure of power is the measurement of power.

In Zarathustra, Nietzsche declares the will to power; he talks about "The Will to Power" in the chapter "on the thousand and one goals". The chapter begins with relational moral. Different nations have different purposes and moral codes. However, all have one thing in common: they are the creations of the will to power. There is a difference between Nietzsche and those who will rationalize their society's values. As opposed to them he claims a relational moral and therefore cannot, a priory, confirm the superiority of his society's values; he also cannot judge or compare between values of different societies unless they will have something in common. He contends against relativity that there is a common element enabling a comparison between the judgments of values and moral codes of different societies.

The will to power is revealed in that chapter as the will to overcome oneself. The will to power is not mentioned again, until later, by extension, in "on self-overcoming". Later on, it is mentioned one more time in Zarathustra. The will to power is revealed as the will to self overcoming; to restore order in your micro universe and not letting your energies control you. The will to power is not something metaphysical, not in terms of Heidegger or positivistic term, rather it, to begin with, is primarily a central concept in a psychological hypothesis, the manic-depressive consciousness is a multitude of ever changing streams, feelings, emotions and impulses, extreme fluctuations and periodicity in mood states: pleasure and suffering, the feeling of euphoria and pessimism, high self confidence in manic state and low self confidence in depression, hope during mania and despair during depression, sexual desire during mania and sexual depression in depressive state, depressed mood as opposed to elated mood, a wish to die during depression and a will to live in mania, bad temper and aggressiveness in both cases or type of serenity in mania. All mental aspects and human activity have to be understood by an intrinsic world of urges, passions, emotions and instincts. A will is an example for an urge appearing as a command (command of urges, passions, emotions and instincts). Nietzsche claims that wisdom is a system of links between different passions; and thinking is no other than links between urges. Moreover, all those urges are reduced by him to the idea of the will to power: "it is possible to trace all its drives (of an animal) to the will to power; likewise all the functions of organic life to this one source." (The Will to Power 619). According to this suggestion, the will to power is a primitive form of our mental urge from which all remainder of urges, passions and emotions are derived and developed; he adds that there is no force or other urge that acts within us beside the will to power. The reality of our urges is not doubtable; all psychological and behavioral phenomena can be explained by them united by one principal - the will to power.

A difference in type and level of spirituality are functions of relative power and the organization of numerous urges leading different people. Therefore any "great spirituality" is the outcome of a controlling urge leading all other urges. While Nietzsche recognizes the numerous psychological phenomena and their complexities, he contends that all of them are urges, functions or expressions of the will to power reduced, at the end, to 'a psychological system of forces.' The game of manic-depression, pleasure and its prevention by depression is part of a bigger game of achieving power. Pleasure and the lack of it are results, only a side effect; the real desire is for the amplification of the feeling of being powerful. Pleasure is the product of the passion for power, motivated by this passion he seeks resistance and finds it in the lack of pleasure, a feeling he wishes to overcome as a way to achieve power. I.e. the game of manic-depression is a natural and essential fact by the patient of which end stands the purpose of self empowerment. The manic-depressive should not try to evade the game, rather play along; victory and the feeling of pleasure are conditioned upon its resistance being overcome. Therefore, the lack of pleasure is not a reduction in power, rather, in most cases, is the factor causing the feeling of power. The will to power are the forces and urges acting within us over which we have to overcome; by the manic, it is the passion for life and the urge to empower them which overcomes the depressive's desire to die, or, for example, the manic-depressive has to overcome his bad temper. We need, ethically and morally, overcome the urges and passions and to organize them, give them style and rise beyond them to a higher level of existence, a human being's existence, i.e. turn us into super humans. The power is the mental power which controls these forces. Such a man, this mental patient is a energy

454

bomb, a bi polar circle without beginning nor end; constant energy, not increasing nor decreasing, not expanding, just changing. The power or energy of the soul does not decrease or increase quantitatively; it is just channeled qualitatively and stays constant quantitatively. The passions, feelings and urges are the expression of the will to power, they are the force or a game of forces or waves of energies; competition! The competition is between urges, passions and different feelings of who will rise above another; who will have the most powerful urges and passions and who will gain control over the other. At the same time, mental energy is one or many, a single or many urges, increasing here, decreasing there and vice versa; a sea of energies forever changing qualitatively, forever flowing and streaming strongly recurring with differences over years; tides, from the simplest energy developing to become more complex returning to become simple and so on; starting with small and calm waves up to stormy waves and whirlpools of contradicting forces, building and enforcing each other and then again returning to calm sea, serenity and peace of mind; the conversion of a complex mind to a simpler one enjoying the serenity and silence after the storm. The mind confirms itself and congratulates itself as such that has to recur forever; it is being formed ever hungry, no self loathing or tiredness. This is the world of Dionysus of self ascending and descending, of everlasting reversals, of renewed destruction and recreation, this is a mysterious world of pursuing pleasures without aim unless the pleasure of the circle is an aim to itself. Such a person, this manic-depressive, is the materialization of the will to power and nothing else. He has to make order of hid chaos of energies; he should not oppress his energetic passions but to make order and enforce authority upon them! To enforce his will upon them!


## 05:10 Morality and sublimation


The central perception of Nietzsche's later thinking is the will to power. In Zarathustra's speech "on the thousand and one goals", he says: "a tablet of the good hangs over every people. Behold, it is the tablet of their overcomings; behold, it is the voice of their will to power."[32] This section influences Nietzsche's perception of the morality and sublimation. These will enable the proper understanding of the philosophy of power. Nietzsche does not try to give us a method of ethics in its classical sense. A summary by Emanuel Kant and John Stewart Mill will show it. Kant insisted that a person is not morally better unless his deeds are marked by the absence of psychological tendency and are only motivated by reason. He objected to any other form of morality and treated it as a total distortion. "The categorical imperative" was termed by the Prussian philosopher Emanuel Kant. The categorical imperative is the central concept around which Kant's ethics revolves requiring from humans to universalize his actions, judging them as if he was a judge in a court of law. The law itself, as initially formulized by Kant, is: "do your deeds only according the practical rule which, by accepting it, you may wish it also to become a general rule". I.e. the imperative demands the principal stemming from a human action will be guiding principal which every person shall

---

[32] Friedrich Nitzsche, thus spoke Zarathustra, translated by Walter Kaufman, Penguin books 1966.

wish to adopt. According to the imperative, the morality rules by which I live must be universal, i.e. valid for all. These are rules which, I wish, everyone will adopt. An example to such rule is: "do not kill". In this case, I would wish all people to preserve their fellow man's life and as such "do not kill" will become a universal law obliging all mankind. And therefore, this rule is in accordance with the categorical imperative. If I would wish people to murder each other, I would accept the fact of someone killing me, but since I cannot wish that someone will kill me, I cannot universalize the law "kill", i.e. there is a contradiction; and if there is a contradiction then reason cannot accept it. John Stewart Mill, on the other hand, does not revoke Kant's ethics, rather he claims that all those moral men believing a priori that it is essential and necessary to contend at all, utilitarian arguments are necessary and cannot be waived; and therefore, he gives Kant's theory of ethics as an example. Mill thought that utilitarianism, i.e. a philosophical doctrine pertaining to the field of ethics determining that a value of an act is determined by its contribution to the general good. I.e. doing a deed, I must ask myself if this deed will bring happiness to people thus utilitarianism is a doctrine assessing deeds according to their result and not according to their ethical importance as opposed to deontological doctrines relating to the ethical importance of deeds and consider certain deeds as good or morally bad without any relation to their outcome. I.e. there are deeds, according to deontological doctrines that there are appropriate deeds that should be done even if causing suffering to others. According to utilitarianism, the result sometimes justifies the means. The benefit - that good that should be achieved - was defined by different thinkers as "pleasure" as opposed to "pain". Therefore, when Mill includes

Kant in his method, he is actually saying 'do your deeds so that your action will maximize happiness brought by it upon people, this will be a moral deed'. Every deed is assessed, according to the utilitarian perception, according to the criteria of "bringing the greatest good to the greatest number of people"; however, such assessment is bound by various moral and other problems; for example, if a severe injury inflicted upon one person brings benefit to other, thus his pain is absorbed, in the final analysis, by the pleasure brought upon others thus justifying his injury. Utilitarianism of the deed is, therefore, a utilitarian worldview contending that the right deed is the one which brings the greatest pleasure to the largest number of people. Utilitarianism of all, on the other hand, contends that the right deed is the acting according to a rule which if acted upon generally, the greatest pleasure will be given to the largest number of people (similar to the categorical imperative). Actually, according to utilitarianism-deed, when a choice between possible action routes is presented to us, we have to consider, firstly, the result of each possible action and choose the action, we believe, will produce the greatest pleasure. Utilitarianism-rule will choose the same case by searching after a universal rule according to which a consistent action under it will produce the greatest pleasure. Nietzsche's perception of morality is best understood in terms of resistance to rival utilitarianism. John Stewart Mill may include Kant's ethics in utilitarianism only because of him misunderstanding Kant. Utilitarianism was never the subject of Kant's interest: the value in morality was, in his eyes, a function of reason, i.e. the cohesion of a behavioral rule according to which an action is set. Any contradiction and the non cohesion, so Kant thought, can become clear by universalizing the rule and determine if its universal adoption will describe a situation in which the rule can no longer be applied. Whether Kant did consider a result, he did not find any interest in the benefit, rather in the formal property: does the rule contradict itself? It is not important for our matter what is preferable, Kant's ethics or Mill utilitarianism, but as a general definition of moral, utilitarianism failed in the inclusion of Kant's ethics. Kant's power manifests in the rationalization or the giving of an intellectual basis for the ethics of the western world, i.e. the Ten Commandments. Men were commanded by God to be good because this is what God wanted regardless of the results. There is another aspect which districts between the moral and immoral, so Nietzsche claims it to be the overcoming of oneself. Kaufman contends that Kant's ethics as the Ten Commandments presenting this trait is clear; we, for example, are required to overcome our tendency to violence. This element of overcoming is no less essential for the utilitarian standing; the power and probability of utilitarianism are not separated from the insistence on the individual having to overcome and subject his interest to the benefit of the people. In moral codes being allegedly primitive, an element of self control and discipline of tendencies is always present. Nietzsche standing can be based on the consideration of form in which moral codes must avoid general definition. Such code cannot put any restrain on the individual and will have to let him act upon his urges. While this standing is legitimate, it will have to agree with the usual use of the term 'morality'. A person adopting it may contend this: I negate morality and prefer to act upon my urge. Kaufman says that "this position should not be confused with classical Greek Hedonism, which considered pleasure the aim of conduct but did not identify pleasure with the gratifications of every impulse. Man was told to control his impulses for the sake of his ultimate happiness, which was conceived in refined and spiritual terms—as the pursuit of philosophy."(Kaufman p.213) A human being always put upon him moral strings, he depresses himself; therefore, it is logical to call a human being not just a "rational creature" rather also a "moral creature". The two titles are inseparable. Man's self criticism by self reflecting on his intentions and actions are the nucleus of morality. Indeed, a non impulsive action is not necessarily good. If a crime is committed "in cold blood" out of calculation and complete consciousness, it does not enable extenuating circumstances. In such case, anyways, the criminal had acted as a moral product and this act was, in a certain sense, moral or given to moral judgment, moral evil. A small child acting upon his urges will not tell us to act morally or immorally, he will simply tell us to behave immorally as small children do. Morality always calls for the resistance to urges: moral codes are methods of imperatives against surrendering to urges or acts that are caused by impulsive passions. Positive moral imperatives as "do not kill" have always preference over animalistic urges. Utilitarianism is an important trait of moral codes, but it is not, as the self overcoming, the essence of morality itself. A difference in moral methods is a different way of self overcoming. In the classic form, reason was supposed to overcome tendencies while Kant insisted, as we have seen, that one should overcome tendencies in such a way by which they will not even be a motivation to action. Had Nietzsche developed his dualistic method, he would talk now about reason controlling the will to power, about Apollo defeating Dionysus. His ignorance of such dualism includes the rejection, through Zarathustra's speeches, of all respect and coming closer to the Kantian and classic views. Actually, Nietzsche's monism raises the question of how control may exist at all. He asked what is in the world that can overcome the will to power. Nietzsche would say that there is nothing else than the will to power and therefore the will to power has to overcome itself. Therefore, the idea of self overcoming receives new sense. The requirement that reason overcome urges or that the consideration of your future happiness or of the happiness of others will overcome and oppress urges and tendencies is logical and accepted. The image of self overcoming, and the word is metaphoric, implies on two forces overcoming each other. "Self overcoming" may be perceived and be with sense when the self is analyzed as having two forces, for example reason and tendencies and urges while the first controls the two. It seems that according to this dualism, i.e. the image of one force overcoming and controlling the second force, there is no meaning and sense to the self overcoming as monism. One needs to ask: is Nietzsche coherent to himself? It may be that the dualism being allegedly rejected by him exists at the edge of his consciousness and harms his argument? It may be that Nietzsche is assuming, to begin with, dualism of Apollo and Dionysus or as in "The Dawn" power and reason (The Dawn page 548). However, according to Kaufman, Nietzsche is trying to explain the whole range of human behavior in terms of the will to power; Nietzsche says that all our urges need reducing to the will to power, this is the "small" and important insight by which he succeeded, in his opinion, to penetrate the heart of human motivation. He thought he did it better from all preceding philosophers. "Let us assume, finally, that we will succeed to explain all our intensive life as a development and divergence of one basic form of will - i.e. of the will to power, as my assertions present; let us assume that all organic functions can be reduced to the will to power and someone can find in it the solution to the problem of bearing children and feeding, this is one problem, then someone will earn the right to determine all effective forces in a clear manner as a will to power. The world being internally viewed the world that is defined and set according to "understandable trait" will be the will to power and nothing else. (The Dawn page 36). Let us concentrate just on the psychological problem for a moment: not on the possibility of self overcoming rather on the actual process of overcoming urges. Nietzsche defines the process and this control in one word - sublimation, i.e. channeling. When we are full of energy, for example violent energy and we do not wish it to burst immediately and directly toward somebody, we may channel this energy to a sexual energy, sexual passion; i.e. the urge for violence is channeled to sexual passion. Instead of the energy bursting as violence it burst and disposed of by sexual relations. Therefore, my ethics says that when a mental patient is full of violent energy of self destruction he can and must channel it to become a sexual urge and from there continue channeling it to creation and art as was explained by him later on. Nietzsche uses the word in the second volume of "Human, all too Human" (first published in 1878) by which he means "sexual sublimation". Speaking in these places or others of sublimation, he speaks, for example, of Eros (the God of love) in a Plato's banquet relating to a sublimation of a sexual urge. In "the Will to Power" he refers to the sublimation of the artist's urges (677). One needs to consider what is happening when an urge goes through channeling or sublimation. Nietzsche believed that a sexual urge can be channeled to a creative, spiritual activity instead of directly bursting. The manic-depressive has to create sublimation for the

462

energy stemming from the urge and passion for death and self destruction in the depressive state and channel it to a sexual desire and from there to an artistic or philosophic creation or the manic must channel his bad temper to a sexual activity and if it might harm him, for example in uncontrolled sexual relations which might harm his family, then to art. Actually, in my opinion, depression and mania are the two sides of the same principal - the will to power. The mental energy being a self destructive energy in the past was channeled in mania to passions and sexual urges and from there to a creative productivity (which explains the creativity and strong desires of the manic). The negative thoughts while in depressive state and the will to die which led Van Gogh to put an end to his life should have been channeled to more artistic creations. Similarly, the passions of the barbarians to torture their enemies can be channeled to competing with them in the Olympic Games. In a similar way, the rivalry between the Greek can be channeled to the competition on the title of the best philosophy writer, the best speech writer, the most cleansing tragedies, etc. is it possible to talk logically about sublimation of the same urge? Nietzsche hands us a method and says in "The Dawn" in a long aphorism entitled "self-mastery and the as its ultimate motive": someone brings about the disruption of his strength by self coercion of a specially difficult and tedious task or by self exposure to a new stimulus or enjoyment thus distracting his thoughts and the game of physical forces to other channels. For example, nowadays, psychiatrics insist that mental patients will participate in sport activities and not only for diet's sake but also to gain control of the mind diverting it from obsessive thoughts. This method is strengthened by other methods. Nietzsche summarizes: "one can dispose of one's drives like a gardner and cultivate... the seedings ofwrath, pity, brooding, and vanity as fruitfully and usefully as beautiful fruit on espaliers" (the Dawn 560). The manic-depressive has to channel his self violence and destruction to his sexual urges and them, he should channel by Eros, in sense of love and productivity, to a philosophical, artistic and lyrical creation. The passion to die and being toward death (Heidegger) of the depressive has to be channeled to passion to create and passion to be productive; in this state, feelings and negative passions in depressive state are being channeled to a will to artistic creation as those of Van Gogh; lyrical as of Helderline and philosophical as Nietzsche's. An artistic creation starts with an idea and thought; i.e. in this piece of rock an idea already exists, the idea of David (Michael Angelo gave birth to David out of the raw marble), and as we know form Plato, the idea is eternal because it was born from love and passion; idea or thought are, according to "the Banquet", the outcome and product of eternal love. The manic, as I have already stated, are very creative and productive, this productivity is also a born child but also a newly born idea. Indeed, in a manic state while being full of passions, urges and desires and the passion for sex increases and since he, the manic, wishes to reconstruct the energy of pleasure more and more, he finds it in the enjoyment of sex wanting to live and prosper, i.e. the enjoyment is kind of vital, the increasing urge for life. Actually, in mania, the will to die during depression is channeled into a will to create to bear children, to leave behind descendants, biological descendants but also intellectual descendants in the form of philosophical creations. Someone can question and contend that sublimation is an unclear term that in some situations does not exist rather a replacement of urges. The criticism may have been relevant should Nietzsche had contended that only energy remains while the purposes of the urge is being replaced - energy is not being defined as the material by Aristotle while the purpose seems to define the essence of urge. However Kaufman contends that Nietzsche thinks about what was left as essence and that the things that are changing are incidental. He considers the will to power, which remains all along, as "essence" while "all goals and purposes" are only incidental and variable properties of the one and only "will to power". In other words, not only the energy remains but also the goal, power; and these which are called "goals" or "purposes" and are cancelled, are only incidental traits of the most basic passion. When Nietzsche starts to relate to the will to power as a basic motive of mankind, he thinks also on sexual motivation or urge; in his writings, one can find it in the pages including the second and third citation of "the will to power".

"Sexual stimulation in the ascent involves a tension which releases itself in the feeling of power: the will to rule—a mark of the most sexsual men: the waning propensity of the sex impulse shows itself in the relenting of the thirst of power".

"The reabsorption of semen by the blood...perhaps prompts the stimulus of power, the unrest of all forces toward the over-coming of resistance...the feeling of power has so far mounted highest in abstinent priest and hermits." (Kaufman page 222).

A paragraph from "Beyond good and evil" should also be remembered: "the degree and kind of the sexuality of a human being reaches up into the ultimate pinnacle of his spirit" (75). Sexuality is the frontal background of something else more basic and therefore kept in sublimation: the will to power. I think that
465

the increased sexuality of the manic is not the essence but an aspect of the will to power; the sexuality goes through sublimation into creation, i.e. one force in the mind goes through channeling and manifests itself as a different power; what is left is the will to power. for example, the depressive's violence and self destruction in being towards death, in which the purpose is death, "is cancelled" when he rises into mania in which he feels vital and alive, and then the sexual urge rises and increases also without the inhibitions of traditional morality being channeled into creative force. The feeling of power is essential with the manic-depressive also in the sense of him presuming of having powers; i.e. supernatural powers, messianic, power, money, respect, etc; actually, all are the same expression of the will to power. The sexual manifestation, the messianic manifestation, the paranoia and anxieties are only aspects of the basic will to power. The sexual and messianic expression, power, money and megalomania is incidental; this essential is the will to power, i.e. mental urges competing with each other for seniority which will be stronger and more powerful. And therefore the feeling of power by sexuality can goes through sublimation into an absolute feeling of power. Sexuality is not the base rather a station on the way. The sexual urge can be a station on the way and is capable of great sublimation. For the Greek, the sexual symbol was a respected symbol and only religion had turned it into something not clean. Nietzsche insists on the point of a man with strong urges having more hope than a man without urges. He believed that a man without urges cannot do the good or create the beautiful more than a castrated man can bear children. A man with strong urges can be violent and bad only because he had not yet learned to channel his urges, but should he achieve self control, he will achieve greatness. Think about the paranoid believing someone is stalking him; his primary instinct or urge is to hit him but overcoming this urge he achieves moral greatness. In "The Will to Power" Nietzsche contends that we should exercise our urges not cancel or destroy them. To exercise them differently! Self overcoming is, therefore, the will of man to empower passion or another certain urge or to give it "style"; i.e. to channel the urge, to sublime it thus succeeding by sublimation to restore order in his intrinsic world. A man with power is the one succeeding to overcome his destructive urges by *changing their form* to something beautiful.

"Moral intolerance is an expression of weakness in a man: he is afraid of his own "immorality," he must deny his strongest drives because he does not yet know how to imploy them. Thus the most fruitful regions of the earth remain uncultivated the longest:--the force is lucking that could here become master." (The Will to Power 385).

## 05:15 Reason and sublimation

The first comment on self overcoming is, as aforesaid, the overcoming of urges and passions by sublimation. However, one must honestly ask how sublimation is possible with Nietzsche's monism. Indeed, "Self overcoming" is only a metaphor talking about two forces and therefore, one should ask whether Nietzsche is fooled by such metaphor or dualism still exists behind his consciousness. Nietzsche used another word beside sublimation: spiritualization (Vergeistigung). Nietzsche recognized

467

only one principal - the will to power; therefore, one should ask how passions and mind will be considered in terms of the will to power. How are they linked to it, as, at the end, he must give accounts to sublimation only on the bases of the will to power. His monism was not deducted from Schopenhauer's metaphysics; he did not consider as legitimate to accept unequivocally tradition's believes about Reason's unique status. After questioning God's status, he felt committed to question the status of Reason. Empirical research brought him to the assumption that every human behavior has to be understood on basis of the will to power. His psychological diagnoses together with historical research and in particular his understanding of the Greek culture convinced him of the will to power being the most basic fact that can be thought of. From here, he concluded that not only our passions and urges but also our Reason are tools in the understanding of the will to power. Intellect, Reason and spirit seemed to him as the phenomena of the same basic urge into which our urges are being reduced. In sublimation of sexual urges, the target, for example this particular woman is cancelled. On the other hand, Reason is unique (Sui generis) and therefore cannot be cancelled in a sublimation process.

Reason as well as sexual urge is the forms of the will to power. The will to self destruction or the sexual passion are an urge and in surrendering to it in a non sublimed form man remains a slave of his own passions without the ability to overcome them. Reason, however, gives man self control; as a will to power which in essence is the instinct of freedom (On the genealogy of morals II 18), it can be fulfilled only through Reason. Reason is the expression of the highest phenomena of the will to power; through Reason, he can realize his goal in the most complete way.

468

Reason is hailed by Nietzsche not because the ability to abstract it from the empirical, incidental phenomena or forms of the universal as well as deductions, but because these abilities enable us to restore order from the chaos of urges and passions and bring them to harmony through which man will become powerful: powerful over him and nature. Intellectuality differentiates between the "higher" man and the "lower". Irrationality is a weakness in his eyes and rationality is a sign of power. Lack of Reason, intelligence and spirit are lack of power. His offensive on "methods", for example philosophical, is based on his resistance to irrationality which is identified in the unequivocal acceptance of assumptions for granted. Those who find refuge in irrationality, dogmatism and methodology based on an unequivocal acceptance of assumptions are considered by Nietzsche as weak. In "science", Nietzsche intends the will to ask by putting one's believes forward for criticism and change them in face of new evidence. Not to do so is a sign for irrationality, weakness and lack of power. The true rational man puts all his believes under the microscope turning it to his second nature. Being strong enough, man's Reason will enable him to control and use his urges. I.e. the mentally ill should not burst in anger but control his urges, including the urge for self destruction and sublime rage and self destruction by making use of the urge to create as Van Gogh did in his paintings or to exercise his rage in sport or sex.

In all his late works, power is the only criterion and rationality is of such value which leads it to be the expression of power. The spiritual people are the strongest. A person being able to develop his rationality only by annulling sensuality is of a weak mind; a strong mind does not fight urges: it controls them, therefore, being the pinnacle of man's power. Nietzsche considers a man acting on urges as well as a man intentionally cancelling his urges as lower and weaker man than the man who acts on his instincts motivated by his Reason. If the manic-depressive acts and is motivated by the desire to die for example, hence being irrational he is consider as weak, but if he decides to be a teacher, or a poet, painter or an artist having purpose and aim, then by rationality he overcomes the passion and urge and becomes overman. Nietzsche's doctrine differs from irrationality as if he contradicts Reason to the basic principal of his method, however Reason is described as the realization of the will to power; the irrational does not seem as something opposed to rationality but a "weak" of rationality: it lacks the power, the toughness and the power to be rational. "The will to power is neither identical with reason nor opposed to it, but potentially rational." (Kaufman page 235) The urges, passions as well as Reason (mind) are also expressions of the will to power; when Reason overcomes urges, we cannot talk on marriage between two different principals but only on the self overcoming of the will to power. This single force, the will to power, previously manifested as an urge and then rising above its other early manifestations. The will to power is the successor of Dionysus and Apollo being an endless passion but having the ability to give it a form. Having one of his most outstanding traits as giving form to itself in different appearances, Nietzsche talks on the character of Proteus (in Greek mythology: the God of the seas being able to change his form). In overcoming sublimation, he seems as having double ability: he is the one overcoming (Reason) as well as the one being overcome (urges), in Aristotle terms he is material as well as form. Nietzsche was influenced by the "dark" philosopher Heraclitus due to his assertion that nature or the "is" is not something stable. The will to power is in war against itself. The battle between Reason and urges is one form of many calashes. Hamlet asks: "To be, or not to be– that is the question: Whether 'tis nobler in the mind to suffer the slings and arrows of outrageous fortune, or to take arms against a sea of troubles and, by opposing, end them", Shakespeare raises, as Nietzsche, the idea of the intrinsic battle of man; in particular within the manic-depressive, i.e. to be toward death or toward life and being a teacher. The manic-depressive can and has to overcome his depressive state, he must channel the passion to die and change it into something else. Vincent Van Gogh and Virginia Wolf did not manage to restore order from the chaos in them and overcome their state and passion to die. Man thrives to be perfect having complete self control despite being bound by asceticism and self denial and therefore a type of self overcoming which seems in its essence ethical. Therefore, I say that the being depressive has to, ethically, overcome his passion and urges to be toward death and instead confirm life. The will to power is the aspiration to improve you. The will to power is not just the will to live or self preservation, but to live in such a way of self improvement. "Only where there is life is there also will: not will to life but—thus I teach you—will to power". (Thus spoke Zarathustra, II 12) Therefore what I ask of the manic-depressive is not just living but the next overcoming arrives in order to be a teacher for the crowd, the mob. There is more to valuable life than to life itself. Oscar Wild, who concurred with Nietzsche that all human beings kill all that they love, has written one poem: "the artist". The artist wants to create a bronze statute but he does not find bronze anywhere in the world except for in previous work. He melts his previous creation in order to create his new one from it. This is considered by Nietzsche the essence of creativity and the way of life. Sometimes one has to "destroy" one passion in order to give expression and form to another; to channel one urge and change it to a new form. The will to cease life has to be melted and changed to the will to sexuality or to creation which is an urge to empowering life and the feeling of being vital, vigorous and energetic. Nietzsche linked the erotic creation with the longing for eternity. The will to create is a sub case of the will to power; it also the will to the God of love Eros which can be manifested in different manners. So was Van Gogh and his love for creation. Nietzsche's emphasis of the suffering bounded by self improvement and cruelty of man toward himself becomes clearer in the second investigation of genealogy, there; he deals in "negative consciousness". The will to power is an erotic creativity (Eros) - "the love of creation and the birth of the beautiful". Nietzsche contends that man cannot be conscious of the good and beautiful without being conscious of the ugly and evil. In order to become powerful, to achieve freedom, to control his urges and improve himself, man has, first and foremost, to develop the feeling that his urges are evil. This cognition is the essence of negative consciousness; man tells himself: my tendencies are despicable and I am evil; at this moment, he divides himself. There are, allegedly, two "selves", the rational and the irrational. The one tries to give form to the other; he tries to reinvent himself, to give character and restore order from his own emotional chaos. His urges are rebellious; he suffers and feels guilty; he destructs himself being violent toward himself. The man has, first and foremost, to imprint "no" in his mind, he has to denounce despicably his urges and become aware of the contradiction between bad and good. The depressive has to see something bad in his passion to die. Prior to man being born beautiful, he has to go through torments. Going through torments is a necessary evil. The road to happiness in mania goes through the road of torments and suffering under depression.

## 05:30 The overman and eternal recurrence

Walter Kaufman contends that Nietzsche's philosophy of power reaches its peak in the dual vision of the overman and the "Eternal Recurrence". In light of Nietzsche's determination that the two ideas are linked to each other, the "Eternal Recurrence" doctrine and the overman became the peak of his whole philosophy. Nietzsche is a psychologist and philosopher; the manic depressive overman overcame the chaos in his mind and restored order to it; he overcame his passion to die and channeled his feeling to empower life. He arrived at the recognition that suffering (depression) and pleasure (mania) are linked and inseparable; they replace each other for ever. The pleasure and suffering in manic-depression repeat in a daily existence circle of the "eternal recurrence" forever and he says "yes" to them. "behold, I teach you the overman: he is the lightning; he is this frenzy" (Thus spoke Zarathustra, Zarathustra Prologue, p.13)

"I will teach men the meaning of their existence—the overman, the lightning out of the dark cloud of man." (Thus spoke Zarathustra, Zarathustra Prologue p.19)

By the manic depressive, pleasure and suffering appear alternately. I will show how the two ideas of overman and eternal recurrence are naturally compatible and being realized in the manic-depressive.

The overman (Uebermensch) is a central term with Nietzsche. Nietzsche's perception of the overman is dependent upon the association of the word "ueber". Nietzsche asks how the individual can give sense to his life; otherwise his existence will remain as an accident.

His answer was how can you determine your true self?

A man must investigate himself which is not somewhere in your deeps hidden from you but is beyond you (Ueber dir). For Nietzsche, the overman is a symbol of rejection the acceptance of the conventions of one's norm: the antithesis of mediocrity.

In "Thus spoke Zarathustra", Nietzsche says: "upon the arrival of Zarathustra to the nearest town at the edge of the forests, he met a crowd gathering in the market; they were promised a dancer on a rope.

And thus spoke Zarathustra to the crowd: I teach you the overman. Man is something that should be overcome. What have you done to overcome him? (Thus spoke Zarathustra V 3).

The overman cannot be detached from overcoming (ueberwindung). Man is something to be overcome and the one who managed it becomes overman.

As for the manic depressive, I have said that depression is a state of having desire to die and self destruction; by overcoming his desires particularly the desire and urge to die or being toward death, the depressive overcomes himself and turns into overman.

The manic-depressive overcomes the illness of self destruction! So he must do, otherwise he will get lost. Zarathustra declares "never yet has there been an overman. Naked I saw both the greatest and the smallest man. They are still all-too-similar to each other" (Thus spoke Zarathustra II 4). Since the manic-depressive is not part of the crowd or the flock rather shamefully expelled from them, he was not yet visible; until now!

The purpose of humanity is not at the end rather in a specific person. The development of mankind can be only within special individuals. Most people, the crowd according to Nietzsche, who are not philosophical nor artistic remain animalistic compared with a man overcoming himself, channeling his passions, recognizing his urges and giving style to his character thus really becoming a man or overman.

The man discovering his true self, i.e. overman, changes his "for" and achieves self control. The same way, the manic-depressive overcoming himself as depressive controlling his desires (being toward death), irrationality and channeling his desire to die into something else such as philosophical or rational artistic creation, he will be overman. He recreates himself by sublimation; he simply creates lyrics, art and philosophy. One should not err, to overcome a depressive illness is a very difficult thing, the depressive has to raise himself from the ground and the abyss, he has to pull his own head by his hair and raise him upwards. Arriving at it, he may be defined as being in control of his urges, choosing being toward life.

At the beginning of the Antichrist (Antichrist), Nietzsche explains: "the problem I thus pose is not what shall succeded mankind in the sequence of living beings (man is an end[Ende]), but what type of man shall be brad, shall be willed, for being higher in value...even in the past this higher type has appeared often—but as fortunate accident, as an exception, never as something willed...from dread the opposite type was willed, bread, and attained: the domestic animal, the herd animal, the sick human animal..."

Nietzsche's sayings applied, of course, by me to the mentally ill, are that the mentally ill were not part of the flock, they were shamefully expelled from a flock fearing them; they still remained wild, undomesticated by not being part of the flock. The mentally ill being a overman is perceived as an unfortunate accident, exceptional and not welcomed by society, they were expelled from human society, from the flock because the anxiety felt by humanity from the exceptional, an undomesticated wild animal.

A mentally ill is not positioned in the continuum of human development in term of progress but is present any time sporadically in every culture. Nietzsche continues: "mankind does not represent a development toward something better or stronger or higher in the sense accepted today."Progress" is merely a modern idea, that is, false idea." (Antichrist 3,4).

In manic-depression in general and in a mixed state in particular, there are contradicting and opposing urges and desires; manic-depressive is a state of chaotic contradictions of consciousness which is due to the change taking place in conscious states: pessimism and optimism, happiness and suffering, hope and despair, high self esteem in mania as opposed to low self esteem in depression.

The manic-depressive as a overman rose beyond his animalistic nature, to restore order from the chaos of his urges and gave style to his nature or as Nietzsche said about Goete that he imposed discipline upon himself completely, he created himself and became "a man of tolerance, not out of weakness but out of power", "spirit turned free". The manic lacking impedance who releases his urges and desires from any restraints (since sexual activity pleases him and, by nature, he wishes to multiply any pleasure many times) becomes "free spirit" when he succeeds to gain control over them.

Even though sexual activity is not evil, the manic has to sublime his sexual urge and channel it into something lyrical as lyric, art and philosophy. Having understood the overman as such particularly the manic-depressive as his realization, the perception of "Eternal Recurrence" becomes clear. Nietzsche is the teacher of the "Eternal Recurrence". Zarathustra's doctrine of "the Eternal Recurrence", i.e. the infinite independent recurring flow of the circle of all things may have been taught already by Heraclitus, at least by the Stoics who inherited most of their principals from Heraclitus.

Nietzsche, by "the Eternal Recurrence", says the nobody achieves redemption at the end, because there is no end, rather he achieves redemption at any moment at which the world allegedly comes to an end; what can we be taught in ten new years that we were not taught before?

i.e., Nietzsche says that there is no infinite progress, what is called "negative infinity" by Hegel, rather Nietzsche emphasizes the infinite value of the moment and the individual. The mentally ill has to be redeemed in every step of his illness. I.e. the chronic illness which, by its nature, is circular and infinite (a positive infinity in Hegel's terms) does not bring him to any type of end; rather he has to see in every step a "moment" on its own. In other words, at every moment, step by step through his illness, the mentally ill has to overcome and redeem himself; while in depression, he has to overcome the "moments" of being toward death.

While in mania, at the manic "moment", he has to channel and sublime his emotions and destructive urges (spending money, uncontrolled sex, intolerance, etc) into creativity.

The doctrine of "Eternal Recurrence" of all things was already aforementioned as the fate of Dionysus. The man - Nietzsche chose Goete as a representative - who restored order to the chaos of his urges, desires, emotions, states of consciousness and thoughts and merged every trait of his personality and looks at ugliness giving it a sense in the beautiful whole; such overman will also completely understand his being as part of the cosmos and by confirming his being, he will also confirm everything that had been, present and will be (Twilight of the Idols IX 49).

As a result of the overman's pleasure, which can be seen as the pleasure in overcoming of the manic-depressive, the secret of recurrence is being revealed, the depression will disappear and be replaced by mania that will disappear and the depression will recur again and again indefinitely.

In the "The other Dancing Song" and in "Drunken Song" from "Thus spoke Zarathustra" Nietzsche links between his perception of "the Eternal Recurrence" to the feeling of pleasure being overman's fate. It seems that there is some general perceptive tension in "the Eternal Recurrence" of eternal pleasure and suffering of manic-depression since, after all, there is a lot of suffering in the illness; as will be explained later on, there is pleasure in the actual overcoming and confirming of the existential circle of pleasure and suffering by saying "yes" to the manic-depressive circle, i.e. there is pleasure in confirming the illness and in the acceptance of one's fate. Therefore, by confirming the eternal and chronic circle of the illness you create pleasure wishing it will recur forever.

Doch alle Lust will Ewigkeit-

Will tiefe, tiefe ewigkeit

"All Joy wants eternity-

Wants deep, wants deep eternity"

"Thus spoke Zarathustra", "The other Dancing Song" and in "Drunken Song."

Nietzsche describes the relation and link between "Eternal Recurrence" and pleasure or, I say the eternal recurrence of the mania and depression which expresses the two poles of the illness, i.e. pleasure and suffering:

"Do you not hear it? Do you not smell it? Just now my world became perfect; Midnight too is noon; Pain too is a joy, curses too are a blessing; night too is a sun..." this is the message from Zarathustra to me: the manic-depression is an illness describing the completeness of the infinite circle of life for the manic-depressive, pleasure bound by suffering following each other replacing each other, the essential link; it is possible and necessary to view it as a blessing and not a curse; as a blessing because it enables me to overcome myself and confirm my fate; moreover, to love my fate and turn me into overman, this is the source of the blessing in the illness and therefore I am happy to have the ability to return to overman!

And also:

"Pain, too, is a joy...have you ever said Yes to a single Joy...then you said Yes, too, to all woe. All things are entangled, ensnared, ensamored. If ever you wanted one thing twice, if ever you said "you please me, happiness! Adibe, moment!" then you wanted back all. All anew, all eternally, all entangled, ensnared, enamored—oh, then you loved the world. Eternal ones, love it eternally and evermore: and to woe, too, you say: go, but return! For all joy wants—eternity...you higher men, do learn this, joy wants eternity. Joy wants the eternity of all things, wants deep, wants deep eternity" (Thus spoke Zarathustr IV 19).

This paragraph from "Thus spoke Zarathustra" tells us, the manic-depressives, that we have to say a big and decisive "yes" to pleasure while we are in mania as well as say "yes" to suffering and sorrow while we are in depression because both are linked and inseparable; both are expressions of the will to power. Should we desire the pleasure in mania, we should want also the suffering and sorrow in depression. Should we want the one, we should want the other as well because the two are a circle, i.e. positive infinity; and so we should love ourselves and our world - the circle of our existence. We say also to sorrow go - but return! Because pleasure and sorrow will recur forever!

This paragraph expresses the elated (mania) mood of the moment. Nietzsche in "Eternal Recurrence" teaches us on the circle of happiness and depression in life and that life in its generality has to be confirmed, i.e. the happiness and the good as well as the suffering and the evil. The choice in the possibility of life is by the "Eternal Recurrence".

The thought of "Eternal Recurrence" is possible only because temporality and circularity exist from the depressive to the manic and vice versa. I as a manic-depressive have said "yes" to life because reality is a stream or coming into being; I knew that I will collapse and rise over and over again because all is temporal and this temporality on the other hand, is eternal, i.e. will forever continue for the duration of my whole life. This is my choice; "being toward death" or to choose and confirm life and be "toward life".

In a negative way, the "Eternal Recurrence" doctrine is a complete rejection of all denunciations of the moment, the final and the individual; this is the antithesis to the belief in infinite progress being the evolution or self improvement of the eternal soul. Nothing progresses toward anything, there is no purpose, and there is no end just an infinite existential circle in which the manic-depressive exists. This is also the antithesis in every belief pertaining to other worlds, i.e. there is no redemption in "the next world" just in this world.

For the manic-depressive there are two worlds: the one of depression, grey and dark and the other of mania, lighted and merry and he has to fund redemption in both of them.

Nietzsche, as aforesaid, was mainly busy with the philosopher, the artist and with those who achieved self improvement and confirm their existent state forever, forward and backward and do not consider tomorrow rather the moment. The moment at which they are in a certain or another existential state; such people want the eternal recurrence and find pleasure in the "moment" and not at the end since there is no end. Therefore, the manic-depressive have to confirm their being and wishing for every step in their illness to recur relating to every moment, sorrow or happiness as welcomed or at least as they supposed to be as Nietzsche was. Nietzsche is "I, the last disciple of the philosopher Dionysus - I, the teacher of eternal recurrence" (Twilight of the Idols X 5).

"Eternal Recurrence" was for Nietzsche less than an idea and more of an experience, i.e. a way of life; an extreme experience in life full of suffering, pain and grief. In such a way, he could redeem himself and overcome his manic-depressive illness, to turn a curse into blessing, to also confirm the moments of suffering and pain and tell them "yes", "go, but return".

Already in "the birth of a tragedy" Nietzsche had tried to see how life can be justified. His first answer was that life can be justified only as an esthetic phenomenon. He used the analysis of the Greek tragedy in order that also the Greek had enjoyed life despite the suffering and sorrow in their life and eventually they were powerful and enjoyable (the birth of a tragedy 7).

Only on August 1881, the thought that man improving himself, changing the form of his nature achieving sheer pleasure popped up in his head (Kaufman page 324). In such a state, while flooded with happiness, man does not feel needier to justify life, i.e. the manic-depressive in light of his happiness in mania and his knowing that suffering under depression is only one "moment" in the illness followed by another "moment" of happiness and so the wheel will recur thus he needs no justification knowing there are none. He enjoys the "moment" loving it as it is like Nietzsche. He confirms the illness forward and backward forever "eternal". He "not mearly bear what is necessary, still less conceal it—all idealism is mendaciousness in the face of what is necessary—but love it." (Ecce Homo II 10)

Nietzsche says that such feeling of pleasure and joy is "amor fati", i.e. "my formula for greatness in a human being is *amor fati*: that one wants nothing to be different, not forward, not backward, not in all eternity."( Ecce Homo II 10)

The experience in amor fati (love of fate) is the experience by which man loves his life with all difficulties, despite them, only for what they are. When a person succeeds to see in suffering also pleasure understanding that he has to control it and loving it then he is powerful and in control of his life. Being in control of his life means that the powerful man becomes overman, he succeeds in seeing pleasure also in suffering and channeling them by sublimation into creativity.

The man experiencing such pleasure is a strong man, instead of relying on an external happiness as heaven he sees in this world an opportunity for pleasure and happiness. Instead of finding sense to his life in the next world, he confirms the world as it is without the need for justifications, he has sense in his life by confirming them and their sense of pleasure. When a person feels pleasure he does not need justifications nor reasons but he simply says yes to pleasure and life made out of pleasure and suffering. Suffering can be channeled to artistic creation giving him satisfaction and pleasure.

This is also the sense of one of the most important paragraphs written before Zarathustra by which "the Eternal Recurrence" is described as follows: "what, if some day or night, a demon were to steal after you into your loneliest loneliness and say to you: this life, as you now live it and have lived it, you will have to live once more and innumwerable times more; and there will be nothing new in it, but every pain and every joy and every thought and sigh...must return to you—all in the same succession and sequence—even this spider and this moonlight between the trees, and even moment and I myself. The eternal hourglass of existence is turned over again and again—and you with it, speak pf dust!" would you not throw yourself down and gnash your teeth and curse the demon who spoke thus? Or have you once experienced a tremendous moment when you would have unswered him: "you are a god, and never have I heard anything more divine!" if this thought were to gain possession of you, it would change you as you are, or perhaps crush you. The question in each and everything, "do you want this once more and innumerable times more?" would lie upon your actions as the greatest weight. Or how well disposed would you have to become to yourself and to life to *crave nothing more fervently* than this ultimate eternal confirmation and seal?"(The Gay Science 341).

As for the manic-depressive, I think that the demon is saying to me and those alike that this life will recur i.e. the eternal recurrence will happen for the two poles, we will experience the circularity of manic-depression and its contents repeatedly until infinity. I do not refer to other dimensions or life after death, but this earthly life thus living repeatedly means just life composed of manic and depressive events happening alternately. Any suffering under depression and any pleasure and joy in mania will recur and if you thought in the past of being a messiah and people persecuted you conspiring to kill you, know that this thought will recur. Now, the existential and important question arises: will you find, in this case, this existence as a blessing or a curse?

Will this thought elate your mood or break it?

Will you continue wishing to live like this forever?

Saying "yes" to this state, confirms immediately life with its circular suffering and pleasure - he finds in this circle an existential sense. The manic-depressive who confirms life and says "yes" to the demon is a overman because he succeeds to overcome the suffering since he sees the suffering and pleasure being linked to each other and the one who wants the one has to want the other, he transforms the suffering into opportunity! Suffering is perceived by him as something which confirms life; he channels it to art and philosophy. And the one who does not? Van Gogh last words before dying were "the sadness will last forever"; Van Gogh said "no" to the demon, he crashed! He did not agree to confirm life which is composed from pleasure and suffering and he believed that suffering will last forever while, in fact, by nature of the illness, suffering is temporary and it arrives together with pleasure. Van Gogh said "no" to life, he broke the circle of existence and the eternal recurrence thus not elevating him to the level of overman. One should ask himself whether his existential state is such to enable him to answer the demon, i.e. confirm or denounce life. Being one of the yet incomplete, being still anxious of the question and the possibility presented to him by the demon, he has an opportunity to become powerful.

Man in general and the manic-depressive in particular need to love life as it is, not wishing it to be any different forward and backward nor ever. Loving his fate (amor fati), despite the suffering, he says "yes" also to suffering, "go but return" thus succeeding to overcome it. The overman overcomes the suffering and confirms life by channeling the suffering into a feeling of pleasure accompanied, for example, by creation. A physician may find pleasure in his difficult life by healing his patients. The manic-depressive can be overman, i.e. a man overcoming suffering confirming it and his life. However, how suffering can be turned into pleasure?

First and foremost, Nietzsche says that one must see in suffering one "moment" among others that can be pleasing. Secondly, it is well known that artistic creation, lyrical or literary often stems from states of pain, distress and grief. A person being capable to channel grief, sadness and suffering into creation is the one who will derive pleasure from it. There is joy in creation. The suffering is going through sublimation turning into pleasure coming from the joy of creation.

"The Eternal recurrence" is an opportunity; it provides stimulus to elates one's state of existence, to cross the abyss between true man and animal or in other words to become overman. The weak who are capable of suffering life only by hoping for a better life in the next world, will crash by the doctrine of "the Eternal Recurrence", while the strong will find in it a better opportunity to overcome and improve themselves. Being already in this state, the doctrine will be their Dionysus' fate.

An existence recurring indefinitely means also that the existence is without sense or purpose, there is no plan or general purpose giving sense to life, but the manic-depressive needs to find sense for his existence circle. The patient should not treat his illness as an unfortunate accident but as a wonderful opportunity.

The manic-depressive is Zarathustra, he finds in the endless circle of the "Eternal recurrence" opportunity to become a teacher. He teaches the crowd about the "Eternal Recurrence" doctrine thus finding sense in his life. His life becomes bearable. He gives his strength to others.

Zarathustra is a teacher! In the twilight of the idols, Nietzsche tells of himself, "I, the last disciple of the philosopher Dionysus—I, the teacher of eternal recurrence!" (Twilight of the Idols X 5) And therefore, Nietzsche, as a manic-depressive, is the teacher. He chooses to overcome the will to be toward death and suffering and channels it into a will for power, i.e. to be toward pleasurable life. The will toward life, this is a confirmation of life, this is the pleasure and joy in life and then, he channels the will to power into creativity and pleasure. The manic-depressive, as Nietzsche, overcame the suffering and through his creative skills and feels the pleasure of creation which is joy, the passion and the excitement in creation. In unpublished paragraphs between November 1882 and February 1883, Nietzsche says: "all signs to super human nature are seen as an illness or insanity".

## 05:40 The disease and the recovery

People get sick! They suffer from existential depression. They are desperate from life and their senselessness; they feel emptiness. Emptiness is the feeling that the world is without content, not interesting, senseless, and purposeless. And there are those, the preachers of death and pessimism, who tell a person "leave life".

Such people who Nietzsche stands against, the pessimists oppressing the will to live: "there are preachers of death; and the earth is full of those to whom one must preach renunciation of life." (Thus spoke Zarathustra I 9[33]) "Gladly, they wish to be dead, let us respect this will of theirs!", i.e. there are "preachers of death" and pessimists depressing man, oppressing his spirit.

Nietzsche says: "they encounter a sick man or an old man or a corpse, and immediately they say, "Life is refuted." But only they themselves are refuted, and their eyes, which see only this one face of existence." (Thus spoke Zarathustra I 9).

And there those who say: "life is only suffering," others say, and do not lie: see to it, then that you cease! See to it, then, that the life which is only suffering ceases. And let this be the doctrine of

---

[33] Nietzsche, Thus spoke Zarathustra, translated by Walter Kaufman, Penguin Books 1978

your virtue: "thou shalt kill theyself!" However, Nietzsche stands against the oppressors and the preachers of pessimism! He tells humanity: "wake up and listen, you that are lonely! From the future comes winds with secret wing-beats; and good tidings are oroclaimed to delicate ears. You that are lonely today, you that are withdrawing, you shall one day be the people: out of you, who have chosen yourselves, there shall grow a chosen people—and out of them, the overman." (Thus spoke Zarathustra I 22).

A wise reader may see that Zarathustra was having depression; some of the classical symptoms of depression (excessive sleep and "fatigue", lack of appetite, "heaviness") appear in this speech from Zarathustra: "no sooner had Zarathustra spoken these words than he fell down as one dead and long remained as one dead. But when he regained his senses he was pale, and he trembled and remained lying there, and for a long time he wanted neither food nor drink. This behavior lasted seven days; but his animals did not leave him by day or night...at last, after seven days, Zarathustra raised himself on his resting place, took a rose appleinto his hand, smelled it, and found its fragrance lovely. Then his animals thought that the time had come to speak to him. "O Zarathustra, they said, "it is now seven days that you have been lying like this with heavy eyes; won't you at least get up on your feet again? Step out of your cave: the world awaits you like a garden. The wind is playing with heavy fragrancesbthat want to get to you, and all the brooks would run after you. All things have been longing for you, while you have remained alone for seven days. Step out of your cave! All things would be your physicians! Has perhaps some new knowledge come to you, bitter and hard? Like leavened dough you have been lying; your soul rose and swelled over all its rims." (Thus spoke Zarathustra III 13).

It seems to me that the sensitive man is more vulnerable to suffering. "what ever in me has feelings, suffers and in prison; but my will always comes to me as my liberator and joy-bringer." (Thus spoke Zarathustra II 2). Nietzsche prescribes himself a recipe for overcoming depression: in order to recover, man must laugh big laugh against fate: "when I saw my devil I found him serious, thorogh, profound, and solemn: it was the spirit of gravity—through him all things fall. Not by wrath does one kill but by laughter. Come, let us kill the spirit of gravity!" (Thus spoke Zarathustra I 7).

I believe that also in cases of depression, even an acute depression, man still possesses a wild, animalistic, biological instinct for life, or an urge to live, i.e. there is an instinctive, primitive instinct for life which has to be awaken, for example, by laughter, in order for us to overcome self destruction and death. The first instinct is: the will to power - this is the fertile and endless will for life; i.e. life is only an expression of power; more life leads to more power: "the will to power—the unexhausted procreative will to life." (Thus spoke Zarathustra II 12)

"And life itself confided this secret to me: "Behold," it said, "I am that which must always overcome itself." (Thus spoke Zarathustra II 12)  Life itself has revealed the secret to Zarathustra - the self overcoming! The self overcoming is a state in which a man overcomes his tendencies, passions and urges calling him to surrender life which is a reduction in power by restoring order in them by his will, controlling them and free of their tyranny. The first instinct - the will to power and the empowering of life has to overcome the other instinct of self destruction. The self overcoming is the recognition of the beauty of the "Eternal recurrence", and so he speaks: "everything goes away, and returning; forever, the wheel of "is" will spin. Everything is dying and blooming anew, forever galloping the year of the "is". All is broken and reattaching anew; forever, we will build that same building of the "is". All is separated, all return and meet in peace; forever remains the ring of "is" faithful to it. In every moment, "is" begins; for every here there is over there turning. Every place is middle. Curved is the course of eternity".

You who suffer from existential depression need to get acquainted with the wonders of "Eternal recurrence": what that was, will be again and recur forever more - as you have suffered, remember that before it you had moments good as honey, the latter as the first ones will recur again and again.

This is the existential comedy of pleasure and suffering! Is it not worthy laughing? "A long twilight limped before me, a sadness, weary to death, drunken with death, speaking with a yawning mouth.'eternally recurs the man of whom you are weary, the small man'—thus yawned my sadness and dragged its feet and could not go to sleep...'Alas, man recurse eternally! The small man recurs eternally!"...'Do not speak on, O convalscent!' thus his animals answered him;"but go out where the world awaits you like a garden. Go out to the roses and bees and dovecots. But especially to the songbirds, that you may learn from them how to sing! For singing is for the convalescent; thehealthy can speak. And when the healthy man wants songs, he wants different songs from the convalescent."so responded his animals 'thus go out; go out to the world which, as a garden, is expecting you. Go out to the roses and the bees and the flock of pigeons! But in particular the singing birds: so you can learn from them how to sing. Because the singing is good for the recovering: the healthy can speak. When asking for (Thus spoke Zarathustra III 13).

"Cure your soul with new songs that you may bear your great destiny, which has never yet been any man's destiny. For your animals know well, O Zarathustra, who you are and must overcome: behold, you are the teacher of the eternal recurrence—that is your destiny! That you as the first must teach this doctrine how could this great destiny not be your greatest danger and sickness too? "Behold, we know what you teach: that all thing recure eternally, and we ourselves too; and that we have already existed an eternal number of times, and all things with us..." and if you want to die now, O Zarathustra, behold, we also know howyou would speak to yourself. But your animals beg you not to die yet. You would speak, without trembling but breathing deeply with happiness, for a great weight and sultiness would be taken from you who are most patient...I come back eternally to this same, selfsame life, in what is greatest as in what is smallest, to teach again the eternal recurrence of all things, to speak again the word of the great noon of earth and man, to proclaim the overman again to man" (Thus spoke Zarathustra III 13)

Zarathustra recovers because he has a mission, the taste of his life, the sense of his life, something to wake up in the morning for - to be the teacher of life and overman and not teach pessimism and toward death.

Zarathustra recur again and again back to the essence of that life, identical in the greatest and smallest in order for him to recur and teach again the doctrine of eternal recurrence of all things, in order for him to speak the great things to earth and man, to recur and bear the news of overman to man. He has spoken, and in his speaking, so ends the decline of Zarathustra.

Zarathustra is presented in the book "Thus spoke Zarathustra" as a messiah, prophet and a megalomaniac coming to redeem man (is it not a psychotic thought?) and give him hope, let him see the beauty and joy in life: "we who were despairing have now come to your cave and no longer despair—that is but a sign and symbol that those better than we are on their way to you; for this is what is on its way to you: the last remnant of god among men—that is, all the men of great longing, of great nausea, of great disgust, all who do not want to live unless they learn to *hope* again, unless they learn from you, O Zarathustra, the *great* hope." (Thus spoke Zarathustra IV 11).

And what does Zarathustra teach? The laughter: "so, learn to laugh away over yourselves! Lift up your hearts, you good dancers, high, higher! And do not forget good laughter. This crown of him who laughs, this rose-wreath crown: to you, my brothers, I throw this crown. Laughter I have pronounced holy; you higher men, learn to laugh!" (Thus spoke Zarathustra IV 14).

But to laugh at what? At fate! What fate? That of the "Eternal Recurrence": "just now my world become perfect;midnight too is noon; pain too is join; curses too are blessing; night too is sun—go away or you will learn: a sage too is a fool. Have you ever said Yes to a single joy? O my friends, then you said Yes too to all woe. All things are entangled, ensnared, enamored; if ever you wanted one thing twice, if ever you said," you please me, happiness! Abide, moment!" then you wanted all back. All anew, all eternally, all entangled, ensnared, enamored—oh then you loved the world. Eternal ones, love it eternally and evermore; and to owe too, you say: go, but return! For *all joy wants—eternity*." (Thus spoke Zarathustra IV 19).

I say, Zarathustra teaches the eternal recurrence of pleasure and suffering as an existential fate in the face of which we have to laugh and not break. The illness is an existential depression, the

492

recovery passes through Zarathustra who, as a manic-depressive messiah, teaches us the overcoming through "the Eternal Recurrence". In my opinion, Nietzsche tells us, through his alter ego Zarathustra who he considers a messiah or prophet, to accept the illness and suffering, to know it but to also know that human suffering and the manic-depressive in particular, is interlaced with moments of pleasure! "In every joy there is also suffering" (The will to Power 658); both being entwined and exchanged by each other; we, therefore, have to laugh, to laugh at fate and accept it as it is, because it is the "eternal recurrence"

## 05:55 The philosopher and legislator

Nietzsche presented himself as a legislator prophet and revolutionary of values as his Zarathustra. In "beyond good and evil", Nietzsche first book after "Thus spoke Zarathustra" (1883-1885).

The laborers philosophy despite its important and wonderful role is composed from the compression into formulas of archaic values previously accepted as truths. The archaic values are adopted like a religious belief. The task is important and those who are devout need following Kant's and Haggle's doctrines.

For the true philosopher, genuine philosophers, on the other hand, there is a different task. He, also, need to meet schedule and walk through the steps as the laborers philosophers, however, he need be a poet, a strong and free man bearing new message; a message of truths and new values; in other words, he must be some sort of a messiah or prophet with an important mission who preaches morality and new truths and criticizing the truths of the past, he possesses "free spirit" who objects almost everything within the range of human values and he is ready to view all values in different eyes and consciousness. Zarathustra is the legislator, the philosopher of the future who teaches about overman and the "Eternal Recurrence". All these are only a precondition to his task. A true philosopher is a legislator of the future. (Beyond good and evil 211)

The old philosophers, laborers, are "those who wish to verify a complex fact of values" and the futuristic and new ones are "those who legislate the values" (The Will to Power 972). "Genuine philosophers, however, are commenders and legislators: they say, "Thus it shall be!" they first determine the Whither and For What of man, and in so doing have at their disposal the prelimintary labor of all philosophical laborers, all who have overcome the past. With a creative hand they reach for the future, and all that is and has been becomes a means for them, an instrument, a hammer."(Beyond good and evil 211)

Any true philosophical thought is first and foremost creative, i.e. novel. What Nietzsche is meaning to say, nevertheless not saying it explicitly, is that true philosopher, in my opinion a sort of messianic and prophetic figure needs to legislate and bring to the public knowledge a different set of values; values and new truths. Nietzsche could not have thought of a more superior and difficult task then the development of a set of values which will give sense to human life. As a prophet, this is his role and mission; a prophet always considers himself as a messiah in the role of Zarathustra who gives the crowd and flock new values. He considers himself as a legislator of new truths; for example in ancient days, Moses who stood against values of people surrounding Israel, and

494

brought with him new religion and values, wished to create revolution. He was that "free spirit" who came to dismantle old values and construct new ones out of the rubble.

Nietzsche actually says that philosophers as Hegel and Kant are slaves and laborers preserving and justifying existing values; while he had nobler task: the legislation of values! Later on (Beyond Good and Evil page 211) he writes "are there such philosophers today? Have there been such philosophers yet? The next paragraph answers the question; such philosophers did not and still do not exist today".

Nietzsche denotes, this perfect person, i.e. the philosopher, Socrates with whom he walks hand in hand and whom he imitates; Socrates reveals some hypocrisy, convenience, and the lack of self discipline truly hidden under the most respectable type of current moral (Beyond Good and Evil 212).

Nietzsche's perception of his relationship with that legislator philosopher is expressed in another paragraph in the same book in which he speaks of himself as the prophet (i.e. Nietzsche considers himself as the messiah with a mission) who precedes the philosopher of the future. Nietzsche considers himself as such philosopher of the future, exactly as the prophet Zarathustra with whom he identifies. Instead of revolutionize accepted values which seem to him as "creating values turned dominant, and they, at the same time, are called 'truths'", he suggests criticism thus preparing the ground for the creation of new values legislating new values for the future.

A psychotic who thinks he is the messiah, for example a psychotic Jew thinking he is the reincarnation of Moses, or a Christian thinking he is Jesus, believes that he is here to give humanity a new gospel, he came here to convert the previously accepted and true and now he declares a new world view, new values and truths. Thus, the messianic see themselves as playing a role with a mission. It is interesting to see that also Nietzsche considered himself as a bearer of new gospel, revolutionary, a philosopher of the future, the one who gives humanity new truths and values, should we not be willing to say that Nietzsche had a feeling of megalomania, or a perception of a prophet, teacher and revolutionary?

Zarathustra as Nietzsche's alter ego is perceived by him as the philosopher of the future as the one who shatters values and prophesizes the gospel of overman and the eternal recurrence. Zarathustra is the teacher of overman and the eternal recurrence. He confirms life and tells them "yes" despite its suffering. The traditional moral which praises the pessimism of Schopenhauer's existential philosophy, Jesus suffering and the tragedy of life seems to Nietzsche as something dying or about to die, unavoidable.

"Beyond Good and Evil" was published in 1886, i.e. three years before his mental collapse! The psychotic being a messiah, i.e. who legislates new values and truths is free of another and comes with a new discussion and narrative to replace the old one, he is free of the old and is committed only to the new that he brings along, he is not part of the flock but preceding it, above it. This same messiah or Zarathustra is of "free spirit"; he is free from the conventional opinions of the flock, he hits the flock with a hammer. Nietzsche does not intend in 'freedom' relief or giving freedom to his urges; the release of holding in favor of urges is disastrous. Our urges contradict each other, disturbing each other when not restrained. Such type of freedom is actually deterioration. The provision, from which such term of "freedom" stems, is not a true human freedom according to Nietzsche's interpretation but tyranny.

'Freedom' for Nietzsche is something opposite to surrendering to passions rather controlling them, you are not being controlled by passions rather are free from tyranny, for him, being the cause of the greatest troubles. We need to take responsibility for our urges and passions, i.e. our deeds. As long as freedom exists in reality, it had to be understood as an achievement, as something extraordinary and hard to get. It is achieved by the will to take responsibility for him and not being controlled by the urge to die, rather to control the urge, raising above it, controlling it, to be the master, not the slave. Nietzsche says that "my idea of freedom.— the value of a thing sometimes depends not on what we manage to do with it, but on what we pay for it—what it costs us ..." (Twilight of the Idols, IX 38).

Man who achieved freedom and became free is rare and exceptional and is 'higher' in level than the average man who is part of the flock. Freedom itself is rare goods and 'free spirits' are few; however they can appear and the talent for freedom can be realized. Nietzsche measures the trait of such supremacy with how far can a person go in taking responsibility for his life, suggesting that the 'higher' man is the one able to carry the burden of responsibility and collapsing under it (The Will to Power 975).

The ability to make decisions in the long term has to relate to greatness (Beyond Good and Evil 212). "Independence is for the very few, it is a privilege of the strong... the "strong" are "recklessness" if they "experience it... without inner constraint" (Beyond Good and Evil 29). Self control which is bound by the achievement of such inner constraint is an important aspect of being free. Through these terms Nietzsche understands the concepts of 'struggle' and 'conquest' characterizing the 'free spirit' in terms of 'independence and command' (Beyond Good and Evil 41).

## 06:15 Moral and values

Through the birth of a tragedy, Nietzsche tries to understand how the Greek could find a way to carry life while embracing and confirming them despite the insight arrived at by Schopenhauer: he wished to justify life although being horrible, controversial and false (The Will to Power 1005).

His standing in the birth of a tragedy is that only as an esthetical phenomenon, existence and the world are justified. Nietzsche did not abandon his commitment for answering Schopenhauer. He asks what the sense of Nihilism is.
Answering: "That the highest values devaluate themselves. The aim is lacking;"why" finds no answer" (The Will to Power 2); i.e. that life is senseless and lack value. It may be that the world and existence do not have the same value attributed to them thus resulting in lack of value. Pessimism is perceived by him as a form of Nihilism. Both are perceived as the negation of life, their values, therefore, are in great danger. He accepts the fact that he, until now, was a definite nihilist (The Will to Power 25), showing, in my opinion, a syndrome of depression since the depressive does not succeed in finding sense and purpose for his life. Nietzsche himself, passed through a period of nihilism and

pessimism while being in depression, but it is only a transient period.

Nihilism can be a transit to new conditions of existence. Nihilism is only a step needed and able to be overcome by adopting a replacing perspective. Nietzsche, himself, says that he lives nihilism through to its end but it should be left behind. We have to find new values instead of surrendering to depression in nihilism. It may be that the world has more value than we have thought to begin with, and therefore our life in it has more value. He believes that this is possible to give value and criteria of renewed evaluation of the world relating to the nature of reality and find for it and the human existence in it sense and confirm instead of denying them. As I have said, the confirmation of life manifests in the idea of "Eternal recurrence" and "amor fati" - "the love of fate", i.e. "that one wants nothing to be different, not forward, not backward, notin all eternity. Not merely bear what is necessary, still less conceal it—all idealism is mendaciousness in the face of what is necessary—but love." (Ecce Homo page II 10), as his formula for Dionysus' relation to existence which is considered by him as the highest level achievable by a philosopher; he wants to turn the view from the nihilistic, pessimistic "No" to a "Yes".

A Dionysus' confirmation of the world as it is; this is a "higher" state to be aspired for. Not only one should say "no" to nihilism and pessimism but he should also say "yes" to the desire to find new values. He says "yes" to subjects that were negated by tradition. These subject are not only desired, they are also true, strong and more efficient for existence.

Nietzsche speaks, in this context, of "an ethical Dionysus' criteria for existence" by which he will take upon him to draft the "reevaluation of all values". He uses Dionysus to convey the message which he calls "the true facet of existence" which is the "deification" of existence peaking in achievable pleasure, "in which existence celebrats its own transfiguration," which "come, as is reasonable, only to the rarest and best-constituted men." (The Will to power 1051)

He suggests, for example, to reevaluate the values of pity, empathy and compassion to which we usually attribute much value. When we pity someone we relate to his suffering. Modern moral represents "cult of suffering"; what is called "pity" is a proper and correct reaction to suffering on the part of tradition; such reaction is the essence of the moral sense (Beyond Good and Evil 293).

The man of conventional moral takes the big kit of pity or compassion as the pinnacle of the dealing in suffering. Let us assume, says Schopenhauer, that every suffering is despicable and redundant, thus its removal is desirable. Schopenhauer insists that suffering is part of life and our fate is full of pain. Pity establishes a community of sufferers; when someone pities someone else, he adds the suffering of the pitied person to his own.

Pity "convinces" a person to attach to anything that makes him miserable thus making misery contagious. And therefore pity negates life's vitality; moreover, pity is the practice of nihilism since it depresses instincts which purpose is to preserve life and the power of their value: it encourages us to see only agony and feel sick under duress while we consider the results and manifestation of these feelings.

In light of this, Nietzsche says that pity damages more the losers and the weak, concluding that from a point of view of life and of what they need in order to bloom and proper is to make change and amendment to pity as it is presented by Schopenhauer and other moralists who praise it.

Nietzsche's criticism on pity and compassion is directed against the tendency of the sufferers to self pity. In order to avoid the adoption of self pity and the pessimism following it, Nietzsche says that one should think and live on a way by which he confirms life not negating it. Suffering should be converted to advantage.

Nietzsche suffered too, but he would not want to be pitied, he would want to be more than another sufferer. He did not have any tolerance and respect for self pity and for those who love their neighbor only because they share his grief and sorrow. Nietzsche despises the type of morality integrating, on one hand, the participating in ones grief and on the other hand tries to cancel it. He does not agree that such morality is the pinnacle of culture. Philosophy of moral has to get new direction and take upon itself new purposes. We have to overcome morality in its traditional sense. In Zarathustra's words, "self overcoming" is the essence of life, and morality, as perceived by Nietzsche, is a way or means for self overcoming, i.e. we have to overcome our tendency to help all sufferers under their existential state. Therefore, we should not identify with... and pity someone; first and foremost for our own benefit, we should not to be infected by his suffering or letting him be more than "human, too human" because man is something to be overcome. Humanity is something needing overcoming. "Not "mankind" but overman is the goal!" (The Will to Power 1001).

This individual, the overman, can, under certain circumstances (the absurd), justify the existence of thousand years, i.e. a complete human, reach and great; this is the true value of the

501

thousand years' existence. Nietzsche contends that he is "immoral", for example, the moral person is an inferior type than the immoral person for two reasons, the one being that he is weaker and the second being that his value is exterior to him, i.e. his value is measured by allegedly 'objective' criteria like God. Therefore, the moral person cannot be "beyond good and evil", the overman lives beyond good and evil, i.e. he is the "immoral". The difference which Nietzsche tries to point out is between those whose value is a function of other's benefit and those who are equal to something which is them; between those who need be led, who are the flock, and those who can be independent; The one who achieves spiritual supremacy, rising above morality and conventional ethics but not returning to a previous moral state. The moral person according to Nietzsche cannot become an option without the other - overman. That type of contradiction and existing relation between the supreme spirituality characterizing the 'higher type' which is considered by Nietzsche as higher in rank and value and the will of the flock to be 'civilized' does not grant to man, in Nietzsche's opinion, any higher value and rank in his reevaluation of values; its sense is merely that everybody were tamed and united socially. And therefore turned into a better flock, domiciled animals; he continues contending that those, the tamed and submissive represent the decline of humanity instead of rising to the highest level (On the Genealogy of Morality I: 11).

Nietzsche insists on the distinction between taming the wild beast, man, and the growing of a certain type of a higher man. By "growing", he does not mean in a sense of genetic or biological reproduction rather pedagogical, the education of a man to be a overman, the education of man to recognize "the Eternal Recurrence" and accept such fate in love.

Nietzsche, as aforesaid, sees a blunt contradiction between culture in its widest sense (civilization) and the empowering of the overman; it is because the fact that the civilized flock is under restrains guarding it from the influence of the free and uncivilized. The higher man will have many urges but it is not sufficient to have urges, passions, he should also know to control them. In this control, the man holding his urges is transforming by sublimation; for example from wantonness to art.

According to Nietzsche, only through self overcoming and such transforming one may say "be what you are" and so a overman can create himself and write new boards prescribing the definition of good. The creation of values, according to Nietzsche, in interlaced with such terms as strength, spiritual supremacy, confirmation and pleasure which he compares to higher humanity and the pinnacle of empowering life. In manic-depression there are conflicts between urges, passions and various moods, but the manic-depressive should control them by channeling. This is a type of man which is presented by Nietzsche as the most steeply 'rising' life line most contributing to his power presenting it in its highest empowered form: "just for the rarest and most authorized of man" who experiences in "the highest and most illustrious human joys, in which existence celebrates its own transfiguration, come, as is reasonable only to the rarest and best-constituated men…from that height of joy where man feels himself to be altogether a deified form and self-justification of nature." (The Will to Power 1051)

This way, Nietzsche considers human life as transforming into an "esthetic form" in terms of "existence and the world" alone are

503

worthy of justification (The Birth of Tragedy 24). Therefore, this, the complete man, the rich, the great whose appearance "justifie the existence of a whole millennia" (The Will to Power 997), and from which life is justified even in its most dreadful form, controversial and false. Nietzsche promotes the adoption of what he calls "a 'Dionysusial' ethical criterion of life" which does not hesitate to negate traditional criteria for the evaluation of life, particularly not of life themselves, rather accepting and adopting the 'Dionysusial' confirmation of the world as it is by the formula of "Amor Fati". "To a Dionysian affirmation of the world as it is, without substraction, exception, or selection—it wants the eternal circulation:--the same thing, the same logic and illogic of entanglements", this is "the highest state a philosopher can attain: to stand in Dionysian relationship to existence—my formula for this is *amor fati*" (The Will to Power 1041).

From Zarathustra onwards, Nietzsche always returns to the same idea of confirming life granting it major importance. This specifies the point in which we overcome nihilism according to which life is not worth living; and uniting it with his overall perception pertaining to the complete trait of the existence specifying happiness as the issuer of the definitive criterion of the value identified and continuing to be applied by him.

The pleasure celebrated by Nietzsche is the artistic way by which the Greek won against suffering. There are different ways of life for different people. These essential differences are translated to different conditions of life, and if someone thinks of morality as a system of evaluations which partially conform to the conditions of the life of creatures, thus the result, as Nietzsche contends, is a type of variety of human life; morality is relative. Different morality is justified in different human context; as far as they are rejected and adopted by others they are "relative"; they are relative, though, under circumstances pertaining to essential human differences between different humans. Nietzsche's morality represents an extension of the context in which moral operates, by the presentation of considerations stemming from a more general interpretation of "life" and the theory if its value. Morality, from his point of view, is a measure used for "the purpose of empowering life."

Nietzsche morality has to relate to life, life in its most extensive meaning, empowerment and strengthening. The morality of Nietzsche's development is "about morality" in the sense that it is not morality for everyone and that everyone can live by it, but a wider and higher principal of moral according to which relation only few people can live reaching a higher level of humanity. For Nietzsche, morality is a matter of perspective in which there are different people with different morality; we have to recognize that morality ruling today is only one type of human moral and beside it coexist different forms of morality above which can and must be a higher morality. Therefore, Nietzsche contends that instead of looking for and impose a "universal law" or "categorical imperatives", we need to limit ourselves to something else: "to the creation of new boards about the definition of good… as new persons, unique, issuing laws for themselves, creating themselves" thus "become what they are" (The Gay Science 335). Sometimes, Nietzsche emphasizes the function of this type of morality as a way of necessary discipline for the realization of the highest human potential. He speaks of it as serving to train man for heights, and to enable man "to transform, placing himself higher, from afar", as opposed to others who adhere to passions and human interests, too human (Beyond good and evil 187).

Such morality of self control and self overcoming is bound by restraining, resistance of passions, negation and prohibition which are not lesser than other forms of morality.

## 06:35 The Myth of Sisyphus

Zeus, the idol of idols himself, punished Sisyphus severely by sentencing him to repeatedly role a big stone ascending the mountain. Each time Sisyphus arrived at the peak of the mountain, the stone rolled down again. The big stone, that heavy burden, is the metaphor of Sisyphus' life of suffering.

Nietzsche teaches us: "your sentence, yourself, is it not, and stoning yourself: aha, Zarathustra, far, far away, have you thrown every stone, but it return to be fallen upon you". I.e. the stone, the burden of life, is it not, is your sentence, even if you try to throw it away from you it will return and fall upon you. There is no escape from the arrows of a cruel fate.

In "The Myth of Sisyphus"[34], Albert Camus asks about the sense of life in a modern absurd world in which we perform a hard and purposeless job in an office or a factory for 12 hours and finally die. In a world with no definite values and we, at certain tragic moments, discover the senselessness of life under which we suffer, is it not logical to commit suicide considering the suffering and senselessness of existence?

---

[34] Albert Camus, The Myth of Sisyphus, translated by Zvi Arad, Am Oved publishing 1978.

He asks about the purpose of preferring such existence on suicide. The person feeling his life being absurd in the face of death surely luring him at the end of the way and due to the lack of meaning and logic in the world facing bluntly the infinite will of man to understand the meaning of the world and the sense in its existence, has to ask himself why not commit suicide?

Albert Camus answers: nevertheless, the absurd man will reject suicide and live a life of rebellion manifesting in him living the absurd, not giving in to it. Camus collimated modern man's life to Sisyphus' fate; thus he writes: "the struggle to the peak for itself is enough to fill man's heart with joy. Sisyphus should be considered as joyful". Sisyphus rebels his absurd life continuing them while deeply aware of their essence. This consciousness grants him happiness. I would suggest another interpretation to the myth.

Kant's categorical imperative says: "do your deeds only according to that practical rule which, by accepting it, you can wish it to become a general rule". But this is just a formal rule, i.e. without content, an empty frame needing to be fulfilled with content. Well, sometimes I wish to be left alone suffering longing in order for me to reach the level of overman.

My moral imperative is: that I will have a strong enough will to be able to give another to suffer temporarily so he can overcome himself. Kant in his categorical imperative and Mill in his utilitarianism commanded to do a deed, I demand non-action. My dream is of a world in which each person will have the opportunity to rise above himself, i.e. to overcome himself, to the level of overman; I have a dream that everybody will tell himself "I have to do nothing and enable suffering of longing in order to be able later on to pull at his hair, to take himself in his own hands and let him confirm life and tell them yes despite the pain".

I do not wish to be the cause of his suffering; I should not depress the other and put him intentionally in a depressive state of any kind by causing him injustice, I am not cruel in the sake of cruelty, but to leave him, temporarily, to the misfortunes of life and his cruel fate and let him by himself to use the suffering as a leverage to the level of overman.

I suggest being an immoral man: the moral man will pity Sisyphus offering him help in rolling the stone to the mountain's peak, while the one who does not act, who does not do anything, looking at Sisyphus with admiration is beyond good and evil of the civilized. The suffering and sorrow are for the benefit of man! The value of my non-action, i.e. not to try and rescue the other from his suffering is, in the final account, contributing to the personal benefit of the other. The pleasure will arrive following the pain. The self overcoming of pain which is demanded by Nietzsche from man is pleasing. Pleasure is the result of self overcoming! How can one value pleasure before knowing suffering?

Nietzsche teaches us that suffering and pleasure are linked and interlaced with each other: if you ever said 'yes' to pleasure? Then, you have said 'yes' to every suffering. All things are restrained, interlaced, in love. According to my perception every non-action on my part will be reviewed by the enabling man to confirm life despite their hardship. I have a dream that all human beings will have such elated opportunity to turn themselves into strong human beings, overman, superhuman; and so, in an act of non-action, I bring benefit to all. I want every man to be able to overcome his cruel fate and the senselessness of his life only to be able to reconfirm them later on. Since we all were thrown to the same world, we all deserve the same opportunity to rise to the level of overman by saying "yes" to pain and "yes" to pleasure; in this sense, man are born equal and deserve the same opportunity; we all were born crying. My moral imperative prohibits man to be 'human, all too human' but super human. Every man, as Sisyphus, has to carry his burden alone. When Sisyphus reaches the peak of the mountain, he is manic state, he arrives joyful and happy in his achievement; when the stone rolls down, he falls to the abyss of despair and depression; and again everything returns "in the eternal recurrence": up and down, mania and depression, joy and despair, happiness and suffering.

In "Gay Science" (341) Nietzsche characterizes the "Eternal Recurrence" in the following manner: "what, if some day or night, a demon (my interpretation, analogy of Zeus) were to steal after you into your loneliest loneliness and say to you: this life, as you now live it and have lived it, you will have to live once more and innumwerable times more; and there will be nothing new in it, but every pain and every joy and every thought and sigh...must return to you—all in the same succession and sequence—even this spider and this moonlight between the trees, and even moment and I myself. The eternal hourglass of existence is turned over again and again—and you with it, speak pf dust!" would you not throw yourself down and gnash your teeth and curse the demon who spoke thus? Or have you once experienced a tremendous moment when you would have unswered him: "you are a god, and never have I heard anything more divine!" if this thought were to gain possession of you, it would change you as you are, or perhaps crush you. The question in each and everything, "do you want this once more and innumerable times more?" would lie upon your actions as the greatest weight. Or how well disposed would you have to become to yourself and to life to *crave nothing more fervently* than this ultimate eternal confirmation and seal?"

The question of 'do you want this once more and innumerable times more?' will lie on your deeds as a heavy burden. Or how much will you be ready with yourself for life wishing zealously nothing else but this definite and certain confirmation. From here, I understand that Zeus asks Sisyphus, are you ready to accept my punishment as an elated thing, as a blessing or a curse? Would you wish to continue ascending and descending? Should Sisyphus say "yes", then he confirmed life and achieved greatness. Should he say "no" and curse Zeus, then he will break and cry not being able to continue carrying the stone of life.

The manic-depressive should behave the same way, shall I, Avshalom, be willing to carry my life while knowing that I shall be forever ill expecting pleasing periods accompanied by periods full of suffering? Saying "no", how can I continue living? Saying "yes", then I confirmed my existence! And loved it!

Nietzsche's formula of greatness of man manifests in Amor Fati - the love of fate, in which man does not wish anything else, nor forward, not backward, nothing else forever more. Not just carrying the necessity and, of course, make it disappear, is the experience by which man loves his life, with and despite all hardship, just for what they are.

Nietzsche is the teacher of overman. I.e. Sisyphus wishes that everything will stay as it is, that the stone will be rolled by him climbing the mountain and subsequently rolling sown again in the "Eternal Recurrence".

And therefore I interpret Sisyphus differently than Camus, my Sisyphus does not rebel fate and Zeus, rather embraces it accepting it with love! The idea of eternal recurrence also in 'thus spoke Zarathustra' and also in 'gay science' expresses the existential circularity of life; it has an existential sense of man. The idea of eternal recurrence serves as a test to determine whether the individual authentically considers his life as having sense. In this form as an existential test, the eternal recurrence is important since it specifies an advisable standing toward life. Should someone being really able to confirm the eternal recurrence, hence he considers his life as having sense and valuable worth living again and again.

In 'thus spoke Zarathustra', Nietzsche teaches us: "and even while the fatigue of death and the long evening shadows descend upon us, you, the advocate of life, are not sinking on us. A new view of stars you have shown us and new wonder of the night; indeed, the very essence of life, as a colorful tent you have spread above us". The strongest man, possessing a powerful spirit, successful in seeing the wonder of life and confirm it.

Sisyphus is the first overman; someone worthy of admiration. The moral imperative demands of every man to recreate himself, being reborn out of the suffering. The criticism by Nietzsche on pity and compassion is a criticism against the tendency of the sufferers to self pity; Sisyphus does not have pity himself, surely not rebelling Zeus and his fate, rather loving it! In order to avoid the adoption of self pity and pessimism following it, Nietzsche says that one has to think in a way by which he confirms life, not negating it. Sisyphus is using suffering in order to elate into being a overman, je turns suffering into advantage. He is more than "human, all too human" because man is something to be overcome. I say to man "dare dreaming"; dream about self salvation, not the type coming from God or from the likes of messiahs.

## 07:00 The birth of tragedy or Hellenism and pessimism[35]

A fundamental question is the relation of the Greek to pain and suffering. The question is whether their increasing passion to beauty, celebrations, pleasures, new rituals, really stems from pain and suffering? What is the origin of tragedy? Maybe pleasure? And what is the sense of Dionysusial insanity from which the art of tragedy and comedy have stemmed?

I wish to prescribe my depression! I have said before that the overcoming of the depressive illness has to go through laughter; I know it is difficult, but the one wishing to continue living has to know how to do so. In the words of Dionysusial demon called Zarathustra: "carry your hearts to heaven, my brothers, raise it to heights! And also the legs do not forget! Carry also your feet, you, the good dancers, and more shall you improvingly do: on your heads shall you stand! And this is the corona of the laughers, the corona of roses: with my own hands I crowned my head, with my own mouth I sanctified my laughter, as of today, there was not found enough brave spirit but me to do so.
Zarathustra the dancer, Zarathustra the light-footed, the winker of his wings, always ready to fly, winks at every bird, willing and ready, golden, in a hurry and happy: Zarathustra the visionary of truth, Zarathustra the laugher of truth, not impatience, not certain or definitive, likes to hop, also deviate; with my own hands I have crowned my head with the crest of the corona! This corona

---

[35] Nietzsche, the birth of tragedy, translated by Dr Israel Eldad, Shoken publishing 1985

of laughter, this corona of roses, my brother, I throw this corona. I have sanctified laughter, you, the sons of ascent, learn, for me, the laughter (The Birth of Tragedy 7).

The Greek idol Dionysus characterized by pleasure, joy, cheerfulness, promiscuity, and exhilaration reaching madness, is the manifestation of madness and insanity; Apollo the idol of dreams, or in my words, the idol of hallucinations and beautiful illusions; they are the remedy for misfortune, suffering and pessimism of life: "in these two divine arts, in Apollo and in Dionysus... those two urges, so different, go hand in hand, mostly in strife, and repeatedly stimulating each other to newer and stronger births, in order to persist in that battle of contradictions over which the common word art does not bridge only seemingly... and, as the fruit of this mating giving birth to the Dionysusian and Apollonian masterpiece, the ethical tragedy (The birth of Tragedy 1).

Apollo and Dionysus complete each other while appearing by the manic-depressive; although they seem different and separate at the beginning, in second and closer look they are certainly two Heraclitical contradictions completing each other. In order to understand these two urges, Apollo and Dionysus, one has to imagine them as two separate fields of art: the one in the dream (which does not differ in its essence from hallucination) and the other in a pleasing intoxication, Apollonian and Dionysusian respectively.

According to Lucretius' description, the magnificent figures of the idols have initially appeared in the human's soul by dream which is an Apollonian element. "Their beautiful image of places of dreams, which by creating any man as a whole man, a precondition to any plastic art, and indeed, as we will see henceforth, also to a quite important half of poetry" (The Birth of Tragedy 1).

A philosopher has some kind of feeling that behind this reality in which we live and exist, exists another reality, totally different, this is the reality of dreams or hallucinations. Sometimes, people and objects seem imaginary or visions from dreams, and to psychotic in particular, as hallucination. "An esthetic man's relation to the reality of dream is as the philosopher's relation to the reality of the existing; he observes it willingly and carefully: because according to these sights he interprets life for himself, according to their moves he trains himself for life. The philosopher refers with full understanding not only to pleasant sights which he experiences, but also to 'the divine comedy' including netherworld which passes by him not only as a game of shadows, indeed living with all those images, suffering with them, but should it, nevertheless, withstand it, not without the hovering feeling of image; out of them, his horrors and anxieties of man's dream, nevertheless succeeds telling himself "this is only a dream, nevertheless, I wish to go on dreaming" (The Birth of Tragedy 1).

According to Nietzsche, we experience dream out of passion and joy; therefore, we have to consider the manic-depressive as one that despite his hallucinations sometimes carry horrific nature, he, nevertheless, accepts the dream or hallucination since the dream supposed to also replace another and difficult reality. This necessary joy of the experience of dreaming was manifested by the Greek in her Apollon: Apollon, as an idol of all shaping forces, is also the fortune teller idol... he is also the governor of the allegedly beautiful phenomenon of a world, of the intrinsic world of Imagination... a year and a dream are of the discoveries by a healing and assisting nature, they serve, at the same time, a symbol for the virtue of fortune telling and in general for the virtue of the arts without which life is not possible or worthwhile. However, also that gentle borderline over which the dreamy sight has no permission to cross without its act turning into pathological, and in order for the image should not deceive us pretending as a clumsy reality, also this line shall not be absent from the image of Apollon (The Birth of Tragedy 1).

Something supernatural arises from Dionysus' charm: "here, he feels himself as God, here, he himself walks now charmed and elated the image of his dream's image of the walking idols. Man is no longer an artist; he himself became an artistic act." (Ibid)

I call such art "the art of life". We have looked so far at the Apollonian and its Dionysusian contradiction, inspecting artistic powers... and in which the urges of the creator in nature by the primary and direct way are satisfied: firstly, as the world of images from dreams which governing is not dependent at all on the intellectual level or the artistic education of the individual, following it as a reality in which intoxication... each artist is in terms of "imitator" of the two ways, or as the artist of the Apollonian dream or as an artist of the Dionysusian intoxication, or also, as in a Greek tragedy, as the artist of intoxication and dream concurrently: in this term, we have to imagine it in our mind, how in his Dionysusian intoxication and mystic and materialistic expansion, he is kneeling down alone and afar from the choirs of the daydreamers, and how it is now revealed to him under the influence of the apollonian dream, and by way of a dreamy image like a metaphor, his own state, i.e. his unification with the element of all the elements of the world. (The Birth of Tragedy 2).

By the manic-depressive, both, the Apollonian and the Dionysusian materialize as dream showers, i.e. hallucinations (which, essentially, do not differ from the dream) and in term of pleasure and intoxication from pleasure and the joy in mania. We may, so says Nietzsche, based on the dreams being perfect, call the dreaming Greek 'Homerians' and Homer as 'the dreaming Greek' (The Birth of Tragedy 2).

In all Dionysusian feasts, almost at every site, at the center of every feast there were promiscuous lewd acts, uncontrolled sexual feasts which waives flooded and sunk the family structure with all its respectable exceptions; for the sake of promiscuity! Dionysus specifically sets free the wildest predators despicably merging sexual lust and unrestrained rage episodes. Apollon's activity is in the dismantling of Dionysus' destructive weapon by way of reconciliation. This reconciliation is the most important moment in the Greek ritual: "wherever you look, you see the signs of vicissitudes following this event. It was the reconciliation between two rivals... the Dionysusian hallucinators, as the medication reminding of the poison, is a phenomenon of torments invigorating pleasure and joy producing torturous cries from the heart (The Birth of Tragedy 2).

Apollo and Dionysus are two Heraclitical elements which despite their difference are completing each other and create, in the manic's consciousness, a feeling of happiness which follows the feeling of pain and grief. The Dionysusian and Apollonian have ruled the essence of Hellenism while renewing and strengthening each other. Nietzsche contends that only in the realization of these two elements into an esthetical phenomenon, life is justified: "for all existence and the world are not forever justified unless in terms of being an esthetical phenomenon" (The Birth of Tragedy 5).

"Essentially, the esthetical phenomenon is simple, if it is only your virtue, to see before your always a living game of images and to live constantly while surrounded by flocks and flocks of spirits, in this you are a poet; and if only you feel the urge to roll yourself into other figures and speak from other bodies and spirits, in this you are a playwright" (The Birth of Tragedy 8).

The manic-psychotic, in my opinion, is a playwright because he hears voices and sees visions which he creates and telling their stories which is actually his own story, by the realization of the images of his creation. Apollo and Dionysus are the contradiction and the tension between men; both play the spur of disgust and undoubtedly rely on the virtues of their immense artistic charms; in this game, both justify the existence of a world even if it is "the worst of all worlds". And pertaining to the Apollonian element, the Dionysusian element is being revealed here as an artistic, eternal, original and mighty force, he who, at all, said to the whole phenomenon world "let it be": however, in its center, there should be a new cleansing image, in order to sustain in life, the world of all creatures. If we only could imagine a human realization of the Dionysusian - indeed, what is a man if not this? Indeed, this Dionysusian will need, for the purpose of living, a wonderful illusion which will cover his own entity in a veil of beauty. And this is the true artistic aim of Apollon, which in his name we now attach the infinite delusions of the beautiful image, these, the delusions which give, at any moment, a taste to life, to be worthy of their vitality, pushing you to live the next moment. (The Birth of Tragedy 25).

The delusions are the hallucinations or the dreams of Apollo who is a component in the manic-psychotic's consciousness and which sense is given to it of life and its purpose. In a manic-depressive state, two idols are materialized, the Dionysusian element and the Apollonian element which the tense between them and their struggle is the secret of creativity and productivity of the manic-depressive. Apollon, the idol of dreams (or alternately hallucinations), the image and imagination, and on the other hand Dionysus, the idol of joy, happiness and the unrestrained passion as the one of sexual carousing became with Nietzsche a symbol of confirming life and their empowerment and as I have shown, of the overman's power. Apollo is the Hallucinatory element, a beautiful and esthetical dream; Dionysus is the passionate and delicate element of life. Their mating is dreams and pleasing hallucinations, an esthetic phenomenon worth living and repeatedly reconstructing. For this which came out "good", an illness is a stimulus for his life; he knows how to exploit bad luck such as of an illness; he is strengthened by accidents threatening to destruct him.

Nietzsche says "at the same time, I grasped that my instinct weny into the opposite direction from Schopenhauer's: toward a justification of life, even at its most terrible, ambiguous, and mendacious; for this I had the formula "Dionysus" (The Will to Power 1005).

Philosophers have always given priority and supremacy to the search for the truth "as it is" and considered phenomena and hallucinations something false worthy of overcoming; opposing them, Nietzsche considered the Apollonian - the idol of dreams: "the belief really materializes, in us, its final conclusions - you know what they are: that if there is something to be admired, it is the phenomena that should be admired, that the lie - and not the truth - is divine" (The Birth of Tragedy page 1011).

Nietzsche, probably knowing something about hallucinations, being hallucinator himself, indeed admired them and not some objective truth. Pleasure appears where there is the feeling of power." (The Will to Power 1023).

"A full and powerful soul not only copes with painful, even terrible losses, deprivations, robberies, insults; it emerges from such hells with a greater fullness and powerfulness; and, most essential of all, with a new increase in the blissfulness of love." (The Will to Power 1030) Therefore, the pleasure in mania is the manifestation of the will to power in term of willingness coping with pain. And finally the conclusion: "if we affirm one single moment, we thus affirm not only ourselves but all existence...and in this single moment of affirmation all eternity was called good, redeemed, justified and affirmed" (The Will to Power 1032).

"The tragic man affirms even the harshest suffering: he is sufficiently strong, rich and capable of deifying to do so" (The Will to Power 1052).

**The time 07:30 Art**

Why art is so important to me? Because it is a medication! What is essential in art is the completeness of existence; "Art is essentially affirmation, blessing, deification of existence" (The Will to Power 821).

"Art and nothing but art! It is the great means of making life possible, the great seduction to life, the great stimulant of life"

(The Will to Power 853 II). "Art as the redemption of the sufferer—as the way to a states in which suffering is willed, transfigured, deified, where suffering is a form of great delight." (The Will to Power 853 II).

"The will to appearance, to illusion, to deception, to becoming and change (to objectified deception) here countsas more profound, primeval, "metaphysical" than the will to truth, to reality, to mere appearance:--the last is itself merely a form of the will to illusion. In the same way, pleasure counts as being more primeval than pain: pain only as conditioned, as a consequence of the will to pleasure (of the will to become, grow, shape, i.e., to create: in creation, however, destruction is included). A highest state of affirmation of existence is conceived from which the highest defree of pain cannot be excluded: the tragic—Dionysian state." (The Will to Power 853 III)

Nietzsche says: "in this way, this book is even anti-pessimistic: that is, in the sense that it teaches something that is stronger than pessimism, "more divine" than truth: art." (The Will to Power 853 IV) In order to understand the creativity in insanity, one needs to understand that it stems from the same roots from which the artist creates art. Nietzsche strongly considered art. Art, to him, justifies and enables life. Evidence for this can be found in the opening of the birth of tragedy: "Art as a whole... enables life turning it into being worthwhile".

Nietzsche considers artists as belonging to the higher humanity thus linking art with the philosophers of the future on one hand and with overman whom he considers as the "sense of earth" on the other hand. Art represents the higher purpose of life. Nietzsche does not try to hide Schopenhauer's influence on his perception of reality and his perception of art in the birth of

520

tragedy. Schopenhauer was the mentor of these subjects. On one hand he was convinced by the logic of most of his Schopenhauer sayings about the world, life and art. On the other hand, Nietzsche was not happy from Schopenhauer pessimism pertaining to life and their worthiness. Instead of agreeing with Schopenhauer, he chose to argue worth him and respond to the challenge; one may consider most of Nietzsche's thinking and ideas as response to Schopenhauer's challenge. Therefore, one of his central ideas pertaining to art and life is: "it is only as an aesthetic phenomenon that existence and the world are eternally justified" (The Birth of Tragedy 5).

Schopenhauer's fundamental reason for his pessimistic standing was that for him, all existence and life in general, are characterized in endless war and struggle and as an unavoidable result of which is destruction bound by tremendous suffering for sensitive creatures. All life, for Schopenhauer, was senseless since nothing valuable can be achieved in such struggle. There is no superior purpose for which we are struggling and suffering; there is no happiness, no pleasure or satisfaction which can balance life pertaining to pain and suffering. Therefore, when there is no Hedonistic justification to live, life is not worthwhile living. In one word, life is absurd, precisely as Sisyphus'. The being depressive feels that his life is absurd, he suffers for nothing and for no reason; his life and suffering are senseless, life has no justification and sense resulting in him saying "there is no sense in living" or as Van Gogh has put it before he died: "the sadness will last forever".

There is nothing in life but constant effort, suffering and inescapable pain, a necessary destruction - all is purposeless, senseless and not justified, there is no redemption or external

521

justification, there is only liberation by death. Nietzsche does not doubt the logic in this pessimistic world view, and despite the later negation of Schopenhauer's metaphysics, he goes on saying that we should not expect some kind of utopia or another life which can serve as justification and sense to "we can look neither to a future utopia nor to a life hereafter that might serve to render endurable and meaningful 'the terror and horror of existence'." (The Birth of Tragedy 3) Therefore, how someone is capable of suffering the world and life as depicted by Schopenhauer - to suffer them and even confirm them as something worthy and worthwhile notwithstanding the terrors and horrors which are part thereof?

Nietzsche expresses this recognition of the world and the individual in it as a "Dionysusian wisdom" and compares the Greek who achieved such recognition with Shakespeare's Hamlet and without reservation with the modern man; "in this sense the Dionysusian man resembles Hamlet: both have once looked truly into the essence of things, they have gained knowledge, and nausea inhibits action; for their action could not change anything in the external nature of things... now no comfort avails anymore...conscious of the truth he has once seen, man now sees everywhere only the horror or absurdity of existence...: he is nauseated." (The Birth of Tragedy 7)

The ancient Greeks did not surrender to Schopenhauer's pessimism; on the contrary, they were vigorous, creative and confirmers of life as they knew it. Nietzsche admired them, he asked about them: how did they do it? What was the secret of their liberation from the oppression of the act and life which allegedly had to be the conclusion from the Dionysusian wisdom?

The answer, so Nietzsche believed, is in the greatest achievement of their culture: art. Nietzsche refers to two concepts, Dionysus and Apollo, for the provision of a satisfying account of art. Each one influences the other and brings change to the other as well as the other is going through changes. The basic unity of the terms of art and life by Nietzsche is best seen in the birth of tragedy when he deals in the basic urges acting in art - "the Dionysusian" and "the Apollonian" as expressions of man's natural tendency and nature's as one.

The overman can be understood as a symbol of human life arising to the level of art in which a crude and resolute struggle undergoes sublimation to creativity which is no longer enslaved to demands and limitation of the human, all too human. The overcoming of the senseless and horrifying existence characterizes essentially art as well as life as Nietzsche understood them. For him, the sense is in life being a deed of art and that art is a manifestation and the essential nature of life. Overman is an example of this basic tendency - the realization of the basic trait of reality of which any existence, life and art are attributed to it.

One of the outstanding traits in Nietzsche's study on art and life is the use of the term "Art" not only to denote painting, music, sculpture etc, but also in a wider sense. For example, he contends that every man is an artist in the sense that he "creates" "beautiful illusions" of the "dreams' world" even if no concrete art work is realized by such illusions.

I think that in this context, it is fair to say that the manic-psychotic is the truest, most authentic human form of art; he is the "master of illusions"; he creates in his consciousness hallucinations which are "beautiful illusions" coming from his intrinsic world, and even if they are not being painted, they are engraved in his consciousness. In this term, the manic-psychotic realizes the Apollonian element, the world of dreams and hallucinations. Moreover, Nietzsche, at the same time, also refers to the Dionysusian element in the artist's world, i.e. to experience what he calls a "Dionysusian ecstasy", i.e. that same element of excitement and elated enjoyment characterizing mania; here, Nietzsche speaks of man, and I speak of the manic, as specific work of art.

Man is not the artist rather the work of art itself. Mania is a type of art. Art in the context of life covers hard reality with a veil of beauty. Nietzsche speaks of it (art) as "'a veil of beauty' over a harsh reality" and as a "transfiguring mirror" (The Birth of Tragedy 3). It changes the form of a hard, fear arousing reality. Nietzsche gives as an example the ancient Greeks who were forced by the horrors and atrocities to be redeemed from them. On light of this, Nietzsche linked between art and life in terms of art being the source for Hellenic redemption from the bleak existential state: "Art saves him, and through art - life" (The Birth of Tragedy 7).


**08:00 Apollonian and Dionysusian art**


Richard Schacht[36] contends that Nietzsche speaks of art in terms of what it does and how; and for him the answer to these two questions has to be given by the two terms of "overcoming" (Ueberwindung) and "transfiguration" (Verklaerung). These two terms have to be understood pertaining to basic human needs.

---

[36] Richard Schacht, Nietzsche, Routledge & Kegan 1983

Nietzsche's interpretation of art according to "transfiguration" distinct him from Schopenhauer. If art in its essence, is a matter of changing form, hence its service of our needs will necessarily progress differently than the increase of our understanding and intellectual power. One needs to remember that the two terms, "change of form" and "overcoming" are applied in his study in a different way and distinct while he speaks of artistic urges and forms and this, in order for him to be able to say something different about each of them as well as linking them anew. He analyzes the two terms in two different ways reaching even the assertion that they represent two artistic worlds differing in their intrinsic essence. The artistic urges (elated happiness) and the art worlds (the world of hallucinations) even if being different in their essence, they still wish to overcome and change the form of the horrible and absurd reality.

"The beautiful illusions" and "the world of dreams" are different and distinct in their essence from the hard reality of regular experience existing beside them and which they wish to overcome.

According to Nietzsche, neither the Apollonian art nor the Dionysusian represent the world directly to us, not as it represents it to us in experiencing or as is. For Nietzsche, the urge to create art is not a cognitive urge, rather it has some sort of connection to knowledge, hence art is an antidote for the poison being the absurd reality. Apollo represents the world of illusions and dreams of psychosis while Dionysus represents the world of debauchery and elated pleasure of mania. Each one of these phenomena manifests in the most deepest and essential an aspect of the manic psychotic; each one respond to a strong urge which aim is an overcoming reality while changing its form. I.e. by changing its form of reality we overcome it; on one hand, the Apollonian is the urge of the world of hallucinations and dreams of the psychotic being detached from reality, and on the other hand, the Dionysusian is the passion and urge of the elated pleasure in mania detaching from a horrific and atrocious world. These two forces, despite their difference, speak the same language, the language of mania- psychosis. On one hand, overcoming and escaping the world of experiencing the mundane reality and on the other hand, an elated happiness being a remedy for suffering and fear of mundane reality.

The Apollonian and Dionysusian experiences linked to the "art" and "creativity" of the manic-depressive, as the ones of Van Gogh and Virginia Wolf, create worlds by dream, thus creating alternate reality; the manic-depressive is basically composed of these tendencies being a manifestation of different emotions responding to different needs.

Moreover, it is true that the manic episode is accompanied by a blessed Dionysusian ecstasy out breaking from the deeps of the manic's nature. These feelings of profound pleasure and hallucination characterize the experiencing of art forms linked to the development of these two aspects, Dionysus and Apollo. The two experiences play the two chords of our nature thus creating the same form of reaction, i.e. mania- psychosis.

The key to the understanding the functions of life empowerment and overcoming the reality of the manic is in Apollo and Dionysus; the Apollonian dream and the Dionysusian pleasure. Nietzsche explains the term Apollo associatively as "all those countless illusions of the beauty of mere appearance that at every moment make life worth living at all and prompt the desire to live on in order to experience the next moment." (The Birth of Tragedy 25)

If by dream or by artistic imagination, Apollo manifests the improvement and the rise to a higher level of creative development a world of beautiful illusions. Equally, Nietzsche suggests that also the Dionysusian art is convincing us of the infinite circular pleasure in existence. We need seeking pleasure not among your world's phenomena, rather among phenomena beyond and over reality, i.e. by direct ecstasy to a level of elation, by a feeling of immense passion for existence and the joy in existing; the pain, the suffering and struggle is now perceived as a condition for pleasure and happiness and saying "yes" to life. In order to say "yes" to life, we need to recognize suffering and pain and the struggle between the "no" of existence to the "yes" of existence. Nietzsche perceives illusion and intoxication of pleasure not as analogies of art or early forms of art or early experiences and activities of art, rather in the deepest sense, they are artistic phenomena, and I call it "the art of life". The manic is the artist and the art of life is the nature of the illness.

Artistic activity, in this case, has to be perceived as a creation which is a basic part of the manic's nature, i.e. the dualism of Apollo and Dionysus. Every manic is the Apollonian artist of hallucination and dream creating beautiful illusions or a Dionysusian artist of pleasure intoxication ecstasies, or both. In this context, Nietzsche speaks of the conscious differential in the creation of "two worlds of art differing in their intrinsic essence." (The Birth of Tragedy 16)

Richard Schacht maintains that in case of Apollonian art, reality changes and transforms a change of state into a world of dreams and imagination; they are "beautiful illusions" because they are not the world of your phenomena, i.e. a world of objective phenomena, they do not conform to any reality, they do not "agree" with any reality.

The dreams are a change of form of reality. In the case of Dionysusian art, one of its expressions is the intoxication by pleasure manifesting, for example, also in the "sexual promiscuity" of Dionysus; as I have said, the manic is trying to deal in happiness causing activity and there is nothing as sex and orgies to bring the feeling of happiness and pleasure resulting from sexual relief. By the way, manic women are more "liberated" sexually; their fantasies are mostly of a sexual nature. By Apollo and Dionysus, we achieve conscious change arrived at not by knowledge, rather by dreams and hallucinations (also sexual fantasies) strong and pleasing, seducing the manic-depressive to continue living.

These "works" of art, the art of life, are creations which do not represent nor symbolize, rather pleasing precisely due to change of form. The manic himself is going through a change of form because prior to it he was in depression or was balanced - part of the flock. Also the Dionysusian artist is creative; Nietzsche does not understand the terms of changing form and illusions as being applied to just to Apollonian and Dionysusian art that are perceived as objects of esthetical experiences, but also as subjects of experiences in a way by which they are integrated in it. The subject, as well, is going through a change of form or a conscious change. For example, the Dionysusian artist being intoxicated by pleasure may be defined as not "being himself", he is immersed in waves and flow of esthetical experience in which he is "loosing himself"; i.e. the manic is in an external state different from a balanced state in which he is part of the flock. His consciousness is trapped in an esthetic outbreak; his consciousness changing accordingly manifesting behavioral power in complete joy with relapses of mundane activity.

This experience is ecstatic in essence, i.e. being external to you. Apollo overcomes the suffering of the individual by the "beauty of dreams" overcoming the suffering of life since man is "absorbed in the pure contemplation of images" (The Birth of Tragedy 5) and becomes aware of their pleasure. This psychological change of consciousness is real; in a fundamental way, also the objects of consciousness and self consciousness are the two sides of that same Apollonian illusion.

Art may be created by man, however man is also being created or changing his form by the art of life. The Apollonian force of changing form enables us to suffer and confirm existence which is ours as part of the provisions of our existence, not only during Dionysusian moments of outbreak of joy, but also when we recognize our individuality and confront the circumstances of human life. In the realization of "the Eternal Recurrence", Sisyphus' tragic live with all the horror and fear in the existence are defeated and change their form to wonderful and transcendental. Indeed, tragedy is the measure by which life can become possible; it is the temptation and incentive for life. For Nietzsche, the true sense of art is life. "Art is the great stimulant to life." (The Twilight of the Idols IX 24)

Art is not just a measure to relieve life, but a measure "recognizing in them the aim of enhancing life." (The Will to Power 298) Nietzsche recognizes that art may be the result of dissatisfaction with reality, and sometimes it is so, but it may be, also, "an expression of gratitude for happiness enjoyed." (The Will to Power 845)

Every sort of art may be considered as a remedy and assistance in the struggle and growth in life. The erotic urges do not manifest exclusively in Dionysus: "in the Dionysian intoxication there is sexuality and volupyuousness: theyare not lacking in the Apollonian," what distinct them is "the difference in tempo in the two conditions." (The Will to Power 799).

Art is a beautifying art while sensuality is only a mask. The demand for arts and beauty is an indirect demand for sexual ecstasy in its spiritual form. Nietzsche specifies three criteria: sexuality, intoxication and brutality, all belong to the ancient celebration of pleasure by humanity and all are being realized in the manic artist. "thus the Dionysian is seen to be, compared to the appollinian, the eternal and original artistic power that first calls the whole world of phenomena into existence—and it is only in the midst of this world that a new transfiguration illusions becomes necessary in order to keep the animated world of individuation alive. If we could imagine dissonance became man—and what else is man?—this dissonance, to be able to live, would need a splendid illusion that would coverdissonance with a veil of beauty. This is the true artistic aim of Appolo in whose name we comprehend all those countless illusions of the beauty of mere appearance that at every moment make life worth living at all and promp the desire to live in order to experience the next moment. Of this foundation of all existence—the Dianysian basic ground of the world—not one whit more may enter the consciousness of the human individual than can overcome again by this Apollinian power of transfiguration." (The Will to Power 25)

Art is directly and intimately linked to life, and as having major sense for them, in the birth of tragedy, it is considered and understood as a life's perspective. Art is the creative force in man.

"Creativity" is the base for the terms confirmation, overcoming, higher humanity, value and overman. "Creativity" as Zarathustra maintains, is the redemption from suffering and the growing light of life.

The artist, so says Zarathustra, creates the purpose of man and gives earth its sense and future. Life has to be overcome, you do it by creation. Creativity turns things into valuable by changing their form creatively.

The creators are higher than the flock, they are higher due to their creativity; the overman is the human realization of creativity. Art is interlaced with the development of creative forces in man, promoting his power, extending the possibilities of his expression and by that not only beatify life but also empowering it and as such it is blessed. Art serves the manic-depressive for elation and overcoming the stress factors and hardship inherent in existence; there are those who will consider it an "escape" and type of escapism, however, I maintain that this is a protective mechanism being realized in hallucinations creating an alternative reality accompanied by pleasure, i.e. art. Where you fail, the manic creates automatically beautiful pleasuring hallucinations. Where there is suffering, the manic knows how to overcome it; by "transcending" and "high" he transcends reality and by the work of art he literally creates his life. His life is the canvas on which consciousness draws its record.

Art is the way of the manic-depressive to overcome reality full of suffering and this is the remedy I recommend to all who are depressed by their existence. Nowadays, we link between the outbreaks of a mania and stress states in life. A stress state, i.e. an unpleasant urge, putting it mildly, is the urge for a state of pleasure. i.e. the artist, the manic, who is urged by stress states in life, develops mania in order to overcome the unpleasant urge. He does it based on two Greek Gods: Apollo and Dionysus. Apollo overcomes reality by beautiful dreams and illusions meaning by detaching from reality he overcomes it. Dionysus overcomes the suffering of existence by sensual ecstasies and life orgies; the state of intoxication resulting from a sexual orgy and any other pleasing activity in life perceived as ecstasy, assist the manic artist to overcome the dark reality. Without art (beautiful hallucinations) and ecstasy, life has no purpose staying forever senseless. As opposed to Plato who had contempt for art since it is "just" an imitation of reality, I confirm it. I confirm the dreams because they are phenomena. Nietzsche recognized the Apollonian God of dreamy phenomena: "the faith in truth attains its ultimate conclusion in us—you know what it is: that if there is anything that is to be worshipped it is the appearance that must be worshipped, that the lie—and not the trut—is divine!" (The Will to Power 1011). Therefore, indeed the manic- psychotic state is the way by which the manic artist overcomes the depression in the horrific reality. This is my prescription for health of man - art!

**08:30**

"All signs of overman's nature appear in a man as illness or insanity".[37]

---

[37] Nietzsche, unpublished text dated from November 1882 to February 1883 (my translation)

**The time 08:45 Me**

I am the overman; the will to power is being realized in me, I have come to teach you the "Eternal Recurrence".

Made in the USA
Middletown, DE
31 July 2018